BIDEN VS TRUMP

BIDEN VS TRUMP

How Political Advertisements Shaped the 2020 Presidential Race

Allan Louden, Editor

CONTRIBUTORS:

Hannah Abernethy, Curtis Anderson, Logan Bolton, Haleigh Cadd, Madeline Coelho, Noah Collier, Melissa Cooney, Jack Crane, Maya Dalton, David Dockery, Maria Jose Falcon Gimenez, Ashley Foley, Jordan Hessinger, Kellyn Jamison, Grace Keilen, Mary Kern, Dave Kilduff, Ryan King, Itamar Lewin-Arundale, Rafael Lima, Elizabeth Maline, Caroline Mclean, Maggie Moran, Tori Pylypec, Kiki Rodriguez, Rachel Singleton, Chandler Stearns, Mark Sucoloski, Elizabeth Thomas, Kaley Vontz, Yuxuan (Sandra) Wang, Elizabeth Whitehurst, Virginia Witherington, Mu-Tsu Wu, and Liyan Zhu

ISBN 978-1-61846-125-4

Copyright © 2021 Allan Louden

All rights reserved,
including the right of reproduction,
in whole or in part, in any form.

Produced and distributed by

Library Partners Press
ZSR Library
Wake Forest University
1834 Wake Forest Road
Winston-Salem, North Carolina 27106

www.librarypartnerspress.org

Manufactured in the United States of America

DEDICATION

To

Michelle Gillespie, Dean of the College

& Her Staff

For Their Above and Beyond
Commitment, Perseverance, and Patience in
Leading the College Through the Pandemic Season

And to

The Katherine Mohr Stahl Communications Department Fellowship
And Her Family's Continued Support of Student Excellence

TABLE OF CONTENTS

INTRODUCTION - *Allan Louden, Editor*...1

SECTION 1: CRUCIAL ADVERTISING THEMES - *Allan Louden, Editor*..............9

    Chapter 1: Middle-Class Rust Belt Voters in the 2020 Election: An Analysis of the Presidential Campaign Economy Advertisements - *Mary Kern*..........15

    Chapter 2: Trump and Biden's Primary COVID-19 Political Advertisements - *Melissa Cooney*..27

    Chapter 3: COVID-19 Ads in the 2020 Presidential Election - *Chandler Stearns and Mu-Tsu Wu* 39

SECTION 2: BROADLY FRAMED – CANDIDATE IMAGE AND FUTURE TIMES - *Allan Louden, Editor*..53

    Chapter 4: Candidate Framing: Profiles, Competency, and Character - *Ashley Foley*..59

    Chapter 5: Presidential Fitness - *Noah Collier*......................................65

    Chapter 6: Future Framing: Socialism vs. Democracy - *Grace Keilen* 77

SECTION 3: NON-TRADITIONAL PURPOSE FOR TRADITIONAL CAMPAIGN THEMES - *Allan Louden, Editor*..87

    Chapter 7: Religious Advertisements in the 2020 Presidential Campaign - *Madeline Coelho and David Dockery* 91

    Chapter 8: A Critical Survey Comparing 2016- and 2020-Women's Campaign Advertisements - *Hannah Abernethy*.. 101

    Chapter 9: The Representation of Assault Weapons in 2020 Primary Election Media - *Tori Pylypec* 109

    Chapter 10: Firearms Advertising in the 2020 General Election Cycle - *Kiki Rodriguez* 117

    Chapter 11: Biden and Sanders's Primary Health Care Reform Advertisements: An Aristotelian Analysis - *Kellyn Jamison* 123

    Chapter 12: Climate Change Primary Political Advertisements - 2019-2020 - *Maria Jose Falcon Gimenez*.. 133

Chapter 13: Advantaging Sustainability in 2020 Climate Advertising - *Jack Crane* 143

SECTION 4: DISTINCTIVE ADVERTISING THEMES IN 2020 - *Allan Louden, Editor* 146

Chapter 14: Criminal Justice Reform in the 2019-2020 Primary Election Advertising: A Critical Narrative Approach - *Kaley Vontz* 152

Chapter 15: Rhetorical Reflections of the 2020 Social Justice Advertisements - *Ryan King* 160

Chapter 16: Critique: Counting the Black Vote in 2020 Primary Campaign Advertising - *Logan Bolton* 168

Chapter 17: Race Emerges as a Critical Issue in 2020 Presidential Advertising - *Curtis Anderson* 176

Chapter 18: Analysis of Ideals: Law and Order Advertising in the 2020 Presidential Campaign - *Elizabeth Thomas* 186

Chapter 19: Relationships between Candidate, Character, and Issue in Spanish Language and Latinx Ads - *Rachel Singleton and Elizabeth Whitehurst* 196

Chapter 20: 2020 Vice Presidential Political Advertisements - *Dave Kilduff* 204

Chapter 21: Corruption Narratives in the 2020 Election Cycle - *Maya Dalton and Mark Sucoloski* 212

    Section 1: Voter Suppression, the USPS, and Voting by Mail 213

    Section 2: Sideshow Corruption Advertising: Character, Prominence, and Impact 219

SECTION 5: SURPRISING SIDEBARS IN THE 2020 ADVERTISING THEMES - *Allan Louden, Editor* 228

Chapter 22: WhiteHouse.gov Video as Political Advertising - *Rafael Lima* 234

Chapter 23: Shifting Lines: Party Migration Voting & Political Ads in the 2020 Presidential Race - *Madeline Coelho and David Dockery* 246

Chapter 24: Supreme Court Political Advertisements in 2020 - *Jordan Hessinger* 258

Chapter 25: The Lincoln Project – Success Story or Hype - *Caroline McLean* 266

Chapter 26: From Delusional to Dominant: Debate Dialogue in Political Advertising - *Maggie Moran* 276

Chapter 27: Modern Political Campaigning: Assessing Michael Bloomberg's Use of Memes - *Elizabeth Maline* 288

Chapter 28: Word Choice in Trump's 2020 Primary Advertisements - *Haleigh Cadd* 310

SECTION 6: FOREIGN POLICY ADVERTISING SIDETRACKED - *Allan Louden, Editor* 318

Chapter 29: Correlations between China Campaign Ads and US Social Issues - *Yuxuan (Sandra) Wang* 322

Chapter 30: "Trade Wars" Define 2020 Campaign China Advertising - *Liyan Zhu* 332

Chapter 31: Why the Children? Foreign Policy Advertising in 2020 - *Itamar Lewin-Arundale* 340

Chapter 32: "Losers" & "Suckers": 2020 Presidential Campaign Military Advertising - *Yanlin Zhang* 348

Chapter 33: An Examination of Immigration Political Advertisements in the 2020 Election - *Virginia Witherington* 372

INTRODUCTION

Allan Louden, Editor

This collection of student research owes its existence to the 2020 COVID-19 pandemic. In March 2020, the academy took classes online. Presented with a steep learning curve, instructors lamented the loss of personalization of their classrooms, yet also discovered unexpected innovations. In early Spring term, in March, I was teaching a class on "Political Communication." The class adapted to online instruction remarkably well. It helped that, after all, politics is largely video-based.

> Students can generate at levels we might not have anticipated in the pre-pandemic environment.

In this new environment we made the important discovery that, with undistracted time, **every** student can generate quality observational work at levels we might not have anticipated in the pre-pandemic environment. Continued conferencing, lessened busywork, and breaking isolation's boredom invited richer academic applications. We rightly grieve students foregoing the expected "college experience," nonetheless, comparative isolation and changing time commitments was the world in which the class took place. The trade-off was the invention of this book. When presented with this notion, students (to their credit), were enthused to create this book and we were off and running. The essays vary in depth and methodological sophistication, and so too did each student's prior background. Each author made substantial effort to produce their best product.

This book also grows out of a long personal fascination with political messaging. Before social media, in a not-too-distant past[i], ads from political campaigns were challenging to obtain and archive. Limited sites, such as *The Living Room Candidate,* the C-SPAN archives at Purdue, or a personal visit to The Julian P. Kanter Political Commercial Archive at the University of Oklahoma, represented the range of options.*[ii]*

During the energized 2008 presidential campaign cycle I began to collect the available political spots. The candidates' campaigns made their messaging available directly, breaking the previous dependence on secondary sources. The kinetic 2008 election primary was full of pitched rivalry, pitting primary rivals Hillary Clinton and Barack Obama, followed by John McCain in the general election. The number of ads produced mushroomed, spurred on by the growing availability of online access.

From this setting began the ad collections, one of which this book investigates. No collection can be fully complete, and each collection certainly misses some ads created. Through experience and more accessible sourcing these collections became more "inclusive" over time and began to represent (if not all ads) the largest collection of ads from previous election cycles that I am aware of.

This collection now covers four presidential election cycles. The upsurge in the number of political messages (ads) being produced and entering the public domain, is unmistakable. The exception to this is the set of ads produced for the 2012 Mitt Romney and Barack Obama campaigns, which dipped compared to 2008. Nonetheless, even that election cycle surpassed ads produced for 2000, 2004, and any campaigns before that time. The trajectory for 2016 and 2020 is self-evident (see Table 1).

Table 1: Political Ads Produced by Election Cycle

Year	Campaign	Collected
2008	McCain/Obama	1060
2012	Obama/Romney	520
2016	Clinton/Trump	1310
2020	Trump/Biden	4350

One wonders who the audience was for the avalanche of 2020 advertising. The primary presidential campaigns and many independent groups found a way to raise immense amounts of money for this advertising. Although estimates vary, one credible source noted "$2.63B has been spent on Presidential advertising this cycle as compared to $855M in the previous cycle" (Record Shattering, 2020).

> "$2.63B has been spent on Presidential advertising this cycle as compared to $855M in the previous cycle"

Perhaps the spending and the number of ads was driven by both a polarized election that featured a larger-than-life personality, and the large-scale political agendas and availability of vast financial resources. Most of the over

4300+ ads probably had little effect. Recent research has suggested political advertising has very small persuasive effects (Coppock, Hill, & Vavreck, 2020; Lau, Sigelman & Rovner, 2007). Despite the inundation of ads and their potential to be ignored, a viral spot can break through. A fuller explanation would assert that ads attain collective weight, thereby reinforcing via repetitive volume and voters' intentions, resulting in collective mobilization or quiescence. Advertising influences minimally helped define the 2020 election's unfolding (Gerber, et al., 2011; Sides & Karch, 2018). Candidates advertise because for their purposes, it works.

Defining the Ad Collections

The question of what constitutes a political ad is not easily answered. A sufficient response was more easily assessed in the not-too-distant past election cycles. Presumably, ads could be identified as having run on television or radio, containing the candidates disclaimer – "I approve this ad" – and standard durations (30 sec) designed for the broadcast medium. These overt signs, however, would exclude candidate messaging that functions the same but doesn't contain ad characteristics of the past. Proliferating social media outlets, ease of production, and ease of funding have led to an exponential increase in video that, if not formally a political ad, has the characteristics and markings of a political ad. Much of a campaign's videos are meant for circulation across social media – not ads exactly, but they behave similarly. Decisions of what constituted political ad in the 2020 cycle included messaging that when judged by appearance and sponsor seemed to be "intended" as political ads.

Not every video that the campaigns or PACs produced were included in the sample sets organized for this book. For example, the campaigns issued videos that were designed for social media sharing, presumptively aimed at their base, but never intended for airtime. Both Trump and Biden provided substantial numbers of speech excerpts, the preponderance of which were Trump's, reflecting both the campaign's strategy and the fact that he held considerably more campaign rallies. Representative samples from these categories were included, with most excluded, resulting in a

Ad Sets Available for Scholars

Ad sets of the four presidential campaigns and (relatively complete) ad sets for several Governor and Senate races in the last few years are available to researchers for scholarly work. Contact the book's editor for authorization of academic institution and appropriate research purpose. (louden@wfu.edu) small proportion of the "speech-excerpt" video becoming part of this book's data sample. Similarly, not all Facebook nor Instagram ads were collected. Ads designed primarily for fundraising or entertainment programming for this volume were omitted. As the ad set was collected it became clear that ads found expression across a wide variety of channels.

Preview

From the 4300+ ads produced in the primary and general election period of 2019 – 2020, ads were grouped into assortments based on the topic they addressed. Occasionally the ads fell into two categories and were placed in both. The focus of content grouping and assignment of spots was based on the editor's judgment. As the campaign unfolded, themes surfaced, building an organic unfolding of categories. Some were obvious, by volume and similarity, for example Coronavirus and the more short-term but vibrant set surrounding the President's *Atlantic* "Suckers and Losers" (military ads). Several sets would be considered standard fare in any modern election, for example: education, immigration, and climate. Other groupings in the 2020 election cycle would have been minor entries in past campaigns, but due to attention and volume to these less common topics, they merited independent consideration in this cycle. For example. Spanish-language advertising, vice presidential ads, and what we termed "migration" ads mostly, but not always, Republicans, to vote Democrat in the presidential race (Republican Voters Against Trump). Also distinctive to this campaign were ad sets that outwardly addressed common topic areas, religion, corruption, foreign policy, but carried ulterior purpose.

Potential topics were more abundant than the number of class members resulting in not all categories developed being assigned to class researchers. Some arenas omitted include Social Security and the elderly, education which included a vigorous video exchange on school openings, featuring many third-party voices, including teachers' unions and business interests. Additionally, spots from the bevy of primary candidates were largely not included, as well as a myriad of interest groups spots addressing peripheral topics. Also, Trump and Biden issued ads that fell outside the categorization employed for this volume. The aggregated advertisements examined for this volume was over 2800.

The aggregated advertisements examined for this volume was over 2800

A vast majority of the ads placed in research sets had the form of political spots, and political ads remained relevant in 2020. *Forbes* observed, "80% of paid advertising still went to broadcast and cable TV (aka "linear TV"). This is a lower percentage than in prior elections, but an impressive share nevertheless given that within even that last two years ago we've witnessed a significant drop in linear TV viewership and a significant increase in homes cutting the cord from cable or satellite TV" (Homonoff, 2020). In a familiar story for most in the advertising world, digital political advertising spending also exploded in 2020. In the 2015-2016 election cycle, digital media accounted for roughly 2-3% of political ad spending. That jumped to 18% in this one." Ads on Facebook and Instagram were included in the book samples when they had the appearance of a standard political ad. Most ads on the social media, however, were announcements, posters, memes and only occasionally for political ads, most of which also appeared in other venues, were included were included. As AdImpact's John Link pointed out, "75% of Facebook spending was aimed at soliciting funds through campaign contributions or merchandise purchasing. A far smaller percentage was aimed at voter persuasion, which is still the focus of most TV ads." (Homonoff, 2020)

Book Design

Before the book was conceived students in the prior semester produced class project research, six of which dealt with the primary ads in 2019 – 2020. They have been revised and included in this volume. In most instances the primary political ads were distinct from those aired in the general election. The audience was Democrat voters sorting through a populated primary process which from one time or another featured 28 candidates (additionally there were five Republicans who entered and quickly withdrew from GOP primary process). In particular, the primary ads contrasted with the general election regarding health care, climate, and criminal justice, with less contrast in the arena of guns and COVID-19, as explained in the relevant chapters.

The book is organized around six sections aimed to underline distinctive features that characterized the 2020 political advertising. The first section, *Crucial Advertising Themes*, examines the two-core advertising vectors, economy and COVID-19. These themes not only produced the greatest volume of advertising they likely had the greatest influence on the election outcome.

The following section, *Broadly Framed – Candidate Image and The Future,* a more symbolic set, captures the underlying themes that defined this election. Identifying the candidate's image and framing the country's future are involved in every campaign, yet their ruthlessness and predominance stood out in this election cycle. It was a campaign built around the candidate's persona and strategically played out through competing visions of the country's future. Leadership versus compassion, democracy's survival versus socialism became the respective campaigns symbolic containers. Additionally, this section reports data for a less than dignified sidebar assessing the candidates "fitness" for office, dementia contrasted with soundness of judgment.

The third section, *Non-Traditional Purpose for Traditional Themes*, looks at campaign choice wherein traditional campaign advertising categories (religion women guns, and healthcare) and how they are commandeered for less traditional purposes. For at least some of these chapters the traditional arena became not so much a policy debate but rather a referendum on the candidate's character. Issues such as climate were essentially settled in voter's intention. Others, notably health and guns, were comparable with prior campaigns.

Section four, *Distinctive Advertising Themes*, looks at advertising themes that developed in ways that have not happened in prior campaigns. The summer of racial unrest and the governmental "law and order" response, social justice in many forms, were talked about with volume and multiple voices heretofore not apparent in political ads. Other categories which garnered heightened centrality included Spanish-language ads, vice presidential ads and an unprecedented emphasis on corruption in its many forms.

Section 5, S*urprising Sidebars*, examines a variety of unusual themes, ranging from consideration of the White House video as political advertising to the advent of heavily funded secondary groups, in particular The Lincoln Project, the realignment of the electorate as expressed in "migration" ads to an examination of unique social media applications, including memes and language use.

Finally, the last section, *Foreign Policy Advertising Sidetracked*, allegedly looks at foreign policy advertising. While the ads examined talk about foreign policy ranging from China to the US military, these researchers uncover that the 2020 ads focused more on candidate's character and their leadership quotient.

—

The hope is that reader's approach to this volume with a couple ideas in mind. First it is fundamentally a descriptive volume, accounting for most of the presidential ads produced in 2020. Occasionally it rises to analytic, but training and time constrained those expressions. Nonetheless this initial overview provides a historical and demographic sense of the cycle otherwise unavailable.

Secondly it is hoped that the readers approach the chapters with a teacher's generosity. Not only is the book about the 2020 cycle but it also served as a training tool for a capable class of students. The students research designs were negotiated but were largely of their choice. The research therefore ought to be viewed as featuring each author's voice and not an imposed overlay for their investigation choices. The chapters hopefully are more than a "nice" student project. The chapters are substantive, offering genuine contributions.

References

Coppock, A., Hill, S. J., & Vavreck, L. (2020). The small effects of political advertising are small regardless of context, message, sender, or receiver: Evidence from 59 real-time randomized experiments. *Science Advances*, 6(36).

Gerber, A. S., Gimpel, J. G., Green, D. P., & & Shaw, D. R. (2011). How large and long-lasting are the persuasive effects of televised campaign ads? Results from a randomized field experiment. *American Political Science Review, 105*(1), 135- 150.

Homonoff, H. (2020, December 8). *2020 political ad spending exploded: Did it work?* Forbes. https://www.forbes.com/sites/howardhomonoff/2020/12/08/2020-political-ad-spending-exploded-did-it-work/?sh=343399cf3ce0

Lau, R. R., Sigelman, L. & Rovner, I. B. (2007). Effects of negative political campaigns: A meta-analytic reassessment. *Journal of Politics, 69*(4), 1176-1209

Record shattering political ad spending in the 2020 election cycle. (2020, October 15). BusinessWire. https://www.businesswire.com/news/home/20201015005996/en/Record-Shattering-Political-Ad-Spending-In-the-2020-Election-Cycle%20BusinessWire,%20Oct%2015,%202020

Sides, J., & Karch, A. (2018) Messages that mobilize? Issue publics and the content of campaign advertising. *Journal of Politics, 70*(2), 466-476.

---

[i] YouTube launched in 2005, in-video ads in 2007.

[ii] http://www.livingroomcandidate.org/commercials/2020; https://cla.purdue.edu/academic/communication/cspan/ccse/index.html; https://www.ou.edu/carlalbertcenter/congressional-collection/kanter

SECTION 1: CRUCIAL ADVERTISING THEMES

Allan Louden, Editor

Many issues populate campaign ads but not all issues wield equal influence. Even the most impactful themes may not be apparent in the heat of the campaign. Albeit speculative, two ad sets appeared to dominate as the 2020 campaign's major decision criteria. The research in this opening section examines the dual centrality of economy and coronavirus ads.

Mary Kern launches this volume with her examination of 147 economic ads from the 2020 general election cycle. She justly observes that Biden ad's focus on bringing back manufacturing jobs likely was a key reason he flipped Upper Midwest but it is also likely that Trump's "economy" advertising may have contributed to the November's closeness.[i] Very few commentators or analysts have given the economic political advertising its due. Kerns substantive research provides insight into the scope and messaging of Trump's economic communication.

Trump's economy spots were not his most dramatic nor did they generate the buzz of other ads, but they may have been the most effective in voting preference. Their style was generally more substantial than his "viral" ads appealing to long-term Republican tropes of taxes, jobs, and the bedrock importance of a rising economy. By mid-September, the campaign shifted *en masse* from "law and order" to heavy spending "in key battleground states and districts promoting the president's economic policies," often with the flavor of economic breakthroughs for women of color. (Easley, 2020).

Kerns emphasis on middle-class and upper Midwest advertising, may undersell the effectiveness of the Trump economic advertising. While the trends she identifies were in play, Trump also focused on specific businesses and the necessity, even in the face of coronavirus, of being open for business. He also aired many ads addressing small business, often in a narrative form, including Pennsylvania's fracking industry. In one highly produced spot *Jen*, a technician rises early commuting to her fracking job. The enterprising young women laments Biden's eliminating jobs and concludes with the appropriate working-class twang "I'm stickin' with Trump" (Jen, 2020). Many voters abhorred Trump style but ascribed a flourishing economy to the president, an interpretation directly fostered by Trump. (Love Me or Hate Me, 2020)

An end of the campaign Republican poll suggested the most important issue was the rampaging virus. "Most voters said they prioritized battling the coronavirus over reopening the economy, even as the president put a firm emphasis on the latter" (Isenstadt, 2121). Despite Isenstadt's claim the economy still was a dominant issue, at least in mid-summer according to Pew (See Table 1). Later in the campaign the Coronavirus issue combined economic issues – shutdowns versus openings – in an ongoing video debate.

According to the Wesleyan Media Project (2020) Biden mentioned health care, jobs, and Social Security at a slightly higher rates… while Trump has focused on taxes (in just under half of his airings), the economy, jobs, prescription drugs and health care. Late in October the Trump ads shifted primarily to, economy and taxes jobs, and businesses while the Biden campaign touched on similar issues their emphasis included healthcare, Social Security, and coronavirus (Wesleyan Media Project, 2020).[ii]

To argue that the economy was central is not to suggest that coronavirus did not share that status. The second, but not secondary, defining influence was more evident, boosted by mainstream media. By April, the *New York Times* reported that "more than, 50%, political ads on TV are about the coronavirus." In just one week, they suggested 33 unique ads centered on the virus (Corasaniti, 2020). From the outset of obvious political fallout, COVID ads were issued in a steady video metronome until the November vote. Evidence of the issue's importance is indirectly affirmed in the sample included over 380 individual ads.

After the election, a Trump campaign pollster, Tony Fabrizio indicated his data showed that in the 10 key states voters "rated the pandemic as their top voting issue" (Dawsey, 2021). Most of the ads, as the following studies indicate, were produced by Biden or affiliate group with fewer Trump or Trump supporters weighing in. Many of his ads were speech excerpts, with an occasional ad touting progress or his "bold step" cutting off China travelers.

Two chapters examine the COVID-19 advertising, Melissa Cooney the preconvention period (65 ads from 130 sample) and Chandler Stearns and MuTsu Wu postconvention (100 ads from 489 sample). The numerous coronavirus ads led both studies to use sampling techniques. Unlike other issue arenas where the campaigns enjoyed the latitude to advantage bearing messaging, the Covid-19 ads stayed relatively consistent across the campaign. Similar stylistic presentations, charts with soaring infection numbers, timelines and countdown clocks, and repetition of "revealing" quotations, held throughout. Visuals favored coffins and chaotic hospital isolation wards.

The unchanging style and content may be explainable. The media narratives constrained and sustained a drumbeat of "ever worsening" news, obviously red-hot political material. Moreover, with Trump assuming the coronavirus briefing spotlight, charges of "lack of leadership" by *the* central actor followed. The groundswell of COVID-19 messaging functioned synecdochally for the larger question in obvious play, the selection of leadership. It also was an issue that allowed many third-party voices to easily pile on, often with ads aimed toward unique communities.

The economy and Corona ads combined for over 500 ads examined in this volume. The spending was markedly different than even the very expensive 2016 election. BusinessWire (2020) recounted that "$2.63B has been spent on Presidential advertising this cycle as compared to $855M in the previous cycle."[iii]

References

Burden, B. C. (2121, April 22). *The 2020 Presidential Election Verdict*, Political Studies Quarterly, https://onlinelibrary.wiley.com/doi/full/10.1111/psq.12715?campaign=wolearlyview.

Coransaniti, N. (2020, April 21). *Coronavirus takes over political advertising*. New York Times. Accessed at https://www.nytimes.com/2020/04/21/us/politics/coronavirus-takes-over-political-advertising.html.

Dawsey, J. (2021, February 1). *Poor handling of virus cost Trump his reelection, campaign autopsy finds*. The Washington Post. https://www.washingtonpost.com/politics/poor-handling-of-virus-cost-trump-his-reelection-campaign-autopsy-finds/2021/02/01/92d60002-650b-11eb-886d-5264d4ceb46d_story.html.

Easley, J. (September 2020). *Trump campaign shifts message to the economy with new eight-figure ad buy*. The Hill. https://thehill.com/homenews/campaign/516455-trump-campaign-shifts-message-to-the-economy-with-new-8-figure-ad-buy.

Isenstadt, A. (2121, February 1). *Trump pollster's campaign autopsy paints damning picture of defeat.* Politico. https://www.politico.com/news/2021/02/01/trump-campaign-autopsy-paints-damning-picture-of-defeat-464636.

Jen (2020, October 1). Donald J Trump, YouTube. https://www.youtube.com/watch?v=CIvctsTdhLk.

Love me or hate me, but you have to vote for me: Trump makes 2020 pitch with 'hottest economy' boast (2020, August 16). News-18-World. https://www.news18.com/news/world/love-me-or-hate-me-but-you-have-to-vote-for-me-trump-makes-2020-pitch-with-hottest-economy-boast-2272023.html.

Pew Research Center (20, August 13). *Important issues in the 2020 election.* Pew Research Center. https://www.pewresearch.org/politics/2020/08/13/important-issues-in-the-2020-election/.

Wesleyan Media Project (2020, October 29). *Presidential general election ad spending tops $1.5 billion.* https://mediaproject.wesleyan.edu/releases-102920/#table1

---

[i] Political scientist Barry Burton summarized, [Trump] did not suffer a landslide loss. The 2020 election was instead a startlingly "normal" verdict. (2021).

[ii] Regrettably, this volume did not have enough researcher to cover the Social Security and elderly ad categories. They were, however, presented with much energy, each candidate claiming they would protect the elderly and Social Security while their opponent would eviscerate the elderly. Their presentations were consistent with the traditional emphasis of the respective parties.

[iii] From mid-April through late October, Biden had spent an estimated $376 million on broadcast, cable, and satellite TV ads, whereas Trump had spent $222 million (Wesleyan Media Project, 2020) Although Trump's ads were increasingly attacks on Biden and Democrats, the Biden ads were light on attacks, leading to an overall ad tone that was more positive than in 2016.

Biden spent $191 million on online ads, almost half of which ran through Google Ads. Trump spent $268 million, also equally divided between Facebook and Google. But much of Trump's advantage was a result of his spending that occurred prior to Biden's campaign launch, dating back to when Trump officially filed for reelection at the Federal Election Commission on the day after his 2017 inauguration. (Burden, 2121).

Chapter 1: Middle-Class Rust Belt Voters in the 2020 Election: An Analysis of the Presidential Campaign Economy Advertisements

Mary Kern

Mary is a Senior in Economics from Richmond, VA

Introduction

According to an August registered voters survey conducted by Pew Research Center asking which topics are of most importance to Democrats and Republicans in the 2020 election, 84% of Republicans and 66% of Democrats said the economy would be a top issue when voting this year (Deane & Gramlich, 2020). On the other hand, it appears that both parties had starkly different views on how the economy has been doing since the pandemic. A survey by The Associated Press found that Americans who view the economy as "good" overwhelmingly voted for President Trump, while those who view the economy as "poor" were much more likely to cast their vote for Biden. These polarizing viewpoints on the state of the economy amid the worst pandemic since 1918 have contributed to the contrasts of the economy-related advertisements between Trump and Biden leading up to the election.

One of the most important groups that Biden needed to win back was White working-class citizens. In 2016, 23% of white working-class men voted Democrat, and in 2020, that number jumped to 28% (Williams, 2020). It may seem like a small increase, but it was enough to flip Wisconsin, Michigan, and Pennsylvania in Biden's favor. From analyzing the data set of Economy ads, Biden's campaign tactic was to focus on White working-class citizens from the Upper Midwest and Rust Belt region. This group historically votes Republican and had wide Trump support in 2016, but Joe Biden took back some of those votes. Biden's relatability to working-class Americans in the Upper Midwest due to his upbringing in Scranton, Pennsylvania along with his consistent middle class focused messaging in his campaign ads on bringing back manufacturing jobs likely was a key reason why Biden flipped Upper Midwest counties to win the 2020 election.

Literature Review

Traditionally, "white working class" citizens are defined as whites without a college degree and report below the annual household income median of $60,000 (Carnes & Lupu, 2020). Over the past few decades, more and more white working-class citizens have voted for Republican presidential candidates. In the 2016 election, 62% of white working-class voters voted for Donald J. Trump. This indicates that Trump won the largest percentage of white working-class voters than any past Republican candidate, a noteworthy 5% increase from the 2012 election (Carnes & Lupu, 2020). A lot of researchers believe that white working-class voters, especially males, helped Trump flip three 2016 key "blue wall" states in the Rust Belt: Wisconsin, Michigan, and Pennsylvania (Carnes & Lupu, 2020).

In 2020, however, Trump lost votes from white males by 5 percentage points. Trump did increase votes in Latinx men by 3 percentage points and in Latinx women by 3 percentage points (Vox). Trump also won 45% of the Latinx vote in Florida, mainly fueled by fear-mongering rhetoric towards Cubans and Venezuelans that voting for Biden would lead to socialism (Williams, 2020). More generally, the Trump campaign's tactic in the 2020 election revolved around the use of fearmongering in their political advertisements. These advertisements heavily centered around the idea of Joe Biden being a socialist and that he will let the "radical left" rule the Democratic Party. However, these fear-based ads were, in part, believed by Trump supporters already. This suggests that Trump's tactics were to persuade vulnerable swing voters to vote for Trump, showing success among Latinx voters. According to polls conducted this past summer and fall, the use of fearmongering during the Black Lives Matter movement under the Trump campaign did not appeal to most voters. The paradox of Trump's broad derogatory statements around Black Lives Matter was not resonating with voters who viewed the pandemic and the economy as more important than the protests (Bennett, 2020). While the 2020 Campaign advertisements touch on a wide range of genres, this paper focuses on the advertisements released in the nine months leading up to the election that can be categorized under the Economy topic. More specifically, I will analyze the effectiveness of the Economy advertisements on the middle class in the Upper Midwest Rustbelt region which I believe played a significant role in Biden's victory.

Even though the Biden campaign in the 2020 election did their fair share of fear-mongering advertisements related to the leadership and morals of the President, the Biden campaign put out many positive advertisements that reflected Biden's plan to restore decency and provide hope in this country (also see chapter 6). More specifically, the Biden campaign's key narrative was focusing on the middle class. Joe Biden has repeatedly stated that one of the main components in his economic plan is to restore the middle class, especially in the Rust Belt states. Born in Scranton, Pennsylvania in a middle-class family, Joe Biden uses his relatability and authenticity to his advantage in his political speeches and advertisements. Studies have shown that authenticity in a political candidate helps inform voters' intentions when deciding who to vote for (Stiers, et al., 2019). The vast amount of economic advertisements depicting Joe Biden as a relatable, authentic, middle-class Pennsylvanian wanting to restore American manufacturing and lift the middle class helped Biden turn key states in the Upper Midwest.

Research Question and Methodology

The research question examined is the 2020 Economy ads: what are the common themes in the 2020 presidential Economy ads, and what are the key distinctions between the Trump and Biden ads?

The data set used for this study encompasses the ads on Economy, Jobs, Taxes, and Small Businesses, comprising 147 total advertisements. These ads are from various sources such as the Trump and Biden presidential campaigns, Pro-Biden and Pro-Trump Political Action Committees (PACs), and other third-party groups.

I conducted a content analysis to analyze the qualitative data in the advertisements. I conducted a first-round coding process on all the advertisements to identify common themes, topics, patterns, word usage, and structures. Next, I formulated a code sheet that appears in Figure 1 which includes the candidate positions, messaging format, theme, source, and other important variables in which I coded each advertisement in their appropriate categories.

(continues on following page with Figure 1)

Figure 1: Economy Ads Code Sheet

5. **Categories/Themes:**
    a. 1=Small Businesses
    b. 2=Middle Class
    c. 3= Taxes
    d. 4=Jobs
    e. 5=Leadership/Ideology
    f. 6=General Economy; multiple issues

6. **Position:**
    a. 1= Pro-Trump
    b. 2= Pro- Biden

7. **Source:**
    a. 1= Trump campaign
    b. 2= Biden Campaign
    c. 3= pro-Trump groups
    d. 4= pro-Biden groups
    e. 5= third party other; Lincoln Project, Meidas touch, SEIU, unions, Pacronym

8. **Timeline:**
    a. 1= Before February- May
    b. 2= June- July
    c. 3=August- September
    d. 4=October- November

9. **Messaging:**
    a. 1= Personal Narrative
    b. 2= Economic statistics (TV News, reporters, etc.)
    c. 3= Omniscient Third Person Narrative
    d. 4= Attack other president (fear mongering, attack ads, scare tactics, intimidation)
    e. 5= Candidate Praise (successes, policies, plans)
    f. 6 = Other messaging formats

10. **Geography:**
    a. 1=targeting Upper Midwest
    b. 2=targeting other geographic regions
    c. 3= non- targeted geographic location

11. **Profession:**
    a. 1= small business owners
    b. 2= farmers
    c. 3= manufacturing/auto industry
    d. 4= fracking
    e. 5= N/A

From my first round of coding, I created six categories for the Economy ads. Each of these categories was formed based on the number of advertisements that included economic policies, personal narrative, economic statistics, candidate strategies, or candidate behavior related to these different categories. The Positions tags were based on if the ad delivered positive messaging related to the candidate or delivered negative messages towards the opponent. The Source category tags the advertisement sponsor: primary campaigns, Pro-Biden/Trump PAC, or a third-party PAC that is not related to either candidate. I included a Timeline category that shows the dates of when the ads were published or aired. The Messaging Format category relates to the type of messaging of the advertisement. These categories represent most Economy ads. I added a Geography category if the advertisement was about a specific location, talked about a specific location, or took place in a specific location. Lastly, I added a Profession category if the advertisement was specific to a type of industry or it focused on a person in a specific line of work. After creating the code sheet, I conducted a second round of coding to group each individual advertisement into each of the categories. I created an Excel spreadsheet and coded each advertisement using the code sheet as my guide, using Stata to analyze the data.

Results

In this section, I conducted various cross tabulations and Pearson's Chi-squared statistical test to find the frequencies of the advertisements and if differentials in the number of advertisements in the different categories between Biden and Trump are statistically significant.

In Table 1, reports on the Position of Candidate and the Category of the advertisement, significance recorded as chi-squares. The frequencies suggest that by far the most common theme in the Economy advertisements are related to Leadership and Ideology.

Table 1: Position of Candidate and Category of Advertisement

		Small Business	Middle Class	Taxes	Jobs	Leadership	General Economy	Total
Trump	Ad Count	3	3	9	15	27	12	69
	χ^2 Contribution	1.2	5.2	4.0	0.6	0.3	0.0	11.3
Biden	Ad Count	9	19	1	11	25	13	78
	χ^2 Contribution	1.1	4.6	3.5	0.6	0.2	0.0	10.0
Total	Ad Count	12	22	10	26	52	25	147
	χ^2 Contribution	2.3	9.8	7.4	1.2	0.5	0.0	21.3

Pearson Chi-squared (5) = 21.2975   P-value= 0.001***

I grouped these two themes together because most of the advertisements that include the leadership qualities, or lack thereof, also include the ideologies the candidate. Some common examples from the Trump campaign are related to apprehension of Joe Biden's drift to socialism. For example, one Trump campaign advertisement says that "Joe Biden and the socialist Democrats would immediately collapse the economy." This idea of Joe Biden being a socialist and his threat to the economy was very common in this thematic category. On the other hand, many of Pro-Biden advertisements attack President Trump's leadership qualities and his ability to guide the economy out of the COVID-19 related recession. The Chi-squared contributions below the frequencies show that the differences on the Middle Class is highly significant. Of the 22 ads in the Middle-Class category, 19 of them are Pro-Biden ads. This finding is important in understanding Biden's main campaign tactic, targeting the middle class. Most of these ads relate to the middle class as being the "backbone of our nation" and that "Joe Biden will fight for middle-class families". These advertisements include personal narratives of Michigan auto workers, the thousands of jobs lost in Good Year plants under Trump, and Biden's economic plan to restore the middle class and supercharge American manufacturing. All 19 Middle-Class advertisements put out by pro-Biden groups all relayed similar messaging and imagery to make Joe Biden seem relatable to middle-class voters. Overall, the Chi-squared statistic is significant at the 0.001 level. We can conclude that there are significant differences between the Biden and Trump advertisements within the different categories of the advertisement.

In other findings, I calculated the candidate position in the advertisement by the ad's source. The Lincoln Project, Meidas Touch, SEIU, and others mainly were more anti-Trump than they were Pro-Biden. Another finding to note is that there are more pro-Trump campaign ads than pro-Biden campaign ads on the Economy. However, the Pro-Biden PAC ads and third-party group's ads make up for this difference.

I also conducted a cross-tabulation of the position of the ad and the date the ad was posted. Most of the advertisements were in the August-November timeline, showing the importance of putting out more content as the election nears. In general, the advertisements were evenly spread across different time periods indicating that economic ads remained central as the campaign unfolded.

In Table 2, I report a Chi-squared test on the Position of Candidate and the Messaging Format. The most common messaging format by far is the "Attack other candidate," with a total Chi-squared for the category at 4.9. This category includes fear-mongering ads about the other candidate or party and other negative advertisements on the other candidate. The Pro-Trump ads had 34 advertisements in this format, compared to 21 advertisements in the

Pro-Biden ads indicating the difference was statistically significant.

Table 2: Position of Candidate and Messaging Format

		Personal Narrative	Economic Statistics	Omniscient 3rd Person Narrative	Attack Other Candidate	Candidate Praise	Other Messaging Formats	Total
Trump	Ad Count	16	8	0	34	11	0	69
	χ^2 Contribution	0.0	1.0	1.4	2.6	2.1	3.3	10.3
Biden	Ad Count	18	4	3	21	25	7	78
	χ^2 Contribution	0.0	0.9	1.2	2.3	1.8	2.9	9.1
Total	Ad Count	34	12	3	55	36	7	147
	χ^2 Contribution	0.0	1.9	2.7	4.9	3.9	6.2	19.5

Pearson Chi-squared (5) = 19.4902   P-value= 0.002**

Another relevant finding from this table is that of the "Candidate Praise" advertisements, 25 of the 36 of them come from Pro-Biden advertisements. We can see the statistical significance again in the large Chi-squared contribution statistics. These findings suggest that a lot of the "Attack other Candidate" advertisements, which are mainly negative ads towards the opposing candidate, are Pro-Trump, and a lot of the "Candidate Praise" advertisements, which are mainly positive ads towards the candidate, are Pro-Biden. This finding confirms what articles and studies have shown regarding Trump's heavy usage of fear-mongering scare tactics in his political advertisements surrounding Joe Biden giving in to the "radical Democrat socialists". The Chi-squared statistic of 19.4902 is significant at the 0.002 level of significance. We can conclude that there are distinct differences between the Biden and Trump advertisements on the different messaging formats of the advertisement.

In Table 3, I look at Chi squares on the Position of Candidate and the Geography of the Advertisement. This statistical table shows the importance of the Pro-Biden advertisements targeting the Upper Midwest region in their Economy ads. Out of the 36 ads targeting the Upper Midwest, 26 of them are Pro-Biden ads.

Table 3: Position of Candidate and Geography of Advertisement

		Upper Midwest/Rust Belt Region	Other Geographic Location	Non-targeted Geographic Location	Total
Trump	Ad Count	10	4	55	69
	χ^2 Contribution	2.8	0.0	0.9	3.7
Biden	Ad Count	26	4	48	78
	χ^2 Contribution	2.5	0.0	0.8	3.3
Total	Ad Count	36	8	103	147
	χ^2 Contribution	5.3	0.0	1.7	7.1

Pearson Chi-squared (2) = 7.0623   P-value=0.029**

We can see the statistical significance of the difference of the number of ads in this category by the hefty Chi-square numbers of 2.8 and 2.5. Most of the advertisements targeting the Upper Midwest relate to Wisconsin, Michigan, and Pennsylvania, three states that Biden flipped in the 2020 election. These advertisements mainly included personal narratives of middle-class citizens from these states and a heavy emphasis on restoring American manufacturing jobs in these states. These findings show the significance of targeting the Upper Midwest region for Biden's campaign strategy. Overall, the Chi-squared is statistically significant at the 0.029 level of significance. We can conclude that there are statistically significant differences between the Biden and Trump advertisements on the targeted geographic locations of the advertisement.

Table 4 shows a statistical test on the Position of Candidate and the professions pro-trade in the advertising. Most advertisements relating to a specific profession are about manufacturing jobs. This ranges from a personal narrative of a manufacturing worker or the importance of restoring manufacturing jobs in the United States. Of the 21 ads related to manufacturing jobs, 18 of them are Pro-Biden ads.

Table 4: Position of Candidate and Profession of Advertisement

		Small Business Owners	Farmers	Manufacturing & Auto Industry	Fracking	N/A	Total
Trump	Ad Count	5	0	3	10	51	69
	χ^2 Contribution	0.2	2.8	4.8	6.0	0.7	14.4
Biden	Ad Count	8	6	18	0	46	78
	χ^2 Contribution	0.2	2.5	4.2	5.3	0.6	12.8
Total	Ad Count	13	6	21	10	97	147
	χ^2 Contribution	0.4	5.3	9.0	11.3	1.2	27.2

Pearson Chi-squared (4) = 27.2153   P-value= 0.000***

The statistical significance is clear from the Chi-square. For example, one advertisement in this category says that "Joe Biden is all about American manufacturing". Since most of the manufacturing jobs in the United States are in the Upper Midwest and Rust Belt region, we can conclude even more that Biden's messaging to Upper Midwestern, middle-class manufacturing workers was consistent throughout his advertising. All the 10 fracking advertisements are pro-Trump, which was Trump's main tactic in the advertisements targeting the western Pennsylvania region. This difference in fracking ads is obviously statistically significant (at the 0.000 level). We can conclude that there are statistically significant differences between the Biden and Trump advertisements on the targeted professions of the advertisements and types of employment.[i]

Findings and Conclusion

The results presented provide evidence for my research question regarding the key differences between the Biden and Trump economy-related political advertisements. From analyzing the data, Biden's main economic advertising tactic was to target middle class, upper Midwestern manufacturing workers. From conducting the qualitative research of watching all the economy-related advertisements, it was clear that Joe Biden had a focus on flipping middle-class voters in the Rust Belt region in the 2020 election. These advertisements were consistently made up of positive rhetoric regarding Biden's economic plan for the middle class and for manufacturing jobs. On the other hand, the statistical tables show Trump's main tactic of attacking the other candidate's leadership abilities through attacking the opponent on leadership and ideology. From the data, we can confirm that Trump used more fearmongering and scare tactics in his advertisements surrounding Joe Biden's leadership and ideology to instill fear and anxiety in swing voters. Of course, the Trump campaign and Associates also produced many ads aimed at particular groups and professions. For example, in Pennsylvania they aired numerous fracking commercials and traditional economy ads.

The stark distinctions between the tactics of the Trump campaign and the Biden campaign show the importance of what may have contributed to Biden's election victory. Biden took back a small share of Upper Midwestern white middle-class voters, which was enough to flip Wisconsin, Pennsylvania, and Michigan. Now that the Democratic Party has those states along with Georgia and Arizona, it is important that the Republican Party understands why Biden won in those key states if they want to stand a chance in future presidential elections. This paper gives a glimpse of the growing importance of the Upper Midwest middle-class voters in presidential elections. In a time of great division, polarization, and despair, the evidence shows that voters supported a candidate that was relatable and could restore hope to middle-class American workers.

References

Bennett, B. (2020, September 5). *Donald Trump's campaign of fear resonates—but not necessarily with the voters who will decide the election.* Time. https://time.com/5886343/trump-fear-swing-voters/

Carnes, N., & Lupu, N. (2020). *The white working class and the 2016 election.* Perspectives on Politics, First View. 1-18. doi:10.1017/S1537592720001267

Cineas, F., & North, A. (2020, November 7). *Election results: White people make up the majority of Trump voters in 2020.* Vox. https://www.vox.com/2020/11/7/21551364/white-trump-voters-2020

Deane, C., & Gramlich, J. (2020, November 6). *2020 election reveals two broad voting coalitions fundamentally at odds.* Pew Research Center. https://www.pewresearch.org/fact-tank/2020/11/06/2020-election-reveals-two-broad-voting-coalitions-fundamentally-at-odds/

New York Times. (2021, November 3). *2020 presidential election results: Joe Biden wins.* The New York Times. https://www.nytimes.com/interactive/2020/11/03/us/elections/results-president

Pager, T., & Egkolfopoulou, M. (2020, September 17). *Biden stresses middle class roots in plea to Pennsylvania voters.* Bloomberg. https://www.bloomberg.com/news/articles/2020-09-18/biden-stresses-middle-class-roots-in-plea-to-pennsylvania-voters

Stiers, D., Larner, J., Kenny, J., Breitenstein, S., Vallée-Dubois, F., & Lewis-Beck, M. (2019, December 9). *Candidate authenticity: 'To Thine Own Self Be True.'* Political Behavior.

Watson, K. (2020, October 1). *Trump banks on fear and anxiety to motivate voters.* CBS News. https://www.cbsnews.com/news/trumps-use-of-fear-and-anxiety-to-motivate-his-voters/

Williams, J. (2020, November 10). *How Biden won back (enough of) the white working class.* Harvard Business Review. https://hbr.org/2020/11/how-biden-won-back-enough-of-the-white-working-class

[i] Significant differences were not found for aspects messaging formatting. Table 5 shows the Category and the Messaging Format of the advertisement.

Table 5: Category and Messaging Format of Advertisement

Category		Personal Narrative	Economic Statistics	Omniscient 3rd Person Narrative	Attack Other Candidate	Candidate Praise	Other Messaging Formats	Total
Small Business	Ad Count	9	1	1	0	1	0	12
	χ^2 Contribution	14.0	0.0	2.3	4.5	1.3	0.6	22.6
Middle Class	Ad Count	8	0	1	1	11	1	22
	χ^2 Contribution	1.7	1.8	0.7	6.4	5.8	0.0	16.3
Taxes	Ad Count	1	0	0	6	3	0	10
	χ^2 Contribution	0.7	0.8	0.2	1.4	0.1	0.5	3.7
Jobs	Ad Count	6	5	1	9	5	0	26
	χ^2 Contribution	0.0	3.9	0.4	0.1	0.3	1.2	5.9
Leadership	Ad Count	10	0	0	36	4	2	52
	χ^2 Contribution	0.3	4.2	1.1	14.1	6.0	0.1	25.8
General Economy	Ad Count	0	6	0	3	12	4	25
	χ^2 Contribution	5.8	7.7	0.5	4.3	5.6	6.6	30.6
Total	Ad Count	34	12	3	55	36	7	147
	χ^2 Contribution	22.5	18.4	5.2	30.6	19.2	9.0	105.0

Pearson Chi-squared (5) = 104.9604   P-value= 0.000***

Chapter 2: Trump and Biden's Primary COVID-19 Political Advertisements

Melissa Cooney

Melissa is a Senior in Communication from Locust Valley, NY

Objective

It was announced on March 11, 2020 that classes at Wake Forest University would be postponed a week and then conducted online for an indefinite time. Throughout that week, public hotspots like Broadway Theatre announced that they would be 'going dark' and the NCAA March Madness Basketball Tournament was canceled for the season. These operations were affected by the same affliction – the outbreak of the novel coronavirus in the United States. COVID-19, first appeared in Washington State on January 21, 2020, perhaps from a citizen who traveled to Wuhan, China (Schumaker, 2020). Since then, the United States government has engaged the continuing threat of COVID-19, a crisis which has permeated all 50 States and most every aspect of daily life.

New York City was named the epicenter of the United States COVID-19 outbreak on March 20, 2020 (Schumaker, 2020). As a resident of Long Island, NY, living only twenty miles away from Manhattan, this virus was alarming, yet intriguing – a natural for my research. Before the world went remote, I interned at WXII 12, the local Winston-Salem NBC News affiliate. Nearly every day, I watched reporters curate stories about COVID-19, a peril that still seemed out of reach and non-threatening, despite warnings. This virus was perhaps less alarming due to the intense politicization that tangled its narrative even before it fully entered our lives.

COVID-19 arrived in a tumultuous time for the nation. A Presidential election was only eight months away; the pandemic became perfect ammunition to make or break the candidates' relationships with voters. The federal and statewide government's ability to handle such a crisis proved difficult, and politically it would be no surprise that COVID-19 themed advertisements would be crafted during the ever-escalating crisis.

Political advertising is "one of the most powerful weapons in the arsenal of any political marketing effort," due to the way these advertisements can with relative ease reach voters on the internet, television, radio stations, and even billboards (Kaid, 2008). The goal of political advertising in general is to market a candidate in a zero-sum game depicting them electable, or not electable, depending on the sponsor. Essentially, "politicians shape the message they want to communicate to voters and spread it out in the form of a public message or political advertising," in an effort to appeal to the ethos of their supporters and to sway those who do not support them (Maarek,1995).

There are very traditional forms of positive political advertisements, created by the candidate or by proxies who support them. Some examples of these positive advertisement styles include the "cinema verité" style, which shows the candidate interact with real people in normal situations, the "man-in-the-street" style, with an endorsement from ordinary citizens, the "testimonial" style which provides endorsements from high profile individuals, and the "neutral reporter" style which provides facts about the candidate, inviting viewers to make judgements on their own (Lahi, 2015). Negative advertisements, on the other hand, are usually created by the candidate's opponents. These negative advertisements frequently utilize intense music, harsh graphics, testimony of how the candidate has disrespected the citizenry. This mode often employs self-indicting quotations inviting judgments of incompetence or insensitivity. The purpose of negative advertisements often is to prompt fear. According to Ted Brader at the University of Michigan, "Fear ads heighten attentiveness and weaken people's reliance on partisan habits, while enthusiasm ads reassure you, and reaffirm the choice you've already made" (2005).

From a pool of 130 pre-convention COVID-19 related advertisements, I analyzed 65 of these. The specific set was chosen by random generation from the ~130 advertisements and I chose the first 65 that were generated.

There are two political advertisement techniques that are most prevalent throughout the COVID-19 ads, regardless if the advertisements were positive or negative. First, many advertisements, often across ads, repeat sound bites from each candidate. The goal of this technique is to paint a candidate is capable and consistent (or not). These sound bites continually reinforce or create viewer notions about candidates. Political theorist Danielle Allen explains the use of sound bites in political advertising as "the pleasure of recognition, or as Aristotle called it, 'easy learning'" (Allen, 2008). Essentially, the goal of this is to create a positive or negative association in the viewers brain based on the sound bite used.

Secondly, many advertisements use a video editing technique where a buzzword (good or bad) is seen on top of a photo of a candidate or situation.

This technique also creates an association that said buzzword is related to the image. The use of implied messaging is a common technique, to "unconsciously cause people to view a candidate more negatively" (Weinberger & Westen, 2008). These implied messages, however, can also be used in a positive way as well, with a positive buzzword overlaid on a positive image (like the American flag).

The objective of this analysis is to recognize the recurring tropes, themes, quotes, and other means of political communication seen in these advertisements, and how each presidential candidate is portrayed. The categorizations were designed to answer the question: What was the composition of pre-convention COVID-19 political advertisements?

Methodology

I reviewed the randomly selected 65 ads, dividing them into 5 categories. These categories of advertisements include: Anti-Trump and Anti-Biden Advertisements, Pro-Trump and Pro-Biden Advertisements, and Testimonial Advertisements from frontline healthcare workers, business owners, and voters, who provide firsthand account of how the government's actions with the virus had personally affected them. In each category, the sponsor of the video was noted, as well as a summary of the video, the type of video (speech, use of voiceover, etc.), the videos goal, and length. Moments of repetition, when advertisements took advantage of the same sound bites or series of soundbites – typically cuts of Biden and Trump speaking – were noted. Many advertisements also took advantage of specific video tropes, like adding text over an image. Dividing the videos into these categories and subcategories aided in understanding which sponsors used which advertising technique and provided an account for how each candidate presented himself and how other sponsors portrayed them.

Results

I describe the results for each of the five categories and explain the subcategories that were noted in the advertisements. Additionally, I select advertisements from each category that represent a common theme as representative examples.

Anti-Trump COVID-19 Political Advertisements

The political advertisements that were against Donald Trump tended to take advantage of his inconsistencies with informing the public about the disease and its spread. The goal of these advertisements was to present Trump as an incompetent leader and blame his inconsistencies as an important cause for deaths and spread of COVID-19. Sponsors tended to take advantage of Trump's apparent lack of awareness of COVID-19, both with the first appearance of the virus and as the severity became apparent.

One advertisement by American Bridge 21st Century, a liberal American Super PAC employed the incompetent leader premise this. This advertisement is titled *Trump Played Golf* (2020) and develops its message by showing important dates on the virus' timeline, coupled with imagery of Trump playing golf, purportedly on those same days. Common sound bites of Trump were also used to enhance this idea of incompetence. These quotations, returned to later in this analysis, include "This is their new hoax" and "It'll go away, just stay calm," both of which convey the idea that Trump is not committed to the idea of the virus's severity. At the end, this advertisement utilizes the technique of sending an implicit message by showing a graph with an exponential curve of the rising COVID-19 deaths. Over this image a text overlay reads "Trump's failure to act cost lives", which asserts that Trump's actions are directly consequential to the deaths of Americans.

An advertisement titled *Crisis Comes* by Unite the Country, a pro-Biden Super PAC, suggests Trump is an incompetent leader by way of comparing him to past presidents (Crisis, 2020). This advertisement explains that "what matters is how they [Presidents] handle it [crisis]." An ominous voiceover explains how Trump relieved the pandemic response team positions in 2018, and how he "let the virus spread unchecked" throughout the country. The advertisement ends after thirty seconds with a black and white image of Trump with text that reads "This one failed." This advertisement shared information about Trump's job performance asking voters to drive comparative judgment. This subtly relays the message that he would not *become competent* as a leader in a second term either.

Another Anti-Trump COVID-19 political advertisement that enhances the goal of proving Trump to be an incompetent leader is The Lincoln Project's infamous ad titled *Mourning in America* (2020). The Lincoln Project is an Anti-Trump Republican Super PAC, and this advertisement does not utilize the soundbite and implied message technique as previously mentioned but creates a feeling of intensity and drama. A menacing voiceover states that "more than 60,000 Americans have died from a virus that Donald Trump ignored," once again promoting the idea that an act of incompetency directly resulted in death. Striking images are shown throughout this advertisement, with footage of people being dragged away on stretchers and a town in shambles. The idea of Trump bailing out "Wall Street, not Main Street" tells the viewer that he has picked and chosen who he does and does not want to help during this pandemic. The advertisement finishes by leaving the viewer with a question: "if we have another four years of this, will there even be an America?" [i]. This advertisement, while slightly different than the others analyzed, proved to be one that is historic and important to acknowledge, considering Trump himself took to Twitter to express his anguish with it (Galen, 2020).

These are three examples of COVID-19 Anti-Trump advertisements that paint President Trump as an incompetent leader. Out of the 20 Anti-Trump advertisements watched, the quote of Trump in a press conference saying, "this is their new hoax" was used seven times. A clip of Trump saying that COVID-19 is "like a miracle, it will disappear" was used four times in varying advertisements. A clip of Trump claiming that the virus will go away in April with the heat was used five times in varying advertisements.

Repeating text and images also occurred and often across various sponsors (in 15 times out of the 20 advertisements – See Table 1). This occurred in several ways. Some advertisements, like the one mentioned earlier by the American Bridge 21st Century as well as *Exponential Threat* by Priorities USA (Exponential, 2020) used graphs to show the death toll and relate it to Trump's leadership. Other advertisements, like *Trump Lies, People Die* by MoveOn inserted phrases like "Trump Lies", "False", and "Blames Hospitals" (to name a few) over footage of Trump (Trump Lies, 2020).

Pro-Trump COVID-19 Political Advertisements

The COVID-19 political advertisements in favor of President Trump were mostly created by The White House communication unit and Donald J Trump for President campaign. Two of the 12 advertisements viewed in this category, however, are sponsored by The Republican National Committee, and one of these advertisements is sponsored by United We Stand, a Republican Super PAC. There are two major themes apparent in this Pro-Trump selection. The first theme is patriotism, and the second theme is proof of competent leadership (a stark contrast in comparison to the Anti-Trump COVID-19 political advertisements).

Table 1: Frequency of Direct Quotes in COVID-19 Pre-convention Ads

Quote Used	# of Ads Using this Quote	Context Used
"It'll go away in April" -Trump	5	Anti Trump Ads, Pro Biden Ads
"Their new hoax" -Trump	7	Anti Trump Ads
"No, I don't take responsibility at all" -Trump	4	Anti Trump Ads, Pro Biden Ads
"Something's going on. Where are masks going?" -Trump	2	Anti Trump Ads
"They're not bad folks, folks" -Biden	3	Anti Biden Ads
"A rising China is a positive development" -Biden	2	Anti Biden Ads
"Like a miracle, it will disappear" -Biden	4	Anti Biden Ads
"It's in our best interest that China continues to prosper" -Biden	4	Anti Biden Ads
"...everything we could have hoped for." -Newsome	3	Pro Trump Ads

There were two advertisements that especially exemplify the idea of patriotism and nationalism, both positive. The first is *President Trump Welcomes America's Truckers* created by The White House (President Trump welcomes, 2020). Firstly, it is important to note that the videos created by The White House are not actually advertisements, but their propagandist nature creates a similar feeling of a political advertisement, with the goal to convince the viewer of a message or value (See Chapter 22). This video is narrated by a voiceover of President Trump giving a speech, explaining how important truckers are during this pandemic and to our economy in general. In many White House videos common tropes included the use the American flag, slow motion clips of Trump, and a voiceover. This advertisement seems to be created to prove Trump's love for the United States and anyone who inhabits it, especially the working class. The second video that exemplifies the idea of patriotism is titled *President Trump Visits USNS Comfort*, also produced by The White House (2020). This advertisement has more American flag use than the previous one, but still follows the same format of a voice-over coupled with slow motion saluting, walking, and helping others. A use of tacit messaging is seen in this advertisement, with Trump's speech being heard while the only thing in the shot is a flying American flag. This advertisement presents Trump the patriot, putting America first, and waving in the USNS to the New York city harbor on its Presidential ordered mission; implying Trump responds to the crisis and helps stop the spread.

Some of the Trump ads use repeated clips, primarily governor's testimonials to validate his competence. For example, the advertisements *HOPE* (2020) and *My Coronavirus Response is a Promise Made, Promise Kept!* (2020) produced by Donald J Trump for President and *President Trump's Bipartisan Leadership is Making a Difference* produced by the GOP include repetitive sound bites of various governors throughout the country commenting on positive aspects of the President's leadership (President Trump's Bipartisan, 2020). All three of these advertisements include sound bites from California Governor Gavin Newsom explaining that Trump has done "everything we could have hoped for." Additionally, varying sound bites from New York Governor Andrew Cuomo, New Jersey Governor Phil Murphy, Maryland Governor Larry Hogan, and New Mexico Governor Michelle Grisham were provided, all praising Trump's responsiveness and aid in a sentence or two. All three of these advertisements additionally prove Trump's competency as a leader by showing imagery of the President working hard and appearing as a leader.

Perhaps the most interesting advertisement is titled *President Trump Never Called the Coronavirus 'A Hoax'*, created by the GOP (President Trump Never Called, 2020,). This advertisement warns viewers to not believe everything the media produces, because a lot of sound bites in advertisements can be taken out of context. A full clip from the Trump; speech is provided, and it is clear that, while there was still a negative connotation associated with what he was saying, Trump did not claim COVID-19 itself to be "a hoax." It appears that he was claiming that democrat accusations are a hoax, the same way he has previously titled his impeachment trial and the election scandal a hoax. That is, Trump's "failures" are the conspiratorial fabrication of his political enemies. This advertisement is interesting, in part, because it does what other advertisement do not – directly calls out misrepresentations in the opponents advertising.

Anti-Biden COVID-19 Political Advertisements

Out of the seven Anti-Biden COVID-19 political advertisements viewed, six were sponsored by American First Action, a Pro-Trump PAC. The seventh advertisement was sponsored by Donald J. Trump for President. All seven of these advertisements have the same angle against Biden: proving that he is a traitor who favors China and would therefore be an incompetent leader (See Chapters 29 & 30). It was found that the recurring sound bite was used in every single one of these advertisements. A clip of Joe Biden referencing the Chinese "They're not bad folks, folks!" was used in three varying advertisements. A clip of Biden stating "It's in our best interest that China continues to prosper" was used in four varying advertisements. A shot of Chinese President Xi and Biden cheering champagne flutes at a press conference was used in four advertisements as well. Additionally, all seven videos shared the same editing and production technique, taking advantage of aggressive graphics, the color red, intense music, and sound bites that may have been taken slightly out of chronological context. These advertisements are all negative and seem to coincide with Brader's theory of instilling fear in viewers as mentioned earlier. While there were not as many Anti-Biden COVID-19 advertisements in this pre-convention period, the ones that were present provided insight on the initial attack on Joe Biden. While Anti-Trump advertisements benefit from using Trump's inconsistencies and mistakes while in office as they pertain to COVID-19, Anti-Biden advertisements acknowledge the virus' origin in China and try to paint Biden as someone who supports them and their journey with the virus.

Pro-Biden COVID-19 Political Advertisements

Of the fifteen Pro-Biden COVID-19 political advertisements viewed, thirteen were sponsored by Biden for President, one by Priorities USA, a Democratic Super PAC, and the other was sponsored by the Service Employees International Union. The main theme found throughout these advertisements is that Joe Biden would be a better President than Trump based on Trump's actions (or lack thereof) with COVID-19, shown in positive and negative forms of advertising.

Some uses of negative advertising as seen in the Pro-Biden advertisements are in the ones that bring Trump down. The advertisement *Better Prepared* by Priorities USA uses imagery to accompany a voice-over that explains how a crisis like COVID-19 causes Americans to lead (Better Prepared, 2020). This advertisement uses an out of context sound bite from Trump that says "No, I don't take responsibility at all" about the virus. *Better Prepared* also utilizes the technique of implied messaging by having this sound bite laid over an image of Trump with text that says "America needs a leader we can trust" over his face. Another advertisement *Buck Stops Here* also utilize this same soundbite of Trump saying that he takes no responsibility (Buck, 2020). Another Pro-Biden negative advertisement is titled *Hoarding – Joe Biden for President* (Hoarding, 2020) This advertisement compares Trump sound bites with Biden sound bites, allowing the viewer to draw conclusions that Biden is much more competent a lead in than Trump based on the audio. Two other negative advertisements that support Biden are *The Uncomfortable Truth is that Trump Left America Exposed and Vulnerable* (Uncomfortable, 2020) and *Trump's Rewriting History* (2020), both of which explain how Trump got rid of the pandemic response team in 2016 and Biden's plans for the future. Through these advertisements, Biden's goal and strategy are to prove himself as a more organized, consistent, and competent leader than Trump.

Biden also has produced a plethora of positive advertisements that focus on his experience with COVID-19 as opposed to bringing down Trump. Using a message of unity in many of these positive advertisements, Biden takes advantage of many of the techniques mentioned previously. The advertisement titled *Joe and Jill Biden Thank Frontline SEIU Workers* (2020) is a perfect example of the "cinema verité" or "man-in-the-street" advertisement types (Lahi, 2015). Here, the Bidens are seen doing a normal quarantine activity (Facetime) while thanking a nurse who could represent a whole population of healthcare workers and union workers. Additionally, some of Biden's advertisements are simply clippings from speeches, like the one titled "Joe Biden Discusses the Coronavirus Outbreak During the

Democratic Debate", where Biden provides the viewers with a comprehensive three-part plan about how he would help COVID-19 crisis as president (Biden, 2020, Joe Biden discusses). Although these types of advertisements do not mention Trump and do not utilize the same tropes that have been already analyzed, they send a message that he is a better fit than Trump based on the clarity and comprehensibility of his speeches. These advertisements are positive and serve as an example for the "neutral reporter" advertisement style, where the viewer is provided information with little visual and aural guidance.

Testimonial COVID-19 Political Advertisements

Also important were the relatively large number of testimonial advertisements that surfaced. While the political slant in testimonial advertisements could be sometimes obvious and sometimes hidden, they differ providing evidence as opposed to more advertising tricks (e.g., repetitive sound bite usage and implied messages). Testimonial advertisements allow viewers to associate a face with an issue that a candidate did or did cause or solve. For example, the advertisement *Lynn WI* by Priorities USA shares a personal story from a retired nurse who also has a chronic illness (Lynn, 2020). She explains how she feels the government was unprepared, especially in the firing of the Pandemic Response Team, and now fears for her health and the safety of her former colleagues at the hospital. This is a perfect example of how testimonial advertising is fully political. This is a tangible story from someone facing direct consequences of Trump's actions and under preparedness. In a similar advertisement, *Sandy #Protect Nurses* by National Nurses United shares the same theme as *Lynn WI*, as nurse Sandy Redding explains her troublesome experience and why she feels the government is not prepared Be a Hero (2020). In a different but also effective advertisement by The Lincoln Project, *Heroes* is a collection of emotional stories from nurses, teachers, and other frontline essential workers explaining

their hardships with the virus (Heroes, 2020). While this advertisement has less of a direct political slant to it, it is very clear to the viewer that the government's action can be to blame for the hardship these essential workers are facing.

Conclusion

Each of the five categories analyzed utilized similar tropes of sound bite repetition, subtle messages, and overall themes of proving (in)competency. In one sense the findings are to be expected, Donald Trump and his sponsors put him in the best light possible, and Joe Biden and his sponsors did the same. The advertisements were often skewed or fabricated, even for testimonial spots with no mention of a political candidate. The offenses were largely self-indicting video clips, cherry picked and reiterated across most of the COVID-19 primary ads. This analysis shows how ads are not necessarily trustworthy even in the arena of public health and national crisis. The onset of COVID-19 in the United States is a unique issue, especially when coupled with the 2020 Presidential Election. COVID-19 was, and still is, very much a mystery at the time of these advertisements, and these advertisements had a strong role (perhaps a larger role than they realized) in shaping the public's perception of the virus. These advertisements proved themselves to be repetitive and take advantage of such a small group of imagery, quotes, and text. Perhaps, if COVID-19 did not enter the United States during such a tense political period, the virus itself would not still be politicized to this day.

References

Allen, D. (2008). *Politics, propaganda, and the use and abuse of sound-bites.* Institute for Advanced Study. https://www.ias.edu/ideas/politics-propaganda-and-use-and-abuse-sound-bites

Better prepared (2020, March 23). Priorities USA, YouTube. https://www.youtube.com/watch?v=I0-7EFmHArc

Buck stops here – Joe Biden for President. (2020, April 20). Joe Biden for President, YouTube. https://www.youtube.com/watch?v=ozzwMBvvUiA

Biden, J. (2020, March 15). *Joe Biden discusses the coronavirus outbreak during the democratic debate – Joe Biden for President.* YouTube. https://www.youtube.com/watch?v=WWDvWNyqQ74

Brader, T. (2005). Striking a responsive chord: How political ads motivate and persuade voters by appealing to emotions. *American Journal of Political Science, 49*(2). 388-405.

Crisis comes. (2020, March 25). Unite the Country, YouTube. https://www.youtube.com/watch?v=uw2W82HE99Q

Exponential threat (2020, March 23). Priorities USA, YouTube. https://www.youtube.com/watch?v=bkMwvmJLnc0.

Galen, R. (2020 May 6). *Trump's Twitter rant against Lincoln Project's 'Mourning in America' ad proved our point. Think:* NBC News. https://www.nbcnews.com/think/opinion/trump-s-twitter-rant-against-lincoln-project-s-mourning-america-ncna1200881

Heroes (2020, April 1). The Lincoln Project YouTube. https://www.youtube.com/watch?v=o4uj7t3rvJ0

HOPE (2020, March 27). Trump, Donald J. YouTube. https://www.youtube.com/watch?v=BSSrimkmxzI

Hoarding- Joe Biden for President (2020, March 30). Joe Biden for President, YouTube. https://www.youtube.com/watch?v=OexuGsd7rEw

Joe and Jill Biden Thank SEIU Workers (2020, April 17). SEIU, YouTube. https://www.youtube.com/watch?v=6Yb4gB0NPC8

Kaid, L. (2002). Trends in political advertising. *Journal of Political Marketing, 1*(1). 209-212.

Lahi, R. (2015). Political advertising: How new and old democracies make use of it. *European Journal of Research in Social Sciences, 3*(6). 13-33. https://pdfs.semanticscholar.org/d368/527bd88ebcff8b2445b361f9597b9b7a9dad.pdf

Lynn WI. USA (2020, April 14). Priorities, YouTube. https://www.youtube.com/watch?v=TTyjGv3acr8

Maarek, P. (1995). *Political marketing. The International Encyclopedia of Communication.* https://doi.org/10.1002/9781405186407.wbiecp062.

Morning in America (2020, June 8) Reagan, R. (1984). New York Historical Society, YouTube. https://www.youtube.com/watch?v=pUMqic2IcWA

Mourning in America (2020, May 4). The Lincoln Project. YouTube. https://www.youtube.com/watch?v=t_yG_-K2MDo

My Coronavirus Response is a Promise Made, Promise Kept (2020, April 29). Trump, Donald J., YouTube. https://www.youtube.com/watch?v=9hQqg7fIQGs

President Trump's bipartisan leadership is making a difference! GOP (2020, April 9). YouTube. https://www.youtube.com/watch?v=HByLIRy2BPg

President Trump never called the coronavirus 'A Hoax' (2020, April 16). GOP, YouTube. https://www.youtube.com/watch?v=bkMwvmJLnc0.

Sandy #ProtectNurses (2020, April 21). Be a Hero, YouTube. https://www.youtube.com/watch?v=ssgQbXYMES0

Schumaker, E. (2020, April 26). *Timeline: How coronavirus got started.* Retrieved from https://abcnews.go.com/Health/timeline-coronavirus-started/story?id=69435165.

The uncomfortable truth is that Trump left America exposed and vulnerable (2020, April 17). Joe Biden for President, YouTube. https://www.youtube.com/watch?v=R2-5GXQASLE

Trump lies, people die (2020, April 8). MoveOn, YouTube. https://www.youtube.com/watch?v=sIfM8GeSk6Y.

Trump played golf. (2020, April 24). American Bridge 21st Century, YouTube. https://www.youtube.com/watch?v=eoJv-48iFcc

Trump's rewriting history (2020, April 18). Joe Biden for President, YouTube. https://www.youtube.com/watch?v=gVgQ0pYGYtk

President Trump visits the USNS Comfort. (2020, March 30). White House.gov, YouTube. https://www.youtube.com/watch?v=5YkB-I58N-o

President Trump welcomes America's truckers (2020, April 16). White House.gov., YouTube. https://www.youtube.com/watch?v=miImQAY8PiU

Weinberger, J., & Westen, D. (2008). RATS, we should have used Clinton: Subliminal priming in political campaigns. *Political Psychology, 29*(5). 631-651.

---

[i] The ad also plays off Reagan's famous *Morning in America* reelection spot (1984), reminding Republican voters of the contrast with past presidents and invoking the glory days of a "true" Republican. (New York Historical Society, 2020).

Chapter 3: COVID-19 Ads in the 2020 Presidential Election

Chandler Stearns and Mu-Tsu Wu

Chandler is a Junior Communication major from Chicago, IL & Mu-Tsu is an MA student in Communication from Yunlin, Taiwan

2020 is a historical year for political advertisements, with spending that was unprecedented. The Wesleyan Media Project's final report before Election Day, produced in conjunction with the Center for Responsive Politics, finds over $1.5 billion in estimated ad spending on TV, digital, and radio in the presidential general election between April 9 and October 25. $991 million (65 percent) of that spending was from candidates, while outside groups account for the rest. The Biden campaign has spent nearly $564.7 million on advertising across TV, digital, and radio, while the Trump campaign has spent approximately $426.3 million. Both campaigns highly valued advertising's effect on voters. Between October 12 and October 25, the campaigns were ending, and the candidates were making their final appeals to voters. According to the Wesleyan Media Project (2020), while COVID-19 was not the top issue for either candidate, the issue appears in "1 in every 3 Biden ads, and in 1 in every 5 Trump ads, taking up 33% of Biden airings and 22.6% of Trump airings." In addition to political ads produced by the primary candidate campaigns, there are a high number of third-party ideological groups and interest groups that contribute COVID-19 themed ads. According to Erika Franklin Fowler, co-founder of the Wesleyan Media Project, "the outside groups and parties tend to play that role of attack dog" due to the fact that "citizens generally don't like negative advertising," for if candidates themselves go negative against their opponent, that candidate tend to "suffer backlash from airing the negativity in the first place. (Booker & Fong, 2020)"

Previous research shows that political advertisements can alter criteria voters use to judge candidates and impact judgment of candidates (Goldstein & Ridout, 2004; Simunich, 2005). However, despite the relevance and the urgency of the coronavirus pandemic, there has been a paucity of previous literature as there is not a historical parallel in the televised era. The goal of this research is to identify the different modes of persuasion and content in COVID-19 spots in the 2020 campaign. Our first goal is to assess the ads' rhetorical visions to determine the social reality that candidates are asking voters to embrace. Our second goal is to identify the means in which each source attempts to persuade voters of their vision, enhance issue knowledge among voters (Brians & Wattenberg, 1996), win over undecided voters, and motivate party supporters to go to the polls (Atkin & Heald, 1976; Johnston & Kaid, 2002). The purpose of this study is to extend previous political advertising research by using the theoretical framework of priming and framing. Additionally, this study contributes to the body of research, including a content analysis to measure the statistical implications of the political advertisements in the 2020 presidential campaign cycle.

Persuasive Images– the Picture Superiority Effect

The theory of the *picture superiority effect* is used to explain the phenomenon that verbal text paired with imagery is more memorable than verbal text alone (Nelson et al., 1976). The phenomenon implies that images strengthen the impact of verbal persuasive appeals (Seo, Dillard, Shen, 2013). Candidates have a strong incentive to evoke emotion in their campaign ads (Jerit, 2004). In addition, emotions such as anger, fear, and anxiety are the most evoked and will survive longer in the minds of voters when compared to other types of arguments (Jerit, 2004). There is a substantial amount of evidence that supports a priming approach to most campaign strategies (Jacobs & Shapiro, 1994).

Agenda setting in political advertising using salient images and emotional appeals therefore is a powerful strategy to evoke feelings, often "uneasy feelings that need to be dealt with" (Carlson et al., 2009). The way to deal with that uneasiness, would be to take action by casting a ballot in response to the political message (Carlson et al., 2009).

Since graphic images typically influence the salience of an issue, we would like to investigate whether visual rhetoric was a prominent feature in the 2020 Presidential Campaign ad cycle.

Priming & Framing in Political Advertising

Researchers have studied political issues and effects under the framework of priming for many years (Boyle, 2004; Iyengar & Simon, 1993; Mendelsohn, 1996; Valentino, 1999). Priming refers to the effect of a prior stimulus or event on a succeeding stimulus (Roskos-Ewoldsen & Carpentier, 2002) as well as that stimulus "prime" schemas, a complex collection of knowledge about some concept that is stored in long-term memory, to influence individual judgement (Boyle, 2004; Roskos-Eqoldsen et al., 2009). In network models of memory, memories consist of a series of nodes and each node corresponds to a unique concept (Price & Tewsbury, 1997; Koerner & Krcmar, 2016). Priming is effective when it increases the activation level of a mode to its activation threshold, sending the message from the first node to the rest along the associative pathways (Koerner & Krcmar, 2016). In political campaigns, candidate characteristics of trustworthiness and integrity are often the most vulnerable to priming effects (Kelleher & Wolak, 2006), it is therefore not difficult to understand why increases in media exposure promote priming of candidates' character during campaigns (Mendelsohn, 1996), as the concepts have become chronically accessible by frequent activation. This leads us to ask the research question: Do the ads emphasize the character of the candidates? If so, how?

If priming affects what issues are thought about, framing then influences how audiences think about the issues (Carlson et al., 2009). When political advertisements frame an issue, they select some aspects of a perceived reality and make them more salient, further promoting a particular definition, causal interpretation, moral evaluation, or treatment recommendation (Entman, 1993). Framing is at its core, a means of social construction (Dunning 2018), influencing and shaping the perception of reality by using schemas of interpretation, anecdotes, and stereotypes (Druckman, 2001).

By framing issues in specific ways, political campaigns declare the underlying causes and likely consequences of a problem and establish criteria for evaluating potential remedies for the problem, creating symbolic issue constructions, knitting together discrete pieces of information into plots or storylines (Gamson et al., 1992; Nelson et al., 1997).

While it has been recognized that the strengths of frames are difficult to measure (Chong & Druckman, 2007), it is worth noting that the relative strength of frames depend on varied factors such as *frequency*, *accessibility*, and *relevance* (Ardevik-Abreu, 2015). In application, the strength of a frame tends to be higher when it is repeated more frequently, when it focuses on considerations that are accessible to individuals, and when it speaks to the core of the matter rather than peripheral issues (Chong & Druckman, 2007; Ardevik-Abreu, 2015). This fact that both priming and framing can strengthen messages by repetition leads us to ask the research question: Do most of the ads tend to feature simplistic, accessible themes and ideas?

Method

Design

This study measured the date, source, target audience, message form, content, and visuals of the COVID-19 themed advertisements from the 2020 Presidential Election.

Measures

In this study we designated the most prevalent message form, content, and visual when coding, however we observed that often a combination of multiple messages, content, and visuals were used.

Date released

Advertisements were identified as either pre-convention (March through June), post-convention (July through August), or main campaign (August through election day November).

Source

Advertisements were coded as being released from five sources: the candidates' primary campaign, Republican and Democratic party sponsored groups, third party candidate associated groups, third party ideological groups, and third-party interest groups. Republican and Democratic party sponsored groups include the Republican and Democratic National Committees. Third party candidate associated groups include Priorities USA, Rebuild America Now, Correct the Record, The Briefing, Unite the Country, and American Bridge 21st Century. Third party ideological groups, representing the largest category, include Republicans Against Trump, The Lincoln Project, Meidas Touch, Don Winslow Films, Independence USA, ReallyAmerica, Pacronym, the conservative attack group American Crossroads, Future 45, and Marco Rubio's PAC, Reclaim America. Lastly, third party interest groups include Protect Our Care, Protect All Workers, Unions, and MoveOn.

Target Audience

The advertisements were identified as either generic or targeted toward an interest group. The main targets identified were families and mothers, the elderly, healthcare workers, schoolteachers, small business owners, agricultural and rural voters, and voters who have lost a loved one.

Message Form

Six forms of message delivery were coded: candidate testimony, third party testimony-public figures against a candidate's position, non-political actor personal testimonies, narratives, internal documentation, and audio-visual combinations. While only the most prominent form of message delivery is identified for coding purposes, many advertisements featured a combination of various message delivery forms, most prominently candidate testimony with narrative.

Content

Nine topics were observed. The topics, or content, observed were: devastation and death in the United States of America, the imminent vaccine, China, pre-existing conditions and the elderly, the Trump administration's leadership or lack thereof, schools, front-line workers, and the economy. As observed with message form, advertisements often featured a combination of topics.

Visuals Used

Advertisements featured eight visuals: front-line workers and nursing home employees, dead bodies and caskets, hospitals and labs, empty chairs and households, cleaning supplies, pictures of people who have passed away, news and social media clips, and graphs. As observed with message form, advertisements often featured a combination of visuals.

Procedure

This specific study examined the COVID-19 related advertisements. From an ad set of 489 advertisements, 100 advertisements were selected at random to be analyzed and coded. The advertisements were coded for the categories described above. Each of the 100 advertisements were watched in full and coded for the previously listed topics.

Results

We originally predicted that visual rhetoric will be a prominent feature in the 2020 Presidential Campaign ad cycle and that advertisements with audiovisuals would be produced pre-convention. To address the first half of the research question we analyzed the various percentages for the visuals used within the advertisements. We observed a wide variety of visuals employed for both the Trump and Biden campaigns, thus supporting our prediction via visual rhetoric. Secondly, for the latter half of the research question, we examined the percentage of audiovisual ads that were produced during the pre-convention period compared to the post-convention and main campaign periods.

We also predicted that most of the advertisements would emphasize the character of the candidates. To test this question, we looked at the content of ads focusing on character. We found that more than half of the advertisements emphasized, and criticized, President Trump's character.

Lastly, we predicted that the advertisements would not differ greatly in content and that the framing for the advertisements would feature simple and accessible ideas. To test this, we looked at the percentages of content in the 100-ad sample. We found that 47% of the content was President Trump and the administration's lack of leadership, supportive of the consistency of the ads. In terms of the framing of the advertisements, we found that the most common visual used to be news and social media clips, both of which include simple, to the point, targeted messages, and are on outlets accessible to the general public.

Moreover, this study has determined that a COVID-19 advertisement's release date did not prove to be impactful. The three possible categories for release were split evenly, with advertisements released pre-convention occupying 35%, advertisements released post-convention occupying 31%, and advertisements released during the main campaign occupying 34% of the sample.

While the release date for a COVID-19 advertisement was not significant, the source was significant (See Table 1). 47% of the 100 strong advertisement sample came from the candidate's primary campaign, and 30% came from third party ideological groups, the majority produced by The Lincoln Project, X, and X. Additionally, 13% of the advertisements came from third party candidate associated groups, 6% from third party interest groups, and 4% from political party sponsored groups.

Table 1: Advertising Sponsor

Primary Campaign	47%
Third-Party Ideological Groups	30%
Third-Party Candidate Associated Groups	13%
Third-Party Interest Groups	6%
Political Party Sponsored Groups	4%

Thirdly, 86% of the advertisement sample was observed as being generic and 14% as targeting a specific audience. The targeted audiences observed were front-line workers, families and grandparents, truck drivers, and schoolteachers.

Furthermore, 32% of the advertisements featured, or were delivered, by the candidates themselves, 20% were narratives, 17% were a combination of audio and visuals, 16% were personal testimonials from non-political actors, 9% were third party testimonials from public figures, and 6% were internal documentation (See Table 2). The Biden campaign, and affiliated groups, were the main producers of advertisements with internal documentation, often quoting President Trump and Vice President Mike Pence's response to the virus. While one may suspect there to be a correlation between the advertisements released pre-convention, due to COVID-19 lockdown restrictions, one was not observed.

Table 2: Stylistic Content

Message Delivered Directly by Candidate	32%
Narratives	20%
Combination of Audio and Visuals	17%
Personal Testimonials	16%
Third Party Testimonials	9%
Internal Documentation	6%

In addition, content, the largest category, observed 47% of the advertisements focused on President Trump's lack of leadership. 13% of the advertisements focused on death, 12% focused on front-line workers and respirator production, 8% focused on the development of the vaccine, 6% focused on the economy, 4% focused on the elderly and pre-existing conditions and the devastation of the virus, and 2% focused on China and schools. 3% of the advertisement sample did not fall under the nine established categories (See Figure 1).

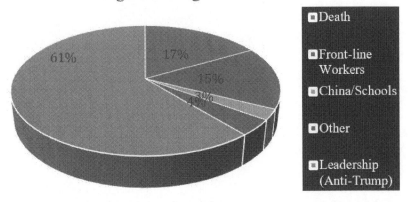

Figure 1: Targeted Content

Lastly, 26% of the visuals in the advertisement sample were news and social media clips, 20% were front-line workers and nursing home employees, 14% were graphs and charts, 11% were hospitals and labs, 3% were pictures of people who have passed away and dead bodies, and 1% were empty chairs and households. No advertisements were observed to use visuals of cleaning supplies, and 22% of the advertisements fell into the "X" category of visuals, which as was the case with content, represented a category of visuals that was not one of the eight established categories. The advertisements assigned an "X" often did not contain any visual aspect or featured positive images of people smiling while wearing masks.

Discussion

Summary of Findings

Overall, this study has determined the importance of visual rhetoric in the 2020 Presidential COVID-19 advertisement cycle, that there is no correlation between the audiovisual message form and the release date of the COVID-19 advertisements, that the majority of the COVID-19 advertisements would emphasize the character of the candidates, that the COVID-19 advertisements did not vary greatly in content, and that the frames employed for the COVID-19 advertisements would feature simple and accessible ideas.

Practical Implications

These findings suggest that, while other categories may have observed most of their advertisements released during the main presidential campaign, the pandemic was a topic for advertisement fuel that the nation had not yet seen before. Additionally, it is significant that the majority of the third party advertisements, at 57% of the 53 ads attributed to third party groups, were produced by third party ideological groups, with The Lincoln Project and Meidas Touch at the forefront of production.

Furthermore, the joint message forms of candidate testimony and narrative were observed in half of the sample, thus showing that the pandemic created a need for people to tell a story, with the ads demonstrating current President Trump's inability to provide a "happy ending". The 6% of advertisements utilizing internal documentation were mainly produced by the Biden campaign and supporting groups to demonstrate an uncaring President Trump and one who is lacking in leadership. The quotes most commonly observed were: "I think we very well have it under control," "It's going to disappear," "Anybody that needs a test gets a test," "No, I don't take responsibility," "Nobody knew there'd be a pandemic or an epidemic of this proportion," "There's never been anything like this in history," "We have it very much under control," and "I think the numbers are going to get progressively better as we go along." Oftentimes these quotes were provided with symbolic soundbites of clocks ticking in the background, or some other representation of calendar and time, alongside the contradicting statements of public figures such as Dr. Anthony Fauci and other health experts and past presidents Barack Obama and George W. Bush. This suggests that political campaigns are well-aware of the potent effects of how frames are strengthened through repetition of similar messages that are made accessible and salient through frequent emphasis.

In addition to featuring the rhetoric of the Trump as contrary to the experts, liberal or anti-Trump sources often feature statistics of cases and of deaths, a Lincoln project used a visual of 100,000 bags that appeared to contain dead bodies that zoom out to resemble to American flag, with ominous audio in the background that is often heard in end-of-the-world Hollywood movies about catastrophic events. Those clips often are seen in dark blue filters that make the pictures grim and depressing, as well as show directly scenes of patients lying in the hospital bed, breathing through ventilators, while the viewer hears the sound of the heart rate monitor that suggest a distressing result. Metaphors are often used in the attack ads, some comparing the Trump administration's response to the pandemic to a war that is brought upon the American people.

It is significant that much of the content for the COVID-19 advertisements was Trump and his administration's lack of leadership, which was aided by the news and social media visual majority. Interestingly, while we did observe advertisements that did not feature any of the visual categories we had established, and thus designated those ads with an "X", we found that the visuals changed but the essential content did not. For example, The Biden campaign and affiliated third party groups often produced advertisements with positive visuals, such as Trump dancing, shaking hands, and mingling with the American people. However, these positive images are used to demonstrate his lack of respect to the Centers for Disease Control and Prevention's guidelines, such as wearing a mask and practicing social distancing. Thus, the advertisements were still successful, despite the more positive imagery, in demonstrating President Trump's lack of leadership.

On the other hand, when coding the pro-Trump ads, most of the ads emphasize on sending the message that Trump was leading the U.S. to overcome the virus. Some of the ads include sounds bits of Kayleigh McEnany, the White House Spokesperson defending Trump by saying that the public should acknowledge "how much this administration has done" when facing something "no one has seen come into" the U.S., while others feature Jared Kushner, saying "President Trump has had a very steady hand in this." Other clips feature sound clips directly from President Trump, using language characterized by superlatives "the United States has carried out more testing than any other country," and comments made by hosts as well as guest speakers on conservative media such as Fox News that seek to frame Trump as a more suitable leader by framing the Biden campaign as reckless in the face of the pandemic, for instance: "Joe Biden is not for any of these shut downs" and that "he [Biden] just decided to cancel all of the testing," the very charges level at Trump. Other Trump ads tend to emphasize the numbers of people who have recovered from the coronavirus and feature clips of Trump visiting patients in the hospital, with the music in the background hopeful and sentimental, like those one would recognize from a film featuring patriotic American war heroes and veterans.

In conclusion, the ads that were sampled in this election cycle have successfully answered the research question of whether ads mainly emphasize the character of the candidate, which the answer would be yes, for both the pro-Trump as well as the pro-Biden camps, aligning with priming theory that the audience would be conditioned to envision candidates in certain ways with certain characteristics and tendencies. Moreover, our analysis with the application of framing theory shows leadership, death, and frontline and medical personnel, to be the most prominent, recurring themes that characterize the ads.

References

Ardèvol-Abreu, A. (2015). Framing theory in communication research. Origins, development and current situation in Spain. *Revista Latina de Comunicación Social, 70.*

Atkin, C., & Heald, G. (1976). Effects of political advertising. *Public Opinion Quarterly, 40*(2), 216-228.

Atkinson, J. D., Hoque, R., McWan, B., & White, J. (2020). Activism's sweet embrace: Political advertisements, audiences, and interpretive strategies. *Democratic Communiqué, 29*(1), 62–77.

Boyle, T. P. (2004). Presidential priming: Incumbent and challenger advertising. *Atlantic Journal of Communication, 12*(4), 200-215.

Brians, C. L., & Wattenberg, M. P. (1996). Campaign issue knowledge and salience: Comparing reception from TV commercials, TV news and newspapers. *American Journal of Political Science, 40*(1)172-193.

Carlson, J., McGloin, R., & Kowal, C. (2009). *An Individual's emotional reaction to political advertisements: Using framing and priming as a theoretical framework.* Conference Papers — International Communication Association, 1–41.

Cacioppo, J. T., & Petty, R. E. (1984). The elaboration likelihood model of persuasion. *ACR North American Advances.* Needs a publisher Review of Clinical Science Chong, D., & Druckman, J. N. (2007). Framing theory. *Annual Review of Political Science, 10*, 103-126.

Dunning, E. (2018). # TrumpStyle: The political frames and twitter attacks of Donald Trump. *The Journal of Social Media in Society, 7*(2), 205-231.

Daignault, P., Soroka, S., & Giasson, T. (2013). The perception of political advertising during an election campaign: A measure of cognitive and emotional effects. *Canadian Journal of Communication,* 38(2), 167–186.

Druckman, J. N. (2001). The implications of framing effects for citizen competence. *Political Behavior, 23*, 225-256.

Entman, R.M. (1993), Framing: Toward clarification of a fractured paradigm. *Journal of Communication, 43,* 51-58.

Gamson, W. A., Croteau, D., Hoynes, W., & Sasson, T. (1992). Media images and the social construction of reality. *Annual review of sociology*, *18*(1), 373-393.

Goldstein, K., & Ridout, T. N. (2004). Measuring the effects of televised political advertising in the United States. *Annual Review of Political Science*, *7*, 205-226.

Hill, R. P., Capella, M., & Cho, Y.-N. (2015). Incivility in political advertisements: a look at the 2012 US presidential election. *International Journal of Advertising*, *34*(5), 812–829.

Iyengar, S. (1987). Television news and citizens' explanations of national affairs. *The American Political Science Review*, *81*(3), 815-831.

Iyengar, S. (1991). *Is anyone responsible? How television frames political issues*. Chicago: University of Chicago Press.

Iyengar, S. & Simon, A. (1993). News coverage of the Gulf crisis and public opinion: A study of agenda-setting, priming, and framing. *Communication Research*, *20*, 365-383.

Iyengar, S., & Ottati, V. (1994). Cognitive perspective in political psychology. *Handbook of Social Cognition*, *2*, 143-187.

Jacobs, L. R., & Shapiro, R. Y. (1994). Issues, candidate image, and priming: The use of private polls in Kennedy's 1960 presidential campaign. *American Political Science Review*, *88*(3), 527-540.

Jerit, J. (2004). Survival of the fittest: Rhetoric during the course of an election campaign. *Political psychology*, *25*(4), 563-575.

Johnston, A., & Kaid, L. L. (2002). Image ads and issue ads in US presidential advertising: Using videostyle to explore stylistic differences in televised political ads from 1952 to 2000. *Journal of Communication*, *52*(2), 281-300.

Kelleher, C. A., & Wolak, J. (2006). Priming presidential approval: The conditionality of issue effects. *Political Behavior*, *28*(3), 193-210.

Krcmar, M., Ewoldsen, D. R., & Koerner, A. (2016). *Communication science theory and research: An advanced introduction*. Routledge.

Lippmann, W. (1922). *Public opinion*. New York: Harcourt, Brace and Co.

McCombs, M. E., Shaw, D. L., & Weaver, D. H. (2014). New directions in agenda-setting theory and research. *Mass communication and society*, *17*(6), 781-802.

Mendelsohn, M. (1996). The media and interpersonal communications: The priming of issues, leaders, and party identification. *Journal of Politics*, *58*(1), 112-125.

Nelson, D. L., Reed, V. S., & Walling, J. R. (1976). Pictorial superiority effect. *Journal of experimental psychology: Human learning and memory*, *2*(5), 523.

Page, J. T., & Duffy, M. E. (2009). A battle of visions: Dueling images of morality in u.s. political campaign tv ads. *Communication, Culture & Critique*, *2*(1), 110–135.

Price, V. & Tewksbury, D. (1997). New values and public opinion: A theoretical account of media priming and framing. In G. A. Barnett & F. J. Boster (Eds.), *Progress in communication sciences: Advances in persuasion* (Vol. 13, pp. 173-212). Greenwich, CT: Ablex Publishing.

Roskos-Ewoldsen, D. R, Roskos-Ewoldsen, B., & Carpentier, F. R. D. (2002). *Media priming: A synthesis. In J. Bryant & D. Zillmann (Eds.), Media effects: Advances in theory and research* (pp. 97-120). Lawrence Erlbaum Associates.

Simunich, B. (2005). Investigating the effects of sponsorship of negative political advertisements on source credibility. In *International Communication Association 2005 Annual Meeting* (pp. 1-20).

Seo, K., Dillard, J. P., & Shen, F. (2013). The effects of message framing and visual image on persuasion. *Communication Quarterly*, *61*(5), 564-583.

Vafeiadis, M., Li, R., & Shen, F. (2018). Narratives in political advertising: An analysis of the political advertisements in the 2014 midterm elections. *Journal of Broadcasting & Electronic Media*, *62*(2), 354–370.

Valentino, N. A. (1999). Crime news and the priming of racial attitudes during evaluations of the president. *Public Opinion Quarterly*, *63*, 293-320.

Wesleyan Media Project. (2020). *Presidential general election ad spending tops $1.5 billion.* https://mediaproject.wesleyan.edu/releases-102920/

Yeojin Kim, Gonzenback, W. J., Vargo, C. J., & Youngju Kim. (2016). First and Second Levels of intermedia agenda setting: Political advertising, newspapers, and Twitter during the 2012 U.S. presidential election. *International Journal of Communication* (19328036), 10, 4550–4569.

Zhao, X., & Bleske, G. L. (1995). Measurement effects in comparing voter learning from television news and campaign advertisements. *Journalism & Mass Communication Quarterly*, *72*(1), 72–83.

SECTION 2: BROADLY FRAMED – CANDIDATE IMAGE AND FUTURE TIMES

Allan Louden, Editor

The 2020 election felt like a referendum on one individual, Donald Trump. An avalanche of Trump hyperbole occupied the political spectrum; all others were bit players offering contrast. Issues often drive elections and partisanship paints a favored outcome, but in the end most campaign's success and failures reside with a specific candidate, a singular actor commanding the stage.

Most everything from 2020 exuded exaggeration, from Donald Trump's basking in the spotlight to Joe Biden's DNC clarion convention call that "character and decency are on the ballot." Nearly all vectors ran through Trump, as if in a centrifuge, the essential defining factor.

In is most elementary form Trump's image claim centered around "strong leadership." Biden's petition concentrated around various iterations of "decency." The candidates were contradictory, differences emphasized across messaging by both candidates. Yet the contest remained close with each finding a sizeable audience. Alan Schroeder, a Boston University election expert explained, "What counts as an appealing personality to one voter may be viewed as a repulsive personality to another," adding that is especially true in the current partisan political environment (Bernstein, 2020).

On a micro-level, one reporter wrote, "Trump was widely seen as more energetic than Biden and slightly more courageous. Biden was overwhelmingly seen as being more even-tempered, a better role model, more empathetic and more honest than Trump" (Bernstein, 2020). A detailed post-mortem from Republican pollster Tony Fabrizio concluded "the former president suffered from voter perception that he wasn't honest or trustworthy…" (Isenstadt, 2121).

Nearly every category of ads examined in this volume returned in some manner to candidate image. Specific Issues were used as exemplars for Trump's governing style and character, often serving as a container for adding further accusations and criticisms of Trump himself. Section 3 explores some of the ways in which traditional issues transform into "it's all about Trump" advertising.

Ashley Foley examines a sample of 152 ads narrowed to spots which directly or suggestively addressed the candidates image presentations. These were more standalone ads on the candidate's personal narrative, character testimonials, and the standard qualifications by which voters often measure political candidates, from competence to integrity. Foley explores the intersection of issues, personal qualities, competence, and the candidate communicated behavior as expressed in their advertising.

One of Foley's findings, notes the marked difference between the two campaigns image establishing strategies, positive advertising by Biden and negative from Trump. Her findings were consistent with Wesleyan Media Project finding, "By and large, pro-Biden ads are positive or contrast, with only about 10 percent being pure attacks. Pro-Trump ads, on the other hand, have seen a rising percentage of attacks since mid-September. In the past week, over 60 percent of pro-Trump ads were pure attacks, and fewer than 10 percent were positive" (2020).

Presidential Fitness

Noah Collier examines a subset of the candidate image spots that we titled "presidential fitness." Clearly, this category could be a subset of both the candidate image framing and predictive future, collections the other two chapters in this section address. The category was created and analyzed because it became an identifiable and heavily advertised pattern, with 58 ads[i] using this theme.

Presidential fitness is not often a major tenet of a campaign, at least in the sense of mental agility or stability. Candidates' age has been called into question in past elections, notably Ronald Reagan, and Bob Dole among modern presidential candidates (Hamblin, 2019). A failing Physical capacity was insinuated regarding FDR's ability to withstand the physical demands of a nation and world in crisis. The tone and directness in the 2020 campaign, however, seemingly had few guardrails, almost zero restraint on impugning their opponent. Not only was the sheer volume of attack ads record-setting (nearly 90 fitness ads), but the tenor was also distinct. Overt messaging accused their opponent of dementia or mental instability, tailoring the attacks towards disqualifying deficiencies.

Noah brings order to the nuances of this sizeable set of advertisements. As Collier indicates most fitness ads did not originate from Biden but rather from his surrogates and primarily from Trump and third-party GOP supporters. A representative example was a longer video that the Trump campaign spent "in the high seven figures" to use on social media (Past and Present, 2020), it was essentially a montage of clips sharing Biden memory lapses and muddled cadence. The argument is that the "commander-in-chief" cannot be mentally diminished (Langlois, 2020). On the Democrats' part, the reservations about Trump's capacities resulted in a quasi-serious discussion of invoking the 25th presidential removal amendment based on mental disqualification (Gerson, 2020).

Future Framing

Campaigning's most fundamental component is a competition to *name* the past, present, and future and thereby influence the meaning assigned to unfolding events and predictions. This process of defining is, in part, the responsibility of the political advertising – to lay out the construction of the future that appeals to voters or to frighten them with the world in which their opponent's values are in place.

I argue that every ad is in some sense convergent with candidate-centric judgments. Likewise, the campaign ads and its surrogates inherently are speaking to the future. Sometimes we reward a "Change" election, as with Obama in 2008, or a status quo reaffirmation as with Reagan's 1984 *Morning in America* (It's Morning, 2020). And seemingly without irony candidates claim the stakes of each election being "the most important in our lifetime." This standard embellishment, however, when embedded in our present polarized rhetoric seemed to rise to an overarching judgment of which future the election endorsed. The hegemony of future framing was imminent, a claim heretofore reserved for going into a major war election (1860, 1928). The campaign's future frames simultaneously felt more contrived than in the immediate past, contrasting failed socialistic states and the "battle for our democratic system." The two campaigns warned of a future dystopia, a nightmare of authoritarian or totalitarian rule, our world changed, for the worse, almost beyond recognition. (Kunkel, 2018).

Grace Keilen takes on this nebulous set of ads, selected for their immediate concern with framing a positive future or soliciting fears for their opponent's nightmare. She examines 183 ads, exploring the orientations offered by the campaigns in 2020. She follows the Joe Biden for President Committee issued ads that forewarned "we are living through a battle for the soul of this nation" as with his dramatic opening advertisements, *Two Years after Charlottesville* (2019).

In non-Biden produced ads, The Lincoln Project, cut to the chase with two entries. *Pizza*, opens with a caring mother tell her son "I'm voting for you," for the "kind of world you deserve." Through smiling tears she tells the young boy "I'm voting for your future." The ads refrain is the simple understated "It's Time" (2020). A second spot, *Goodness* (2020), the Mom in says to her young son. "Sure you would, you'd be a very good president. You would have to be a good person, first." Cut to a defined B/W image of Biden, "It's time for decency."

Trump's offered strength as his most defining character trait, wrapped in patriotic symbols and defiance for those too weak to lead. In a sharp example, *Promises & Hope* (2020), Trump affirms "I didn't back down from my promises and I've kept every single one. Promises Made, Promises Kept."

References

Bernstein, L. (2020, August 20). *2020 election shaping up to be personality contest between Trump, Biden.* ABC News 7. https://wjla.com/news/nation-world/2020-election-shaping-up-to-be-personality-contest-between-biden-trump

Gerson, J. S. (2020, October 26). *We may need the Twenty-fifth Amendment if Trump loses.* The New Yorker. https://www.newyorker.com/news/our-columnists/trump-biden-election-twenty-fifth-amendment-mental-fitness

Goodness (2020, September 18). The Lincoln Project, YouTube. https://www.youtube.com/watch?v=O9yEALZ2vXA

Hamblin, J. (2019, November 15). *The presidents cognitive develop decline.* The Atlantic. https://www.theatlantic.com/health/archive/2019/11/kings-speech/602050/

Isenstadt, A. (2121, February 1). *Trump pollster's campaign autopsy paints damning picture of defeat.* Politico. https://www.politico.com/news/2021/02/01/trump-campaign-autopsy-paints-damning-picture-of-defeat-464636

Langlois, S. (2020, August 18). *The 'harshest' campaign ad yet? Either way, President Trump's reelection team put a lot of money behind it.*

MarketWatch. https://www.marketwatch.com/story/the-harshest-campaign-ad-yet-either-way-president-trumps-reelection-team-put-a-lot-of-money-behind-it-2020-08-18

Kunkel, B. (2018). *Dystopia and the end of politics*. Dissent. https://www.dissentmagazine.org/article/dystopia-and-the-end-of-politics

It's Morning Again in America (2020, June 8). New York Historical Society, YouTube. https://www.youtube.com/watch?v=pUMqic2IcWA

Past and Present (2020. August 15). Donald J. Trump. YouTube. https://www.youtube.com/watch?v=0CszSlVp4tA&feature=emb_logo

Pizza (2020, October 28). The Lincoln Project, YouTube. https://www.youtube.com/watch?v=beiO4DmbFYo

Promises & Hope (2020), Donald J. Trump, YouTube. https://www.youtube.com/watch?v=H3tZplwdS18

Two Years After Charlottesville: A Battle for the Soul of This Nation (2019, August 12). Joe Biden, YouTube. https://youtu.be/KC9NeWG-4BY

---

[i] The sample was limited to examples of Trump's speech excerpt video and a few social media entries. The primary sample was video for broadcast outlets.

Chapter 4: Candidate Framing: Profiles, Competency, and Character

Ashley Foley

Ashley is a Junior in Communication from Charlotte, NC

Candidate framing is always important but perhaps more so in an election that served, in part, as a personal referendum on Trump. Candidate character and traits are at the forefront at understanding election results because "personality traits may even prevent, or make more likely, a president's taking policy positions which may ultimately threaten war" (Rapoport et al. 920). In fact, "even the most highly educated and politically sophisticated voters often seem very concerned about issues of personality and character" (Rapoport et al. 920). Louden and McCauliff write that "the most important characteristics [are] that the candidate be honest, be a person of the highest moral integrity, and be able to talk about problems facing the country" (Louden and McCauliff 89). This is also extremely important for the media:

> Unquestionably the media are powerful in setting agendas and framing candidates' character. What is not predictable is how campaigns and candidates react in the face of prevailing narratives and events. The reality is that candidates continue to appear on television, proffer messages, and make strategic decisions. In other worlds, the central characters in the narrative act and their choices are windows to judging motive." (Louden and McCauliff 96).

Louden and McCauliff also argue that despite many believing "that voters are little more than pawns to the unfolding campaign and media saturation," they believe "that voters have the ability and opportunity to make these more intricate assessments of authenticity" (Louden and McCauliff 96). This is crucial to understand with candidate framing, as many ads are up to the interpretation of the viewers and voters.

Considerable academic debate asks whether candidate traits outweigh candidate's stances on issues. Rapoport, Metcalf, and Harman argue that voters interpret a candidate's stance on issues through understanding their traits, and that they will also interpret a candidate's traits through their stance on issues. Yet, they write:

> Compared with campaigns which directly focus on traits, those emphasizing issues will bring a bonus in terms of greater inferential appeals. This advantage is particularly important since the inferences that people make, going beyond what they see, in an advertisement for example, are better remembered than the facts presented in the ad. If one can emphasize an issue that has consistently accessible links with particular targeted traits, it can, therefore, be more effective than a straight trait appeal (Rapoport et al. 921).

Louden and McCauliff also address the traits versus issue dynamic, as they state that "nearly every article in the last decade has joined a chorus recognizing the limitation of the issue/image dualism, calling for an abandonment of viewing these as independent elements in voter's decision making" (Louden and McCauliff 88). They do point out that "researchers have consistently confirmed that voters are far more interested in candidate characteristics than in party identification or specific issues and are more likely to vote on the basis of the candidate's image" (Louden and McCauliff 86). These arguments demonstrate the complicated and sometimes confusing dynamic of traits versus issues, as they are different but also one and the same.

Establishing the importance of character framing and the dynamic between character and issues is extremely beneficial to understanding the results of the 2020 election. Now more than ever, it seems voters are recognizing how they associate with the character of a candidate as they discover character cannot be separated from policy. Essentially all political ads aim to frame their candidate's character in a strategic and beneficial way. Not only do these ads portray the character of the candidates, but they also compare the character between candidates. Whether it be through Biden's attempts to frame Trump as anti-American, Trump's desire to portray Biden as incompetent, or the many in-betweens, the strength and number of the character ads for this election influenced much of the 2020 campaign.

Method

I looked at 152 ads centered around candidate advertising presentations to gain more insight into how those images were framed. I looked first at the source of ads. The source ads were five categories" Trump Campaign, Biden Campaign, Trump Campaign Affiliate, Biden Campaign Affiliate, or another actor. I looked at each category's orientation, either pro or anti-Biden or Trump. This was necessary, as the ad could be from the Trump Campaign, but it might not mention Trump and focusing instead on attacking Biden. Next, I noted if the ad had any aspects of a personal narrative or anti-personal narrative. I defined this as mention of the candidate's life outside of politics, such as Trump's business or Biden's family.

Lastly, I categorized ad spots by the categories suggested by Louden and McCauliff: Issue Stance, Personal Qualities and Traits, Competence, and Communicative Behavior. Keeping the categories consistent was important to me for analysis when comparing this election to future elections. By using the same categories, comparisons to past elections and their candidate framing can be made. I recorded if the ad orientation was positive or negative. For the most part, ads that were pro-candidate would be in the pro-category, and ads that were anti-candidate would be in the anti-category. The only exception was when the ads focused on both candidates, then there would be some combinations of the pro and anti-categories. I analyzed these categories to see how framing interacted with other variables.

Results

First, I looked at the distribution of the positive and negative ads by sponsor. The data showed that far more ads from the candidates themselves were from Biden. There were 44 Pro-Biden ads from his campaign, but only 9 Pro-Trump ads (see Table 1). The largest number of ads came from Independent groups, such as the Lincoln Project and Meidas Touch. Not only were many of the Biden ads positive (33), but many of the Trump ads were negative (58). It is very clear from this table that character ads focused more on framing Biden in a positive way, and Trump in a negative way. This is possibly due to the Biden campaign emphasizing Trump's character in framing differences.

Table 1: Positive and Negative Ads by Sponsor

Pro-Biden	Pro-Trump	Anti-Biden	Anti-Trump
44	9	5	7
1	1	0	2
33	2	5	58

There were 31 ads with a focus on positive personal narrative. Every one of those 31 were pro-Biden. There were 10 ads with a focus on anti-personal narrative. Each one of those 10 ads were anti-Trump.

Table 2: Positive and Negative Personal Narrative Ads by Candidate

Positive/Negative	Trump	Biden
Positive Personal Narrative	0	21
Negative Personal Narrative	10	0

Looking at the character categories, there are quite a few different ways to view this. I decided the best way to cross reference the category with whether it is pro or anti the candidate. It is important to note that when a category is pro-candidate, it means it is praising the candidate for the trait, but when a category is anti-candidate, it means it is attacking the candidate for the trait.

Table 3: Ad Orientation by Content

Orientation	Issue Stance	Personal Qual	Competence	Comm. Behavior
Pro Trump	8	1	12	0
Pro Biden	18	53	39	3
Anti Trump	6	19	51	15
Anti Biden	4	2	5	2

Discussion

As mentioned above, candidate trait is an especially important decision factor for voters. The results of the data analysis prove that the Biden campaign, or Pro-Biden creators, chose to either attack Trump's character or praise Biden's character. I cannot speak for other categories, but I suspect ads praising Trump and attacking Biden were focused elsewhere.[i] I believe this is due to the fact that in this election, Biden had the best chance to win over Trump by connecting character to presidential success. Many of his ads focused on highlighting how being president involves being a good person, and how he possessed the positive character attributes to excel in these positions. Ads attacking Trump portrayed how his lack of character led to his failure in the White House, and how America could not handle four more years of this horribleness.

The personal narrative ads were informative as demonstrations of how the candidate's personal history would influence their presidency. The ones with a positive personal narrative on Biden focused mostly on his life growing up in Scranton, the tragedies he has faced in his life, and his experience as a member of the middle class. The anti-personal narrative ads of Trump focused mostly on his corrupt business activity.

Louden and McCaullif write how issue stance and character trait must be reflexive (Louden and McCauliff 88). The ads for this election cycle suggest this as well. Many candidate framing ads still included issue stance (37 total), functionally connecting this to character. Trump's issue ads had the largest percentage of ads attacking Biden at 40%. The Trump campaign outwardly assumed he could most effectively attack Biden in policy specific issues. Many of these issue stance ads attempted to portray how Biden's past policy decisions have negatively impacted America, making him a suspect choice. Still, there were more anti-Trump ads in Biden's issue stance category (60%) that mostly focused on his failure to address COVID-19 and the nascent political movements.

For personal qualities and traits, I was not surprised to find that 53 out of 54 of the pro personal traits were positively framing Biden. The Biden campaign, affiliates, and other creators assumed that they could beat Trump by reinforcing that Biden was simply a better person. Additionally, the anti-personal qualities and traits were most focused on Trump, proving how he was a bad person, and therefore a bad leader.

An interesting question that came up when looking at competence was leadership.

Like the issue stance and character argument, leadership and character go hand in hand. This was the category where Trump has his most pro-category attributes. He portrayed himself as a leader for the American people, not Washington. Biden ads, in turn, attacked this by proving his failures the past four years. There were also a decent amount of anti-Biden ads attacking his competence, often demonstrated through his failures as a Vice President for Barack Obama. The pro-Biden ads were focused on showing that leadership necessitates decency. For Trump, leadership meant that caring for America was the characteristic factor a leader must embrace.

There were not many ads about communicative behavior (only 20), but many of them attacked Trump's communication techniques through Twitter and how his speeches compare to other US presidents. The comparison tactic was a very interesting one, as it demonstrated how the communicative behavior of previous presidents showed their character, while Trump's constant tweets and rowdy speeches made him much less sanguine as a leader.

Overall, the character framing ads prove this was a very important category for the Biden campaign, as they could praise Biden and attack Trump. As a meta-strategy, arguably this succeeded as Biden won the presidency.

References

Louden, A & McCauliff, K (2004). The "Authentic Candidate": Extending candidate image

assessment (2004). In K. Hacker (Ed.). *Presidential Candidate Images* (pp. 85-103). Rowman & Littlefield.

Rapoport, R, & Metcalf, K. L. (1989). Candidate traits and voter inferences: An experimental study. *The Journal of Politics, 51*(4), 917-932.

---

[i] Editor's note: Each chapter, illustrate the intersect of character and issue, underscoring Trump's persona, most often in the context of an issue, for example, Coronavirus (the issue is COVID-19, the target is Trump' failed s leadership). Attacks on Biden's character were also told through an issue lens, for example China and economy. As indicated earlier in this essay, soliciting a positive or negative character judgment can be most effective when contextualized in a specific issue or action.

Chapter 5: Presidential Fitness

Noah Collier

Noah is a Senior in Politics and International Affairs from Richmond, VA

Introduction

The political arena and political advertising have recently become more vicious, shifting away from policy to the negative framing of an opponent's character. In their report titled "The Mass Media and the Public's Assessments of Presidential Candidates, 1952-2000," Martin Gilens, Lynn Vavreck and Martin Cohen (2007) study this trend. Using a ratio of policy content to character as content as a measure of advertising and news quality, the authors find that since the 1950's, the quality of campaign and political news has fallen drastically. For instance, their measure of quality via *60 Minutes* had fallen from about 1.0 in 1968 to 0.4 in 1998 (Gilens, et al., 2007). From such data, one can conclude that ads have become "meaner" and more hostile towards the opposing candidate.

One such move away from policy could be towards the fitness of a candidate. The President of the United States needs to be physically and mentally fit to serve in the largest leadership position in the world. In the instance of the 2020 election, both Joe Biden and Donald Trump were well over the age of 70, being 77 and 74 years old, respectively. As Catherine Lucey and Ken Thomas of the *Wall Street Journal* noted in May of 2020, while the Biden campaign focused attack ads on Trump's handling of the COVID-19 pandemic, the Trump campaign launched a series of ads showing Biden as "old, looking confused and appearing to slur his words." (2020). The journalists further speak on Trump's strategy, citing the words of Republican strategist Alex Conant. "They need to convince voters that Biden is a riskier choice than Trump." Conant makes the Trump campaign strategy quite clear here – show as many Biden gaffes and mental slip ups as possible to level the playing field and show that Biden is unfit to serve.

Employing this disqualification strategy, the Trump campaign was active on social media releasing ads questioning the former Vice-President's fitness. Facebook ads released in May asked voters if Mr. Biden was "too old" to be elected President and said, "Geriatric mental health is no laughing matter" (Axelrod, 2020). Other ads depicted a photoshopped Biden being fed in a nursing home, asking again "Too Old?" Trump spokesman Ken Farnoso defended the President's attack ads on Biden, claiming "Any honest voter juxtaposing President Trump and the Democrat candidate can see the stark difference in mental acuity and wit" (Olorunnipa & Linskey, 2020). Again, the strategy was explicit and well-focused in targeting Biden as a politician who is past his prime.

The mental health attack ads were not necessarily reciprocated by the Biden team. In fact, following Trump's COVID-19 diagnosis on October 2nd, 2020, the Biden team was quick to take down any attack ads it had on Facebook or TV. Syracuse University assistant professor Brian McKernan notes that the Biden campaign was "usually way more civil than uncivil" in the use of his ads, further noting that on most days, about 90% of Biden's ads are rated as civil (Kates, 2020). This seems to portray the Biden campaign's strategy and overall message being cast to voters – Biden tried to take the high road and display positivity against a President who has been seen as provocative by many, while seemingly giving the "dirty work" of personally attacking the President to outside groups. Lastly, Olorunnipa and Linskey of the *Washington Post* note that the fitness attack ads on Biden may not be working, noting the lack of change in Biden's lead in swing states and Biden's lead amongst older voters. Most of this analysis took place during the campaign. Research that dives deeper into the details of this election's ad patterns does not exist yet, which gives me the impetus to perform this study.

Research and Methodology

I built this study around the research question "How was each candidate framed in terms of their fitness for office?". To examine this question, I examined a sample of 88 political ads that dealt with the theme of the candidate's health and fitness during the 2020 Presidential election.

Within this ad set, I coded each ad based on a set of criteria organically constructed. A content analysis was performed, and the resulting data statistically analyzed via SPSS. In this analysis, I coded each advertisement with the following criteria: 1.) Was the ad was targeted at Trump or Biden, 2.) the ad's length, 3.) the ad's source, and 4.) if ad content was primarily focused on the candidate's mental health, physical health, or the candidate's fitness of their "character." For advertisements that dealt with the candidate's mental health, I included ones that focused on any age-related mental slip up, including stutters, incoherent speech, forgetting facts and topics, and anything else that focused on the candidate's mentality as it is affected by aging. For physical health, included ads focused on content such as injuring themselves doing basic tasks, health as it relates to coronavirus (such as not wanting to go outside/participate in rallies), coughing, etc. Lastly, ads that focused on fitness of character had content that dealt with if the candidate had a record for lying, if they had a "backbone", if they had a strong moral compass, and if they had said anything inappropriate (i.e. sexually, race-related, etc.) on record. (Also See Chapter 4 which focuses on presentation of candidate character).

For each category, the variables were assigned numerical values. Advertisements regarding Trump and Biden were coded to whether they were shown in a positive light or in a negative light. Ad length was coded as either less than 15 seconds, around 30 seconds, between 45 seconds and a minute, or if it was greater than one minute in length.

Advertisement source was coded for if it were of a primary source (a verified ad from an official campaign account, primarily directly from the official Trump or Biden campaigns), sources associated with the National Parties (fairly uncommon – RNC, DNC, or associated groups), and ads from independent, third party sources. These ads were mostly ideological, sometimes explicitly endorsing a candidate, while other times just speaking against one. Ads of this type were generally from sources such as "The Lincoln Project," "Meidas Touch," "Restoration PAC," and the "Committee to Defend the President PACs.

Finally, I coded for ad "content." Each were assigned to one of three categories of fitness characteristics: "Mental Health," "Physical Health," and "Fitness – Character." The answer also was assigned values of if the trait was shown in a positive or negative light.

After coding, the data set was evaluated using SPSS, resulting in cross tables of each candidate's ads.

Results

Included below are the results for both Biden and Trump focused ads. Included first are the summary tables for each candidate, followed by specific tables for each variable.

Ads That Focused on Biden

Biden-Focused Ads Summary

	Cases					
	Valid		Missing		Total	
	N	Percent	N	Percent	N	Percent
Biden * Mental Health – age	40	59.7%	27	40.3%	67	100.0%
Biden * Physical Health	4	6.0%	63	94.0%	67	100.0%
Biden * MH – Character	23	34.3%	44	65.7%	67	100.0%
Time * Mental Health – age	40	59.7%	27	40.3%	67	100.0%
Time * Physical Health	4	6.0%	63	94.0%	67	100.0%
Time * MH – Character	23	34.3%	44	65.7%	67	100.0%
Source * Mental Health – age	40	59.7%	27	40.3%	67	100.0%
Source * Physical Health	4	6.0%	63	94.0%	67	100.0%
Source * MH – Character	23	34.3%	44	65.7%	67	100.0%

(Biden-focused ads continue on the next two pages)

Source * Mental Health – age Crosstabulation

Count

		Mental Health – age 2	Total
Source	1	34	34
	2	1	1
	3	5	5
Total		40	40

Time * Mental health – age Crosstabulation

Count

		Mental health – age 2	Total
Time	1	10	10
	2	14	14
	3	10	10
	4	6	6
Total		40	40

Source * Physical Health Crosstabulation

Count

		Physical Health 2	Total
Source	1	4	4
Total		4	4

Time * physical health Crosstabulation

Count

		physical health 2	Total
Time	1	1	1
	2	2	2
	3	1	1
Total		4	4

Source * MH – Character Crosstabulation

Count

		MH – Character 1	2	Total
Source	1	1	14	15
	2	1	0	1
	3	0	7	7
Total		2	21	23

Time * MH – Character Crosstabulation

Count

		MH – Character 1	2	Total
Time	1	0	2	2
	2	0	10	10
	3	1	4	5
	4	1	5	6
Total		2	21	23

Biden * Mental health – age Crosstabulation

Count

		Mental health – age	
		2	Total
Biden	2	40	40
Total		40	40

Biden * physical health Crosstabulation

Count

		physical health	
		2	Total
Biden	2	4	4
Total		4	4

Biden * MH – Character Crosstabulation

Count

		MH – Character		
		1	2	Total
Biden	1	2	1	3
	2	0	20	20
Total		2	21	23

Ads That Focused on Trump

Trump-Focused Ads Summary

	Cases					
	Valid		Missing		Total	
	N	Percent	N	Percent	N	Percent
Trump * Mental health – Age	4	22.2%	14	77.8%	18	100.0%
Trump * Physical Health	5	27.8%	13	72.2%	18	100.0%
Trump * Mental Health – Character	9	50.0%	9	50.0%	18	100.0%
Time * Mental health – Age	4	22.2%	14	77.8%	18	100.0%
Time * Physical Health	5	27.8%	13	72.2%	18	100.0%
Time * Mental Health – Character	9	50.0%	9	50.0%	18	100.0%
Source * Mental health – Age	4	22.2%	14	77.8%	18	100.0%
Source * Physical Health	5	27.8%	13	72.2%	18	100.0%
Source * Mental Health – Character	9	50.0%	9	50.0%	18	100.0%

(Trump-focused ads continue on the next two pages)

Source * Mental health – Age Crosstabulation

Count

		Mental health – Age	
		2	Total
Source	3	4	4
Total		4	4

Time * Mental health – Age Crosstabulation

Count

		Mental health – Age	
		2	Total
Time	2	1	1
	3	1	1
	4	2	2
Total		4	4

Source * Physical Health Crosstabulation

Count

		Physical Health	
		2	Total
Source	1	1	1
	3	4	4
Total		5	5

Time * Physical Health Crosstabulation

Count

		Physical Health	
		2	Total
Time	1	1	1
	2	1	1
	3	2	2
	4	1	1
Total		5	5

Source * Mental Health – Character Crosstabulation

Count

		Mental Health – Character	
		2	Total
Source	3	9	9
Total		9	9

Time * Mental Health – Character Crosstabulation

Count

		Mental Health – Character	
		2	Total
Time	3	4	4
	4	5	5
Total		9	9

Trump * Mental health – Age Crosstabulation

Count

	Mental health – Age	
	2	Total
Trump 2	4	4
Total	4	4

Trump * Physical Health Crosstabulation

Count

	Physical Health	
	2	Total
Trump 2	5	5
Total	5	5

Trump * Mental Health – Character Crosstabulation

Count

	Mental Health – Character	
	2	Total
Trump 2	9	9
Total	9	9

Key Takeaways

Initially, we can see that more ads focused on Biden than Trump, with 67 focusing on Biden to Trump's 18. With advertisements that focused on Biden, only three focused on the candidate's fitness in a positive light, whereas none focused on Trump in a positive light.

As for Biden, most advertisements that focused on him targeted his age and how his age affects his mental health, at 57%. The fitness of his character was the next targeted characteristic, accounting for 34.3% of ads, with Biden's physical health accounting for 6%.

Further, 34 out of the 40 age-related mental health ads that were targeted towards Biden came from a primary source, thus accounting for 85% of the category. For Biden's physical health, all four ads came from primary sources, and for his character, 15 of the 23 came from primary sources, or 65%. In each ad category 30 seconds was the most prevalent length of ad, accounting for 35% of ads in age related mental health, 50% in physical health, and 43% of character related ads. Lastly, the only ads that focused on Biden in a positive light focused on his character fitness to be President. Two of these three ads came from primary sources, with the remaining one coming from an independent source.

On the other hand, many ads that focused on Trump targeted the fitness of his character, accounting for 50% of the focus of all Trump ads. 27.8% focused on Trump's physical health, with the remaining 22.2% focusing on his age-related mental health.

For sourcing, nearly all Trump-targeted ads came from outside groups and independent sources, apart from one advertisement attacking him from the opposing campaign, which in this case was on his physical health. For the length of each ad, 8 of the 18 ads were longer than one minute, 7 were about 45 seconds, with only three remaining ads being 30 seconds or less. Lastly, every ad that targeted Trump's fitness was negative.

Analysis and Conclusion

So, what does this all mean? For starters, it shows that each candidate was generally viewed through each advertisement as having poor fitness for office, whether it be mental fitness, physical fitness, or character fitness. One of the most glaring findings is that out of the 85 ads in this set, 67 focused on Biden, or about 79% of all ads. Biden was the center of the "fitness for office" debate, at least when it came to the ads found in this category. This makes some sense – one of the biggest questions that may have been raised in this election was over Biden's age, as he would potentially become the oldest President to take office at 78 years old.

The results also show that it was the strategy of the Trump campaign to heavily target Biden's fitness, more-so than the Biden campaign targeting Trump's. The results show a ruthless attack on Biden through primary sources, which in this case came from the Trump campaign. And of these attacks, they primarily focused on Biden stuttering, forgetting facts and topics of sentences, and speaking incoherently.

For Trump, it may have been his campaign's strategy to personally attack Biden for his fitness. Just like what helped elect him in 2016, Trump continued his trend of labeling his opposing candidate. In this case he labeled of Biden as someone unfit for the duties of President, for instance, the label "sleepy Joe" was used often in ads that targeted Biden's mental health. Further, the large percentage of these ads coming from primary sources display that this was something Trump largely took into his own hands, as opposed to other independent sources targeting the candidate.

Again, this seems to contrast with the Biden campaign's strategy in targeting Trump. As the results show, few primary sources attacked Trump on his fitness, with the majority of these attacks coming from independent organizations such as the Lincoln Project. I would personally speculate that this discrepancy could have been part of a broader strategy of the Biden campaign to take a more respectful tone to contrast the perceived inflammatory manner that has characterized Trump's campaign and Presidency. This may account for the lack of ads targeting Trump's fitness, not only from all ads, but specifically when it came to ads from campaign endorsed sources. As mentioned earlier, Biden's advertising in general has been characterized as more civil than Trump's, which ultimately makes sense given these results.

References

Axelrod, T. (2020, May 14). *Trump campaign launches ads questioning Biden's age, fitness.* The Hill. https://thehill.com/homenews/campaign/497883-trump-campaign-launches-ads-questioning-bidens-age-fitness

Gilens, M., Vavreck, L., & Cohen, M. (2007). The mass media and the public's assessments of presidential candidates, 1952–2000. *Journal of Politics, 69*(4), 1160–1175.

Kates, G. (2020, October 7). *Biden eliminated attack ads during trump's hospital stay. Trump's campaign saw no need for a softer tone.* CBS News. https://www.cbsnews.com/news/biden-attack-ads-trump-covid-hospital-stay-campaign/

Lucey, C. & Thomas, K. (2020, May 13). *Trump campaign boosts emphasis on Biden's age, fitness.* The Wall Street Journal. https://www.wsj.com/articles/trump-campaign-boosts-emphasis-on-bidens-age-fitness-11589376050.

Olorunnipa, T., & Linskey, A. (2020, June 15). *As Trump casts Biden as "Sleepy Joe," his critics raise questions about his own fitness.* The Washington Post. https://www.washingtonpost.com/politics/as-trump-casts-biden-as-sleepy-joe-his-critics-raise-questions-about-his-own-fitness/2020/06/15/f6f63f28-af19-11ea-8758-bfd1d045525a_story.html

Chapter 6: Future Framing: Socialism vs. Democracy

Grace Keilen

Grace is a Senior in Politics and International Relations from Sudbury, MA

"Time" was an important theme in the 2020 Presidential Election advertisements, referring to focus on the past, present, and future by candidates Donald Trump and Joe Biden. Specifically, future framing played a salient role in politics ads and varied dramatically based on the candidates' differing visions of an effective and hopeful future, and conversely, their visions of a flawed and harmful future. These frames are important because they explain candidates' orientation towards the future and help explain the rationale behind their advertisements. To begin with, Trump's vision of a successful future is directly correlated to economic success and prosperity while his view of a negative future is characterized by socialist and communist, far-left policy. In contrast, Biden's vision of a positive future is focused on themes of unity, justice, and adhering to the tenets of the Constitution. Despite their diverging future orientations, both candidates' advertisement sets orient around their views of a positive and negative future which are expressed in an "aspirational laundry list," "soul of the nation," "country over party," and "dangerous liberals, communist, and socialist" set (the combined ad set totaled 183- See Table 1). Though the candidates' definition of what constitutes a dangerous or successful future differ, both of their advertisements sets advance the narrative of their future orientation and in doing so, strive to advance their vision over the others.

To begin with, the "aspirational laundry list" set is comprised of 37 ads, 14 of which are pro-Biden, 1 anti-Biden, 8 pro-Trump, and 14 anti-Trump. The "aspirational laundry list" refers to the celebration of candidates' past political successes, or conversely, their opponent's shortcomings in office, and operates under an aspirational tone that suggests past behaviors may be indicative of their future actions if elected president. It is important to note that 37.8% of set ads are categorized as pro-Biden, meaning they feature Biden's past political successes, while 37.8% are anti-Trump ads that critique his actions and choices as president. Most pro-Biden ads in the set operate around the idea that in times of crises, it is vital to have a leader who unites country. This, in turn, communicates Biden's vision that a positive future is founded on unity and justice.

Table 1: Ad Orientation by Future Theme

	Aspirational Laundry		Soul of The Nation		Country Over Party		Extremists	
Pro-Biden	14	37.8%	30	62.2%	34	100%	13*	30.9%
Anti-Biden	1	.27%	-	-	-	-	-	-
Pro-Trump	8	21.6%	4	8.1%	-	-	29*	69.0%
Anti-Trump	14	37.8%	15	30.6%	-	-	-	-
Total	37		49		34		42	

*Of the 29, 10 Ads offered "The left has gone too far" and 19 warned "Biden will turn America into a Socialist and Communist nation"

To advance this idea, Biden's advertisements feature celebration of past events and accomplishments during his time in office. For example, the Meidas Touch ad focuses on how Biden handled past crises and tragedies, including Sandy Hook and 9/11, which is contrasted to how Trump has "surrendered" to COVID-19 (America Needs Biden, 2020). These "laundry lists" of achievements suggest that Biden is well trained and skilled in handling crises which is particularly relevant given the need to contain the pandemic.

Furthermore, within the pro-Biden set, the *Heal America* Joe Biden for President ad discusses how America is currently living through four crises, related to public health, the economy, the climate, and the national reckoning on racial injustice (Heal America, 2020). This ad asserts that America needs a leader who can unite and rebuild the nation back better and points to Biden's skills and character in being capable of handling these multifaceted crises. Again, this ad's message relates to Biden's orientation of a positive future because it associates overcoming challenges through unity. Similarly, the anti-Trump ads, which comprise 37.8% of the set ads, promote Biden's vision that a positive future can be achieved through unity and strengthening the tenets of democracy. The anti-Trump ads, like the pro-Biden messages, assert that America needs a strong president to bring the nation together again. The Meidas Touch ad *Trump Devastation* – a climate ad critiques Trump's failure to achieve unity stating that its not just about wildfires and hurricanes (dramatic footage), rather Trump's distrust of science represents failed leadership (Trump Devastation, 2020). The ad expands this argument saying that Trump's failed leadership further includes violent protests, plummeting stock markets, and widespread unemployment. This ad accentuates what Biden perceives as a failed future, one that is founded on division, denial of facts, and a lack of empathy for the people, which in turn, advances his central call for unity.

In contrast, the 1 anti-Biden ad, representing 2.7% of the set ads, focuses on how Biden's "old liberal ideas" would crush the economy. This is included in the laundry list set because it cites Biden's regulations, outsourcing jobs, and tax raises. Additionally, this ad works to promote Trump's vision of a positive future rooted in economic success and celebrates Trump's work in advancing "the biggest job increase ever" because he did it "his own way, not the Washington way." Further advancing Trump's view of an economy-based successful future, pro-Trump ads in the "aspirational laundry list" set focus on his economic accolades, including improved employment rates, the "record" creation of jobs, and rising wages. For example, the January 2020 *The Best is Yet to Come* ad (2020), [i] celebrates the Trump administration for their largest tax cuts, historic working population, and the 2.4 million Americans who were lifted out of poverty this year. The ad concludes that since Trump has set economic reforms in motion, it is time for America to start winning again, which can only be achieved if he is elected for a second term. It is clear based on the selected accolades included in the advertisements that Trump's orientation towards the future was positioned in economic prosperity and advancement. Overall, the ads within the "aspirational" laundry list refer to candidates past leadership decisions and associated skills, whether position or negative, to paint a picture of how the future may look if they are elected.

"Soul of the Nation" is the second advertisement category and refers to how candidates use America as a symbol to advance their vision of the future. Within this set, there are 49 total ads, 30 of which are pro-Biden, 4 pro-Trump, and 15 anti-Trump. Based on the breakdown of the data, and the absence of anti-Biden ads within this category, it is evident that Biden uses this type of symbolism more frequently. The pro-Biden ads within this category frame the election as a battle for the soul of the nation, which, based on his future orientation, can only be won through achieving unity and returning to the tenets of democracy that serve as the nation's foundations. Within this category, there is a lot of imagery of the land, iconic references to American history including the American Revolution, westward expansion, and crises such as Hurricane Katrina. This imagery celebrates America's strong foundation and captures the unique national character. For example, the *Joe Biden Wishes You a Happy 4th of July* ad is begins with stating that "our country is founded on the idea that all men are created equal" and then proceeds to evaluate the historic defects in living up to this ideal, pointing to the civil war, systemic racism, and the murder of George Floyd as events that impede this promise (Joe Biden Wishes You , 2020). Though the ad does not directly mention Donald Trump, it references how recent inflamed racial tensions have pulled the nation apart and thus, it is now time to come together. This ad is within the "Soul of the Nation" category because it critiques how America has been unable to achieve its founding principles of unity and equality and thus, urges that to have a positive future, there must be a commitment to coming together.

Similarly, anti-Trump ads operate under the same assumption that the election is a battle for the soul of the nation but heighten the stakes of the outcome. They assert that Trump posses a direct threat to democracy and if re-elected, he will completely tarnish the soul of the nation. For example, the *Listen to Bernie* issued by Really American PAC features Bernie Sanders warning to America that if Trump is re-elected, all the process that was made will evaporate and that the election is about protecting America (2020). He additionally cites Trump's direct infringements of the Constitution which include his administration's delayed voting, post office threats, and suggestions that he will not leave office if not re-elected. The basic premise of the ad is that Trump is a threat to the future of democracy, putting people's lives and health in jeopardy, and thus, America must come together. This ad promotes Biden's view that a positive future relates to unity and protecting the tenets of democracy and is rooted in the assumption that Trump's actions directly oppose these aspirations.

In contrast, the 4 pro-Trump "Soul of the Nation" ads primarily orient around projecting American power and strength through including nostalgic images of American flags and triumphs. The May 3, 2020 "American Comeback" Trump COVID-19 ad begins by explicitly saying that this is America's greatest comeback story and features images of fighter jets and Governor Cuomo saying that Trump's work in combating COVID-19 was an accomplishment (American Comeback. 2020). The overall message of this ad is that Trump has been successful in dealing with the pandemic which carries many implications about the future of American economy and relates to his conviction that a positive future is one where COVID-19 is defeated and business are able to reopen, and unemployment rates decrease. Overall, the ads within the 'Soul of the Nation" set rely on imagery and an understanding and attachment to the tenets of democracy to advance each candidate's future orientation.

"Country over party" is the next advertisement set and primarily uses testimonials to urge Americas to evaluate their vote and prompt them to consider which candidate is best for the future of America beyond their traditional party allegiance. The set includes 34 ads. Given that all the ads in this set are pro-Biden, this advances Biden's vision of a successful future of unity as he strives to dismantle traditional partisan fractions and urges Americans to come together to vote for the country's future. Within this set, there are testimonials from public officials who endorse Biden, "average" Americans who voted are migrating parties after voting for Trump in 2016, and "Republicans against Trump," those who do not necessarily support Biden but view him as the "lesser" evil option between Trump. Within the category of official endorsements, there are ads from ex-navy SEALS, John Kasich, Steve Kerr and Doc Rivers, General Michal Hayden, and Mitt Romney. The Lincoln Project's *Crossroads – John Kasich*" ad testimony advances the idea that the stakes in this election are higher as Kasich, former presidential candidate, states that the president has pitted the people against each other (2020). He explains that he is endorsing Biden because Biden understands the people, humanity, and can restore and unite America. He concludes the testimony saying that "no one has all the answers, we need to put the partisan behind". This ad advances Biden's vision that a promising future is free from partisan divisions and promotes the notion that to be strong and powerful, America must restore and embody its founding principles.

Furthermore, the "average" Americans who voted for Trump in 2016 but are voting for Biden in 2020 are geared towards the Republican and undecided voters who may be questioning who to vote for (Also See Chapter 23). In the Grandson-Grandma Testimony ad an elderly woman explains how she voted for Trump in 2016 because she had great expectations, however, she was very disappointed because he did not live up to his promises, and in many ways, divided and harmed the nation (Letter, 2020). In the ad, she is writing a letter to Biden explaining how the next four years are very important for his growth and urges all voters to take the election, and their vote, seriously. Again, this ad highlights Trump's shortcomings in office because of the widespread division he created and frames a successful future being one where the president cares about the people and strives to adhere to the constitutional foundations. Finally, the "Republicans against Trump" ads are not overtly Pro-Biden, rather state that he is the better option over voting for Trump. The Lincoln Project "Conservative Veteran narrative" ad begins with an ex-Navy SEAL stating that we are a nation of laws and that the Constitution is scared and must be respected (Conservative. 2020). He explains that though he does not agree with Biden on many things, Trump is weak and disrespects the rule of law and the American Dream. This category of ads highlights what Biden views as a negative future trajectory, one where democracy is directly threatened and urges voters to re-evaluate their allegiance to their past party to consider the implications of the election on the future.

The final category is the "extremists" set which is 42 ads in total which feature candidates portray all their oppositions' supporters as violent individual. For example, Pro-Trump ads cite the "socialist," "communist", and radical liberal left which articulates his vision for a successful future as he views them as an obstacle to ensure economic growth. In contrast, Pro-Biden ads portray Trump supporters as alt-right extremists who adamantly oppose constitutional rights such as equal rights and protection of all citizens and people under the law which advances his calls for a united and caring future America. This set is unique in the sense that there are no overtly positive "pro-candidate" ads that portray an individual in a celebratory light because the ads in this set work to put down the other candidate and in turn, drive voters to support the other. In turn, a Pro-Trump ad implicitly means a pro-Biden ad and vice versa. Additionally, this set is unique because there is a wide range of tones deployed to describe the opponent, ranging from moderate appraisal to complete condemnation and the idea that they are an imminent and dangerous threat to the future.

To begin with, there are 29 Pro-Trump [Anti-Biden] and Pro-Republican party ads. Within this sub-set there are 10 ads within the "left has gone too far left, Republicans are the best/only option" and, the more extreme, 19 "Biden will turn America into a Socialist and Communist nation" ads. The "left has gone too far left, Republicans are the best/only option" ads operate under the core idea that thus year has been extremely difficult with the COVID-19 pandemic and there is a need to go back to "normal" which can only be achieved by Republicans. For example, the Future 45 Pac, *Best Hope* ad acknowledges that this year has been hell but states that this election is a chance to rebuild, to create more jobs, reopen the economy and schools. It concludes that the left has gone too far left and we as a nation will never be able to go back if they are in control. Thus, Republicans are the only hope for the future generations to live in a prosperous and free world (Best Hope, 2020). The essence of this ad set captures Trump's vision for a successful future, marked by the reopening of the country to garner a prosperous future. Conversely, these ads imply that if Biden is elected, he and the Democratic party will oppose re-opening the nation which will have disastrous impacts on the nation's ability to advance and grow which will harm future generations. This subset is within the "extremist" set because the underlying implication is that the Democratic party has become too far left leaning and as a result, rigidly opposes any efforts to re-open the nation, making the Republican party the best choice for the future.

Next, the "Biden will turn America into a Socialist and Communist nation" ads explicitly and implicitly claim that Biden will convert the nation into a Socialist and, or Communist regime and will work alongside, or be manipulated by, prominent ultra-liberal leaders, including Bernie Sanders, Alexandria Ocasio-Cortez, and Elizabeth Warren. The Club for Growth's *The Goal is Control* contends that the left is power hungry and strives to control all aspects of American life, ranging from the car that one is permitted to drive to what they are allowed to say. The assert that AOC will assume a major roll in this government "intervention" and essentially, that the Democratic party will not stop until they have total control (The Goal Is Control: Cars, 2019). This category wields a more combative tone towards the Democratic party and Biden to accentuate the idea that if elected, Biden will destroy all possibilities for growth and individuality in the future. Although "Communism" is not explicitly stated, it is alluded to through the monitoring and suppression of individuality; thus, communicating that it is imperative to vote for Trump. This relates to Trump's vision of a "negative" future because Communism carries many negative connotations especially given the US' history with the Cold War, and additionally, carries implications on limiting individual prosperity and economic growth.

In contrast, the Pro-Biden "extremist" set communicates that Trump is an "authoritarian-like" leader who is charged with inciting division and hate within the country. Given Biden's view that a positive future is founded on unity and respect of civil liberties, his ads work to reprimand Trump and his followers' role in the rising tide of violence and White Supremacy in cases such as Charlottesville, the El Paso shooting, and the armed teenager in Kenosha. The Joe Biden for President, *This is Trump's America* flashes through various images of Trump supporters chanting with "Jews will not replace us" signs, clips of the tragedies discussed above, and rising unemployment and COVID-19 casualties. The ad concludes with saying, "do you feel safe in Trump's America" and strives to insight fear within voters of the future division and disruption that may occur if re-elected (This is Trump's America, 2020). Overall, in the "Extremism" ad set, both candidates strive to accentuate radical elements and actions of their opponent to insight a sense of fear in voters and motivate them to vote for them.

The year 2020 posed many unexpected and often scary and unprecedented events for the United States, leaving the American people yearning for the future and some sense of hope and optimism. Due to this infatuation, the future played a salient role in the 2020 President election and throughout political advertisements. Both candidates Biden and Trump recognized this widespread fear resulting from the coronavirus, racial unrest, rising unemployment rates, and general uncertainty and strived to deliver the people with a "plan" for what the future would look like if elected president. These ideas were expressed in an "aspirational laundry list", "soul of the nation," "country over party", and "dangerous liberals, communist, and socialist" set. In these ads, Trump communicated his vision of a successful future is directly correlated to economic success and prosperity while his view of a negative future is characterized by socialist and communist, far-left policy. In contrast, Biden's vision of a positive future is focused on themes of unity, justice, and adhering to the tenets of the Constitution and a failed future would is one marked by division and deviance from foundational American values. Overall, despite the candidate's diverging perspectives and attitudes towards the future, they both captured the idea that despite the challenges that 2020 posed, there is hope in moving forward.

References

American comeback. (2020, May 3). Trump, YouTube.
https://www.youtube.com/watch?v=Ws66liLKGzA

America needs Biden (2020, September 10). Meidas Touch, YouTube.
https://www.youtube.com/watch?v=gvzCT6p0qxo&t=1s

Best Hope (2020, October 28) Future 45 PAC, YouTube.
https://www.youtube.com/watch?v=gtir2sij3n8

Conservative (2020, July 27). The Lincoln Project, YouTube.
https://www.youtube.com/watch?v=tlmHVtVIJdU

Crossroads (2020. August 20). The Lincoln Project, YouTube.
https://www.youtube.com/watch?v=pGfDGvXzRps

Heal America (2020, August 24). *Joe Biden, YouTube*,
https://www.youtube.com/watch?v=kCYN5MY5BHg

Joe Biden wishes you a happy 4th of July (2020, July 5). Joe Biden, YouTube. https://www.youtube.com/watch?v=KtvRayssI3g

Letter (2020, October 13). American Bridge21st Century, YouTube.
https://www.youtube.com/watch?v=Q-_LvuE3MIE

Listen to Bernie (2020, September 23). Really American, YouTube.
https://www.youtube.com/watch?v=u5Kpb2LMkNY&t=1s

The Best is Yet to Come (2020, January 21), Donald J. Trump, YouTube. https://www.youtube.com/watch?v=KDSpqZI78_g

The goal is control: Cars (December 19, 2019). Club for Growth, YouTube.
https://www.youtube.com/watch?v=r7I11ajRNvw

This is Trump's America (2020, August 28). Joe Biden, YouTube.
https://youtu.be/5EDjAfyZrww

Trump Devastation (2020, October 7). Meidas Touch, YouTube.
https://www.youtube.com/watch?v=wvtkpkFcJgc&t=16s

[i] The Trump campaign and affiliates offered several ads, across more than a year of the election, offing a "bragging rights" version of American's prosperous and patriotic future, all entitled *The Best is yet to come*: December 21 2019, The White House, https://www.youtube.com/watch?v=enJwnRjkE9g; January 21, Trump, https://www.youtube.com/watch?v=QTj4h5loLp8, July 5, Trump, https://www.youtube.com/watch?v=MvUhoexCSac; https://www.youtube.com/watch?v=Wz1mzdT8rG0, August 22, Freedom Forum, https://www.youtube.com/watch?v=QTj4h5loLp8;

SECTION 3: NON-TRADITIONAL PURPOSE FOR TRADITIONAL CAMPAIGN THEMES

Allan Louden, Editor

The entries in this section address themes that routinely appear in presidential elections. For the most part they mirror past campaigns in perspective and content. Some categories, however, differ substantially in tone even as they purportedly address familiar issues. Their uniqueness or typicality can render these ads less influential as the campaign unfolds, making them more of an interesting political sideshow than an influencer. While this sounds contradictory, these ads serve more as reminders of voters' beliefs than reason to change their voting intentions. It goes without saying that religious and women voters, as well as those committed to health reform, guns, and climate control, were vital in the election, but likely more for turnout than conversion.

The first two chapters – Religion and Women – are two theme categories that, in part, reinvent the conventional. Madeline R. Coelho & David D. Dockery examined 52 religious ads (a category usually situational from campaign to campaign). The solidity of an evangelical vote combined with their secularized counterparts produced several independent vectors in religious ads. They provide a thorough and unique accounting of the operative themes, tying those appeals to specific audiences.

Hannah Abernathy's set is a topic that also tends to alter with the times. Her analysis compares women's ads in the 2016 (31 Ads) and 2020 (77 ads) cycle. She discovers, somewhat surprisingly, that the two campaigns largely aligned. She explored the cross channels of ads dominated by harassment accusations and candidate's gender. The presence of Trump and Harris in 2020 and Clinton and Trump in 2016 seem to invite a similar "appalled" dynamic in the advertising. Appropriately, she also offers some correctives to the media reporting on women's advertising.

The last five chapters address three issues, health, guns, and climate. The ads tend to be orthodox but fluctuate in prominence at various stages of the campaign. The health ads, for example, run throughout but modify between the primary to the general election. As Kellyn Jamison records, the health ads dominated the primaries with competing plans and shifted in the general to a more generic "health care" access matters message. Testimonials, personal narratives, and moral choice health ads in the general became more generic

(e. g. Defending or attacking the ADA, pre-existing conditions). Also emerging were campaigns within the campaign from independent permanent third-party organizations who promoted as interested in future policy choice (e. g., Union ads – National Nurses Union, SEIU – and groups like MoveOn.org and Protect our Care PAC). The general election ads were not analyzed and were standard fare and comparatively few (31). In her sample, Jamison utilizes traditional Aristotelian rhetorical analysis to critique for one representative ad from each of the major primary Democrat contenders.

Two chapters analyzed gun and two climate ads. Tori Pylypec and Kiki Rodriguez assess gun advertising while Maria Jose Falcon Gimenez and Jack Crane train their attention on the climate ads, respectively for the primary and general ad sets. With both guns and climate most of the action took place in the primary, issues salient for Democrat voters. The topics drop off precipitously in the general election, as not many voters were open to persuasion. The issues were more of an ideological definition than an open political decision. Pylypec looks at the accuracy of presentation and gun ads in the primaries, examining 14 advertisements, two speeches, and one interview, while Rodriguez provides a profile of 47 ads aired in the gun arena, primarily focusing on the National Rifle Association (NRA) advertising.

The most prolific candidate across the campaign with gun ads was Michael Bloomberg. His biggest purchase *George* (Bloomberg, 2020) was a Super Bowl ad featuring a mother of a slain young man whose goal was to play professional football. Most of his ads were young folks' testimonials, often survivors of school shootings, including Parkland. Perhaps his most memorable was his ad *Every School Shooting Since Trump Took Office* (2019), listing all the school shootings on a roll, picking up speed until the names become unreadable mesh together in a tragic history.

Maria Jose Falcon Gimenez reviews the breadth and tone of the various campaigns via climate in 47 primary ads. Her findings point to the decidedly emotional appeals, avoiding in almost all cases presentation of scientific data. She accounts for the content of the ads from the use of nature imagery to the geographic specificity as a framing device.

Jack Crane examines 65 climate ads from the general election, noting that while there were many, they were almost all in favor of Biden or attacks on Trump. Unlike other groups of ads, on balance the climate discussion seemed to reflect already set notions of the party identification via the issue. Jack argues optimistically that the climate ads had import in the election. That may have been the case for certain sets of voters, but I would also observe that the climate issue impact was relatively opaque compared to other areas of contention.

References

Every School Shooting Since Trump Took Office (2019, December 17). Mike Bloomberg, YouTube. https://www.youtube.com/watch?v=X4ytjCVoxOE

George (2020, January 30). Mike Bloomberg, YouTube. https://www.youtube.com/watch?v=9Yp0yN8UxVg

Chapter 7: Religious Advertisements in the 2020 Presidential Campaign

Madeline Coelho and David Dockery

Madeline is a Senior in Communication and Education from Hilmar, CA & David is an MA student in Communication from Cookeville, TN

Introduction

The 2020 presidential race held important implications for religion in America. According to Pew Research, the decline of religious identification in America continues, with a total of 26% of American adults declaring themselves as nonreligious, including the "nones" (Smith et al., 2019). The rising nonreligious demographic raises critical questions about the place of religion in American civil life, the influence it continues to wield in politics, and how campaign officials approach communicating with the religious public. Is the religious vote even worth pursuing anymore? It is not our purpose to answer these questions here; the full religious implications of the 2020 election are yet to unfold. Hints of that accounting are found in the communicative interaction, specifically in a retrospective on the religious-political advertisements of the 2020 presidential race. By examining the central themes of these advertisements, we can see what arguments political advertisers believed were persuasive.

Background Information

Historically, the word "religion" has referred to Christianity in an American context. Although other religions exist in America, none wield as much influence. The reasons for Christianity's influence are both population and culture. Christians vastly outnumber the adherents of other religions. Pew Research found in 2018 that among American adults, 65% identified as Christians (Smith et al., 2019). Religious Jews constitute approximately 1.8% of the population (Smith, Hackett, Gunk, et al., 2013). Muslims only constitute 1.1% of the American population (Mohamed, 2018). The numbers of adherents of other religions only diminish from there.

Christianity wields greater cultural influence as well. The English colonists who later revolted against the British were overwhelmingly Christian. Indeed, one of the driving ideologies of the American Revolution sprang from the Puritans of New England (Bailyn, 1992). The American Bible Society provided "over a million Bibles per year" in 1860 (Wilson, 2011). Some of America's most cherished political texts, such as the Gettysburg Address, are perfused with Biblical language (Wills, 1978). All of this does not even touch on America's two Great Awakenings or the Billy Graham revivals. Therefore, there is a measure of truth to the claim that America is a Christian nation. No other religion can claim an equal place in the nation's social constitution.

It should not be surprising, then, that Christianity remained relevant in the 2020 presidential race. Both candidates had connections to religion. Donald Trump famously picked Mike Pence as his vice president, a man well-known for his evangelical Christian faith, and surrounded himself with evangelical leaders (Fahmy, 2020). Trump personally identified as a Presbyterian (Fahmy, 2020). On the other side, Joe Biden identified as a Catholic (Schor & Crary, 2020). This is more significant than it might seem at first glance. Biden is only the second Catholic in U.S. presidential history to hold the office, the other being John F. Kennedy (Schor & Crary, 2020). It is somewhat surprising, then, that he was only able to draw about half of the Catholic vote (Schor & Crary, 2020). Trump claimed the other half plus "8 in 10 white evangelicals" (Schor & Crary, 2020). These results are counterintuitive. Traditionally, it is assumed that members of a demographic will vote for those they identify with, especially when that demographic has a chance to make history. There are many possible reasons why Biden failed to capture the Catholic vote and alienated Protestants. Examining the religious advertisement terrain is one avenue to diagnose what Biden did right and what Trump did wrong.

Method

This study looks at religious, political advertisements from the 2020 presidential campaign. To conduct this study, advertisements of both video and image style were collected, totaling 52 ads. The start date for the earliest of the ad collection was November 2019 and only ads that discussed the two presidential candidates, Donald Trump, and Joe Biden, were analyzed. Religious ads from other presidential candidates and other political races were not used. Once the data set had been collected, a reflexive thematic analysis was conducted (Thematic analysis). This began with becoming familiar with the ads by viewing all ads. From this, general patterns began to be noticed and a codebook was created. Each code corresponded with a definition, for example, code "Prayer," definition "the ad contains a prayer for the candidate, country, politicians, etc.". Once the codebook had been completed, there were a total of 40 codes to be tested on each ad. The codes were sectioned into group themes for example theme "Ad Type" contained the codes "Video" and "Graphic," graphic advertisements include billboards, posters, and images, to indicate what form the ad was in. The coding process was then ready to be conducted. Each ad was viewed individually and analyzed to indicate which codes it contained. The ad names were listed in a spreadsheet where the codes could easily be indicated. With this data now procured, the final step was to calculate the frequency with which each code occurred in the whole data set.

Results [1]

The data set used was made up of 96.2% video ads and 3.8% graphic ads. These ads came from a variety of different sources; 57.7% were from sources with no religious affiliation and 42.3% from religious sources. Two groups who were repeat ad producers included the Jewish Democratic Council of America and Republican Jewish Coalitions. Looking specifically at sources from candidates' campaigns or PACs; 9.6% of the ads were from Biden and Biden PACs compared to a high 25% from Trump and Trump PACs. Shifting to the content of the ads; 23.1% of religious ads were explicitly in support of Biden and 32.7% were explicitly in support of Trump. The remainder 44.2% of ads did not endorse a specific candidate, rather attacking a candidate or speaking generally on issues that affect how people vote without endorsing a candidate by name.

The religious makeup of the ads was a straightforward code; however, there was room for interpretation. Looking at ads aimed at "Christians" as a whole group, 75% of ads applied. Because there is so much overlap in beliefs and values between Protestant denominations and Roman Catholics, ads could be aimed at both groups. It was found that 67.3% of the ads were aimed at Protestants and 51.9% were aimed at Catholics. These percentages are made up of ads that apply to both groups as well as only that specific group. This code was more difficult than others to distinguish, but personal judgment was used. Some of these ads stood out as being specific towards one denomination and not able to be aimed at all Christian groups. 25% of the ads were aimed at Jewish people. One ad (1.9% of the data set) was not specific to any religious group. This ad discussed abortion, which is normally a Christian issue; however, the presentation of the video did not emphasize religion, only stating "prayer" once, and used the Declaration of

Independence as the reasoning for protecting life, not religion. None of the ads identified under the code "Other Religious Affiliation" as no ads were aimed at any other religious peoples such as Muslims or Indians.

One code theme was "Age Group," which looked at the approximate age of the people in the ad. 55.8% of the ads were not focused on any specific age group or the style of the ads did not apply to this theme. 34.6% of the ads featured people between the ages of 35-65 and 9.6% of the ads featured people above the age of 65. Typically, in advertisements and persuasion, people share opinions and are more receptive to seeing people of a similar age or lifestyle. Thus, this group is helpful to get a rough idea of what age group the ads were being aimed at. An important lack of data to note is, there are no videos for the age group below 35. A likely reason for this is the younger generation's decrease in religious involvement. The ads are not in this data set because they are rare, and the young are reached through other ad types.

One of the most significant codes was "Religious Contrary." This code was defined as: the candidate is the opposite of the religious group's values and ideas or does not reflect the group. Much of the content in this set could have also been labeled under a code "hypocrites." 51.9% of the ads in the data set were identified to be "Religious Contrary" ads. On the opposite spectrum of that code, is the code "Religious Advocate" which was present in 25% of the ads. This set was defined as: the candidate is helping the religious group, stands up for the group's rights, preserves the group, holds the group's values to be important. These were the two codes that occurred the most under the theme "Religious Orientation." This theme looked at the overall direction the ads were trying to bring viewers.

Another code theme was "Description of Candidate Orientation." This focused on how the candidate was described and what the script of the ad was implicitly or explicitly saying about the candidate as a person. The largest code frequency was "Exploitation," which is defined as the candidate is using the religious group for their own benefit. This code had almost a third of the ads with 32.7% of the data set. Following this, a quarter (25%) of the data set was coded "Empathy." This was defined as: the candidate relates to or understands what a group feels or experiences.

The issues discussed in the religious advertisements were multiple and across the board, so a code theme was created for "Issue Content." The largest code, with 73.1% of the data set, were simply categorized as discussing, focusing on topics, and maintaining religion. This created a general group with all things to do with religion. One would think a large portion of ads would be on abortion, but only 7.7% included this topic. At the same rate, 7.7% of the data set had the key issue of being "Foreign Policy." This code could have been called "Israel" because all these ads discussed Israel or Jerusalem. All but one of the ads under this code came from Jewish organizations and the one aimed at Protestants referenced the embassy being moved to Jerusalem being good for both Christians and Jews. The issue content with the most importance to note was "Social Justice" with 34.6%. These ads focused on social justice matters such as equality, racism, COVID (public health/safety), immigration, and more.

The final theme of codes looked at the style of the ads. 42.3% of ads were categorized as being "Classic Ads" which followed typical ad style with persuasive appeals, nothing sticking out as being significant or out of the ordinary. 15.4% emphasized "Urgency," meaning action was required in a timely matter and the election was very important. 15.4% of the data set were "Prayer" ads. A quarter (25%) of the ads were categorized as "Other" with a variety of forms including songs, movie trailer style, a segment of news coverage (sometimes by itself with no added commentary), etc. The final style is "Testimony." These ads account for 30.8% of the set and are personal stories of either the presidential candidates or normal people sharing their own life experiences or a personal stance of persuasion.

Discussion

With a mere 52 advertisements in this religious ads data set, one wonders who saw these ads (besides us doing research) when there were thousands of other ads all being published at the same time. While it is unclear exactly who viewed these ads, they are being aimed at a specific group of people. Mature Christians [2]. As mentioned previously, none of the ads featured people below the approximate age of 35. This has to do with the decreasing religious affiliation Americans are having. While the currency says, "In God we trust" and the pledge of allegiance says, "one nation under God," people are becoming less and less religious. In 2019 only 49% of millennials identify as Christians and 44% of millennials seldom or never attend religious services (Smith et al., 2019). Because of these decreasing numbers, especially in the younger generations, the ads depict the older generations because they are the ones more likely to be influenced if they were to see the ads.

While young religious generations are a small population and are rarely advertised to, the opposite is true for the Jewish population which is also only a small portion of the total population. Interestingly, 25% of the religious ads were aimed at Jewish groups. If the population of Jews in America is only 1.8% one would think that the percentage of ads aimed at them would reflect this number (Smith, Hackett, Gunk, et al. 2013). After coding, it was found that the Jewish ads had two different issues they typically emphasized. The first of these was foreign policy. As noted earlier, the foreign policy code could have been called Israel. The ads were either pro-Trump or anti-Democrat because of preserved positive relationship that had been created between the U.S. and Israel during the last presidential term. One beneficial thing Donald Trump accomplished, according to a portion of the Jewish population, was supporting and aiding Israel. These ads spoke on the topic of foreign policy positively, making this one reason Trump may have gained a portion of the Jewish vote.

The second issue that the Jewish ads emphasized was social justice issues, specifically about anti-Semitism and white supremacy. In recent months, there have been increases in white nationalist groups forming along with spikes of anti-Semitic violence, and most notably alongside the Black Lives Matter movement, increased racism towards Black Americans. These ads discuss the history of the Jewish people facing genocide, suppression, and many hardships, but they always stand up again and work to improve their lives as well as the lives of others, until equality and justice are reached for everyone. The ads then discussed how the Jewish population needed to and were doing to same thing today with these issues and how voting in the election would be part of the solution. Almost all ads were either anti-Trump or pro-Democrat/Biden.

The topic of white nationalism was brought up throughout the data set and was aimed many times at Donald Trump. Trump's rhetoric was pointed to as being a cause of encouragement for groups, such as white supremacists, to become more active and cause harm to the country. This is not the only instance where Trump's words and actions were questioned. Time after time, the ads used clips of what Trump had said in the past. They referenced things such as how he spoke about and treated women, his vulgar use of language, change in policy stance, and moments where he lied. These ads were oriented to show a religious contrary. The ads coded as showing "Religious Contrary" were either pro-Biden or anti-Trump ads, with no ads making Biden a religious contrary. These religious ads commonly argued that Trump did not reflect the values and ideals of the religious groups and thus did not reflect what the people wanted, true, traditional religion.

The code "Exploitation" had a direct correlation to the "Religious Contrary" code. "Exploitation" occurred in 32.7% of the videos and every time the videos fell under the other code as well. Similarly, this code found that the candidate was using religion for their benefit. The code was only used in anti-Trump ads that did not endorse any candidate. These ads referenced times such as when Trump implicitly said he had never asked God for forgiveness, when he said "one Corinthians" instead of "first Corinthians" (showing lack of knowledge on biblical terminology), and when he took photos in front of St. John's Episcopal Church with a Bible. These ads show that while Trump says he is a Christian, his actions and words do not always reflect the ideal of what a Christian is, and he instead is using Christianity to gain support and votes.

In contrast with being the opposite of religious values and using religion, part of the data set showed the candidates as being a "Religious Embodiment." Some of these ads were in support of Trump but most were for Biden. The ads for Biden included audio of Biden discussing his faith through his life and other ads had people talking about why they believed Biden would be a good president. Most all the ads that were endorsing Biden as the presidential candidate either showed that Biden was a "Religious Embodiment" or that Trump was a "Religious Contrary." Interestingly, only one of the Biden ads was coded as being a "Religious Advocate." The rest of the data set in this code was for Trump. These ads emphasized Trump's support for freedom of religion, protecting the churches, not removing God from the pledge of allegiance, and being pro-life. These matters made Trump out to be a "Religious Advocate," standing up for the religious groups and preserving their values.

Through all the content covered in the religious ads, one form of ad style was repeated the most (besides the "Classic Ad" style). This was "Testimonies." These ads were used to support both Biden and Trump and featured mostly "regular" people (could be volunteer or possibly paid actors) who were discussing why it was they were or were not supporting a candidate. In a religious ad set, this style works well because religion is a personal and important matter, so hearing messages directly from people who seem like oneself can be very persuasive. Many of these ads appeared to be almost home videos where the people set up a camera in their office or whatever space, recorded a video, and posted it online to tell their friends and family about their political opinion. In multiple cases, this is exactly what was done. Hearing directly from other, normal citizens in a testimony style worked for these religious ads because people were sharing their views through the religious lens with other people who held the same religious values.

Conclusion

When taking a first glance at the religious ads set, it would seem Donald Trump had a substantial number of ads supporting him. 32.7% of the ads support him and 44.2% do not endorse a specific candidate. When looking deeper, it was found that of the ads which do not support a candidate, all but one of those ads were directed against Trump. This realistically leaves Biden with almost two-thirds of the ads, even if he is not specifically endorsed. The ads show Biden as a good religious man who treats people fairly and shows what it means to be a Christian.

Trump was noted as doing a few things well, typically within the policy, not the theological arena. On top of this list was his protection of churches and freedom of religion, supporting Israel, and being pro-life. What stood out more for Trump, however, was what he did not do well. Even though he said he was a Christian, his actions and words led people to think he did not have the same values that people of religious groups wanted. He could talk the talk, but he failed to walk the walk (even though at times he failed to talk the talk too). One of the reasons he was elected into office was because he was out of the ordinary and unlike other politicians, but this election he may have gone too far and needed to calm it down and take up some of the traditional American religious values.

Though the religious ad set was small compared to some other ad sets, it still carried its weight in the 2020 presidential election and was part of a tradition that has long been noted as being American. With each election cycle, media messaging becomes more present in all aspects of our lives and religion is an increasingly powerful tool being used. With an ever-changing nation, the 2024 election is sure to have new traditions and likely to contain an entirely different set of religious advertisements.

References

Bailyn, B. (1992). *The ideological origins of the American Revolution.* Harvard University Press. http://ebookcentral.proquest.com/lib/wfu/detail.action?docID=3301184

Mohamed, B. (2018, January 3). *A new estimate of U.S. Muslim population.* Pew Research Center. https://www.pewresearch.org/fact-tank/2018/01/03/new-estimates-show-u-s-muslim-population-continues-to-grow/

Fahmy, D. (2020, March 25). *Most Americans don't see Trump as religious; fewer than half say they think he's Christian.* Pew Research Center.

https://www.pewresearch.org/fact-tank/2020/03/25/most-americans-dont-see-trump-as-religious/

Schor, E., & Crary, D. (2020, November 6). *Survey: Biden and Trump split the 2020 Catholic vote almost evenly.* America: The Jesuit Review. https://www.americamagazine.org/politics-society/2020/11/06/catholic-vote-donald-trump-joe-biden-election-split

Smith, G., Cooperman, A., Besheer, M., Sciupac, E. P., Alper, B. A., Cox, K. & Gecewicz, C. (2019, October 17). *In U.S., decline of Christianity continues at rapid pace.* Pew Research Center's Religion & Public Life Project. https://www.pewforum.org/2019/10/17/in-u-s-decline-of-christianity-continues-at-rapid-pace

Smith, G., Hackett, C., Funk, C., Sahgal, N., Connor, P., Martinez, J. H., Mohamed, Robbins, M., Kuriakose, N., Sciupac, E., & Ghani, F. (2013, October 1). *Jewish American population estimates.* Pew Research Center's Religion & Public Life Project. https://www.pewresearch.org/wp-content/uploads/sites/7/2013/10/jewish-american-full-report-for-web.pdf

Thematic analysis – a reflexive approach. The University of Auckland. https://www.psych.auckland.ac.nz/en/about/thematic-analysis.html

Wills, G. (1978). *Inventing America: Jefferson's Declaration of Independence.* Doubleday & Company, Inc.

Wilson, B. C. (2011). *KJV in the USA: The impact of the King James Bible in the USA.* Comparative Religion Publications.

---

[1] Not all results from research coding were included due to lack of significance and space.

[2] Mature as a relative term meaning just not the young generations

Chapter 8: A Critical Survey Comparing 2016- and 2020- Women's Campaign Advertisements

Hannah Abernethy

Hannah is a Junior in Politics and International Affairs from Hickory, NC

Review of Literature

According to 2020 exit polling data, Trump won among white women. Christina Wolbrecht, professor of political science at Notre Dame, says that women tend to vote more like men in their racial group. While Trump may have gained among Black female voters, much of the Black female vote went for Biden and possibly put him over the edge in key battleground states like Georgia as Kathryn Pearson suggests (Schmidt, 2020). Looking at how ads target certain women may help explain certain outcomes of this election. The manner and frequency with which women are portrayed can add to this understanding, and from our interpretation of the ads, Black women in particular may have had a major role to play in campaign advertisements in 2020.

The Lincoln Project has been a leader in the 2020 campaign by creating advertisements targeting women. Most famously, they aired an ad that includes young girls where the narrator says, "Imagine a young girl in the mirror, searching for role models in the world to give her hope that she too can one day make a difference" (Mathers, 2020). The focus was place on Black women in a series of ads called "Life or Death" featuring an all-Black cast and spoke about issues specific to them like maternal death rates, systemic racism, and coronavirus (NewsOne, 2020). The Biden campaign also targeted women when indicting the administration's response to the coronavirus. The ads that ran in Michigan featured women offering testimonials about the difficulties of starting school during the pandemic and blaming those struggles on the President. Another spot, "Donna," focuses on two things, coronavirus and motherhood. The ad is a testimonial from a woman who lives in the Villages in Florida and laments not being able to see her grandchildren because of COVID (McManus, 2020).

The Trump campaign also had its share of ads targeting women. These ads largely focused on safety. The ad entitled "Cards" features a woman who holds up a poster that reads "I won't risk my children's future with Biden." Trump's famous "Defund the Police" ad poses the hypothetical featuring an elderly woman who is a victim of the lack of police protection (Forgey, 2020). What might be unique about these ads targeting women voters would be the subject matter like coronavirus, racism, and safety. Ads about safety may have resonated more with white women and ads about racism likely resonated with Black women. The ad's targeting suggest that was the campaign's assumption.

When surveying women's ads throughout history in the US Senate, House, and gubernatorial races, it has generally been found that women highlighted their "femininity" postures compliant with gendered stereotypes. However, there have been changes in the frequency with which female candidates talk about gender. In the 1980s, women's campaign ads did mention issues that were not specific to females. However, beginning in 1992, women drew distinctions between themselves and their male counterparts by making women's issues, particularly healthcare and education, the forefront of their ads. This change was prompted by the Anita Hill allegations and the increased number of women running for office in that year. Many female candidates stressed the exclusion of women in politics. Additionally, after 1992 political messaging became even more feminized. Meaning that women emphasized female issues like education, healthcare, childcare, sex discrimination, as opposed to male issues such as foreign policy and spending. Differences have also been found in the way that male and female candidates portray themselves. Men have been found to emphasize their toughness or experiences (male coded traits) and female candidates have been found to emphasize "gendered" traits such as sensitivity. In the 2012 election, each candidate made appeals to women. Because there were two male candidates these appeals were often made through female surrogates, including those close to the candidates. Barack Obama featured his wife, Michelle, indicating that women's issues such as reproductive rights and equal pay were on the line (Shames, 2020).

Methodology

This study seeks to answer the question: How are women's ads in 2020 distinct from those aired in 2016? To answer this question, I conducted a thematic analysis. This was a process that started with transcription of the ads from the 2016 and the 2020 presidential election cycles. The set from 2016 consisted of 31 ads that were sponsored by the candidate's official campaign and special interest groups such as Emily's List and the NRA. The 2020 set consisted of 77 ads. 2020 also included delayed ads sponsored by the candidate's official campaign and interest groups. I then coded major themes such as "Questioning the Opponent's Behavior", "Making History", "Role Models," "Young Women," "Black Women." Coded themes were based on political issues identified as female such as "Education," "Healthcare," "Sexual Discrimination." I then noted the frequency of the appearances of each theme. The resulting categories were applied consistently across the two presidential cycles, allowing comparisons to be made.

Defining theme content

The "Questioning the Opponent's Behavior" code included quotes of controversial statements from the opponent, the controversial history of the opponent, or the hypocrisy of the opponent. "Making History" included symbols of women throughout history or mentioning of record-setting among women in politics. "Role Models" included any expressed admiration of a woman in the candidate's ad. "Young Women" includes any reference to daughters or young women, or images of young women in the ads. "Black Women" would include images of Black women or references to Black women. "Education" would include any mention of schooling, student loan debt, free tuition, or students in general. The "Healthcare" theme would include any mention of premiums, medications, deductibles, Medicare, Medicaid, or insurance. "Sexual discrimination" would include any mention of equal pay, workplace discrimination, sexual harassment, pregnancy discrimination, or violence against women.

Results

The data from the set of ads from 2016 and 2020 show that there are many areas of uniformity among the themes, the key one being the theme of sexual discrimination, which accounted for over 35% of each year's sample. There was no significant difference in the degree to which each ad set emphasized sexual discrimination. Sexual discrimination could include issues such as equal pay, workplace harassment, or pregnancy discrimination. One example from the 12 ads from 2016 that showed this theme would be an advertisement for Clinton by the United Steelworkers union, "Hillary supports equal pay for equal work, and that's really important to me." The woman narrator was reflecting on her young daughters in the workforce and wanted them to have the same opportunities as their male counterparts. Another example of sexual discrimination themes is in the set of 2020 primary commercials. The ad shows Elizabeth Warren on the debate stage saying, "When I was 22 years old, I was fired from my job as a special education teacher and I loved that job. By the end of the first year, I was visibly pregnant. The principal wished me luck and gave my job to someone else." In both election cycles, the theme of sexual discrimination came up in almost equal numbers.

Table 1: Frequency of Themes

Theme	2016	%	2020	%
Question Oppt's behavior	2	6%	10	13%
Healthcare	1	3%	5	6%
Role Models	1	3%	7	9%
Making History	7	21%	6	8%
Young Women	1	3%	4	19%
Black Women	1	3%	6	7%
Education	4	12%	3	4%
Immigration	2	6%	2	2%
Abortion	2	6%	8	10%
Sexual Discrimination	12	36%	26	34%
Total	33		77	

Another area of continuity would be "Questioning Opponent's Behavior." Many of the ads used audio of Trump's most controversial statements. A 2016 ad entitled, "No Defense for the Indefensible" brings up Trump's access Hollywood audio, "I'm automatically attracted to beautiful women. I just start kissing them. I don't wait." This is an example of putting the words Clinton's opponent for voters to see. The ad shows his allies being hesitant to criticize him, which also brings his questionable words to the forefront. The ads in 2020 were similar in this regard. A commercial titled, "Pedo Trump" brings in the question of his relationships with Jefferey Epstein and Ghislaine Maxwell. Notably, the ad uses recent audio of the president saying about Maxwell "I just wish her well."

Both 2016 and 2020 ads included references to education. In an advertisement titled" Getting Started" Clinton says, "I say that all children deserve a good school and a good teacher regardless of what zip code they're in." These are examples of political advertisements becoming more "feminized" in the issues that are highlighted when targeting women voters. In a 2020 ad for Biden, a woman says, "I support Joe because he will pay teachers what they deserve." Both sets of ads for each cycle had a roughly equal amount of references to education.

Another area of similarity between the two sets of ads was abortion. In a 2016 ad called "Let's Meet Mike Pence" shared the statement "Mike Pence has had an obsession with defunding Planned Parenthood." Ads from 2020 also portrayed abortion in a similar light. In a 2019 ad for Kirsten Gillibrand, she mentioned what she sees as an assault on women's reproductive rights and that she would appoint justices that would uphold them. "I would ask them if they believe Roe. V Wade is settled precedent." Sexual discrimination, questioning an opponent's behavior, education, and abortion are all themes that both sets of ads have in common.

Images of "Young Women" were almost equally conveyed in both sets of ads. This should not come as a surprise either. Since the president has made comments about young women, it would be expected that this theme would appear in 2016 and 2020. Notably, an ad from 2020 "Daughters" says "Dear Daughters we want so much for you, we want you to grow proud and strong. We want you to grow up in an America that believes in you." Another ad from 2020 that was dedicated to young women says, "After all the dust is settled, what will they wake up to? What will a whole generation of girls and young women wake up to? Will they wake up to a government trying to take their rights away? 2016 also featured several ads that included images of young women. In a commercial a woman talks about equal pay but also her daughters, "I have two young women in the workforce and they're incredible, and they're strong and they're very smart. The thought that they could be objectified by someone as disrespectful as Donald Trump scares me." Additionally, in a 2016 ad a young girl mentions her dad, "he is voting for my future. His vote is my voice." While both sets of ads evoke images of young women, the messaging is different. In 2016, the ads are more defensive and seemingly want to protect young women. While 2020 ad set did contain some of this messaging, it seemed to push young women to reach their goals. Perhaps this is due to the many women primary candidates and a female vice-presidential nominee.

Immigration and healthcare were also significant themes throughout both campaigns. In 2016 featuring Diane Guerrero says, "When I was 14, my family was deported." In a 2020 primary advertisement, a woman speaks of her grandmother. "She was a migrant worker and she was a single mother. Regarding healthcare, a woman in a promotion for Mike Bloomberg says, "Black women are dying all across this country because of maternal health issues." Planned Parenthood features a 2016 ad that addresses women's health. The narrator refers to Mike Pence as "The guy who tried to defund Planned Parenthood and make it so that women couldn't get cancer screenings.

"Making History" appeared as a concept in both sets of ads as well. A 2016 commercial features Hillary saying, "Thanks to you we have reached a milestone. The first time in our nations' history, that a woman will be a major party's nominee" There were also ads in 2016 dedicated to women of color senate candidates then having a potential to make history. In 2020, when an ad brought up Kamala Harris, the narrator said, "will they get up to a new age of leadership? The first woman Vice President in history."

However, other areas are distinct to the 2020 and 2016 election ads. For the 2020 ads, images of "Women Role Models" appeared more in 2020. For example, an advertisement from the Biden campaign, "Happy Mother's Day" says, "I am Catherine Eugenia Finnegan Biden's son, she is amazing. She instilled in us the notion that we could do anything we want" The ad is entirely focused on his mother and brings up the lessons she taught to his younger self. The ad's focus, Biden's mother, suggests a sense of admiration necessary for a role model. Role models also appeared in primary ads for Mike Bloomberg. A woman mentions that Bloomberg was raised "by an extraordinary woman." 2016 only had one reference, in an ad for Carly Fiorina, where the image of a female role model was depicted as "Margaret Thatcher...the first Iron Lady." The ad also admires that historical figure as if she is a role model for Fiorina and for all American women. Another area where 2020 ads are distinct is for "Black Women." While 2016 only included one reference to Black women, the 2020 set of ads included six. Most notably, in an ad called "Mayors for Biden" featuring Black female mayors, including one woman saying, "Black women have always been on the front lines for social justice, it's what we do. Let's all vote for Joe Biden and Kamala Harris."[i]

Conclusion

In my research, I was surprised to find that the 2020 women's ads were not entirely distinct from the 2016 ads. The ads from 2020 were only distinct in certain areas, the themes of "Black Women," and "Role Models." Targeting women based on race reflected a more open and sensitive political environment in 2020. Black Lives Matter became part of the public's consciousness in 2020 after the death of George Floyd. Consequently, race played a greater role in the 2020 election with both parties including race as a subject in their platforms. Additionally, Kamala Harris was the first Black woman vice presidential nominee in history. With these factors unique to the political landscape in 2020, it legitimized advertising targeting Black women. Also, having women role models as a greater theme in 2020 should not come as a surprise either. There were two male major party candidates and mentioning woman role models is a reasonable targeting strategy for male candidates to reach out to woman voters. There are three major forms of campaign appeals to women and one of these is to connect a candidate with a woman, as Joe Biden and Mike Bloomberg did with their mothers. Since 1992, also known as the "Year of the Woman," politics became more feminized meaning that campaigns began to talk about feminine issues such as education, healthcare, and sexual discrimination (Shames, 2020). Therefore, as expected, the ads were not much different in terms of the frequency with which each set addressed these "feminine" issues. Also, identity-based appeals towards women are found to increase ad message support (Holman et al, 2015a). Scholars believe that studying what appeals to women in campaign advertisements is important because women make up over half of the voting population, their voting patterns are different than men, and they are underrepresented in government (Holman et al, 2015b). In the future, it should be expected that women's ads will vary based on circumstance and the candidate's gender.

References

Forgey, Q. (2020, August 3). *Trump campaign restarts TV advertising with spots slamming Biden.* Politico. https://www.politico.com/news/2020/08/03/trump-campaign-tv-ads-slam-biden-390879

Holman, R.M., Schnieder, C. M., & Pondel, K. (2015a). Gender targeting in political advertisements, *Political Research Quarterly, 68.* 816-829.

Holman, R.M., Schnieder, C.M., & Pondel, K. (2015b). *Political candidates can successfully use targeted appeals to increase support from female voters.* LSE USCentre, United States Politics and Policy. https://blogs.lse.ac.uk/usappblog/2015/10/22/political-candidates-can-successfully-use-targeted-appeals-to-increase-support-from-female-voters/

Mathers, M. (2020, October 16). *Maligned, belittled, harassed, insulted: New Lincoln Project campaign calls out Trump's treatment of women.* Independent. https://www.independent.co.uk/news/world/americas/us-election-2020/lincoln-project-trump-women-assault-allegations-us-election-2020-b1076683.html

McManus, D. (2020, October 25). *This year's political ads: The good, the bad, and the deceptive.* Los Angeles Times. https://www.latimes.com/politics/story/2020-10-25/doyle-column-political-ads-2020-biden-trump

NewsOne (2020, October 22). *New Biden ads emphatically answer the question to Trump's question to Black voters 'What do you have to lose.*

https://chicagocrusader.com/new-biden-ads-emphatically-answer-trumps-question-to-black-voters-what-do-you-have-to-lose/

Schmidt, S. (2020, November 6). *The gender gap was expected to be historic. Instead, women voted as much as they always have.* Washington Post. https://www.washingtonpost.com/dc-md-va/2020/11/06/election-2020-gender-gap-women/

Shames, S. (2008). The "un-candidates": gender and outsider signals in women's political advertising. *Women in Politics, 25, 115-147.*

---

[i] Editor's note: the 2016 ad set which the student researcher was provided was arguably incomplete. One distinct difference between the 2016 and 2020 ads which featured women were the appearance of many celebrities and identity group members in 2016. The researcher rightly notes the increase in black women, among others in the 2020 ads. Also, there were many ads in 2016 that were that used female role models. In particularly, Hillary Clinton often lauded her mother as a role model and many narratives were produced featuring role models across occupation, class, and generations.

Chapter 9: The Representation of Assault Weapons in 2020 Primary Election Media

Tori Pylypec

Tori is a Senior in Communication from Austin, TX

The immediacy and proliferation of social media has diluted information with opinions and propaganda, with definitions often blurring together. As consumers of confusion, specifically during an election season, how are we to identify what we accept as true? What rhetoric do we digest and take-in often without fully knowing its meaning? The topic of gun control was at the forefront of advertisements and debates, primarily in the 2020 Democratic primary phase. As the talk of "banning assault weapons," often in response to a rise in mass shootings, has increased, the politicians who make these claims lack a true definition of the term. This lack of precision in what is an assault weapon also influences voters.

In his TED Talk speech, "The Much Misunderstood Second Amendment," American attorney William Harwood explains "just one simple, short sentence…has become the subject of passionate advocacy and intense political controversy" (Harwood, 2018). This simple sentence he references states, "the right of the people to keep and bear Arms shall not be infringed" (U.S. Const. amend. II). An influx of mass shootings has heightened the political controversy regarding gun ownership in the United States. These acts of violence have proven to "increase gun-related media coverage" (Luca, 2020).

Understanding the classification of guns is essential to the discussion of Second Amendment rights. Terms such as "assault weapons," "semi-automatic weapons," and "automatic weapons" are often used interchangeably, delivered without clarity to the American people. A semi-automatic firearm will "fire one bullet for each time the trigger is squeezed" (PBS, 2014). This type of gun is inclusive of handguns that many individuals select for self-defense within their homes, as well as rifles and shotguns used for hunting. This accounts for approximately "80 percent of handguns currently manufactured" (Kopel, 2018). Automatic weapons, which are generally illegal in the United States, "fire continually until the trigger is released" (PBS, 2014). Automatic firearms may only be owned if they were fully registered before 1986 and the owner is cleared with significant background checks and fingerprinting technology (Stillwell, 2020).

Politicians have coined the term "assault weapons" to represent semi-automatic firearms. Banning assault weapons has remained a top priority for Democratic candidates for multiple decades. In 1994, President Bill Clinton signed into law the Assault Weapon Ban which lasted until 2004. This law was ineffective in its attempt to combat murder rates which during the ban "were 19.3% higher" (NRA-ILA 4, 2019). However, support for reinstating this ban has grown.

Method

This research analyzes the representation of assault weapons in the 2020 primary election period. The study included 14 advertisements, two speeches, and one interview about gun policy. Additionally, excerpts from campaign websites were used to further explain each entity's stance on gun policy. These resources were collected from the NRA and the Trump, Biden, Sanders, and Bloomberg campaigns. The videos were analyzed both visually and verbally (See Tables 1 & 2). The media was categorized visually into one of three categories: "Assault Weapons represented visually as rifles," "Assault Weapons represented visually as handguns," or "Assault Weapons not visually represented." The verbal contents of these videos were categorized into one of the following categories: "Assault Weapon stated verbally and NOT defined," "Assault Weapon stated verbally and defined," and "Assault Weapons not stated verbally." The study aims to discover if campaign media includes verbal or visual clues regarding their definition of assault weapons. The analyzed sources are not inclusive of every gun advertisement from the Trump, Biden, Sanders Bloomberg, and NRA media campaigns.

Joe Biden

Throughout his 2020 primary campaign, Joe Biden broadcasted advertisements to advance his proposed gun policy and his past involvement with the Assault Weapon Ban of 1994. On his website, Biden has advocated for "Ban[ning] the manufacture and sale of assault weapons and high-capacity magazines." (Biden, 2020). Six of his campaign gun-related advertisements were selected to be studied, two of which are in the Spanish language. In the verbal analysis, all six advertisements included "Assault weapons," or "Las Armas de Asalto" without a definition of the weapons (See Table 1). The advertisements lack a verbal explanation regarding the types of firearms included in the proposed ban.

Visually, Biden's gun policy videos showed more variety. Four of the six advertisements did not include any visual representation of an assault weapon. Two of the advertisements, entitled "Streets" and "Joe Biden Banned Assault Weapons," incorporated images of rifles as a visual explanation of the term. Biden has endorsed the gun policy of Beto O'Rourke who famously claimed in 2019: "Hell yes, we are going to take your AR-15, your AK-47" (ABC News, 2019). It is important to note that the AR-15, or the American Rifle, is a semi-automatic weapon. The AK-47 is a fully automatic weapon designed for the military, which is illegal to own unless it is a semi-automatic model of the gun, or if the automatic gun was fully registered before 1986. (Stillwell, 2020).

Mike Bloomberg

In February of 2020, Michael Bloomberg released a Super Bowl advertisement entitled "George" that displayed his longstanding advocacy for stopping gun violence in America (Gun Ads, 2020). According to his campaign website, Bloomberg aims to "ban assault weapons, protect kids, and protect schools" (Bloomberg, 2020). Five of his campaign advertisements were selected for verbal and visual analysis. Each of these videos contained the same verbal and visual representation of assault weapons (See Table 2). Despite the policy outlined on his website, none of his advertisements contained the words or images of "assault weapons." In his video, "A Plan to Save Lives," Bloomberg outlines his proposed gun policy for three minutes. There is no mention of an assault weapon ban in this video, rather an emphasis on background checks. Although Bloomberg released many advertisements about guns, he avoided the rhetorical term "assault weapon" altogether.

Bernie Sanders

Bernie Sanders was less vocal about gun policy during the 2020 race. On his campaign website, his gun policy stated his plan to "regulate assault weapons in the same way that we currently regulate fully automatic weapons — a system that essentially makes them unlawful to own" (Sanders, 2020). From this statement, it is logical to conclude that Sanders' definition of assault weapons references semi-automatic weapons, as he aims to regulate them in the same way as automatic firearms. Due to his extended career in politics, and his current lack of commentary on the topic, this study includes a source from 2016. During a campaign rally in Connecticut, Bernie addressed his gun policy to a crowd of supporters. In his explanation of an assault weapon ban, he refers to guns that have "magazines with 30 bullets at a time" (Sanders, 2016). Although this is not a universally accepted explanation of the term, his provides a verbal description of the assault weapons. Visually, the speech provides no additional images to aid in the understanding of the vague term.

A year ago, Bernie released an advertisement entitled "We Must End the Gun Violence Epidemic." Verbally, this video both stated and defined the terminology in question. Unlike his fellow democratic candidates, Sanders provides a verbal explanation of the term. He referred to assault weapons as machines "designed to kill human beings." The advertisement includes images of many types of firearms, but it specifically represents assault weapons as rifles (See Table 2). There was a noticeable absence of advertisement regarding gun policy by this candidate during the 2020 election cycle.

NRA

The National Rifle Association has been a prominent voice in the discussion of gun laws during the 2020 Election. The NRA releases their own advertisements and media concerning gun education and advocacy for Second Amendment Rights. In their video entitled "Disabled Woman Weak to Coronavirus Issues Message to Politicians Using Pandemic to Push Gun Control," the NRA included both visual and verbal representation of an assault weapon (See Tables 1 & 2). This video discussed the importance of owning a firearm amid a nationwide crisis. Verbally, the video stated assault weapons without a definition. Visually, the woman holds a semi-automatic rifle while she speaks. Towards the end of the video, the woman signaled air quotation marks with her hands when she stated the term "assault weapon." This likely alluded to the lacking validity of the term. Although the NRA has plenty of commentary about guns and gun laws, the organization likely lacked content with the term "assault weapon" because their content uses technical gun terminology.

A second video released by the NRA was a response to the viral video of Joe Biden engaged in a heated argument about gun policy at a campaign event. This advertisement is titled "Union Worker Respond to Biden's Threats Against 'AR-14,'" and it is narrated by the man who challenged Joe Biden for his statements regarding assault weapons. Verbally, this video was an outlier and placed in the "Assault Weapon stated verbally and defined" category. He defines the term as "America's most popular rifle." In the video, he is shown firing a semi-automatic AR-15 rifle. This video provides both a verbal and visual definition of the term in question.

Donald Trump

Throughout his presidency, President Donald Trump has argued on behalf of Americans' right to bear arms. In his speech to the National Rifle Association in 2019, he stated, "We believe in the right to self-defense and the right to protect your family, your community, and your loved ones. We believe in the wisdom of our Founders. And we believe in freedom and liberty and the right to keep and bear arms" (Trump, 2019).

The President has been criticized for his lack of policy response to mass shootings throughout his term. In his 2020 reelection efforts, Trump has maintained a pro-gun stance. He has strategically used this issue and emphasized that Democrats "don't respect the Second Amendment, which will be one of many contrasts drawn during the campaign" (*The New York Times*, 2020).

In the primary President Trump did not release many advertisements related specifically to gun control. His comments about assault weapons can be found in his speeches and interviews. This is a limitation on the visual aspect of this research, and therefore his media was only categorized into the verbal analysis section. In his 2020 State of the Union address, President Trump vowed, "So long as I am president, I will always protect your Second Amendment right to keep and bear arms" (Trump, 2020a). President Trump does not use the term assault weapon in his address. When asked about banning assault weapons after the Dayton and El Paso shootings in 2019, Trump responded by saying "You could do your own polling, and there is no political appetite probably from the standpoint of the legislature." This interview is categorized verbally as stated and not defined.

Table 1: Verbal/Written Representation of Assault Weapons

Candidate/ Organization	Number of sources analyzed	Assault Weapons stated verbally and not defined	Assault Weapon stated verbally and defined	Assault Weapon not stated verbally
Biden	6	5	0	1
Bloomberg	5	0	0	5
Sanders	2	0	2	0
NRA	2	1	1	0
Trump	2	1	0	1

Table 2: Visual Representation of Assault Weapons

Candidate/ Organization	Number of sources analyzed	Assault Weapons represented visually as rifles	Assault Weapons represented visually/handguns	Assault Weapons not rep. visually
Biden	6	2	0	4
Bloomberg	5	0	0	5
Sanders	2	1	0	1
NRA	2	2	0	0
Trump	2	-	-	-

General Conclusions

For the 16 examples analyzed in this study only three provided a verbal definition of the term "Assault Weapon." These verbal explanations included phrases such as "America's most popular rifle," weapons "designed to kill human beings," and weapons that contain "magazines with 30 bullets at a time." There was no representation of assault weapons as handguns in the selected media. Visually, the five media samples that provided images represented them solely as rifles such as the AR-15.

Significance

Rhetoric in politics can be viewed as a "deceitful," yet skillful practice. The term "assault weapon" is believed to have been coined by Adolf Hitler, a dangerous master of political rhetoric and propaganda (Shurkin, 2016). Certain terms are used to evoke emotion from listeners. The focus remains less on the definition and more on the associated connotations. Analysis of multiple primary election advertisements supports the idea that the term "assault" is a tool used to invoke connotations of death, destruction, and military-grade weaponry. Political rhetoric is an important skill for gaining a following, but it has potentially negative repercussions when combined with policy and law-making. Do people know what movements they are supporting and what laws they are advocating for? Do politicians themselves know exactly which weapons they intend to ban?

There is a blatant lack of clarity regarding which firearms are included in this terminology. Due to the complexity of firearm classifications, and the emotional appeal of political rhetoric, the visual and verbal definitions of assault weapons are lacking. There is a likelihood that some politicians may not understand which guns they hope to regulate but do understand the "political work" that naming evokes. The term "Assault Weapon" is malleable, and therefore its meaning is assigned by the politician, voter, or lawmaker who includes it in their political communication.

References

Bloomberg, M. (2020, February 6). *A plan to save lives*. YouTube, https://www.youtube.com/watch?v=Fn4WIZkxvag

Biden, J. (2020). *Joe Biden's plan to end gun violence*. Joe Biden for President. Biden for President. https://www.joebiden.com/gunsafety/

Bloomberg, M. (2020). *Gun safety*. Mike Bloomberg for President, YouTube. https://www.mikebloomberg2020.com/policies/gun-safety

Frontline: *Hot guns: GUN FAQs*. PBS, Public Broadcasting Service, https://www.pbs.org/wgbh/pages/frontline/shows/guns/more/faq.html

Harwood, W. (2018, December 17). *The much misunderstood second amendment*. TED. https://www.ted.com/talks/william_harwood_the_much_misunderstood_second_amendment

Kopel, D. B. (2018, November 14). *Defining 'assault weapons*. The Regulatory Review, Penn Program on Regulation, https://www.theregreview.org/2018/11/14/kopel-defining-assault-weapons/

Luca, M., & Malhotra, D., & Poliquin, C. (2020). The impact of mass shootings on gun policy. *Journal of Public Economics*, *181*. https://www-sciencedirect-com.go.libproxy.wakehealth.edu/science/article/pii/S0047272719301446

NRA-ILA. (2019, September). ILA: *'Assault weapons': 'Large' magazines*. *NRA-ILA*, National Rifle Association. https://www.nraila.org/get-the-facts/assault-weapons-large-magazines/

NRA. (2020). *Disabled woman weak to coronavirus issues message to politicians using pandemic to push gun control.* NRA, YouTube. https://www.youtube.com/watch?v=z8fvDk4E5Pk

Sanders, B. (2020). *Gun safety.* Bernie Sanders – Official Campaign Website. https://www.berniesanders.com/issues/gun-safety/

Shurkin, M. (2016, June 30). *A brief history of the assault rifle.* The Atlantic. https://www.theatlantic.com/technology/archive/2016/06/a-brief-history-of-the-assault-rifle/489428/

Stilwell, B. (2020, August 12). *Everything you want to know about the legendary AK-47.* Business Insider. https://www.businessinsider.com/where-how-ak47-rifle-is-used-around-the-world-2020-8

Trump, D. (2020a, February 5). Full transcript: Trump's 2020 State of the Union Address. *The New York Times.* https://www.nytimes.com/2020/02/05/us/politics/state-of-union-transcript.html

Trump, D. (2019, April 26). Remarks by President Trump at the NRA-ILA Leadership Forum. *The White House*, The United States Government. https://www.whitehouse.gov/briefings-statements/remarks-president-trump-nra-ila-leadership-forum-indianapolis/

Trump, D. (2020b, February 4). *Trump promises to defend religious freedom and the 2nd amendment,* YouTube, PBS NewsHour. https://www.youtube.com/watch?v=FECR_bfspS4

Washington Post. (2019, August 7). *Trump Sees 'No political appetite' to ban assault rifles.* The Straits Times, https://www.straitstimes.com/world/united-states/trump-sees-no-political-appetiteto-ban-assault-rifles

Chapter 10: Firearms Advertising in the 2020 General Election Cycle

Kiki Rodriguez

Kiki is a Senior in Economics from Coral Gables, FL

When it comes to political issues, few, if any, are more polarizing than the debate on gun control. People's opinions on firearms are deep-seated, often leading to fiery debates between members of the public and those who represent them. This debate is largely unique to America, as it is one of the few countries that not only openly allows the possession and use of firearms, but it also holds the belief that its citizens have a god given right to bear arms. Constitutionally speaking, this principle was a key part of the founding of the country.

Given voters' passion, it is no surprise that it was a substantial talking point in the 2020 election advertising campaigns. Both Donald Trump and Joe Biden's campaign teams spent time and money promoting their positions on gun policy. Third-party organizations also sponsor ads to promote the policy that align with their own self-interests. The NRA is the most notable of these third-party organizations—by some estimates the NRA spent more than 50 million in 2020 to back Donald Trump and several Republican Senate candidates (Nass, 2020). This study analyzes 47 general election ads from the 2020 election cycle, including ads for the Trump Campaign, Biden Campaign, and ads from third-party organizations.

According to the John Hopkins Bloomberg School of Public Health, political firearm ads are up eightfold in the last four elections (Political TV Ads Referencing Guns, 2020). The anti-any-form-of-gun-control voters reject restrictions on their abilities to purchase firearms, as reinforced in gun sales data. As the probability of Biden winning the election matured, more people purchased guns. As of November 8th, 2020, gun sales hit a new all-time high (Gibson, 2020). Previous years' data indicates that the record high was set in 2016, which was the election in where Hillary Clinton was favored to win. This indirect evidence suggests that gun owners are very passionate about their guns. When there is any inkling that gun rights will be restricted, they head to the gun stores.

A typical line from Trump issued ad claimed, "They are trying to take your guns away." It is a refrain utilized by Republican candidates and it appears to work. Gun ads frequently try to evoke fear from the audience. By indicating the Democrats will take your guns away, some gun owners feel defenseless from "threats," an argument often a stand-in for many other reasons for owning a gun. A perfect example is seen in one of Trump's ad *Come Hell or High Water* (2020) where the Lieutenant Governor of North Carolina Mark Robinson gives a passionate speech, telling the crowd that taking guns from law abiding citizens leaves gangs like the "Bloods and the Crips" as the only ones left with firearms (Molina & Moody, 2018).

Trump's campaign also used the summer confrontations energized by the BLM movement to its advantage. A big fear among Republican voters was that the chaos and the looting that occurred in major cities like Minneapolis, Dallas, Atlanta, Portland, and many more, would come to their neighborhoods (I Am the Only Thing, 2020) (See Chapter 18). Defunding the police was referenced heavily in Trump and other Republican ads. "Leftists," and often any Democrat, were pictured calling for police districts to be defunded. This may have left many citizens uneasy. Absent the police who would protect them from thugs, criminals, and the unsavory? Trump's *I Am the Only Thing Standing Between YOU and Chaos* (2020) reveals Biden and Harris stating they want to increase gun control measures, which, as the ad claims, is not only unconstitutional, but leaves people defenseless.

In the gun ads there were more ads posted by the Biden Campaign than the Trump campaign, so I tend to them more thoroughly. Like the Trump ads, the Joe Biden campaign put out ads that tried to evoke fear among listeners. Some of his ads showed children and a teacher in their classroom preparing for a drill (Classroom, 2020). The thought of having someone shooting children in an elementary school is almost unthinkable. Independent groups produced an even more startling PSA with visual "back-to-school" preparation for the next school shooting, complete with an active shooter and wounded students (Sandy Hook Promise, 2019).

Joe Biden ran ads that listed major mass shootings in the last few years, emphasizing the devastating effects those have had on the people in the area. When people vote, they vote based on their own self-interests, so I think this is an effective way to advertise the Biden position. Although this instills fear into the viewer, it also shows facts and data, which is something not often seen in ads pro-firearms. This data-based approach occurred more from Biden and the NRA, than from Trump.

By and large the biggest third-party organization that has put out ads related to firearms in the 2020 election cycle was the National Rifle Association (NRA). The NRA always plays a big role in every election. However, they had less of an impact in 2020 compared to 2016. The NRA is very controversial in America, with the proportions of Americans who view it favorably and unfavorably in equivalent magnitude. Democrats have made the NRA a point of campaign emphasis in 2020, attacking the NRA with headlines like *Joe Biden beat the NRA* (2020). and *Stop the NRA* (2020) (Rubin, 2019). These titles seemed to be more to wield his can do credentials. Many Democrats view the NRA as their ultimate counterpart on establishing legality of firearms so they have done whatever they can to delegitimize their messaging.

The NRA, for their part, have used attacks on their organization to an advantage. One ad, *Urgent: The NRA is Under Attack* (2020), was nearly two minutes of Democratic party leaders and members calling them a terrorist organization, claiming they support mass murder, are extremely radical, and that people should be afraid of the NRA. This rhetoric may benefit the NRA as memberships skyrocket (Ingraham, 2018). Just like before, the NRA also uses emotion and fear to get its point across. This is portrayed perfectly by one NRA ad in which a woman is being chased down by thugs, only for her gun to vanish into thin air, leaving her defenseless, while a background voice says this is what a Joe Biden's America would be like (Defend your Family, 2020).

One ad visualized protest in the streets as a reason to retain gun ownership. *The McCloskeys* (2020) reveal a war-torn St. Louis, the home of the vigilante couple who brandished firearms on their front porch as protesters marched by, "They were simply trying to protect their home." The McCloskeys were often shown in Trump opposition ads, as with The Lincoln project spot *Radicalize*, itself an argument for why citizens should not have guns. Video of the white couple pointing guns at demonstrators marching past their mansion, underscores Trump's celebration of the couple at campaign events and the GOP convention; his tacit endorsement of violent actors. The ad summarizes "America *or* Donald Trump? Stand up for" America.

The NRA has also put out ads claiming that Joe Biden's knowledge on firearms is very limited, and looking at it at face value, it looks like a credible argument (Barely There Biden, 2020). There are clips in the ad in which Joe Biden claims that he is going to take away the "AR-14's," he says guns should not be able to have "30, 40, 50, clips in it," and that some "magazines have 100 clips in it." Those familiar with firearms would know that this is not an accurate description (See Chapter 9). The ad suggests that someone who clearly knows very little about guns, should not be legislating restrictions. I think that is one of the NRA's more effective ads as it does not just rely on fear and emotion, but it seems to have a logic to it. In addition, it is framed in self-indicting Biden video to which the viewer is an eyewitness, complicating any denial of the spot's truthfulness.

In the 2020 election cycle, gun ads were propelled by fear and emotion. Of these ads, this researcher found the NRA ads to be the most powerful. The Trump and Biden campaigns have many topics to address while the NRA must focus only on one. The subject of firearms played a big role in the 2020 election cycle, and these advertisements are proof that a lot of money is spent on them, and likely they will continue to be made in future elections, perhaps even more NRA advertisements in support of Republican candidates. In 2016, their candidate came out victorious, but in 2020, when faced by scandal and financial constraints, they aired considerably less advertising and their candidate lost.

References

Barely There Biden claims, "I'm not going nuts." This video proves otherwise (2020, July 9). NRA, YouTube. https://www.youtube.com/watch?v=91nPiokrF-U

Classroom (2020, January 8). Joe Biden for president, YouTube. https://www.youtube.com/watch?v=k5u5kW8yll4

Come hell or high water (2020, November 2). Donald J Trump, YouTube. https://www.youtube.com/watch?v=ARdDxDo_Wjs

Defend Your Family (2020, August 21). NRA Victory Fund, Twitter. https://twitter.com/MediumBuying/status/1296772099055525893?s=20

Gibson, K. (2020, November 3). *U.S. gun sales surge to record high in 2020*. CBS News. https://www.cbsnews.com/news/gun-sales-record-high-2020/

I am the only thing standing between YOU and chaos. Donald J Trump, YouTube. https://www.youtube.com/watch?v=dbJY9VUosPo

Ingraham, C. (2018, February 16*)*. *Nobody knows how many members the NRA has, but its tax returns offer some clues*. The Washington Post. https://www.washingtonpost.com/news/wonk/wp/2018/02/26/nobody-knows-how-many-members-the-nra-has-but-its-tax-returns-offer-some-clues/

Joe Biden banned assault weapons. Joe Biden, YouTube. https://www.youtube.com/watch?v=ARdDxDo_Wjs

Joe Biden beat the NRA (2020, March 25). Unite the Country, YouTube. https://www.youtube.com/watch?v=ezZ0MfrIZW0

Molina, C., & Moody, A (2018, April 6, 8). *'Come hell or high water,' citizens will keep gun rights, NC man vows in viral video.* The News and Observer. https://www.newsobserver.com/news/politics-government/article208049249.html

Nass, D. (2020, August 8). *How much did the NRA spend to support Republicans in 2020?* The Trace. https://www.thetrace.org/2020/08/nra-2020-election-spending-trump/

Political TV ads referencing guns increased eightfold over four election cycles (2020, February 3), Johns Hopkins Bloomberg School of Public Health. https://www.jhsph.edu/news/news-releases/2020/political-tv-ads-referencing-guns-increased-eightfold-over-four-election-cycles.html

Rubin, J. M. (2019, September 13). *Americans' views of NRA become less positive.* Gallup. https://news.gallup.com/poll/266804/americans-views-nra-become-less-positive.aspx

The McCloskeys (2020, August 24). Donald J Trump, YouTube. https://www.youtube.com/watch?v=MDwZOdVT1qQ

Sandy Hook Promise school shooting PSA. KRPC 2 Click2Houston. YouTube. https://www.youtube.com/watch?v=turCfxwkfPE&ab_channel=KPRC2Click2Houston

Stop the NRA (2020, February 15). Joe Biden for President, YouTube. https://www.youtube.com/watch?v=hSGmYHIiRMw

URGENT: The NRA is under attack (2020, August 7). NRA, YouTube. https://www.youtube.com/watch?v=nqI6ASbo6XA

Chapter 11: Biden and Sanders's Primary Health Care Reform Advertisements: An Aristotelian Analysis

Kellyn Jamison

Kellyn is a Senior in Communication from Canfield, OH

Introduction

An analysis of issue advocacy advertising spending for the Democratic presidential primary showed that spending on healthcare advertisements reached over $65 million in the 2019 primary period, far exceeding spending on other issues (Fischer & Owens, 2019). It is evident that healthcare was the prominent issue during the early presidential advertising for the 2020 election. However, even though many Americans were viewing the same healthcare advertisements, varying perceptions of each Democratic candidate arose. The Democratic candidates shared the same political party and boosted the importance of the same topic, but the presence of a zero-sum electoral contest produced different messaging and solicited distinct opinions.

The variation in judgment reveals the importance of another determining factor at play – persuasive appeals in the television advertisements. It can be understood that the persuasion techniques, or rhetorical devices, in advertisements resonate more with certain viewers than others, but this does not fully account for how rhetorical choice in the televised healthcare reform advertisements contributed to each Democratic candidate's public perception. To answer this question, I performed an examination of health advertisements – exploration of the relevance of the healthcare topic in politics, as well as the differences in the healthcare plans proposed by the final two Democratic candidates, Joe Biden and Bernie Sanders. The following is analysis and interpretation of the rhetoric used in advertisements by each candidate to inform viewers of their respective visions for healthcare reform.

Literature Review

Political Television Advertisement

Political advertisements are an important campaign tool that have scaled up in terms of both ad channels and ad numbers over time. In particular, the use of television for the purpose of political advertisement was revolutionary when first deployed 70 years ago. And it remains effective with the American people, offering diverse advertising opportunities. Although it was developed in 1940, television was not utilized for politics until 1952 with the spot ad campaign "Eisenhower Answers America," which was a turning point and start of a new era in presidential politics (Wood, 1990). Since then, the number of political advertisements that circulate each cycle has grown exponentially. During the 2016 presidential election, more than 500,000 broadcast and national TV advertisements aired (Beckel, 2016). The way in which campaigns strategically use these advertising opportunities has the power to either strengthen or weaken a presidential candidate.

Rhetorical Devices in Political Television Advertisements

Televised political advertisement opens the door to several strategic persuasion techniques that can be exploited by presidential campaigns. Advertising spots are commonly used as an opportunity to not only let the candidate's personality shine through, but also to secure votes, justify policy, or attack an opponent (Parry-Giles, 2010). To convey any political message, rhetorical devices inherently have potential to both help or hurt how a candidate is perceived. Further expanding on this idea, Trevor Parry-Giles explains:

Voter perceptions of candidates emanate from somewhere; they do not spring fully formed in the minds of voters from sources like party affiliation or public policy preferences, even as such sources might influence judgments about political images. These perceptions, instead, come from the rhetorics that construct them, the reasons given for a candidate's persona and public character, the evidence provided to justify a particular political image, and the interchange between public figures about public persona. (40)

It is evident the rhetoric surrounding the presidential candidate's messages is worth consideration. Nonetheless, the rhetoric involved in television advertisements is not the only determining factor in public perception. The choice of content is strategic and how this is portrayed relates to the voter understanding. From another point of view, rhetorical choice is also strategic and dependent upon the content, making these components reflexive.[i]

Significance of Healthcare Reform Television Advertisements

The various rhetorical appeals chosen in designing television advertisements is often dependent upon the message. It is understandable that adequately communicating each part of a presidential candidate's platform within the 30-60 seconds allotted time limits is challenging. Therefore, candidates often highlight an aspect of their platform for an entire ad to communicate their ideas in a memorable manner. "Healthcare reform … [remains] top of the political agenda, and numerous interest-groups funded health related advertising campaigns in order to influence public opinion." Beginning with the 1993-1994 infamous Harry and Louise ads successfully opposed Bill Clinton's health legislation (Goldsteen et al., 2001), as have subsequent efforts. The advertising campaign waged to oppose the Affordable Care Act (Overby, 2014) proved less successful, yet remained ongoing often dominating subsequent campaigns to the ACA passing (Newburger, 2018).

It is evident healthcare reform retains interest and has a large influence in public perception. This fact remains true today, as most of the Democratic candidates who were once in the running developed an advertisement surrounding healthcare reform in some fashion (Bycoffe, 2019). Due to the high volume of healthcare advertisements presented to the American people it is helpful to first compare the messages with one another to understand the varying plans proposed.

Healthcare Reform Plans of Joe Biden and Bernie Sanders

Joe Biden and Bernie Sanders advocated for reforms that were drastically different from one another. Former Vice President Joe Biden advocated for the expansion of the Affordable Care Act, also known as "Obamacare." This healthcare reform was enacted March 2010 under President Barack Obama and Vice President Joe Biden ("Affordable Care Act (ACA) – HealthCare.Gov). Since then, Obamacare has insured around 15 million people, but has also brought challenges and limitations of the reform to light warranting a revision or expansion (Scott, 2020).

On the other hand, Senator Bernie Sanders, seen as the more progressive candidate, proposed the elimination of private health insurance companies and placing Americans on a single-payer government health insurance plan. The argument behind this is the decrease of federal spending, lower administrative costs and profits, and the government's ability to negotiate with drug companies, which is now currently outlawed (Kurtzleben, Schapitl, & Hurt, 2019). These benefits were offered as a fix to large medical bills, leading to bankruptcy, a lack of healthcare access, and lower medical expenses. However, Sanders' plan presented new challenges to the federal government as some claimed it increased the federal budget, required new taxes, would have a costly implementation, as well cause a hit to the economy by eliminating private insurance business (Glied & Lambrew, 2018).

Method

The healthcare reform ads mentioned had compelling differences in policy and made distinct rhetorical moves in their attempt to shape public perception. One advertisement aired by each candidate during the time of the primary Democratic debates are evaluated. Both focus on the benefits of implementing the respective healthcare plans that allows for a consistency in analyzed content.

An Aristotelian rhetorical theory approach is used to assess each of the political television advertisements. First, the rhetorical situation, the candidate's purpose for their communication, were noted. Next, the medium's elements of image and sound were evaluated, including the context in which the images of the advertisement were taking place. Finally, credibility, emotional, and logical appeals presented through messaging is considered. Each evaluation occurs in this order respectively and highlights how each of the rhetorical devices can be interpreted positively and negatively. Ultimately, this process has the goal of acknowledging the possible perceptions the American people can form about each candidate through the rhetoric of their television advertisement communication.

Results

Joe Biden: Rhetorical Situation

The *Keep It* advertisement put forth by the Biden campaign in February explains the benefits of Joe Biden's healthcare reform plan (2020). When analyzing the rhetorical situation, there are several persuasive elements that are readily apparent. First, Joe Biden is the only speaker in the commercial, therefore, the message being conveyed can be directly associated with him. Secondly, the purpose of this advertisement can be understood to be both the promotion and explanation of key benefits related to Joe Biden's healthcare reform. Due to this focus, the nature of the advertisement is noticeably intended to be positive. Finally, the medium also conveys a sense of optimism. The background music is upbeat which may communicate the message of determination, ambition, and excitement to viewers.

Additionally, the images and video cuts in the advertisement transition very quickly as to keep up with the music, which further works to convey the same optimistic messages. In combination, these three aspects of the advertisement create a positive effect which in turn reflects on Joe Biden. However, this also could work against him as the upbeat, persuasive elements are so obvious that it can be interpreted as being too forceful or insincere in the ways it attempts to influence. Additionally, this advertisement aired mid-February 2020 shortly after the Iowa caucuses. Following these events, Biden was not doing well, therefore given the context, this advertisement could be interpreted as a forceful push strategically aimed with regaining "the middle" and hence control of the primaries overarching issue of healthcare. Vaccinated

Joe Biden: Image Context

The second rhetorical aspect, image context, continues this purposeful theme of positivity. The advertisement begins with a clip of a room full of people standing and clapping as Joe Biden is speaking about his healthcare reform. Various clips of Joe Biden shaking hands and speaking with smiling people in the crowd follow this initial clip as well. These images work to persuade in favor of Joe Biden, but also can be interpreted differently. First, this advertisement helps persuade by painting Joe Biden in a positive light. The images of clapping and smiling from people in the audience make it seem as though he is favorable amongst a large group of people. Also, the clips of him shaking hands and speaking with people directly shows a sense of personability and empathy due to his attempt to connect with his voters. On the other hand, many of the video clips are recognizably from the same event. This may have been done to create a sense of consistency among the images being presented, however, this can also be interpreted as a limited number of supporters. When thinking about this advertisement in a larger context, the group present in the advertisement who is applauding Biden is quite small. Therefore, utilizing footage from only one event weakens the persuasive appeal to "jump on the Biden bandwagon" as it constrains the reality of his following.

Joe Biden: Rhetorical Message Appeals

Finally, the credibility, emotional, and logical appeals presented through the messaging may have various interpretations. Joe Biden establishes a sense of credibility from the beginning by stating "Where I come from, I don't like people telling me what I have to choose." Biden signals is more moderate approach, appealing to citizen's choice. He is also demonstrating his understanding of the struggle many people are facing which is being told what healthcare they can obtain. This works to align him more closely with the American people and make him seem like one of their own rather than a larger political figure. However, his role of former Vice President is still at play here and does work in his favor here, despite this attempt. He has an inherent credibility due to his previous experience in the White House and, although not acknowledged in the advertisement, it is understood he has knowledge about the healthcare issue due to his close work with implementing the Affordable Care Act. Furthermore, the initial statement mentioned also works to appeal emotionally. He uses this statement to set up a transition to acknowledging the various things people have lost or given up obtaining better healthcare. This implies the long struggle this topic has created and his understanding of the American people's desire for it to end. Finally, Biden uses short statements to mention the key benefits of his healthcare plan, delivering them easy to understand and logical. Together, these rhetorical aspects of the message can positively persuade audiences because it conveys Biden's credibility, understanding of the American people, and logical arguments. However, his messaging is very one-sided and does not offer counterarguments to his plan. It was found in a 1991 study regarding the cognitive processing of one- and two- sided persuasive messages that refutational two-sided messages are more persuasive than one-sided messages (Hale, Mongeau, & Thomas, 1991). Therefore, the messaging in this advertisement can also be viewed as less logical or less persuasive to some audiences because it does not consider counterarguments. situations.

Bernie Sanders: Rhetorical Situation

The January a Sander's spot, *Generations* conveyed the urgent need for healthcare reform (2020). At the time, Sanders was leading in the primary by substantial margins and the press began to recognize him as a serious contender for the Democratic nomination. Aspects of this advertisement work off one another to strengthen his "front runner" status. First, the speakers in this commercial include Bernie Sanders and the three former presidents Harry Truman, John F. Kennedy, and Barack Obama. This works to associate the message being delivered with presidential status. Secondly, the purpose of this advertisement can be understood to be the recognition of the ongoing struggle with healthcare reform in the United States and Bernie Sanders's ability to produce the change desired. Finally, the medium of the advertisement also conveys this idea of a healthcare revolution, a position he could more openly embrace given his status among the field of candidates. The music in the background begins modestly, but as the track begins to ascend there are also sounds of cheering and clapping, further contributing to the impact of the music. Additionally, the transitions between video clips flow at the same speed of the music, working from slow to fast, which emphasizes this idea of increasing. Together, these elements of the rhetorical situation align Bernie Sanders with other presidents to convey him as the next upcoming solution for healthcare reform, keeping in line with the purpose of this advertisement. However, this also could work against Sanders because although he is painting himself to be the solution, he does not mention any sort of previous achievements in this arena that would make him the assumed fix.

Bernie Sanders: Image Context

The second rhetorical aspect, image context, presents multiple modes of persuasion. The advertisement begins with Bernie Sanders in front of a black background conveying a sense of seriousness. The next three clips include the three presidents, previously mentioned, each speaking to the public regarding healthcare reform. The first two clips with Harry Truman and John F. Kennedy, show them speaking in a large room full of people. Both instances communicate public interest and issue importance surrounding healthcare. Additionally, both are noticeably dated in terms of image quality, color, and technology visible in the footage, e. g. the presence of large microphones. The next clip with Barack Obama is not set in the context of a large group gathering, but rather, recognizably a public address available to all citizens. He is speaking about the topic of healthcare reform conveying the same message of public interest and importance. After these images of former presidents, Bernie Sanders is then present again speaking at various rallies where cheering and clapping are noticeable, showing his favorability. The advertisement then transitions back to Bernie in front of the same black background seen in the beginning which helps bring back the tone of seriousness. Some of these images, however, can be interpreted in a different way. Two of three clips showing rallies for Sanders are noticeably from the same event. This results in the "bandwagon" of supporters for the Sanders campaign to be perceived as smaller than was intended, like Joe Biden's advertisement.

Bernie Sanders: Rhetorical Message Appeals

Finally, the credibility, emotional, and logical appeals presented through the messaging are all worth considering. Bernie Sanders attempts to establish a sense of credibility by acknowledging in the beginning of the advertisement that healthcare reform has been an issue for the last 100 years, showing he understands the topic. After this statement, the three clips of previous presidents speaking work to prove his point that it is a long-discussed, mature issue whose time is now. Additionally, this alignment of his message with previous presidents attempts to give him the credibility of presidential status.

Considering emotional appeals, Bernie Sanders uses the phrase "Now is the time…" which resonates with audiences as it fosters hope and relief that their needs will be met soon. He also paints the healthcare industry in a negative fashion by calling them greedy which works to solicit anger from the audience. Both instances have worked against Sanders as well. He is stating that "now" is the new wave of healthcare, but due to his acknowledgement of painful incremental change over the last century it begs the question of how he is actually going to solve the healthcare problem, an often repeated refrain appearing in the press and primary debates. Additionally, those who work in the healthcare industry may not look favorably upon Sanders referring to their line of work as greedy. He does not explicitly state what aspect of the healthcare industry is greedy it has the potential to be taken as personal criticism, especially if viewers were unaware that he typically celebrates healthcare workers as distinct from the industry.

Conclusion

Political advertisements that are highly scalable, such as television, welcome a variety of interpretations. However, it is important to recognize the attitudes toward certain candidates stem from much more than their party affiliation or the platform they discuss. Rhetoric surrounding each presidential candidate adds to how they are perceived by the public and can be interpreted in a variety of ways. The analysis of the healthcare advertisements presented by Joe Biden and Bernie Sanders indicate this is the case. Both 2020 presidential candidates belong to the Democratic party and created advertisements around healthcare reform. However, upon analysis of the rhetorical devices used in each of their healthcare television advertisements, it became apparent multiple interpretations were possible which then lent to a variance in perception. Therefore, rhetorical appeals are a vital component in understanding the variety of perceptions that can surround a candidate.

Addendum

After April of 2020, Bernie Sanders dropped out of the race and Joe Biden became the 2020 Democratic party presidential candidate. In the general election, Biden's healthcare advertisements continued to inform the public on the expansion benefits of The Affordable Care Act. In addition to these efforts, Biden also attempted to reveal the lack of progress President Trump had made regarding the healthcare system. The consideration of rhetorical situations in his healthcare advertisements is recognizable and beneficial to candidate perception.

References

Affordable Care Act (ACA)—HealthCare.gov Glossary. (n.d.). HealthCare.Gov. https://www.healthcare.gov/glossary/affordable-care-act/

Beckel, M. (2016, November 8). *Team Clinton sponsored 75 percent of TV ads in 2016 presidential race*. Center for Public Integrity. https://publicintegrity.org/politics/team-clinton-sponsored-75-percent-of-tv-ads-in-2016-presidential-race/

Bycoffe, A. (2019, September 26). *Tracking every presidential candidate's tv ad buys*. FiveThirtyEight. https://projects.fivethirtyeight.com/2020-campaign-ads/

Fischer, C., & Owens, S. (2019, September 11). *Health care is dominating ad spending this year*. Axios. https://www.axios.com/health-care-dominates-2019-ad-spending-417f0487-b46b-432d-9849-41cbdb7d83c1.html

Generations (2020, January 27). Sanders, B., Youtube. https://www.youtube.com/watch?v=bX36FwgDmrU

Glied, S. A., & Lambrew, J. M. (2018, November 16*). Public insurance options: A guide for 2020 Democratic candidates.* The Commonwealth Fund.

Goldsteen, R. L., Goldsteen, K., Swan, J. H., & Clemena, W. (2001). Harry and Louise and health care reform: Romancing public opinion. *Journal of Health Politics, Policy and Law, 26*(6), 1325–1352.

Hale, J. L., Mongeau, P. A., & Thomas, R. M. (1991). Cognitive processing of one- and two-sided persuasive messages. *Western Journal of Speech Communication, 55*(4), 380–389.

Keep It (2020, February 18). Joe Biden for President, YouTube. https://www.youtube.com/watch?v=LUlKIfiFg0Q

Kurtzleben, D., Schapitl, L., & Hurt, A. (2019, September 10). *Health care: See where the 2020 Democratic candidates stand*. National Public Radio. https://www.npr.org/2019/09/10/758172208/health-care-see-where-the-2020-democratic-candidates-stand

Newburger, E. (2018, Sept 24). *Republicans tout loyalty to Trump. Democrats attack GOP efforts to dismantle Obamacare. Here's how* campaign ads tell the story of the 2018 midterms.* CNBC. https://www.cnbc.com/2018/09/24/watch-the-most-notable-campaign-ads-in-2018.html

Overby, P. (2014, May 20). *Obamacare buried by avalanche of negative ads, study finds.* National Public Radio. https://www.npr.org/sections/itsallpolitics/2014/05/20/314366027/study-obamacare-buried-by-avalanche-of-negative-ads

Parry-Giles, T. (2010). Resisting a "Treacherous Piety": Issues, images, and public policy deliberation in presidential campaigns. *Rhetoric and Public Affairs, 13*(1), 37–63.

Scott, D. (2019, December 19). *The real differences between the 2020 Democrats' health care plans, explained.* Vox. https://www.vox.com/policy-and-politics/2019/12/19/21005124/2020-presidential-candidates-health-care-democratic-debate

Wood, S. C. (1990). Television's first political spot ad campaign: Eisenhower Answers America. *Presidential Studies Quarterly, 20*(2), 265–283.

---

[i] A broader interpretation of the term rhetoric would consider strategic and content also as rhetorical choices. For this research rhetoric is conceived more narrowly as those rhetorical devices implemented in the messaging.

Chapter 12: Climate Change Primary Political Advertisements - 2019-2020

Maria Jose Falcon Gimenez

Maria Jose is a Senior in Communications & Psychology, Greenwich CT

Introduction

In the past few years, there has been increasing attention centered around climate change in newspapers and social media (Boykoff, Daly, McNatt & Nacu-Schmidt, 2020). This increase in momentum, led by people such as Greta Thunberg, focused on youth activism, and others in law, policy, etc. have contributed to climate change being at the forefront of the 2019 – 2020 Democrat primaries.

Literature Review

Certain aspects of political ads that overlap with commercial ads, for comparison we turn to previous research on the subject. One study focused on analyzing the difference between emotional appeals and informational approaches to advertising summarized, "When it comes to issues involving energy, the environment, and global warming, recent research has established that informational appeals have disappointingly minimal effects" (Hoewe & Ahern 2017). Using emotional appeals, some argue helps ensure voters approach the topic in a way that makes them feel personally impacted. While emotional appeals come in many different shapes and sizes, the most interesting have been the use of music and narrative, as well as the lack of specific scientific findings. The study also found differences when looking at how Republicans and Democrats reacted to the presentation of climate change statistics. Democrats, "were more likely than conservatives or Republicans to believe in the scientific consensus regarding global warming and its impacts," (Hoewe & Ahern 2017). On the other hand, "… emotional environmental advertisements appealed more to Republicans and those who did not support a political party," (Hoewe & Ahern 2017). Nonetheless when appealing to either of those demographics, it would seem practical and approaching climate change is through favoring emotional appeals over informational ones. The affinity to emotional delivery might explain the reason for increased politicization regarding climate change in recent years. It has been shown that since 2010, possibly due to increased climate change media attention, there has been a rapid increase of consciousness raising about climate change. This phenomenon continues to accelerate fortified by a scientific consensus that climate change is real and that there are measurable anthropogenic sources of said climate change (Chinn, Hart & Soroka 2020). Polarization, in turn, leads people who do not believe climate change is real – and vice versa – to become defensive and dismissive any information that attempts to prove otherwise. As a result, it has been shown that, "political actors are increasingly featured and scientific actors less so…" when it comes to talking about climate change in general and especially in the political sphere (Chinn, Hart & Soroka 2020). Emotional appeals seem to be the best way to make climate change relevant to people who may not have originally felt the connection.

Another study focused on the importance of the location featured in the ad. In this case, the goal was to make sure that the information presented was *personally relevant* to the audience and increased perceived urgency. According to this study having the ad, "…highlight the local and regional impacts that are already occurring as a result of climate change…" is the most efficient way to combat people, "view[ing] climate change as a low priority issue… that will mostly affect people in faraway places in the distant future," (Bolsen & Palm et al., 2019). Taking this research into account, it does not seem like the traditional ad featuring a polar bear standing on melting ice is the most effective at delivering this message of urgency. Of course local/national focus is not the only way to increase urgency, however. It has been found that using threatening images depicting climate change are also an effective way to increase urgency amongst consumers.

There are two types of imaging that are most common when it comes to speaking about climate change: future consequences and human 'fingerprints' (Manzo 2009). When referring to future consequences, maps of increasing temperatures or rising sea levels are the most common. Fingerprints refer to consequences that are already visible and impacting human life, such as fires, floods, melting ice caps etc. For these images to truly make people feel a sense of urgency, using images that are threatening and dramatic is important (Leiserowitz 2007). By displaying the worst possible consequences in a relevant location, the audience will most likely take this issue more seriously since they can see a potential personal impact close to home.

There is considerable analysis pertaining to how climate change is talked about in the media and in commercial advertisements meant to sell a consumer a product. While some articles, such as the one about politicization, touch upon the political sphere, there have been no parallels drawn between this specific research and how political advertisements utilize or reject the above theories. By analyzing advertisements in the 2020 primaries through a consumer advertisement lens, we approach the following question: Are political ads informative or do they mainly appeal to our emotions?

Research question and Methodology

This research's goal was to analyze political advertisements centered around climate change that were aired during the 2020 primaries. Accounting for the content and format of these ads and comparing it to rhetoric found in commercial climate change ads, this study sought to determine how candidates use different framing to persuade voters.

Analysis was conducted on 47 climate change centered ads from the 2020 presidential primaries. Ads were obtained through an ad archive as well as going on each candidate's YouTube page to find additional advertisements. Out of the 47 advertisements, 45 were aired in the more active Democratic primary.

Figure 1 shows the breakdown of 45 climate change advertisements aired by the Democratic party by candidate. Regarding emotional/ informational framing, there were three different categories utilized: music, use of narrative, and mentions of scientific research.

(continues on following page)

Figure 1: Democratic Primary Ads by Source

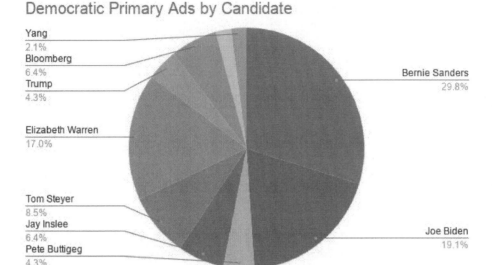

In terms of music, there were four possible subcategories: suspenseful, sad, hopeful, and no music. For narrative three categories were analyzed: use of personal narrative by the candidate, use of personal narrative by a non-candidate American, no use of personal narrative. Scientific research was categorized in three ways: vague mention (*"science shows climate change is real"*), specific mention (*"as stated by Dr Chann there has been a 2 degree increase in temperature in NJ"*), or no mention of scientific findings.

In terms of location, there were three possible categories: local, national, and global. These pertained to the location that the ad places the most emphasis during its duration.

In terms of imaging there were four possible categories: calm (*such as a flowing river*), threatening (*fires, floods, droughts*), both (*a combination of the two*), and no images of nature.

SPSS was used to conduct basic descriptive analysis on these variables. The frequencies were measured and compared.

Results

One of the primary characteristics that emerged was the use of emotional appeals. In most ads there was inclusion of music, narratives, an exclusion of specific scientific findings, all of which magnify the emotional reaction felt by the audience. When looking at the music that the audience first hears when the ad plays, 23.4% of the ads had suspenseful music, 21.3% sad, 34% hopeful, and 21.3% did not have music (See Table 1). The music category looked only at the first type of music played and did not have a way to note a change in music once the ad had commenced.

Table 1: Frequency and Percent of Content/Format Categories.

Variable	No.	%	No.	%	No.	%	No.	%
Music	Suspenseful		Sad		Hopeful		No music	
	11	23.4%	10	21.3%	16	34%	8	21.3%
Narrative	Candidate		Citizens		None			
	5	10.6%	16	34%	26	55.3%		
Scientific	Fully		Vague		None			
	5	10%	11	24%	31	66%		
Location	Local		National		Global			
	9	19%	25	53%	13	28%		
Imagery	Calming		Both		Threatening		None	
	2	4.5%	10	21%	14	29.8%	21	44.7%

Considering personal narrative, it was shown that 55.3% of the ads did not have any form of personal narrative. When looking at the 44.7% which did, it was shown that 34% of those narratives were centered around non-candidate American citizens. The other 10.6% accounted for personal narratives told by the candidates about their lives. Joe Biden made up 80% of this category.

Specific and informational scientific research was not commonly shared in these ads. It was found that only 10% of the ads fell under the 'specific scientific findings' category, while 66% did not include *any form* of scientific information. The remaining 24% made up for the vaguely mentioned scientific category.

Location is another highly important aspect of making ads seem personally relevant to voters. After conducting analysis, it was found that 19% of the ads focused on local settings, 53% focused on national settings, and 28% focused on global settings.

When looking at imaging, it was found that 44.7% of the ads did not include any images of nature. Of the remaining 55.3%, 29.8% of the images that included climate change were threatening. 21% of ads had both threatening and calming images of nature, leaving only a small 4.5% of ads to exclusively include calm images.

Discussion

The findings follow the trends seen in commercial ads. Despite there not being specific literature about what kind of music was used in climate change ads, it would seem that the music followed the trend of presenting the problem in a dramatic way (suspenseful) and appealing to the audiences emotions (sad + hopeful). While the distribution amongst all three categories was effectively even – it was a bit surprising to see that hopeful music was used with most frequency. When talking about an issue that is global and threatening to humanity, hopeful was the last kind of music many would associate with climate change. Not being able to consider the fact that music switches occurred did not affect this result since the most common switch was from suspenseful to hopeful. Most ads that featured hopeful music in the beginning did so throughout. Humanity thrives when hopeful. In a political setting, it would be counterproductive to have an ad that highlights everything that is wrong in the world. The hopeful music is being used to have voters associate the candidate with hope and change despite the conflicting time we find ourselves in.

Analyzing the narrative portion reveals a clear difference in application between Biden and the other candidates. While only a little less than half (44.7%) of advertisements included narratives, the narratives that were included were most commonly revolving around the American people. For example, Elizabeth Warren's advertisements centered around the racial injustice where negative climate impacts have been exacerbated in minority communities. She had people living in 'cancer alley' tell their stories. Similarly, Bernie had American people tell their stories about how they had been personally affected by climate change disasters and then continue to endorse Bernie as the nominee. There was a slight difference when it came to Biden's ads. He made up 80% of the ads that included personal narrative being told by the candidate themselves. He has ads where his family is mentioned as well as other things that he has experienced. This could possibly be an attempt to win over the Republican voters who do not want another term served by Trump, or the Independents who are undecided. Additionally, including personal stories could be a way to open himself up to the public and make himself more approachable. People have seen him in office before, and despite not having been president, it is important for Biden to increase his likability and show off his personality, especially when he is being accused of not participating enough in debates.

The results from the scientific findings category were stunning, but perhaps not surprising. In a nation where there are people who do not think climate change is real, only 10% of the advertisements included specific scientific evidence. This could be due to a lack of people's interest in these statistics, as narratives are more attention grabbing, but also demonstrates just how politicized climate change has become. By not having scientists comment on this matter, it opens the possibility for people to be skeptical that climate change is a problem in the first place, whether that is the candidate's intention or not. Since people are getting the most exposure to climate change through political figures talking about the subject, it would be easy to misunderstand scientists' lack of response for doubt. Could be as simple as, if nothing more, these findings confirm that political advertisements' main goal is to sell a candidate as opposed to fully educating the public.

The locations of the ads analyzed were similar to what was expected. Despite only 19% being locally focused, 53% were nationally focused, which still allows for Americans to find the ad personally relevant. Local ads were very common in Warren's campaign as she tackled environmental injustice in various parts of America. However, Biden and Bernie also paid homage to Iowa farmers prior to the Iowa Caucus. National ads tended to be focused on the economy and how nation-wide green jobs and other changes could make America continue to grow in that sector. Ads that focused on more global approaches often referred to America taking back the role of becoming an example when it came to green energy, which plays into nationalism. The ads focused on leading by example also mentioned the Paris Agreement frequently.

The images that were chosen most frequently for these ads reflected research that states that showing threatening images is the best way to increase urgency. 29.8 % of the ads had threatening images. As mentioned by Manzo, the most common images are either predictions or fingerprints, and for the most part it was fingerprint events that were represented through these ads. Most of the ads included wildfires, both those seen in Australia and in California, which allowed the audience to realize the immediate attention that this issue requires. By scaling it both to a national and global level, the candidates used both strategies mentioned above (location as well as dramatism) to convey the true urgency of climate change. The ads, however, are moderated to include hopeful imagery to not invite backlash/rejection of their viewers. In a journal comparing different imagery in climate change media, solar panels, smokestacks, and protest imagery were noted as promoting different levels of urgency (Hart and Feldman 2016).

Biden most used image was of a solar panel. He utilized this as a symbol of how America's economy could change as it is used to show possible new green jobs. This type of framing seems to fit into his campaign, for he is appealing to moderates by addressing the economic concerns that may come with climate change legislation. On the other hand, Bernie Sanders commonly used protest imagery. This also fits into his campaign since he preaches youth activism as well as placing an emphasis on a grassroot economy. Elizabeth Warren most commonly uses smokestacks in her ads out of everyone. This follows her campaign which places a large emphasis of disbanding harmful corporations. The study on imagery concluded that solar panels and protest imagery were both significantly better at increasing efficacy in comparison to smokestacks, floods, or no imagery (Hart & Feldman 2016).

Overall, the political ads that were analyzed aligned closely with previous research that focused on the rhetorical methods used to discuss climate change. It is important for people to understand the urgency on the matter which can be achieved through emotional appeals. However, this lack of scientific evidence allows for non-believers to interpret the lack of representation as doubt. In order for people to be truly informed on the matter of climate change as it related to the candidate that they vote for, it is vital that more basic scientific information about what climate change is and its consequences be circulated in a politically neutral way. It is evident that the main goal of climate change ads is not to educate people with science, but instead to sell a candidate through means much like any other product that is on the market.

References

Bolsen, T., & Palm, R. (2019). Motivated reasoning and political decision making. In *Oxford Research Encyclopedia of Politics*.

Boykoff, M., Daly, M., McNatt, & Nacu-Schmidt, A. (2020). *United States newspaper coverage of climate change or global warming, 2000-2020*. Media and Climate Change Observatory Data Sets. Center for Science and Technology Policy Research, Cooperative Institute for Research in Environmental Sciences, University of Colorado.

Chinn, S., Hart, P. S., & Soroka, S. (2020). Politicization and polarization in climate change news content, 1985-2017. *Science Communication*, *42*(1), 112–129.

Hart, P. S., & Feldman, L. (2016). The impact of climate change–related imagery and text on public opinion and behavior change. *Science Communication, 38*(4), 415–441.

Hoewe, J., & Ahern, L. (2017). First-person effects of emotional and informational messages in strategic environmental communications campaigns. *Environmental Communication 2017*, 11(6), 810-820.

Leiserowitz, A. (2007). Communicating the risks of global warming: American risk perceptions, affective images, and interpretive communities. *Creating a climate for change: Communicating climate change and facilitating social change.* Cambridge, England: Cambridge University Press, 44-63.

Manzo, K. (2009). Imaging vulnerability: the iconography of climate change. *Royal Geographical Society, 42*(1).96-107.

Chapter 13: Advantaging Sustainability in 2020 Climate Advertising

Jack Crane

Jack is an MA student in Sustainability from Kirkland, WA

Sustainability has gained traction through the last two decades, currently at an all-time high of importance and awareness. The Earth's climate is deteriorating at unpredictable levels and many argue we are headed for a rude awakening. In the last couple of elections, presidents have used global warming as a crucial factor of their political debates and agendas. People are becoming keener about a politician's stance on climate change. Al Gore attempted and almost succeeded at becoming president in 2000 rooted in of his standing regarding climate change. Environmental standards have been upgraded throughout the years. And some abandoned as the last four years of the presidency has shown. Throughout the latest presidential election and debates, it is clear which candidate stands more firmly on environmental issues and the one who does not. Climate change has become woven into political agendas and it is likely to happen subsequent election cycles.

Data shows that Joe Biden's political advertisements outnumbered Donald Trump in many areas of the climate advocating sector. Joe Biden took a firm stance on climate change which is what a popular amount of people wanted to see (Tyson, 2020). Issues exist in a complex combination, and it can only be speculated how climate tipped the voting scale, but as the Pew Center reported "registered voters in the United States say climate change will be a very (42%) or somewhat (26%) important issue in making their decision" (Tyson, 2020).

Donald Trump stands on climate change were clear, as he has disagreed with the science in the past. Joe Biden, on the other hand, touted a "belief in the science" and had plans in place to contribute to the environment instead of work against it (Roberts, 2020). The social outreach was heavily in Joe Biden's favor. The advertising promoted Biden and belittled Trump. Out of the 65 ads that I analyzed, there were 27 ads that support Biden. In correspondence, there were only 4 ads that supported Trump (See Table 1). The differential is large, potentially creating a stigma for the public that Donald Trump does not care about the environment as much as Joe Biden does.

Table 1: Ad Orientation by Content

Orientation	New Jobs	Clean Water	Drilling	New Homes	Emissions	Clean Air	Total
Pro Trump	2	1	0	0	0	1	4
Pro Biden	9	6	2	1	6	4	28
Anti-Trump	6	4	2[i]	1	6	5	24
Anti-Biden	2	0	0	0	0	0	2

Minimally it illustrates the campaign's utility assessment of an issue identified with only one of the candidates. Another interesting statistic was there were 23 ads that belittled Trump and his stance on environmental sustainability while Trump only had 2 ads that prodded about Joe Biden's reliability toward the topic.

Specifically, I divided the information into content categories (See Table 1). There were many ads supporting Joe Biden that communicated very clearly how much of a positive impact there would be in creating new green jobs around the country. It was the most advertised topic. Voters concern about the impact of "Biden's" Green New Deal, which he did not directly defend. Many feared the abolition of fracking would put people out of jobs, but Biden ads attempted to break that stigma and reassure the American public about the benefits of his plan.

The second largest topic that Biden advertised was a tie between clean water and emissions. There were 7 advertisements each with very similar implications. Most of these advertisements were primarily used for patronizing the Trump Administration and the negative impacts it has had on these parts of the environment. Joe Biden continues to claim, "get back on track", which jabs at the prior administration and the little they have done for the environment, especially regarding emissions and clean water. With instances such as the Flint Water Crisis and the issues surrounding natural gas pollution, people were intrigued to hear about the presidential candidate's stand. Joe Biden's advertising dominated the arena of environmental justice because of his vocality. People largely knew what they were getting when they voted for Joe Biden.

The final categories examined dealt with drilling and new homes. Both categories were addressed by Biden, a supporting his case. Drilling is on the forefront of public importance because of the discrepancies on the environment. Drilling has been known to have impacts on wildlife, human health, water sources, and public land (7 ways, 2019). It follows that drilling has been an important talking point among recent presidential candidates.

Biden branched out into every avenue that he believed would help him win the popular vote.

In conclusion, Joe Biden was able to win the public over, in part, with his environmental policies. I believe this is where the scales were tipped in this election and I believe this is where they will come to fruition in the future. It is required that people of authority begin to care about the environment and understand how important our surroundings are. Donald Trump was made to look like he did not care about the environment, and Joe Biden's political advertisements were partly to blame for this notion. However, in the end it does not matter because the people believe in Biden to get the job done, a safe bet given Biden's early and extensive focus on climate (Nilsen, E., 2021). Political agendas will require a strong stance on climate change in the future if they have any desire to stay or get in office.

References

7 ways oil and gas drilling is bad for the environment. (2019, August 9). The Wilderness Society. Retrieved February 27, 2021. https://www.wilderness.org/articles/blog/7-ways-oil-and-gas-drilling-bad-environment#:~:text=Oil%20and%20gas%20drilling%20has,trust%20for%20the%20American%20people

Nilsen, E. (2021, January 27). *Biden's "all of government" plan for climate, explained, Vox.* https://www.vox.com/22242572/biden-climate-change-plan-explained

Roberts, D. (2020, November 06). *Joe Biden will be president, but there will be no Green New Deal.* Vox. Retrieved February 26, 2021, from https://www.vox.com/energy-and-environment/21547245/joe-biden-wins-2020-climate-change-clean-energy-policy

Tyson, A. (2020, October 21). *How important is climate change to voters in the 2020 Election*? Pew Research Center., Retrieved February 27, 2021, from https://www.pewresearch.org/fact-tank/2020/10/06/how-important-is-climate-change-to-voters-in-the-2020-election/

[i] Editor's Note: The Trump campaign, primarily in Pennsylvania, produced 10 ads supporting fracking/jobs.

SECTION 4: DISTINCTIVE ADVERTISING THEMES IN 2020

Allan Louden, Editor

Every election has unique issues that define the contest. This section looks at some of the exclusive advertising sets in 2020. The issues *per se* are not new in campaigns but contrasted with previous cycles the emphasis or content dimensions were distinctive. The Black Lives Matter/George Floyd summer of 2020 engaged the issue of race in a directness manner that was thought to be politically impossible in previous cycles.

The first five chapters can be thought of as an interchangeable alliance wherein the ad sets could be collapsed into one coherent grouping. The number of ads, the time period covered, and their relative emphasis, nonetheless resulted in the creation of more manageable three research areas: (1) social justice more globally (primary and general election), (2) racial issues (primary and general), and (3) "Law and Order." Each set reveals the advertising debate over the very definition of what social justice entails in the American setting.

Social justice

Examining primary ads on criminal justice reform, an important subset of social justice, Kaley Vontz observes as a formerly "bipartisan" issue converts into partisan-laden moralistic injunctions. Utilizing Walter Fisher's narrative paradigm, Kaley, examines distinctions among testimonial ads, selecting four representative ads from a 41set for more in-depth analysis. Her work serves as a solid foundation for the more narrowly tailored chapters which follow.

Ryan King's rhetorical analysis of 67 social justice ads from the general election spotlights the moralistic appeals, echoes of appeals that energized the civil rights movement, as well as the way verbal and nonverbal elements uniquely augment social justice appeals. In an early ad, *Always* (2020). Biden legitimizes and brings front-and-center social justice. "Joe Biden was taught that if you see injustice you've got to stand up and act." Social justice infuses the campaign in ways not seen before. Perhaps best summarized in a late entry ad, *Adrianna* (2020), which typified the newfound social justice authority through personal narrative.

Predominantly, social justice advertising was concerned with racial justice and economic injustices, but other voices also joined in service of various issues. For example, the League of Conservation Voters tied climate to social justice. The SEIU union, among others, stressed links to environmental justice. Ranging from religious groups such as the Bend the Ark Jewish Action to healthcare advocate Protect Our Care waded in drawing attention to social justice issues.

The Trump allies were not without voice in this advertising, often in unexpected ways. For Example, in a video issue, *The Trump administration is committed to the health and safety of tribal communities* (2020), daughter/advisor Ivanka announces efforts to address social and environmental injustice among Indian communities.

Race

Logan Bolton examines the racial appeals of advertising in the primary (10 ads each from top 4 primary candidates), ads much more in the spirit of 2016 then the subsequent development in 2020. She highlights spots from the Democratic primary which illustrate various forms of addressing black voters, critically assessing if these strategies are likely to be fruitful or for naught. She argues that issues that resonate in the lives of black voters are more useful than drive-by photo ops, the typical regimen available to white candidates

Curtis Anderson looks at race advertising as a post–George Floyd "movement," often with visceral visuals and the (re)elevation of equality. He examines sample of 89 advertisements primarily focused on race analyzing their makeup and how they constructed voter appeals.

Finding examples of racial messages in the 2020 advertising is not that difficult. Trumps negative advertising often overtly likened Black Lives Matter protests with civic disorder in the streets (See Chapter 18), while his positive ads recruited a litany of endorsements from black spokespersons, underscoring his claim that he had done more for Blacks than any president since Lincoln (Nobody has done more, 2020). Trump's ad strategy likely contributed to his outreach to black voters, especially men. "According to AP VoteCast, Trump won 8 percent of the Black vote, about a 2 percentage-point gain on his 2016 numbers" (Collins, 2020).

Some PACs produced ads so explicit that the descriptor *dog whistle* hardly applies. An ad posted by Committee to Defend the President[i] was egregious linking Obama's blackness to Biden. *Enough Is Enough* greets the

YouTube viewer with the warning, the content is identified "inappropriate or offensive to some audiences." The spot opens in large white on black block lettering THE VOICE OF BARACK OBAMA followed by Obama's voice running over images of riots and looting, "That's just what it was, too. Black people in the worst jobs, the worst housing, police brutality rampant. But when the so-called Black committeemen came around election time, we'd all line up and vote the straight Democratic ticket, sell our souls for a Christmas turkey. Folks spitting in our faces and we reward them with a vote."

US campaign history is awash with messaging with racial overtones, in the modern era, more masked than explicit. One exception was the ad *Willie Horton* in 1988, often credited to the HW Bush presidential campaign, but was in fact independently produced (Willie Horton, 2016). One Bush ad which quickly followed the Horton spot, *Revolving Door* (2016), filmed at the Utah State prison to appear not about race, was more nuanced dog whistle, following up the Horton opening and broad media coverage. [ii]

Ads in 2020 were much more overt race than in the past. Expressions included progressive movement voices, outright accusations of racism from both camps, and a renaissance of the civil rights movement. Trump pressed Biden hard with ads like *Joe Biden Insulted Millions of Black Americans* (2020) and *Joe Biden Has Destroyed Millions of Black American Lives* (2020). "Mass incarceration has put hundreds of thousands behind bars, for minor offenses. Joe Biden wrote those laws."[iii]

Incivility was distinct even from the 2016 campaign. Modern campaigns typically avoid race, at least directly, in deference to perceived sensitivities. In 2008 for example "Even as his campaign fell far behind in the polls, Sen. John McCain refused to authorize the use of a fully-produced 30-second television commercial that criticized Barack Obama for his relationship with the controversial pastor, Reverend Jeremiah Wright" (Schecter, et al., 2008). (Jeremiah Wright Controversy, n.d.)

Law and Order

Finally, Elizabeth Thomas speaks to the way in which Republican and Democrat ad makers sought to define the public's definition of what the summer protests and burning cities meant. She looks at some of the harshest most adversarial advertising, complete with fiery streets, troops, and appeals to Law and Order (101 ads). In a careful analysis she examines how the advertising sparred to gain naming rights over the events of the summer, protests versus riots. This definitional debate revolved around power and who is legitimately included as Americans. Are those who march, or alt-right activists included in the *American dream*?

Spanish-language ads

For many cycles Spanish language ads, most generously characterized as repetitions of mainstream "white folks" messages, have been aired. Rachel Singleton and Elizabeth Whitehurst examine the campaign's approach to the Hispanic vote, ranging from Trump altering South Florida voting patterns to Biden's sometimes off-key appeals to Latino constituencies. The number of Spanish language ads increased exponentially as did their place in the overall campaign (the authors examined 172 ads). The chapter authors capture much of the nuance in this "new" ad content.

Vice President

David Kilduff looks at an area advertising that has been almost always ignored or a brief afterthought in past campaigns – ads regarding the vice-presidential candidate. He finds generally a traditional use of ads for and against Mike Pence (9) and a surge of ads for Kamala Harris (71), mostly positive, pondering why VP advertisements over-performed the customarily absent issue. He also examines why the ads were largely positive.

Corruption

Finally, Maya Dalton and Mark Sucoloski, beginning with the flap surrounding the United States Postal Service ability to timely return ballots (25 spots), then expanding their analysis into the centrality of corruption more generally (50 spots). Matching scandals, often invoked through invented narratives, surmise how corruption was aimed to neutralize the opponent's messaging. Corruption typically find its way into campaign advertising, but not as narrowcast and brutal as 2020.

References

Adrianna (2020, August 30). Joe Biden for President, YouTube.
https://www.youtube.com/watch?v=fUSudynxSY0

Always (2020, June 21). Joe Biden for President, YouTube.
https://www.youtube.com/watch?v=_j2kmkJh5sQ

Collins, S. *(2020, November 4). Trump made gains with Black voters in some states.* Here's why. Vox.
https://www.vox.com/2020/11/4/21537966/trump-black-voters-exit-polls

Enough is enough (2020, July 31). Defeat Joe, YouTube.
https://www.youtube.com/watch?v=SiGPR3Tdkrg

Jeremiah Wright Controversy (n.d.). Wikipedia.
https://en.wikipedia.org/wiki/Jeremiah_Wright_controversy

Joe Biden has destroyed millions of Black American lives (2020, May 22). Donald J Trump, YouTube.
https://www.youtube.com/watch?v=4hht0HKECNk

Nobody has done more for the Black community than me since, at least, Abraham Lincoln (2020, September 22). Donald J Trump, YouTube.
https://www.youtube.com/watch?v=wrAiO7OoPco

Revolving door (2016, June 10). Museum of the Moving Image, YouTube.
https://www.youtube.com/watch?v=TKXx8GnOgA4

Schecter A. Longabradi E., & Ross, B. (2008, December 4). *Watch: Rev. Wright TV Ad That McCain Would Not Run.* ABC News.
https://abcnews.go.com/Blotter/Vote2008/story?id=6395775&page=1

Searchable database of racist and xenophobic dog-whistle ads (2020, n. d.). America's VOICE.
https://2020adwatch.com/ads?field_candidate_targeted_target_id=Donald+Trump+%28224%29&field_sponsor_target_id=&field_congressional_district_target_id=&field_state_target_id=&field_race_target_id=All&field_party_targeted_target_id=All&field_topic_target_id=All&field_medium_target_id=All#content

The Trump administration is committed to the health and safety of tribal communities (2020, July 27). Donald J Trump, YouTube.
https://www.youtube.com/watch?v=mmWR1zGIEy0

Willie Horton: Political Ads That Changed the Game (2016, July 14). Retro Report, YouTube.
https://www.youtube.com/watch?v=sdJ97qWHOxo&t=5s

---

[i] The Committee to Defend Trump PAC spent $7.5 million on the campaign, less than many but a voice in the campaign (committee to defend the president, n. d.).
https://ballotpedia.org/Committee_to_Defend_the_President

[ii] To view more ads than those presented here, a limited cache of spots collected to illustrate racial dog whistles can be found at America's Voice (Searchable, n.d.).

[iii] To view more of ads than those presented here, a limited cache of spots collected to illustrate racial dog whistles can be found at America's Voice (Searchable, n.d.).

Chapter 14: Criminal Justice Reform in the 2019-2020 Primary Election Advertising: A Critical Narrative Approach

Kaley Vontz

Kaley is a Senior in Communication from Jacksonville Beach, FL

Introduction

Political advertising highlights differences, yet most candidates agreed there exists a need to reform the criminal justice system, an issue that is generally nonpartisan. Yet candidates seem unable to make significant strides in finding a fix. Social media shared cases of violence and police brutality assure the issue is getting more time in the spotlight, as it should. The events following George Floyd death in June 2020 heightened this matter even more, pushing the discussion to the forefront of the 2020 election.

This research was undertaken during the primary election season, prior to the escalation of events. It therefore includes different styles of ads than what was viewed after June 2020. While there are many biases, including racial, regarding criminal justice the issue has remain politically elusive. It is hard to reach the voters on the criminal justice issue for many reasons. One of the main barriers is that it is difficult to communicate messages and have people trust you, especially when a white man is trying to garner support from people of color. This contributed to an interest in the way candidates choose to represent their stance on criminal justice reform. What I found was that many candidates use testimonial ads to share their message, suggesting perhaps the form is more successful or adaptable for campaigns in this sensitive arena.

This research analyzed testimonial ads, looking into theories of storytelling, and understanding how they can be applied in advertisements about criminal justice reform. Testimonial ads, as contrasted with fact-based ads, typically differ in their persuasion tactics. An overgeneralization might be that testimonial spots tend to appeal to emotions and fact-based appealing to logic. While a type of ad may affect certain people more, it is normally found that testimonial ads are more persuasive (Bansley, 2015). For my purposes I define testimonial ads as advertisements that tell their message in the form of a story; most of the time in political ads, it is someone testifying about the work that the candidate did. Factual ads are defined by a list or teaching of what plan the candidate has on a certain subject. Testimonial ads persuade the audience with storytelling, but why does this work?

Narrative Theory, Genre, and Testimonial Ads

Walter Fisher defines the importance, and promise of narrative paradigm theory in his article, "Narration as a Human Communication Paradigm: The Case of the Public Moral Argument." Fisher describes the power of the narrative paradigm as it combines two important factors of effective communication, "the argumentative, persuasive theme and the literary aesthetic theme," (Fisher, 1984). The combination appears to go against the "normal" notions of rationality. but rather dismissing rationality, Fisher extends the notion in describing the rationality of narrative and emotion (Fisher, 1984). Two important aspects of a story are *narrative probability* and *narrative fidelity*, meaning "what constitutes a coherent story" and "whether the stories they experience ring true with the stories they know to be true in their lives" (Fisher, 1984).

Fisher applies these elements of the narrative paradigm to politics stating that "these perceptions and appraisals of political discourse and action become stories, narratives that must stand the tests of probability and fidelity. And these stories are no less valuable than the stories constructed by persons who are 'logical' rational in the traditional way. There is no evidence to support the claim that 'experts' in know better than anyone else who should be elected president" (1984). Fisher emphasizes the importance of storytelling within politics as the very way participants interact. Storytelling and creating narratives are a practical way to involve the public and encourage them to vote, but if done wrong then it can make people feel that "they are meaningless spectators rather than co-authors" (Fisher, 1984).

Fisher goes on to define what makes up the political sphere of "public moral arguments" (Fisher, 1984). He notes that "the presence of 'experts' in public moral arguments makes it difficult, if not impossible, for the public of 'untrained thinkers' to win an argument or even judge them" (Fisher, 1984). Political advertising can play a key role in breaching the control by expertise of experts and sanctioning access to any voter. And that is what makes testimonial ads effective. It is about encouraging a conversation rather than teaching it to someone. Fisher lays out how the structure should be saying that the expert should follow the role of a "counselor", and that "the experts are storytellers and the audience is not a group of observers but are active participants in the meaning-formation of the stories" (Fisher, 1984). Fisher answers an important question in his piece, why does storytelling work? He answers it simply, "First, narration comes closer to capturing the experience of the world, simultaneously appealing to the various senses, to reason and emotion, to intellect and imagination, and to fact and value. It does not presume intellectual contact only. Second, one does not have to be taught narrative probability and narrative fidelity; one culturally acquires them through a universal faculty and experience" (Fisher, 1984).

If we apply Fisher's narrative theory to political advertisements, it combines personal and public memory, as well as personal and public knowledge. As Charla Faye Bansley discusses in her article "Cultural Influence of Storytelling: An Examination of the use of Narratives in Political Campaigns", storytelling encourages "sociological bonds: narratives unite people through shared experiences and mission" (Bansley, 2015). Stories have a way of uniting people that make them feel like they are voting on certain things based on "a common center rather than selfish whims" (Bansley, 2015). She puts it succinctly, "Stories are engaging. Social change happens when people are engaged with their own education" (Bansley, 2015). This is the unique impact that testimonial ads can have on viewers. It is a way to get people directly involved and make them feel invited into the conversation.

Looking further at testimonial ads, Michail Vafeiadis breaks down the logistics of testimonial ads in his article "Narratives in Political Advertising: An Analysis of the Political Advertisements in the 2014 Midterm Elections." He observes that "the purpose of narratives is often to entertain, not to persuade. As a result, narratives are less likely to generate counter-arguing and reactance. Similarly, narratives oftentimes are more emotionally involving, and therefore their inherent messages are likely to be accepted" (Vafeiadis, 2018). He emphasizes that "the inclusion of voters in issue ads was effective and increased viewers' identification because it is hard to discount the real experiences of a story whose protagonist was a voter" (Vafeiadis, 2018). This can be especially important in ads pertaining to specific polarizing issues because they can increase the credibility of the candidates by using people as speakers that voters trust.

Not only can the narrative paradigm create great political ads, but when combined with other elements it can create a very memorable ad. In "Pulp Politics: Popular Culture and Political Advertising", Glenn Richardson emphasizes the importance of association with the genre of ads. He compares these advertisements to movies, saying that, "Viewers of a horror story, for example, are aware of imminent danger as the musical score becomes tenser and the scene darkens, even before the monster appears, because they know how the pieces fit together" (2000). Political ads can achieve the same effect. There are certain social norms that are within cultural communities in the United States of America that can come together to create a genre for a political ad (Richardson, 2000). Richardson describes genres as "networks of interacting conventions at all levels of argument and aesthetics, not lists of typical designs or appeals. Genres are prepackaged bundles of theme, emotion, evidence, and experience—if not always action" (Richardson, 2000). When using the genre approach, it is easy to target certain audiences (Richardson, 2000). Using a specific genre by combining sound, light and other notable aesthetics, political ads are able "convey substantive meaning, meaning that is often found beneath the surface veneer of political argumentation and in the deep grains of unspoken cultural knowledge" (Richardson, 2000). This ability to join through shared meanings can be enhanced with testimonial ads, especially with advertisements that deal with important, yet often polarizing political issues. In this article, these theories will be applied to criminal justice reform ads.

The Politics of Criminal Justice

Criminal justice was one of the pressing issues at in the primary period in the 2020 election. As Paul Testa discusses in "The Politics of Race and the Criminal Justice System", "the criminal justice system is one of the most visible and direct ways government influences citizens' lives" (2016). About 62.9 million United States residents, over the age of 16, have interacted with the police in the past 12 months (Testa, 2016). While most of this number have minor interactions with police, there are a few people that get stuck into this criminal justice cycle called the "custodial citizens" (Testa, 2016). Because it is one of the most direct ways the government interacts with citizens, it affects people's view of the government more than many realize.

You cannot talk about the criminal justice system without the discussion of race. With the plethora of public police brutality cases in the past five years and the Black Lives Matter movement, this issue has been increasingly relevant. This issue was highly debated among the democratic candidates pursuing the nominee spot, targeting like-minded voters. However, Testa found that "the same demographic factors–age, education, income and race– that past studies find lower levels of trust, efficacy and participation" (Testa, 2016). There is also impact from the media that polarizes this discussion even more, reinforcing racial stereotypes (Testa, 2016). Testa raised the question, "For a white person, does hearing about a minority's experience of being racially profiled change he or she thinks about the relative fairness of the police and courts? Does it matter if this information is conveyed personally from a peer or impersonally through the news?" (Testa, 2016).

When discussing criminal justice, the goal is to reach those who are most affected by the injustices. However, as Testa (2016) finds,

Contact with the criminal justice system is non-random and correlated with socio-economic factors that also predict citizens' withdrawal from politics. However, whether that contact occurred in the days before or after an election is plausibly as good as random. Thus, the timing of general elections in the U.S. creates an exogenous source of variation that can be used to identify the causal effect of contact on turnout"

The way to effectively engage with this group can be hard, but it is key to winning. As Testa further analyzes there are "a disproportionate number of stories about Blacks related to crime" (Testa, 2016). Furthermore, most of the research done about criminal justice involves a conversation between the two races of African American and White people, excluding the Hispanic and Asian race that faces these injustices as well (Testa, 2016). When looked at more broadly, it is shown that turnout for elections is "consistently lower by about three to four percentage points among people charged with a criminal offense" (Testa, 2016). The question many campaigns seem to be facing is how do you effectively engage with an audience that needs to vote to make a change but is discouraged from doing so?

Criminal Justice and Testimonial Ads

As discussed earlier, testimonial ads featuring narratives seem to be an effective way to get a message across, but not yet proven. Looking at primary campaign ads in the 2020 presidential election, these ads come from both parties and are testimonial ads. Out of 41 political ads regarding criminal justice reform I originally selected to look at, I chose 4 ads that used testimonial ad techniques in different ways in order to compare and contrast different ways these ads can work or not work. The 4 different ads feature different types of testimonies: for the candidate, for the historical narrative, for their lived experiences with the justice system, and form their own personal experience. I discuss them in conversation with Fisher's narrative paradigm, and how they use techniques of genre and storytelling.

The first ad, featuring a candidate testimony, was issued by former presidential candidate Pete Buttigieg, now Secretary of Transportation. He was a Democratic candidate from South Bend, Indiana, striving to get his name on the presidential stage. While he has a connection with the LGBTQ+ community, he had a challenging time identifying with the people of color. His campaign released a short one minute and 15 second testimonial ad which features Channyn Lynne Parker, an advocate for the trans community in criminal justice. Channyn Lynne Parker immediately starts her story talking about how she met Pete through "community" and then discusses injustices within our society and Pete's willingness to fix them (Becoming Whole, 2020). Throughout her speech is stock footage video of Pete meeting various supporters at rallies, ending with Parker coming on stage to talk on behalf of Pete. While this fills the broad notion of a testimonial ad, it features little narrative. It is awkward for voters to test this ad's narrative probability or fidelity because there is no personal story that is accessible for viewers. Parker speaks in broad statements that may be true, yet are too vague to share her direct connection, nor Buttigieg's immediate connection to criminal justice reform. All of this seems probable, however because it is so generic, there is little fidelity for the viewers. This ad is strong as it focuses on backing up Pete's character without him just listing things he has accomplished, yet when looked at compared to other candidate's ads it is arguably not as strong.

The next ad looked at was a 30 second ad for Tom Steyer, an independent businessman seeking the nomination. What is interesting about this ad is that you do not see Tom Steyer, as the ad focuses on telling the country's narrative. The testimonial ad features the narrative of the country, not a specific person. The ad features dark and ominous music with an opening line describing the country's "racist system of profits" (Reparations, 2020). It seems almost like a horror movie, relating to Richardson's' notion of genre earlier. However, while this ad captures attention immediately, it seems to limit the audience by stating "incarcerated black bodies" (Steyer, 2020). While this ad has a limited audience, the audience it is reaching is still large enough to have an impact, though it contrasts with Testa's earlier idea that the discussion needs to move beyond just being a two-race discussion. When the speaker is revealed, you see that it is Brandon Upson, who is the National Organizing director to his campaign. The narrative of the country's relationship with prisons holds true to Fisher's notion of probability, and fidelity for some, as it flips back and forth between historical figures and modern-day people, as well as showing clips from The Old Slave Mart Museum. This ad makes it seem like this conversation is happening between Tom Steyer and his campaign staff but does not invite others to it. There is a buffer between the experts and the people, as the history speaks for itself. There is stock footage of others throughout the video, yet Upson telling the story is the focus. However, for the short 30 seconds that it has, it gets the message across by captivating and focusing on a variety of audience memory.

Another powerful campaign ad featuring a testimony for lived experiences is Donald Trump's Super Bowl ad (Super Bowl Ad, 2020). While the majority of the focus is on the football game itself, this is the prominent stage for advertisements as well; a prime chance to get people to see political messages that would not normally seek them out, focusing on the younger generations. This ad is short yet features a narrative that follows the basic narrative sequence. Alice Johnson was supposed to serve life in prison for a nonviolent drug offense, yet "thanks to Donald Trump" she is free (Trump, 2020). It then features her crying and thanking former President Trump. This story rings true with its' probability, as this is one of the things that former President Trump has succeeded to do in office, which is shown by the personal connection of her story to Trump. It is hard to deny her life experience and her credibility, therefore making most people feel empathy. The whole ad is in black and white with solemn music, evoking emotion.

Kamala Harris, former presidential candidate and now Vice President, is also successful in her testimonial ads featuring people's personal experiences. One of the most moving ads begins with Shawn Richard, who runs an organization called Gun Violence Prevention, talking about how his younger brother was shot and killed one Easter, and another brother was killed four years later (Criminal Justice Reform, 2019). One of the most telling parts of this ad is that you do not see Kamala until 33 seconds in and you do not hear her name until the last 30 seconds, yet you can still understand the relationship that Richard had with her. This type of testimonial ad seems to be the most effective. The narrative in this ad is centered around the audience instead of the expert. It features those "custodial citizens" that Testa was discussing (Testa, 2016). This ad does a great job of including everyone into the story. There is, like other ads, probability for most everyone and fidelity for some. The story is coherent, and unfortunately, a lot of people have had experiences with people dying because of gun violence. Even those not directly affected can access and find fidelity with the emotions by some unhappiness in their own lives. Even though Harris' name is not mentioned often, that is what makes it so memorable, that you must look out for who was behind helping this man in his story.

Conclusion

The logic of Fisher's narrative theory combined with the complex issues of the narrative of criminal justice, testimonial ads just make sense to use. Though there is no research on the effectiveness of testimonial ads and criminal justice reform compared to the effectiveness of factual ads and criminal justice reform, testimonial ads may appeal in a more emotional way, which could lead to remembering. Someone who has been to prison does not want to hear vague promises from a white man who has never had the same interactions and profiling within the criminal justice system; "what would you expect them to say." While trying to garner the younger demographic, as well as the people of color demographic that have had experience with the criminal justice system, it is important to show them the way that it can be changed instead of just talking to them. There is no better way to feel involved in politics, or culture, than seeing someone who is like you represented in media and advertisements. Candidates are increasingly proficient at offering testimonial support, as illustrated by these advertisements.

References

Bansley, C. F. (2015). *Cultural influence of storytelling: An examination of the use of narratives in political campaigns.* Master's Thesis. Liberty University.

Becoming whole | Channyn Lynne Parker, on Justice (2020, January 27). Peter Buttigieg, YouTube. https://www.youtube.com/watch?v=ClAb5B11WEU

Fisher, W. R. (1984). Narration as a human communication paradigm: The case of public moral argument. *Communication Monographs, 51(1)*, 1-22.

Criminal justice reform: Shawn (2019, October 21). Kamala Harris, YouTube. https://www.youtube.com/watch?v=pLBJEbt6gxI

Jasperson, A. E., & Hyun, J. Y. (2007). Political advertising effects and America's racially diverse newest voting generation: PROD. *American Behavioral Scientist, 50*(9), 1112-1118, 1120-1123.

Pathé, S. (2018, October 25). *Just how average are the average voters in campaign ads?* Roll Call.

Reparations (2020, Feb 5). Tom Steyer, YouTube. https://www.youtube.com/watch?v=JBbjtlUqlqU

Richardson, G. W. (2000*).* Pulp politics: Popular culture and political advertising. *Rhetoric and Public Affairs, 3*(4), 603-626.

Super Bowl ad: Criminal justice reform (2020, February 2). Trump, YouTube. https://www.youtube.com/watch?v=Xtv_PJE8xns

Testa, P. F. (2016). *The politics of race and the criminal justice system.* Dissertation, University of Illinois.

Vafeiadis, M., Li, R., & Shen, F. (2018) Narratives in political advertising: An analysis of the political advertisements in the 2014 midterm elections. *Journal of Broadcasting and Electronic Media, 62*(2), 354-370.

Chapter 15: Rhetorical Reflections of the 2020 Social Justice Advertisements

Ryan King

Ryan is a Senior in Communication from New Bern, North Carolina

Categorizing campaign advertisements is possible as the topics, themes, and persuasive ends of any given ad vary from one another. Not all ads seek to communicate with the same audience nor convince them to adopt the same idea. And as the topics of political ads vary, so do their communicative characteristics. Inherent to each topic is the way ads develop persuasive strategies to convince varied audiences of an idea related to their concerns. When distinguishing between ads—that is, when determining what they intend to accomplish and with what audience they intend to do so—it is important to know how they persuade. Namely, it is valuable to know how messages are framed, what modes of persuasion they employ, and how they utilize different code systems. These characteristics provide insight not only into what the ads intentions, but also how they convey those. This chapter analyzes 67 political advertisements selected for their direct focus on *Social Justice*. The following sections are focused on describing the characteristics of ads within this set.

Frames

Understanding the way ads are framed involves understanding from what perspective the ads are viewing a problem. Framing seeks to make certain ideas or features within an ad's narrative more salient, to promote an understanding of a given idea. For example, some of the most common framing used in social justice ads is that concerned with gain and loss. Gain framed messaging promotes candidate support by focusing an ad on the positive outcomes of electing that candidate. In other words, the candidate's future actions are framed in a way that promotes its positive qualities and shifts focus away from the negative. Or, of course, an ad may do the opposite if it seeks to create an unfavorable perception of an opposing candidate instead.

Such an example is Biden for President's ad *At Stake* (2020). This ad illustrates both the framing of a candidate and their actions as a potential gain, as well as that as a potential loss. It begins by using powerful, negative imagery that emphasizes "fear and anger," such as we hear Biden speak of in his speech that scores the video. "Is this who we are, as is who we want to be, is this what we want to pass along to our children and grandchildren – fear and, anger, finger-pointing – or do we want to be the America we know we can be." This negative state—that references the current state and recent past of the country—is attributed to Trump via the positioning of his image within this negative portion of the ad, leading the audience to understand that a vote for this candidate will lead to the negative outcome of furthered division and dispute. The ad then presents an alternative to this outcome as its tone shifts. It features images that once again reflect Biden's words—of people standing together and making progress toward the hopeful future he references. Thus, framing a vote for the alternative candidate as a potential for the audience to gain a positive outcome. Each candidate, and specifically a vote for them, is attributed a specific outcome that represents a strictly positive case for one, and a negative case for the other.

Gain and loss framing, while a common feature of Social Justice ads, is not necessarily unique to this ad set. Political ads of most any type pose a candidate as the source of some gain or loss, varying in what realm of the viewer's life it pertains to (see, for example, Chapter 6 – future framing). However, there is framing to be seen in Social Justice ads that is more unique to this genre, as they are tied to the themes commonly covered.

Moral framing is an essential consideration for Social Justice ads as they are inherently concerned with ethical problems. Instead of trying to aim audience understanding at the positive or negative qualities of a candidate's actions as they relate to a social issue, moral framing seeks to promote the understanding of a social issue as just that—an issue worth the audience's concern. Moral framing wants to focus the ad's narrative such that it makes the morally objectionable circumstances more salient to the audience, thereby provoking an empathetic response, and motivating them to induce change with their vote.

Another ad from Biden, *I'm Voting for Racial Justice* (2020), demonstrates an attempt at moral framing. The narration in the video is limited but suggests not only that the viewer's vote has moral implications in that it is tied to a fight for racial justice, but also that this fight itself is morally significant. "I'm voting because my life matters," and "the fight for justice doesn't end here, it starts here" are statements heard in the ad, given by an African American man who shares his inner thoughts on why he must engage with the moral action of voting. This directly implies that the viewer's vote too is an essential step in a fight for racial justice—and that it influences the lives of others.

Modes of persuasion

The most pervasive themes reveal to us that many Social Justice ads make appeals based on emotion. It may be expected, given the events often tied to Social Justice, that these ads rely largely on negative emotion. And indeed, they do emphasize it in many cases, however it is even more common that these ads take a hopeful tone. Logically, we can see why this might be a reasonable persuasive choice. Many social justice ads are referencing events and ideas that the audience is likely already aware of, given the media coverage of protests and of the events that contributed to their incitement. Therefore, less time is needed describing these events, leaving more energy to highlight potential efficacy—a way for the audience to improve these circumstances.

Racial Justice (2020), a Joe Biden Twitter ad demonstrates this. The beginning touching on Social Justice issues that his administration plans to address. Within the imagery we see families and children who are framed to be those facing the injustice it describes, and the music serves to support this somber tone. However, what follows are images of happy families and the candidates in powerful and compassionate positions, as they are framed to be the solution to these problems, "I believe with every fiber in my being [that] we have such an opportunity now to change people's lives for the better," we hear Biden say over the video. The music also changes, once again serving to strengthen the hopeful tone.

The appeals to positive emotion are essential because they provide instructions for the audience after they have developed the desire to address the problems the ads present. They answer the question, "what can I do about this?" However, it is also essential, of course, to have the audience possess that desire in the first place. This is a reason why ads may spend time appealing to negative emotions, which may include sadness and to a greater degree guilt.

Unlike appeals to sadness and fear, the audience is not alone an appeal to guilt in the sense that their perceived efficacy may relieve their own negative feelings or sense of uneasiness created by the ads' tone. Rather, given that tone, the audience is made to understand that the incorrect action (voting for the ad's opposed candidate), or even inaction, will lead to negative consequences for *others*. The ads place a sense of responsibility on the audience to do their part in not only helping improve the country more generally, but also in helping the people mentioned and shown in the ads. Though, perhaps in some cases a viewer's concern being for others, instead of their own relief, may not be a result of the ad's framing, but instead whether they relate and identify with the struggles described in the ads or understand them as issues relevant to other Americans.

Fear is an appeal certainly common in political ads, typically accomplished by proposing a negative outcome caused by voting for the opposed candidate. In Social Justice ads specifically, these outcomes are often presented as worsened civil division, hate, and disagreement, such as in the Republican National Committee (GOP) ad, *This Isn't About Justice, It's About Destroying America* (2020). It features imagery and phrasing that frames the audience understanding of Social Justice protests as negative by featuring chaotic and violent imagery ending *destruction* of America, as well as phrases like "we are trained Marxists", which can be considered rhetorically as a 'devil term' in the context of American discourse (where terms like freedom are 'god terms').

An appeal to fear is no different than other appeals to negative emotion in that it works best when the proposed threat is met with perceived efficacy; a way for the audience to challenge or avoid that threat. In these ads the solution is, of course, to vote for the supported candidate, though, this is often enthymematic. In many cases it is a given that political ads are persuading the audience to vote a certain way, therefore ads generally don't waste much time literally stating this action as the solution, despite investing so much into heightening the stakes. The perfunctory "vote for X" or simply "vote" on the end card seems to be enough.

However, persuasive attempts are more effective when they combine appeals. Pathos is by far the most prominent in Social Justice ads, so where do ethos and logos appear? Each ad uses all three appeals in some combination, although appeals to emotion are arguably the most evident. An appeal to logos, or the appearance of an evidentiary based argument, exists within the few ads that clearly cite statistics or facts regarding who is being affected by social issues or how they are being affected. Such an ad is one by the Democratic Congressional Campaign Committee that references the *Anniversary of the Voting Rights Act of 1965* (2020), connecting historical with the struggle against voter suppression in the current day. Documentary in form, not only are chronological facts presented, but the ad is also imbued with a certain somber sentimentality given by its clips and descriptions of the civil rights movement and the injustices endured during that time.

Explicitly stated appeals to ethos appear even less. They arguably exist both in the real people and their experiences featured in the ads, and in the organizations or groups that create or endorse political ads. However, issues arise in the former once the audience fails to trust that the experiences that an ad describes are exaggerated or otherwise untrustworthy, and for the latter when the audience is not familiar with or convinced by the reputation of the endorsing organization. This does not mean however that ethos or credibility are not powerfully used in the social Justice ads. An example would be that the DCCC Anniversary video which explicitly recruits civil right leaders from Martin Luther King, John Lewis, and Barack Obama, among others because of their "social" credibility. A myriad of other ads uses personal narrative to establish the credibility of the movement from grand orator Barbara Jordan (Demand Change, 2020) to contemporary rebuttals to Trump commentary (Doc Rivers, 2020).

In many cases the appeal to emotion is arguably more in need of expressed salience than an appeal to logic or credibility. For example, many ads that appeal to fear by bringing up civil unrest and division are directly referencing the life experience (or fears) of much of the audience. Those watching are reminded of what they already know to be true (but would perhaps rather forget, hence why they are emotionally effective) and do not necessarily need additional logical or credible support, unlike facts or events whose verifiability lacks the same immediacy for the audience.

Code Systems

Analyzing the code systems of these ads means looking at the types of content used to communicate to the audience, and how they are represented via the ads. Any given medium may have a greater ability to utilize a certain code system over another based on its inherent characteristics. More generally the code systems vary in that they are either verbal or nonverbal, meaning they rely either on (spoken or written) language, or some other visual or auditory code system. And because these ads are presented through the medium of video, they can make extensive use of nonverbal code systems (as opposed to say, a print medium with still images and no audio).

The verbal code systems present in the ads consist of text on screen, narration, and other verbalizations often provided by persons featured in the ads. Between these types there are varying characteristics. On screen text often supplemented spoken narration by highlighting key points, and in some cases replaced it entirely. When narration is featured it often provides most of the ads' verbal content. Other speech is most often that featured in testimonials. This is often less concise and far more conversational than narration.

Most interesting are the trends seen within the verbal content. In this set there are repeated terms, phrases, and themes. Political ads are typically short and focused on an idea or statement. Many ads within this set are around a minute or less. They have limited time to make an impression on the audience and therefore rely on strong, concise language that repeats across videos of similar themes. For example, as I mentioned when talking about frames, ads relied heavily on the terms "unity" and "division."

"Unity" and more specifically "unite" in this case represents a god term; one that is especially powerful and relevant to the audience it is aimed at. And the more immediately and innately the audience can be affected by these terms because they fundamentally understand or relate to them, the greater chance that they can solicit intended conclusions.

An ad by the Nextgen America, a PAC composed of young voters exemplifies this style of using powerful wording to effectively express ideas in a short amount of time (End the Nightmare, 2020). "These four years of chaos and hatred have shaken me. But I've found hope in the enormous power of people in this time." The ad is 15 seconds in total and it references both the negative state of the country with "chaos" and "hatred" and the "hope" of the election and the "power" of the viewer and their vote.

Other terms that are common in this ad set are change, justice, and systemic racism. The first two of these are what you might expect to see in ads related to social justice, as they are essential regardless of the specific issues. The latter term is one that may be more relevant to this election cycle than those of the past. Just before the election did the issue of systemic racism become acceptable fare, more widely recognized allowing ads focused on this idea. And indeed, it is pervasive throughout this ad set. Systemic racism operates as one of the fundamental ideas present in the framing in the ads, existing as the undesirable current state that can begin to be mended if the audience takes the correct course of action, or exacerbated if allowed to fester.

The nonverbal content of the ads also very in the type of information communicated, perhaps more so than the verbal. In general, the visuals most often serves to support the explicit wording, themes, and ideas present in the verbal content, but is an inseparable part of contextualizing and setting the tone for verbal content.

One of the primary sources of nonverbal content in the ads is their imagery. This serves to embolden the ideas of the narration or text. For example, the idea of division is many of the ads is supported and made more intense by images and clips of chaotic protests and public unrest. Notably however, in many cases protesting imagery is instead used in a positive light, as an exemplification of others standing up for social justice, prompting the audience to join in, and do their part by voting. This is the case, for example, with Nextgen's *End the Nightmare* previously mentioned.

Another important feature of these ads is the musical score that accompanies the visual and verbal. This is the least explicit form of content in terms of what information it can communicate, however in terms of setting a general tone, it can be one of the most efficient. Even without explicitly stated ideas, the music alone can create a sense of uneasiness, fear, or alternatively hope in the audience. Music's affect serves to further the immediacy of these ads, especially as they relate to emotion.

All the content present in an ad, be it nonverbal or verbal, relates in that it acts redundantly. The same tone and, when possible, the same themes and explicit messaging is reinforced by each form of content, often simultaneously. These ads intend to affect the audience deeply and quickly, because in the short time that they have the audience's attention, they must, above all, motivate them. Whether it be via fear, sadness, guilt, hope, desire, these ads use what aspects of the medium it can to communicate with the audience and effect their point of view.

And it is worth mentioning that the content presented by the ads' code systems, modes of persuasion, and framing is, in some regards, unique to this election. The country's current social environment has prompted the discussion of these ideas with a frequency and focus not previously seen. And we see as much in the Social Justice ad set—more voices are heard giving direct appeals to topics of social justice and systemic racism, and direct objections to racism and white supremacy. This genre of ads has undergone significant evolution in this election cycle, and we can only wait to see how its salience continues to change in elections to come.

References

Anniversary of the Voting Rights Act of 1965 (2020, August 6). DCCCVideo, YouTube. https://www.youtube.com/watch?v=7biApzZXcSg

At stake (2020, June 21). Joe Biden for President, YouTube. https://www.youtube.com/watch?v=BhEF2POEo7A

Demand change (2020, August 28). Meidas Touch, YouTube. https://www.youtube.com/watch?v=aj1WAhS-2eY

Doc [Rivers] (2020, August 30). The Lincoln Project, YouTube. https://www.youtube.com/watch?v=h84qIt6o3qw&t=19s

End the nightmare (2020, September 24). NextGen America, YouTube. https://www.youtube.com/watch?v=wQ0234JimQ4

I'm voting for racial justice (2020, October 23). Joe Biden for President 2020, YouTube. https://www.youtube.com/watch?v=gigFXCjoSYg

Racial justice (2020, September 3). Joe Biden for President. Twitter. https://www.dropbox.com/s/hhp5g98o4p16e8f/Racial%20Justice%20-%20Biden%20-%20Twitter%20-%20Sept%203%202020.mkv?dl=0 (will need to send email to editor to provide access).

Chapter 16: Critique: Counting the Black Vote in 2020 Primary Campaign Advertising

Logan Bolton

Logan is a Senior in Communication from Fayetteville, GA

Anyone who voted in 2008 recalls the lines at the polls wrapping around the building. Barack Obama's inaugural campaign was a time of excitement for most, it signified change, and for countless citizens a beacon of hope. The 2008 election produced the most diverse electorate in U.S. history resulting in a record turnout of African American voters. While the number of White voters statistically stayed the equivalent, around 2 million more Black voters showed up to the polls, resulting in a 65% turnout. Young Black voters in particular (age 18-24) increased by about 5 million from the previous presidential election (McGuirt, 2008).

The 2008 election also showed a surge in voting among the Hispanic and Asian communities, but the Black vote often determines the outcome, especially in certain regions and in recent elections. Louisiana Gov. John Bel Edwards (D) and Alabama Senator Doug Jones (D) can both personally attest to the influence of Black voters and the momentum they generate with their support (McCrory, 2019). This potential power has been a fold in the fabric of democracy for decades, especially in Black-majority cities. In 1992, Bill Clinton secured the Democratic nomination by receiving around 80% of the vote from Black southerners (Harshbarger & Perry, 2020). These efforts do not always go unnoticed, but as Senator Kamala Harris stated in a Democratic debate in November of 2019, "at some point, folks get tired of just saying 'Thank me for showing up.' And say, 'Well, show up for me.' (Harshbarger & Perry, 2020).

The Black vote can only be "secured" by a candidate who openly advocates for and supports reform that directly touches the African American community. Some of those issues are obvious, like supporting policies that address police brutishly gunning down innocent victims and waving punishment, or drafting legislation that recognizes and truly combats systematic oppression and racism. However, this demographic cares about much more than criminal and racial justice reform. In fact, a census of more than 30,000 respondents and more than 30 black-led grassroots organizations revealed that the biggest perceived problem among black voters is economic disparity, specifically, low wages. Most participants (85%) were in favor of raising the minimum wage to $15 an hour. There was broad support for raising the taxes on individuals who make $250,000 or more annually. Large majorities also wanted to make "college affordable for any person who wants to attend," "consider it the government's role to provide healthcare for all Americans," and agreed that "government should provide adequate housing" (Monifa, 2008). There is wide consensus among the African American community on what issues are most damaging and what solutions *could* be enacted by government officials to alleviate them. The question remains, who is genuine in their "desire" to address these concerns?

The African American vote, a vital component when vying for the Democratic nod, led candidates to produce advertising that catered to issues they perceived as allied with the black community. As an African American woman, I have endured my fair share of targeted ads this past campaign season. So, what comprises the most effective ad for reaching black voters?

A critical analysis can tell part of the story. I selected six of the most prominent, white, Democratic candidates in the running for the 2020 presidential election: Joe Biden, Mike Bloomberg, Pete Buttigieg, Bernie Sanders, Tom Steyer, and Elizabeth Warren, and reviewed ten ads from each. Ads were selected if they targeted the black community by addressing specific issues or included specific imagery. From this point, I compiled notes and observations for each ad and generated a list of overarching, recurring themes.

Start with the Basics

Whether catering to black, white, or anything in between… some aspects of campaign ads remain similar. Nearly always, the ad swells with subtle instrumental music which corresponds to the theme of the commercial. Sharing message of positivity and hope? Cue the trumpets. Want to compare the injustice of our modern society to the prejudice of the 1960s? Find some somber piano music. While music aids in delivering the candidate's message, there is no better way to do that than to literally write that message word for word. Subtitles are also essential to advertisements that feature snippets of a candidate's speeches, outline policy specifics, and are just a safe bet to have in general. As with most informative material, delivery should be short, sweet and to the point. Most of the commercials I viewed were right at 30 seconds, designed to be shown on television. The rest were usually one to two minutes long (and two minutes was pushing it). If you cannot say what you want to say in that amount of time, you have not yet finished fleshing out the most important parts of your campaign.

Don't Recruit Know-It-Alls, but Know-Enough

A common tactic utilized in these commercials was the use of testimonials or voice-overs from an African American individual. However, you cannot have just anybody speaking on behalf of the candidate and their campaign. These individuals must be intelligent, with influence, and trustworthy. Hearing from elected officials can be tricky because everyone knows how corrupt politics can be and suddenly that individual's history would become entangled with the candidate. Still, there should be a specific reason that voters want to trust the word of the person in the ad. Maybe they are a former politician who's been around the block a few times, a valuable advocate for their community who is well aware of what changes need to occur, or even just a mother who is expressing concern for the youth. It is imperative that they do all (or most) of the talking in the advertisement. No one wants to hear Bob claim that Jill thinks he is a good fit for the job. We want to hear it from Jill. Not only should they be esteemed and worthy of respect, but voters have eyes too, so they should be conventionally attractive. No one is expecting to see supermodels sharing their testimonies of injustice in the Black community, but it makes the commercial easier to digest when it is aesthetically pleasing, which includes the look of everyone involved. Take Pete Buttigieg's *Gladys: South Bend Stories* (2019) ad for example. We hear from a mature woman who's "been around for a long time" and serves as community organizer for the city where Buttigeig currently serves as mayor. She recounts their personal relationship, her appreciation for his continual participation in community events, and of course his military background (because there is nothing more American). The ad attempts to convey race credentials by the transitive properties of testimonials.

When in Doubt, Pray It Out

Religion is a foundational element of the African American community. Many Black adults who may not self-identify as religious are still aware and appreciative of religious undertones that are ingrained throughout society. For the common Black child, faith is an integral part of our upbringing. So, it goes without saying that most of the voters these candidates are appealing to were raised in the Black church. It is advantageous for a candidate to align themselves with these same values. How many commercials have you seen with the candidate being paraded through a Baptist church during a Sunday service? Religion is not something to be played with. It should not be mentioned haphazardly, or falsely. If a candidate is not religious, it is more viable to express appreciation and respect than to portray a fictitious reality of their faith. Religious references should not be overwhelming either. Tasteful integration can be as simple as including a few lines of a famous Gospel song at the end of a speech, as Joe Biden does in *Step Forward* (2020). There was an uproar of applause when Biden reached the climax of his address at the National Baptist Convention and began to recite the powerful words of the late James Cleveland, who was referred to as the "King of Gospel Music." "We've come too far from where we started. Nobody told me this road would be easy. I don't believe he brought us this far to leave me, and he won't leave me, because of you." Biden mixed his words with the gospel reference, voiced over among black-and-white imagery of Biden among varied black citizens. These words undoubtedly would not have been recognized by the average White voter, but of course in ads like these, that is not the goal.

Pull Out the Scrapbooks! (or in this case the thousand-dollar cameras)

"Did you know that this candidate knows black people?! He/She even hugs them sometimes. Look, here's a picture!" That is what the vast majority (if not all) of these campaign ads scream to me. As if the testimonials, church appearances, and random shots of Black people holding up signs at rallies aren't enough, no ad really portrays a connection to the community without a random smattering of pictures showing the candidate shaking hands, talking, hugging, and smiling with a few African Americans – bonus points if they're children. In Pete Buttigieg's *Mayor Pete Visits Atlanta* (2019), the very first shot showcases Buttigieg with a group of smiling, college-aged Black men. The minute and a half that follow showcase similar optics; seemingly happy, Black young adults with admiration in their eyes as they express comments of support for his campaign. Being depicted in a Black space like a church is likely a desire for identification within the Black community, but it can quickly be perceived as appropriation. In these promotional elements, the intention is to show the candidate in a casual light. These pictures tend to either be integrated throughout the commercial or stockpiled at the end. The last image you will see is your favorite candidate with someone who looks just like you.

Go for the Waterworks

Just like your favorite brands use feelings to get you to make a purchase, your favorite candidate will try to use feelings to get you to vote. Studies show that people often rely on emotions, rather than information, to make decisions. Emotional responses to ads are more influential on a person's intent to act (whether that be to buy a purse or cast a ballot) than the content of the ad (Murray, 2019). These candidates have mastered the art of telling the perfect sob story, crafting themselves as the saving grace. In Mike Bloomberg's *Super Bowl Spot* (2020), we hear emotional testimony from Calandrian Kemp, a loving mother who lost her aspiring Titan NFL player son at a young age to gun violence. As the commercial progresses, the weight of the tragedy settles, and we get a firsthand account of how a young life has been stripped, and a mother's life has been shattered. We also see tears. Lots and lots of tears. Who better than to make sure no other mother must experience these tears because of gun violence? Mike Bloomberg of course! At least, that is what the commercial portrays, as Calandrian goes on to express her support for Bloomberg by referring to him as "the only dog in the fight" that "isn't scared of the gun lobby." Truthfully, most of the Democratic candidates possess similar positions on gun control, but… did *their* commercials make you cry?

History Repeats Itself… In Campaign Ads

I hope you passed history class, because if not some of these campaign ads will surely confuse you. It seems that the candidates have an identification desire to prove that they know the most about the oppression and prejudice the African American community has endured. Three words… the *Civil Rights Movement*. Try to find a campaign ad on racial injustice that does not recruit this historical moment as "our own" at least once. Do not get me wrong. I appreciate that our history is acknowledged and that efforts are being made to never repeat these traumatic experiences. However, something does seem a bit off when the only representation of black excellence in leadership and advancement is portrayed through Martin Luther King Jr. You'll find MLK in Mike Bloomberg's *Greenwood* (2020*)*, Joe Biden's *Step*

Forward (2020), Elizabeth Warren's *Selma* (Elizabeth Warren, 2019), and just about every Bernie Sanders ad that highlights his activism in CORE and the Civil Rights Movement protests. Candidates must prove that they are aware of the oppression, a fighter impeding history from repeating itself under their presidency.

Don't Forget Why You're Here

Tie the message of the commercial back to the policy! (Duh) It is easy to get caught up in the fun and creativity of creating a unique commercial. Everyone wants to be different. Everyone wants to be talked about. Everyone wants their commercial to go viral. But the truth is, if the commercial didn't serve some kind of purpose in outlining why this particular candidate is worthy of Black voter's confidence, how to solve their real problems, it was ultimately just a waste of a couple hundred thousand dollars. Many of the commercials I reviewed always found a way to mention how this candidate's election as president could fix or alleviate a problem that the commercial addressed. Elizabeth Warren, often tagged as the policy wonk, aired ads that perhaps more than any others provided rather specific policy injections from redlining to environmental justice. Even her ad with the historical Edmund Pettus Bridge motif also included calls for housing investment. (Elizabeth Warren, 2019). Yet these efforts did not produce many results, feeling more like a flyover than residency in the communities she was to save.

The Black community is one of immense creativity and artistry, this is undeniable. As a result of decades of oppression, we are accustomed to having to make something out of nothing, and making it look like gold. Therefore, it takes a lot to impress us. However, it is easy for candidates to get so caught up in trying to impress, that they forget to inform. Finding the balance is key.

Now for the question everyone has been thinking... Does it work? Is it effective? The honest answer is no one truly knows. If you're basing your answer off of accessibility and the rate of visibility for a candidate in the Black community, the answer is no. Bloomberg spent approximately $3.5 million advertising his presidential campaign in black news media (Bunn, 2020), setting a record for any presidential candidate, and the fruitless results of his efforts led him to drop out of the race less than 12 hours after Super Tuesday. What some would call an applied effort to give African Americans ample opportunity to learn about him and his platforms was interpreted as a rich, White guy trying to buy the Black vote. If you are basing your answer from promotion of the most "fitting" or relevant candidate, the answer is still no. On paper, African Americans undeniably had the most to gain from the Sanders agenda and the numerous programs he proposed for economic and societal prosperity. Sanders' past experiences as a civil rights activist were also fortuitous to his campaign because no one could discount his intentions to prioritize equality. However, even the multiple commercials featuring the black and white footage of his arrests in the 1960s still could not keep him in the race.

If anything, this research has proven that these candidates are much more alike than they are different. I originally hypothesized that I would unveil the inner workings of the white savior complex through campaign ads exposing the illegitimate and deceptive tactics used to fool the Black community. I no longer believe that their goal is to fool us. Their goal is to get our attention – to utilize artifacts that are easily recognizable (like referencing a Gospel song or being praised by a motherly community organizer) – all in the efforts to get us to pay attention to what they actually want to say. From that point, they can only hope that we like what they said. These candidates can only utilize the angle that is given to them. Warren is a woman. Sanders was a civil rights activist. Biden is attached to Obama. Yet, none of them are Black. Who am I to fault them in their desire to connect with the Black community the only ways they know how? Could some of these campaign ads be described as superficial and opportunistic? Absolutely, but I dare you to name something associated with politics that is not. Black voters did line up to vote for Biden in November, but not with the enthusiasm reserved for Obama in 2008, and not without the motivation of Trump in the opposing corner. However, his decrease in turnout is not because of faulty campaigning or a lack of effort. His ads did not make him Black, but there was a genuineness in his identification, cemented through John Lewis's voice or Barack Obama's embrace. He was a relationally distinct candidate with a relatable platform, and that is ultimately what makes the difference for the Black voter.

References

Bunn, C. (2020, February 26). *Bloomberg spends record $3.5m on ads in black media.* NBC News, https://www.nbcnews.com/news/nbcblk/bloomberg-spends-record-3-5m-ads-black-media-n1142196

Elizabeth Warren visits Selma, Alabama, with Rep. Terri Sewell (2019, April 6). Elizabeth Warren, YouTube. Https://www.youtube.com/watch?v=ZMIbnC2c-Jk

Gladys, South Bend Stories (2019, December 5). Pete Buttigieg, YouTube. https://www.youtube.com/watch?v=jEhZHAgFMS4

Greenwood (2020, February 19). Mike Bloomberg for President, YouTube https://www.youtube.com/watch?v=kM7bN-DHJhk

Harshbarger, D., & Andre Perry., A. (2019, November 25). *Why the race for black voters is the most important Democratic Primary of them all.* Brookings., https://www.brookings.edu/blog/the-avenue/2019/11/25/why-the-race-for-black-voters-is-the-most-important-democratic-primary-of-them-all/

Mayor Pete visits Atlanta (2019, November 25), Pete Buttigieg, YouTube. https://www.youtube.com/watch?v=-DhdDta8Jw0&t=2s

McCrory, C. (2019, November 17). *How John Bel Edwards won the Louisiana Governor's race.* 4WWL, WWLTV. https://www.wwltv.com/article/news/politics/how-john-bel-edwards-won/289-cfccb2c0-798f-43b5-a55d-20aec55d03fb

McGuirt, M. (2008, October 30). *Young black turnout a record in 2008 election.* ABC News. https://abcnews.go.com/Politics/story?id=8140030&page=1

Monifa, K. (2008, October 29). *What Do Black Voters Want?* The Progressive. https://progressive.org/api/content/9f208ffa-c9b0-11e9-b43e-12f1225286c6/

Murray, P. N. (2013, February 26). *How emotions influence what we buy.* Psychology Today. https://www.psychologytoday.com/us/blog/inside-the-consumer-mind/201302/how-emotions-influence-what-we-buy

Step Forward (2020, January 22). Joe Biden for President, YouTube. https://www.youtube.com/watch?v=vaypgbF8xhs_10

Super Bowl Ad (2020, January 30). Mike Bloomberg for President, YouTube. https://www.youtube.com/watch?v=9Yp0yN8UxVg

Taylor, K-Y. (2020, March 14). *Why Sanders isn't winning over black voters.* The New York Times. https://www.nytimes.com/2020/03/14/opinion/bernie-sanders-black-voters.html

Chapter 17: Race Emerges as a Critical Issue in 2020 Presidential Advertising

Curtis Anderson

Curtis is a Junior in Communication from Forest City, NC

In the 2020 election *Race* permeated, becoming a central topic and for some candidates marking the make or break for their political run. Voters consider how candidates handle controversy, what they have done through their lives, and the type of policies and laws they support. For many Americans, specifically those of color how candidates treat people of color is a determinate factor. 2020 was just that, bringing race to the forefront as seldom seen in presidential elections. This paper discusses the candidates and their affiliate's ads for how they created messaging to (minority) voters about benefit and awareness of who they are.

The notion of race has always been an elusive throughout our history. There are of, course, meanings that are categorical. For example, "According to the *National*

Geographic, Race is defined as "a category of humankind that shares certain distinctive physical traits." The term ethnicities are more broadly defined as "large groups of people classified according to common racial, national, tribal, religious, linguistic, or cultural origin or background" (Blakemore, 2021). Your race is the genetic traits you possess from your parents.

In this election more than any other, the topic of race emerged in new ways in part because of events that happened in the summer of 2020. A contributing factor was also Trump's rhetoric and a drumbeat of allegations that Donald Trump was a racist, or minimally, represented those who were. In past elections politicians were guarded when it came to talk about race by using the "dog whistle" technique (Race in our Politics, n.d., Dog Whistle, n.d.). A dog whistle is when an ad uses language which is viewed as normal to most the but for a select group it communicates directly to them, targeted. For example, ads usually use language such as "I have faith in minorities" meaning the inverse and or ads about voter turnout actually aimed at discouraging African-America, both of which, while talking to everyone, were heard differently by white voters. For this essay dog whistle can be thought of messages which offer plausible deniability whenever they seem too overtly racist.

That dog whistles exist in presidential campaigns goes without saying. Historian Robert Toplin offers the reminder "Richard Nixon won the 1968 presidential election by promoting a 'Southern Strategy.' That, too, was an example of dog-whistle politics. The Republican candidate blamed many of America's problems on blacks, but not through specific language." (Toplin, 2016)

Yet modern presidential contests had boundaries of civility According to John F. Harris and Maggie Haberman of Politico neither Obama nor Romney spoke much about race. The article states the reasoning for not "race-baiting" for Obama is, "[Obama] has prospered when white voters see him through the prism of post-racial politics and doesn't benefit from a climate filled with incendiary charges on America's most sensitive issue." It also states the reasoning for Romney, "know it would be toxic if their side is judged by most voters to be waging an overt appeal to racial prejudice" (Harris & Haberman, 2012). Similarly, John McCain largely avoided race, and in a town hall unequivocally defended Obama's origin of birth (McCain Tells Supporter, 2015).

In a campaign determination of race is fluid, understood in the negotiation of messages and their audience. One's race is governed by many factors, but your racial identity makes up much about you. It is how we identify and view ourselves as a human being. Taking race into every equation is inherent because that one term makes up so much of what you are.

Method and Findings

This study looked at a sample of 89 ads asking how race was portrayed as a determining factor for many voters. What you see on televisions, read in articles, garner from your community and family, and see on social media plays a role in how you determine identity. Can election messaging determine your judgement or is it more a product of the situation? 2020, a historic election, was characterized by Ads everywhere discussing either Donald Trump or Joe Biden.

Table 1: Ad Orientation by Content

	BLM	Riots	Racist Trump	Racist Biden	Better America	End Racism	Solution	Historical
Biden	12	1	2	0	22	15	2	2
Pro Biden	9	3	7	0	12	7	1	2
Combined	21	4	9	0	34	22	3	4
Trump	4	0	0	7	10	3	3	0
Pro Trump	6	2	0	6	5	4	5	1
Combined	10	2	0	13	15	7	8	1

The sample was examined through a categorization of its orientation, source, content, and style. With orientation indexed who the ad promoted, was the ad more for Trump or Biden. Source was divided into four options: Biden, Trump, Pro-Biden groups, or Pro-Trump groups.

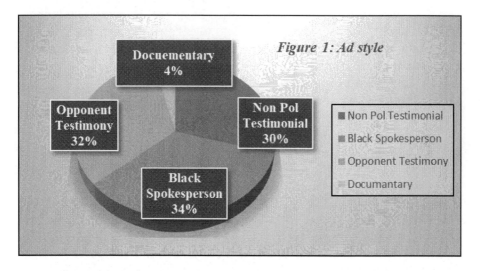

Content was asked by what issue the ad was promoting. For example, an ad discussing how Black Lives Matter and Trump is a racist, I choose those two topics as the content. The content categories were Black lives matter, Riots, Racist Biden, Racist Trump, Vote for Change/Better America, End Racism/ Unity, Solution Based ads, and Historical Race ads (See Table 1). Lastly, *style* cataloged how the ad content was presented. If a person of color was prominent and the main voice it was labeled "race of a spokesperson" or if a non-political actor was being used throughout the ad, testimonial was chosen. This category consists of testimonial of a non-political actor and the race of Spokesperson was recorded as were Opptest (opponent testimony against self) and documentary style ads (See Figure 1). Representative examples were then selected and are discussed in this essay.

Representative Ads

Full Throated Movement Ads

Unlike former presidential contests, 2020 saw the emergence of a considerably more progressive voice in the advertising. From the Bernie Sanders called arms in the primary to the post George flood of voices, ads speaking out on Race in America characterize a large portion of political messaging. A reenergized Civil Rights Movement, from voting rights to systemic racism, surfaced in the advertising.

The ad *Better America*, a Joe Biden for president spot utilized multiple content. The montage including Black Lives Matter, vote for change, and a better America, end racism and unify. The style included the spokespersons race and opponent testimony. The ad started by giving the background for Black America. The purpose of this ad was to tell people, specifically African Americans, that there will be no more taking anything from Trump. That there is a trusted friend running who will get Trump out of office and work to help African Americans. (Better America,2020)

Attacking Trump's Racism

An ad issued by Biden for President campaign in late October exploited debate excerpts exhibiting for viewers racists comments Trump has made in his debate rejoinders to Biden which went quasi-viral (400 K) and illustrates how race, from multiple points of view was directly inserted into the presidential contest. Race plays a determining factor for many people when it comes to voting. The ad, *Donald Trump is the Most Racists President in Modern* History helps further explain what is meant by this (Donald Trump, 2020). This ad was focused on letting the viewers see why they believe Trump to be a racist and in his own enactment. I believe this was created to appeal to those of color. Would you decide to vote for someone who is openly racists?

Throughout the campaign both candidates point fingers trying to tell the media who is more racists than the other. They both did so by producing ads which brought up past comments and tried to use them in a way that would arguably "cancel" their opponents accusations. *Committed* (2020), a Biden spot, the content also used multiple vectors promoting Black Lives Matter, voting for a change and building unity in America, and ending racism. Style was testimonial with Kamala Harris the voice for this ad. This ad was issued late in the campaign to get Black Americans out to the voting polls. Who is a better spokesperson to do this than Kamala Harris a Black voice that can inspire Black voters to the polls? Kamala was symbolic as she became the voice for any African Americans. We have never had an African American Vice President or a female

Adding Harris as VP Vice President gained the support from both African American's and from women. In my own life the response of my peers supported that she was key in energizing many. Growing up we are told women cannot do this and woman cannot do that, Biden did not listen to these conventions, deciding instead to make history and chose Harris. Hope was given to young and old women that anything is possible (Committed, 2020).

Black women, the backbone of the Biden campaign, were often featured in his spots. *Mayors* featured testimonials from Atlanta, San Francisco, Charlotte, Washington DC, New Orleans, and Chicago with black female mayors as spokespersons, is a prime example. Collectively they recite the message taking quick-cut short turns from separate venues. They argue, "black women have always been on the front lines for social justice." Black male mayors speak up in response in the second half of the ad promising to hear the women's call for social justice, and challenging men to vote in the numbers the black women vote (2020).

Self-Indictment

In the ad *Dumb Things*, the Club for Growth Action offered the counter to the widely held media narrative that Trump is a racist. The content sought to persuade voters that Biden be considered racists by applying the style whereby an opponent's personal testimony was used against them. The self-indictment treatment, coupled with historical footage, was often used by Trump to call out his antiracist credentials. The Biden affiliate campaigns also widely use the technique to picture Trump as his own worst enemy via statements he offered during his presidency and on the campaign trail.

The ad discusses how Biden supported segregationist in the fight against busing. Also pointing out that Biden publicly announced he had marched in the Civil Rights movement but went on to explain that Biden did not march in the Civil Rights movement. That not only is he not supportive of African American issues, but he also lied, lacking credibility. Past incidents in his Senate role including his sponsorship of the crime bill and Anita Hill pointing out how terribly he treated her in the Clarence Thomas Supreme Court confirmation. Trump's strategy was to *accuse the accuser*. Trump was routinely labeled a racist, and these ads function to neutralize those charges by portraying Biden to as racist as well. This would put them on an "even plane field" muting the importance of Trump many racists allegations. Trump however retain the power of the dog whistle in his of calling out racism ambiguity.

Another widely repeated "Biden quotation" that Trump deployed was "Well I tell you what, if you have a problem figuring out whether you're for me or Trump, then you ain't black" (Bradner, et al., 2020; Joe Biden Tells, 2020).

Testimonials

Trump and affiliate sponsors produced several "policy success" stories, stories told through black voices. In a Super Bowl ad, *President Trump got it done* (2020), Alice Johnson offers a testimonial celebrating her early release from jail, a pardon approved by Trump. This testimonial by a Black woman who represents many people mistreated by the justice system shows her praising President Trump. This ad, some argued, exploited Alice Johnson taking advantage of her gratitude for being released from prison. Trump employed a black face to draw in Black voters. Although this is a technically a solution based ad because it brings a solution to the issues many experienced, it also is trying to recruit Black votes by demonstrating Trump's policy achievements of helping a black women get out of prison for something she shouldn't have been locked up for. It was not unusual for Trump to employ black spokesperson in his ads, some of which were excerpts from the litany of speakers at the GOP convention, and even on the Martin Luther King holiday issued an ad which appropriated the civil rights leader in claiming Trump's own achievements (His Dream, 2020).

These "policy success" stories included other minority groups as well. The ad *All-star Cast* (2020) was a Pro- Biden ad offered by Asian Americans and Pacific Islander (AAPI) in a get out the vote effort. The style was testimonial with many South Asians showing their support and their reasoning to elect as president. Issues included education, healthcare, planet, economy, and the racism our country is facing right now. One speaker made unity case, "let's stick together, and be sticky rice together." More seriously, one speaker said, "We speak multiple languages and may come from different places, but let's be clear this is our home."

Corrective Parody

A third-party ad which went viral, *Another Day in Trump's America* (2019), deserves mention. The social media video was designed to reorient voter's perspective, a political correction to perceived stereotypes of Trump voters.

The film noir narrative, produced by a Trump supporter Paul Martinez, suggested what you see may not be what is truly going on. This mini drama begins with "an African American man being chased and yelled at by a Caucasian man. A woman records the interaction from her window and posts it to social media revealing the rude white yelling at the black Uber driver. Her video goes viral and is reported on mainstream media as evidence Trump's racist supporters. Rejoining the story, one learns that the white man, in the middle the night dressed and went out to help the African American get out the snow. The ad implies Trump supporters are not what you think they are. The reality, the video reveals, was an innocent interracial helping interaction. Today social media can make or break you, anything racially posted will go viral causing chaos and have many wondering about the happenings in the video.

When running for anything you want as many people as you can to vote for you. You do not want to only have white, or just black, or just Latino to vote for you because you will not see victory. You want as many people as possible of different races and ethnicities to vote for you. That is why bringing up old interviews and old comments to show who is more racists was a big key point for both candidates. Unfortunately, in 2020 this remembrance was offered to reduce the opponents share of the vote and less to increase their own.

Conclusion

When it comes to elections politicians learn what to say, what the market will bear. They predict what each group wants to hear, and work at delivering those messages. With Biden he accentuated African American groups. Electing an African American woman as his Vice President, was a huge eye opener, for both African American people and women. The ad *Step Forward* (2020) was representation of his unity message. It opens with a Biden voiceover, an excerpt from his address to the National Baptist Convention in Arlington Texas. The content included a range of topics, including Black Lives Matter, riots, racist Trump, voting for change, and a better America, and the end of racism and forming unity. The style was a personal testimony seeded with clips from civil rights struggle and adding contemporary of racists incidents and protests. The content fairly summarizes the collective of Biden's political ads on race, "We have to restore the soul of the nation."

Throughout the entire 2020 campaign race was an issue that was discussed from positively from both campaigns, but in such different ways. Find a solution and help work toward creating a "better America" was the point many were trying to make, Biden's aspirations, Trump's claimed accomplishments. It was up to the American people to decide what they wanted and who they wanted to be a representation for them. I chose my race as a determinant factor in this election because who I am and what I am made of.

References

All-Star cast of Asian Americans and Pacific Islanders for Joe and Kamala (2020, October 31). Joe Biden for President, YouTube. https://www.youtube.com/watch?v=NJBe2Y43Lu8

Another day in Trump's America (2019, March 21). Paul Martinez, YouTube. https://www.youtube.com/watch? v=p8_EoMmuqVU

Blakemore, E (2021, February 22). *Race and ethnicity facts and information.* National Geographic. https://www.nationalgeographic.com/culture/topics/reference/raceethnicity/#close

Better America (2020, August 6). Joe Biden for President, YouTube. https://www.youtube.com/watchv=VyJk3H2MtzI

Bradner, E., Mucha, S., & Saenz, A. (2020, May 22). *Biden: 'If you have a problem figuring out whether you're for me or Trump, then you ain't black'.* CNN politics. Https://www.cnn.com/2020/05/22/politics/biden-charlamagne-tha-god-you-aint-black/index.html

Committed (2020, November 3). Joe Biden for President, YouTube. https://youtu.be/1OfaaepZJ74

Dumb Things (2020, June 25). *Club for Growth.* https://youtu.be/IKVaVlKpVos

Donald Trump is the most racists president in modern history (October 22, 2020). *Joe Biden for President, YouTube.* https://www.youtube.com/watch?v=7oU3N1_roPY

Dog whistle (politics) (n. d.) Wikipedia. https://en.wikipedia.org/wiki/Dog_whistle_(politics)

Harris, J., & Haberman, M. (2012, August 29). *Race-baiting hooks 2012 campaign*. Politico. https://www.politico.com/story/2012/08/race-baiting-hooks-2012-campaign-080322

His Dream is Now Our Dream (2020, January 20). Donald J Trump, YouTube. https://www.youtube.com/watch?v=qYsUpaVLWis

Joe Biden tells Black Trump Supporters "You Ain't Black", (2020, May 22. Donald J Trump, YouTube. https://www.youtube.com/watch?v=x0X75QI861o

Mayors (2020, October 10). Joe Biden for President, YouTube. https://www.youtube.com/watch?v=qq1gw0ouNcE

McCain tells supporter Obama is 'a decent..., (2015, February 19). CNN, YouTube. https://www.youtube.com/watch?v=JIjenjANqAk&t=1s

President Trump got it done (February 2, 2020) President Trump, YouTube. https://www.youtube.com/*watch?v=Xtv_PJE8xns*

Race in our politics: A catalog of campaign materials (2020, n.d.). CLC Advancing Democracy Through Law. https://campaignlegal.org/race-our-politics-catalog-campaign-materials

Step Forward (2020, January 22). Joe Biden, YouTube. https://www.youtube.com/watch?v=vaypgbF8xhs

Chapter 18: Analysis of Ideals: Law and Order Advertising in the 2020 Presidential Campaign

Elizabeth Thomas

Elizabeth is an MA student in Sustainability from Raleigh, NC

The 2020 "law and order" advertising debate revolves around definition, most notably definitions of strength. Who defines, or redefines, and which narrative receives prioritization. Can arguments of a subjective idea like "strength" be relied upon to capture the vote of Americans when the cry of "fake news" increases doubt and confusion. Can our political institutions, and those connected with them, invoke the necessary integrity and "strength" to govern? Moreover, with the advent of social media, traditional framing in political advertising and campaign narratives are often edited on an individual level, released into the world with little input from critical eyes. This ability to sway populations through a single edit invites questions of what can be believed. If national narratives can be influenced on a citizen-by-citizen basis, where does national stability reside?

Voters, historically, look to symbols of traditional institutions for stability, including the presidential elections. The president becomes a figurehead to follow in times of need, as with. FDR's 20th century example. More recently, in the aftermath of the attacks on American civilians on September 11, 2001, George W. Bush, quickly became the instrument for American's understanding of "strength" in unprecedented times. The subjective trait of strength was associated to both presidents, often translating into traits of wisdom and leadership. Reliance on subjective traits such as "strength" (or "unity") have historically succeeded. Yet, given the instability infused into our recent national narrative, namely the Trump administration's determined volatility, it could be argued that past contexts are an insufficient compass for examining 2020's presidential campaign.

101 ads produced for both traditional media and social media platforms between June and November 2020 were examined. This ad set effectively framed a prime issue, specifically "strength" through the repeated renditions of "law and order" themes. Both Biden's and Trump's campaigns defined "law and order" by their perceived source of power.

The Republican Party, following the lead of President Donald J. Trump and Vice President Pence, builds a narrative of trust in existing institutions that serve Trump's link to power, such as law enforcement on the ground at 2020's Black Lives Matter protests. Ads that support the Republican party and the Trump campaign, frame their narrative as trust in established political institutions and familiar national symbols, especially the institution of law enforcement.

The Democratic Party, as the party of President-Elect Joe Biden and Vice President-Elect Kamala Harris, builds a narrative of trust in American communities. Their definition of communities largely encompasses the nation, piecing it together through local testimonies, but also apart through who comprises the legitimate community. Attack ads from the Biden campaign and its supporting PACs, exclude American white supremacists from this American community. By excluding them, American white supremacists are used as attacks against Trump, linking them to Trump's rhetoric. Trump is linked to white supremacists, most frequently The Proud Boys (Presidential Debate, 29 Sept. 2020). Connecting Trump to white supremacists, the Biden campaign marks them as an opposing community, ostracized from the American nation yet tied to Trump, separating Trump from the unified American nation Biden envisions in his campaign advertising.

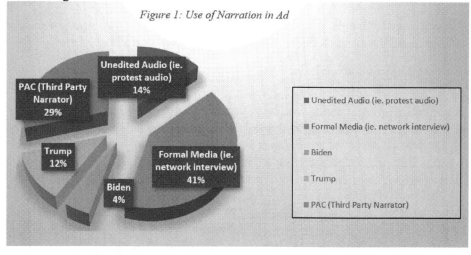

Figure 1: Use of Narration in Ad

Biden's campaign excludes militant, violent protesters from their envisioned American community as well as prohibiting white supremacists linked to Trump, such as The Proud Boys. In a direct address crafted as a response to his critics (mainly Trump), Biden condemns protesters who have escalated protests to the point that they destroy private property. The protection of private property is deemed a foundation of "law and order" and protecting the stability of what is framed as an American nation in crisis. This narrative connecting private property to the foundation of "law and order" at times confuses itself by agreeing with Trump's campaign narrative that also connects the protection of private property to the foundation of "law and order." In the Biden campaign's *Be Not Afraid* direct-address ad, President-Elect Joe Biden makes "clear" that "rioting is not protesting, looting is not protesting, it's lawlessness plain and simple" (2020).

Figure 2: Common Images

MOST COMMON IMAGES IN LAW AND ORDER ADS

- Fire (including smoke, effects of fire such as burned structures and cars)
- Law Enforcement (local, state, federal)
- White Supremacy (including Confederate symbology)
- "Proud Boys"
- "Antifa"/"Radical Left"
- Religion/Church Building

Biden's narration in this ad plays over images of burned-out cars with a bright yellow "Police Line Do Not Cross" tape stretched across the foreground, a firefighter carrying a fire hose and a civilian with a skateboard walking past burned-out buildings. Biden then connects Trump to "forment[ing]" his supporters to act as an "armed militia in this country…show[ing] how weak he is" in leading America. In Biden's definition, militant and violent protesters, are those who actively choose to forfeit legal rights by acting outside of "law and order." Yet Biden also characterizes protesters as an integral part of community. This confusion links the Biden campaign narrative to that of the Trump campaign, both intentionally as an attack on Trump, but also with Trump's own narrative of private property destruction Trump claims are caused by protests.

The American First Action PAC (pro-Trump) produced a one-minute, direct address testimonial ad featuring a white, female small-business owner based in Kenosha, Wisconsin, *Kimberly* (2020). The PAC's ad identifies the events happening in Kenosha (through the testimony of Kimberly) as "riots," and uses security footage to link the "riots" to destruction of private property by showing graffiti being placed on windows, and an attempted break-in. To define their envisioned American community, the Trump campaign excludes most, though not all, participants of 2020's numerous protests, by linking such protests to the destruction of private property and threatening small-business enterprise. The Trump campaign's exclusion targets the protests participants who were calling for acknowledgement of systemic racism and police reform. Trump's campaign highlights these protesters as opposing "law and order" by their rejecting the symbols of traditional law enforcement, police and the national Guard. Trump's focused support of law enforcement and fear-driven dramatizations of an America with a defunded police force, frames protesters as threats, and dangerous. Trump's campaign links protesters to Biden, and perhaps like Biden as having forfeited their legal rights by breaking the social contract, even engaging in criminal activity against their neighbors. Visually these arguments witness wrongdoers breaking into neighbor's homes or looting and destroying storefronts. Trump's campaign narrative conflates "peaceful protesters" as criminals, and links them to soundbites from Biden, Harris, and other Democratic leader's approval, especially Speaker of the House Nancy Pelosi. In a dramatic spot *President Trump Will Uphold the Law* (2020), framed by flames and anarchy, the voiceover repeats large-screen text, "While America's cities burned, Joe Biden and Kamala Harris FANNED THE FLAMES. Supporting bail funds to help let rioters, looters and, dangerous criminals out of jail."

These attack ads frame the 2020 protests, and most importantly Biden and Democratic allies, as the source of these criminal activities, through actively encouraging protesters to outright negligence of traditional "law and order" institutions such as law enforcement (i.e., threats of Biden defunding the police to defend against criminal activity). Trump's overall narrative is a compelling (though dubious) adrenaline rush linking Biden's campaign to general threats against the stability of established legal, commercial, and social traditions. In the Trump campaign's attack ads, the narrative expands the definition of "law and order" to include legal (political leaders seemingly undermining law enforcement), commercial (the destruction of small business enterprises in American cities), and social (calling out the irony of a "peaceful" protest against the backdrop of businesses in flames) (Far-Left Fascists, 2020; Lawless, 2020). Trump's message in framing these ads is clear, that only his re-election will protect and stabilize traditional American ways of life, particularly through supporting traditional law enforcement and strengthening their ranks to restore order by dispersing protesters linked to destruction.

Political advertising that is produced by the Trump campaign and supporting PACs frame visual content in their ads to directly discredit these "peaceful protesters" by using flames, suffocating crowds and tear gas, and unlit city streets. The darkness of much of their ads' visual content only heightens the images of flames. Images of destroyed landscapes in daylight that follow images of darkness heighten the burned-out businesses as the aftermath of protests. The sequence of visual content in these ads implies that the cause of the blackened and crumbling buildings are the protests seen moments ago in the same ad. The actual sequence of the protests is in doubt but not in the ad's enthymeme.

Ads both for and against Trump aligned law enforcement's power with his use of executive power, emphasizing Trump's claim that he ordered law enforcement to quell protests in support of "law and order." 54 of the 101 ads include visual and audio content (including crowds chanting and screaming expletives at uniformed law enforcement) that focus on the presence of law enforcement at these protests. Enforcement personnel are either the last line of defense from criminals or the government's clampdown on its citizens, differing by source.

The law enforcement seen in the visual content (video and photography from established media and raw footage that appears to be from individual citizen phones and uploaded to social media) are often local police officials. Multiple ads also highlight uniformed law enforcement holding shields in front of them that are labeled as "military police", indicating law enforcement from federal rather than local resources, thus implicating Trump as an arm of the federal government. The framing of these ads indicates a corrupt use of power by the federal government, through Trump's orders as President, and calls into question Trump's use of "law and order" and whether it is being used as a phrase to excuse suppression of American freedoms such as speech and assembly. Such attack ads relate to the protests and law enforcement presence in Portland, Oregon.

It has been noted by traditional media and citizen testimonies that "paramilitary groups" appear at these protests, intermingling with both protesters and traditional law enforcement. Testimonies regarding "paramilitary groups" have been used in attack ads against Trump, further tying him to white supremacists, implying that white supremacy is the foundation of these "groups." The presence of "paramilitary groups" undermines the narrative from the Trump campaign that claims Trump solely backs traditional law enforcement. "Paramilitary groups" are not known as part of any traditional American police force, or institutional law enforcement. Such "groups" make claims to defend traditional American law enforcement yet are understood to originate separately from law enforcement and known legal processes that bind them, such as due process of the law.

The Democratic coalition ad *Stop Trumps Terror* explicitly and dramatically makes the argument that trump's "endorsements" is the choice "racism or the LAW" (2020). In recent years, social media platforms such as Facebook have played a part in connecting members of "paramilitary groups", strengthening their ability to act as disciplined units and building national networks. The "paramilitary groups" often use connections through social media to orchestrate self-training in various forms of combat, before they attend protests, such as the Unite the Right Rally held in Charlottesville, Virginia in August of 2017.[i]

"Paramilitary groups" are often associated with The Proud Boys. Trump "stumbled" when asked by both moderator Chris Wallace and President-Elect Joe Biden to condemn white supremacists, and specifically to condemn the Proud Boys during the first Presidential debate in September of 2020. Trump's reticence, or confusion (or both) when faced with condemning The Proud Boys has been associated with his reticence to condemn white supremacy as a general movement. In an ad linking the Proud Boys to Trump, *Trump's Radical Right,* Meidas Touch warns "TRUMP'S RADICAL RIGHT IS COMING FOR YOU" (2020). The connection of white supremacy to "paramilitary groups" indirectly implies Trump's reticence to condemn these external "groups," undermining the Trump campaign's narrative of support to traditional law enforcement units. Debates, interviews, and Trump's own political support rallies are sources for Trump's verbal testimony that is used by the Biden campaign and PACs to frame Trump as a hypocrite counter to his own political narrative. The Trump campaign defines "law and order" by association with established institutional law enforcement and legal processes. Through audio content such as the now infamous quote from President Trump, telling The Proud Boys to "stand back and stand by" rather than outright condemning them as was requested during the September 2020 debate, such content frames Trump as unable to outright condemn white supremacists who separate themselves from the traditional power he claims to support.

Of the 101 ads examined, Trump is heard as the *primary narrator* in 13. Footage from interviews and rallies that focus on Trump are included in at least 44 of the ads. Even if Trump is not framed as the primary narrator, his voice is a focal point in the audio content of nearly half of the political ads crafting the narrative of "law and order" in Trump's existing America. Trump's vocal prowess, the sheer volume of how much audio content he produces, is cited as one of his assets when he seeks to rally his base. Trump's volume of audio content also leaves him vulnerable to that same content being used against him, to the point of self-indictment. This is apparent in attack ads associating him with white supremacists. This relationship is underscored by visual content offering footage from the violent Unite the Right rally in 2017 in Charlottesville and includes other rallies that show Trump branded MAGA hats being worn by persons who also hold Confederate flags. The picture of the Confederate flag is worth a thousand words when explaining that someone is fine with their patriotism until they perceive a threat to their particular status quo, what they believe they deserve. When the Confederate flag becomes a symbol of a campaign for the office of President of the United States, this could become confusing. Further examination of the source of the footage that showcases the Confederate flag is needed to provide context for its use.

It would be reasonable to believe that supporters of Confederate flags and ideology see themselves as being outside of traditional American institutions and systems. They may feel that traditional candidates who are representative of American institutions and systems, are not representative of them and so they seek alternatives, such as President Trump. Trump's detractors cite this as part of his hypocrisy. If Trump's campaign narrative is to support American "law and order" through traditional, now centuries-old American institutions and systems, then his detractors question his mobilization and acceptance of those who actively seek alternatives to the American systems he vowed to protect and uphold by his vow to the U.S. Constitution (an American institution itself). The answer of how a base that considers itself ultimately outside of traditional institutions, could be mobilized by a symbol of the traditional institutions may lie in the social media platforms already utilized by the base [ii].

Social media democratizes the distribution of narrative beyond traditional American media institutions and platforms. This democratization has produced much of the footage seen in the debate of American "law and order" for both campaigns of the 2020 presidential election. This footage can be used by the presidential campaigns, or by individual citizens showing their support for their chosen candidate. The volume of raw footage taken by professional photographers and videographers, and footage taken by private citizens that finds its way to social media platforms like Facebook is a massive and diverse population. This population of raw footage often means that, much like numerical data, a selection of video and audio data can be found, and thus edited to fit a presidential campaign's or individual supporter's narrative.

The raw footage that contributes to visual and audio content within the Trump and Biden campaign narratives is framed through fear. Raw footage has been deemed more effective than crafted dramatizations as indicated by the overwhelming number of times such footage is chosen over the dramatic, staged narrative ad. A paltry eight ads (all supporting the Trump campaign) are dramatized narratives based in fear. Fear of the unknown has long been understood as a powerful motivator for action. Fear of loss (i.e. what strangers invading the nation will take from voters, what a distant national government such as China will take from American voters) was a continual theme in the Trump campaign narrative[iii]. The Biden campaign narrative has benefitted from a fear of unknown, but plausible possibilities how Trump's re-election could ultimately weaken "law and order" in America (a threat to democracy itself).

Amid a global pandemic, and a divisive election season, Americans were living with the knowledge that protests (or riots, depending on the campaign perspective) were occurring nearly every day in the summer and fall of 2020. Many Americans may have been participants in these demonstrations or were personally connected to a protester. Americans were viewing these demonstrations, understanding their effects, and continuing to exist; to go about their daily routines and to watch those they care about do the same. These protests were a known narrative to Americans who, while perhaps disliking such a narrative, had learned to adapt it into their daily lives. while Trump's campaign used footage of protests as a fear of what was known to be occurring, PACs supporting the Biden campaign pushed the fear of Trump's potential escalation of traditional law enforcement's power to challenge protests under a corrupt definition of strengthening and returning to "law and order." PACs supporting Biden linked this fear of law enforcement escalation to historic and current regimes they defined as corrupt and totalitarian. These regimes included historic Nazi Germany, and the current governments of North Korea, Russia, Saudi Arabia, and the corruption they felt challenged the pro-democracy demonstrations in Hong Kong. This fear of an unknown, yet plausible reality, based in actual historic precedence which further emphasizes how easily such totalitarianism could happen weaved through the fear-driven ads of Biden's campaign narrative. Plausible scenarios of waking up to living in an American police state was linked to Trump's re-election, challenging Trump's campaign cries of strength through "law and order" by questioning how America could be strong if it began to resemble those it deemed dangerous, or at the worst, its historic enemy.

References

Abolished (2020, July 13). The Washington Post.
https://www.washingtonpost.com/video/politics/campaign-ads-2020/donald-j-trump-for-president-abolished–campaign-ads-2020/2020/07/13/b669df90-ab19-4a06-ba9f-b611b1b977c5_video.html

Be not afraid (2020, September 2). Joe Biden for President, YouTube. https://www.youtube.com/watch?v=LgHXJ3rdOn0

Far-left fascists have turned Portland into a violent hellscape (2020, July 22). Donald J Trump, YouTube. https://www.youtube.com/watch?v=odUMyzqzjcc

Kimberly (2020, September 21). American First Action Super PAC, YouTube. https://www.youtube.com/watch?v=UGRC1VZo6_Q

Lawless – Kenosha, Wisconsin (2020, September 2). Donald J Trump, YouTube. https://www.youtube.com/watch?v=JTfDgCCpXTE

Stop Trumps Terror (2020, October 8). The Democratic Coalition, YouTube. https://www.youtube.com/watch?v=IrZSgzpyOHQ

Tien, J. H., Eisenber, M. C., Cherng, S. T., & Porter, M. A. (2020). *Online reactions to the 2017 'Unite the right' rally in Charlottesville: measuring polarization in Twitter networks using media followership. Applied network science.* https://www.math.ucla.edu/~mason/papers/tien2020-final.pdf

*Trump's Radical Right (*2020, September 8). Meidas Touch, YouTube. https://www.youtube.com/watch?v=LW-T8QszNLA

President Trump will uphold the law (2020, October 27). Donald J. Trump, YouTube. https://www.youtube.com/watch?v=EDP9iqcvZuU

---

[i] Social media response to the Charlottesville rally gives insight into the use by far-right groups. See: Tien et al. (2020)

[ii] Alternately, those very citizens may see themselves as the legitimate source of power, supporters of the genuine Constitution. The advertising becomes part of the definitional contestation of legitimacy as represented by "law and order."

[iii] A classic appeal combined protests with Biden defending the police, rendering citizens unprotected. In one ad *Abolished* the Trump campaign suggests a 911 response to imminent danger would be on hold for estimated wait time of five days. (Abolished, 2020).

Chapter 19: Relationships between Candidate, Character, and Issue in Spanish Language and Latinx Ads

Rachel Singleton and Elizabeth Whitehurst

Rachel is a Junior in Communication and Spanish from Nashville, TN & Elizabeth is a Junior in Politics & International Affairs and Spanish from Greenville, NC

Review of Literature

The Hispanic and Spanish-speakers impact in American culture and identity is projected to grow exponentially in the coming years, including enhanced electoral influence. Their vote has long been vital component in Presidential elections, having increased bearing in the last couple decades. The US expects to have the largest number of Spanish speakers by 2050, or an estimated 132.8 million (Melendez, 2015). The demographic's influence is also expanding in the economy. U.S. Hispanic buying power is currently larger than the GDP of Mexico, partly due to increasing entrepreneurship (Weeks, 2017).

These commercial trends may help explain Trump alarm with the COVID stricken economy as his advertising disproportionally focused on small businesses, often with Hispanic proprietors. An example includes testimonial ad from Spanish-speaking small business owner that exclaim "*La pandemia totalmente, mató mi negocio*" (The pandemic totally killed my business (Gomez, Martínez, & Mukherjee, 2020). Thus, it is no surprise that political organizations Democrat and Republican, are investing more heavily in Spanish advertisements.

Reports during 2020 stated that political advertisements were gearing up to craft targeted messages. Both parties were taking distinct approaches to cater to Latinx voters. Specifically, President Trump aimed to amplify fear of a potential Latin American style "socialism" under Biden's America. In contrast, the democratic party focused on attack ads castigating Trump (Gomez, Martínez, & Mukherjee, 2020). Each candidate used fear tactics to move the Hispanic population. The results were arguably decisive and sent a precedent for the future of targeted advertisements.

The results of the 2020 Presidential election left much to be understood. Critical battleground states such as Florida had a record-breaking number of Hispanic voters, including Puerto Ricans and Cuban neighborhoods. There was also a large increase of Spanish-language ads in Arizona, Florida, and Texas. Reports in September stated that both parties spent weekly over two million on ads in Miami alone.

Biden offered many Spanish language ads over across the campaign, concentrating in critical swing states, including Florida and Arizona (Gomez, Martínez, & Mukherjee, 2020). These ads micro-targeted diverse Latino groups, with their narrators, for example, speaking with distinct Spanish accents. Biden also campaigned in partnership with Latino celebrities, featuring songs from musicians Bad Buddy and Alejandro Fernandez to seize cultural identity in messaging (Miller, 2020).

Trump was already showing support among many Cuban Americans, especially in Florida, the state with the largest Cuban population. To expand that advantage the Trump campaign, ran Spanish language ads in Florida, many of them calling Biden an extremist. A study conducted by Latino Decisions, a polling firm that studies Spanish-language media, found that more than two-thirds of Latino voters across the country relied on Spanish-language TV for their political news. Further, "half of the respondents said that they trusted Spanish-language media more than English-language media" (Miller, 2020).

The study also found that in areas where candidates invested in Spanish-language ads, there was a higher turnout among Latino voters. In the final two weeks of October, "roughly 20 percent (2,437 airings) of the pro-Biden activity on TV in Arizona has been in Spanish" (Carranza, 2020). Beginning as early as the early 20th century, the United States government began to group together individuals from across the country, based on whether they spoke Spanish. Thus, the government has created a sort of formalized Latino collective, which is linked to the Spanish language, even though not all Latinos speak Spanish. Such cultural collectives are achieved through formal institutions such as news media and advertising, but also through informal methods. Specifically, this would include colloquial language, lyrics in music, and discriminatory language (Carranza, 2020).

The first presidential campaign to feature a Spanish-language appeal was in 1960, with Jackie Kennedy speaking on behalf of her husband (Flores & Coppock, 2019; Jacqueline Kennedy Campaign Spot, 2010). Since then, a voting bloc called "Hispanic" or "Latino" has emerged, and candidates have broadened their methods for communication to these voters. Candidates who produce Spanish-language advertisements must "weigh the benefits of directly appealing to Spanish-speakers against the potential costs of reaching exclusively English-speaking constituents." (Flores & Coppock, 2019). Where Latinos receive their news is highly important because whether the source is in English or Spanish can be indicative of the goals of the news organization. Additionally, it says a lot about how they may view an issue.

Research Questions and Methodology

The study's principal focus was on the character traits (Empathy, Leadership, Integrity) and content/issues as presented in advertisements (e.g., immigration, economy, Puerto Rico) and how the two correlated with "candidate" (Trump Orientation: Pro Trump and Anti-Biden; Biden Orientation: Pro Biden and Anti Trump). The candidate's persona often controlled their advertising, and firmly dominated the media's narrative. This led to the following research questions:

> **Q1:** What is the relationship between the candidate and the character traits targeted in an ad?
>
> **Q2:** What is the relationship between the source responsible for an ad and the character traits targeted?
>
> **Q3:** What is the relationship between the candidate and the content or issue presented?
>
> **Q4:** What is the relationship between the source responsible for an ad and the content or issue presented?

To answer these questions, the researchers relied on a coded examination (correlation comparisons) to determine the relationship between categories. Additionally, ads were viewed using content-based analysis, making distinctions between source, candidate, character focus, message form, and noting key words used in particular ads. Categories for message forms included music (ads centered around a song in Spanish/Latin style), AV (exaggerated opponent audio and visuals), testimonials (personal stories from non-political actors), and parodies (use of humor, animation, reenactment, dramatization, or sarcasm).

Measures were defined as: *Character Focus*: Empathy, Leadership, Integrity; *Content/Issue*: Puerto Rico, values, immigration, economy, COVID, ideology; *Source*: Immigrants' list civic action, Trump for President, CMT to Defend the President, Biden for president, Trump for President, America First Action SuperPAC, SEIU, Democratic Coalition, Priorities USA, Lincoln Project, NextGen America, Republican Voters Against Trump,

Independence USA. Patriots for Change, WomenVOTEProject, Medias Touch

The data set consisted of 172 political advertisements from the 2020 presidential election. The sample exclusively comprised ads that directly targeted Hispanic and Latinx voters, either in Spanish, English, or both. Each ad was coded with each category and characterized by its candidate (i.e. pro-Trump/anti-Biden denoted as "Trump"), holistic character focus, main issue, and its source. Keywords such as communist, socialist, dictator, or the Spanish equivalent were noted for reference. The measurement of each category was based on general characteristics of political ads. For example, the *character focus* grouping includes typical topics such as empathy, leadership, and integrity. Each sub-category was chosen based on ad language and direct use of the word, either in a positive or negative manner. Character appeared to be a pressing issue as hopeful voters looked towards a shift in greater empathy and leadership amid the COVID-19 pandemic. (Mahncke, 2020) In order to evaluate our data in a precise yet simplified manner, we used Pearson's correlation to quantitatively evaluate the data.

Results

The outcomes of the correlation are shown in Table 1.

Table 1: Correlation Outcomes

Measures	t	df	p-value	Correlation
Candidate & Character Focus	-1.2899	108	.1999	-0.123
Source & Character Focus	0.6711	105	0.5036	.0653
Candidate & Content Issue	-0.40165	116	0.6887	-0.0372
Source & Content Issue	3.4973	122	0.000675*	.3133

*=Statistically Significant (p <.05)

The correlation analysis between source and content or issue was statistically significant, with a p-value of .0006. There is a positive relationship between advertisements from certain groups or PACs and the issue that they advertise. Therefore, question four of our study led to a significant correlation. The insignificant outcomes of the other questions are most likely due to the large overlap between each candidate and their ad choice. For example, both Biden and Trump ads targeted the character of the opposing candidate with similar subcategories. The result could also be skewed by the broadness of the three subcategories. Empathy, leadership, and integrity are extremely common targets for political advertisements, and usually are not exclusive to one candidate. In contrast, the broad spread of issues in this election cycle could have contributed to each source targeting specific content to advertise. The numerous groups and PACs have niche subjects that they advocate for and likely led to a statistically significant outcome.

While many of the ads in our sample set were translated versions of an ad in English, some ads were rather unique in their content, appealing to a niche part of the electorate. For example, many ads used music and song lyrics of a specific style to appeal to the Spanish-speaking audience, and sometimes specific Latino identity groups. Additionally, the *Trump for President* source often attempted to prove their loyalty and recognition of Latinx voters by addressing specific parts of their culture, such as the *Dia de los Muertos* holiday.

Another unique component of many Spanish language ads was the incorporation of testimony. By use of narration and stories, many ads focused on topics that are specifically moving and meaningful for the immigrant population and their families. Testimony ads use appeals to pathos to argue how the candidate understands the distinct struggles of many Hispanic voters. Most of the testimonial ads in the sample set for this study were pro-Biden, as they played upon the promise for improvement under Biden's administration. Predominantly, the stories used for pro-Biden ads focused on Trump's failure to deliver on the "American dream" and that immigrant struggles were only worsened under the Trump administration. By dividing the ads in our sample set into categories based on their message form, it is evident that testimonials and personal stories was a widely used tactic in Spanish language ads, especially by organizations creation pro-Biden and anti-Trump ads.

Conclusion/Findings

The significant correlation between source and content issue tells us that many sources hone in on a particular issue or topic in order to be more effective in their argument and play to the strengths of their candidate's focus. For example, many pro-Biden or anti-Trump ads either attacked Trump for his management of COVID-19 or discussed what Biden would do to fix it. However, in our sample set, there were no pro-Trump/ or anti-Biden ads that discussed COVID-19 as their main issue focus.

Given the difficulty of framing Trump's handling of COVID, many pro-Trump sources focused on topics such as ideology and leadership. It was clear that Trump made efforts in outreach to specifically Cuban voters, also "drumming up the (inaccurate) idea that Biden was a 'trojan horse' bringing socialism to the US" (Joe Biden is a Trojan Horse, 2020; Thomson-DeVeaux, Skelley, & Bronner, 2020). An appeal to a specific population that, having come to the States to avoid socialist dictators, fears such leadership, was evident in a portion of our ad set. In fact, in many ads from the Trump for President Organization, the focus was framing Biden as a socialist or communist leader. While Biden still won a large majority of the Latinx vote, the Trump campaign created ads to play upon the fears (or experiences) of specific parts of the Latinx community which influence particular communities among Hispanic voters (for example Cubans in South Florida as we indicated earlier).

Because there was no statistical significance between candidate and character focus, source and character focus, or candidate and content issue, it could be concluded that a large majority of Spanish language ads are comparable to any other presidential ad. Regardless of the target audience, many of the Spanish language and Latinx ads are created with similar aims, as well as many of the same rhetorical tactics as presidential ads in English. Part of this phenomenon could be due to the increased prevalence of the Spanish language and Hispanic culture. The widespread influence in America and growing population of Spanish speakers makes it so these ads naturally appeal to a wider audience. Additionally, it means that many of the ads do not need to focus on issues specific to people of Hispanic origin; a wide variety of political issues are relevant and decisive for Latinx voters.

While it is difficult to determine which ads swayed Latinx voters, we can speculate about their effectiveness by looking at where votes went in heavily Hispanic counties. According to the American Election Eve Poll (2020), Trump won 27% of the overall Latino vote, while Biden won 70% (American Election Eve. n.d.). Additionally, Trump performed quite well in some heavily Hispanic counties—"In Florida's Miami-Dade County, for instance, which is 68 percent Hispanic, Trump narrowed his deficit by 22 percentage points between 2016 and 2020; in Texas's Starr County, which is

99 percent Hispanic, Trump improved by a stunning 55 percentage points" (Thomson-DeVeaux, Skelley, & Bronner, 2020). Further research on the distinctiveness of Spanish language and Latinx ads, we now find the influence and scope of Spanish language ads growing and will continue to grow in succeeding elections.

References

American Election Eve. (n.d.)., *Latino Decisions, The American Election Eve Poll,* Latino Decisions. https://electioneve2020.com/poll/#/en/demographics/latino/

Biden's Spanish ads target Latino voters. Los Angeles Times. https://www.latimes.com/projects/election-2020-trump-biden-ads-latino-voters/

Carranza, R. (2020, October 31). *Campaigns blanket Spanish-language TV with political ads to court Latino voters in Arizona.* The Arizona Republic. https://www.azcentral.com/story/news/politics/elections/2020/10/31/political-ads-dominate-spanish-language-tv-arizona/6079571002/

Flores, A., & Coppock, A. (2019, September 18). *Candidates can be rewarded for speaking Spanish, but evidence suggests there might be a cost.* LESCentre USAPP. https://blogs.lse.ac.uk/usappblog/2019/09/18/candidates-can-be-rewarded-for-speaking-spanish-but-evidence-suggests-there-might-be-a-cost/

Jacqueline Kennedy Campaign Spot (2010, June 8). JFK Library, YouTube. https://www.youtube.com/watch?v=Xu1BuGbq_i4

Mahncke, J., (2020, July 11).*US election: For Joe Biden, empathy wins the presidency.* DW.COM. https://www.dw.com/en/us-election-for-joe-biden-empathy-wins-the-presidency/a-55408733

Joe Biden is a Trojan Horse for the Disciples of Marx and Castro who control his party and campaign (2020, August 19). Donald J Trump, YouTube. https://youtube/LL5ubs-w5c4

Melendez, P. (2015, July 1). *More Spanish speakers in U.S. than Spain, Report Finds*. CNN. https://www.cnn.com/2015/07/01/us/spanish-speakers-united-states-spain/index.html

Miller, E. (2020, September 15*). Biden, Democratic groups target Latinos with Spanish language ads*. OpenSecrets. https://www.opensecrets.org/news/2020/09/biden-trump-spanish-language-ads/

Thomson-DeVeaux, A., Skelley, G., & Bronner, L. (2020, November 23). *What we know about how white and Latino Americans voted in 2020*. FiveThirtyEight. https://fivethirtyeight.com/features/what-we-know-about-how-white-and-latino-americans-voted-in-2020/

Weeks, M. (2017, March 2). *UGA report: Minority groups driving U.S. economy*. UGA Today. https://news.uga.edu/multicultural-economy-report-17/

Chapter 20: 2020 Vice Presidential Political Advertisements

Dave Kilduff

Dave is a Senior in Economics from Bedford, New York

While they play an integral role in American government, Vice-Presidential candidates rarely are the focus of political advertisement campaigns. These candidates do not often tip the scales in the of voter's minds as they are typically regarded as an extension of their party's nominee. In the 2020 election cycle, however, the respective Vice-presidential candidates, Mike Pence and Kamala Harris, have received much more attention in political advertisements. This is most likely due to a multitude of converging circumstances, all of which have led to this historic development in political advertising.

Several reasons have been offered as to why Vice-Presidential advertisements in 2020 received more attention. Many speculate it relates to the perceived or potential health of Donald Trump and Joe Biden. Both candidates are old relative to former candidates, Donald Trump, 74, and Joe Biden, 77. As worries regarding the physical and mental health of the top-of-the-ticket grew, some voters may have anticipated an increased likelihood of the vice president having to take over the presidency (Gersen, 2020).

While this is a legitimate concern, an examination of the vice-presidential ads suggests the main motivation for the increase in Vice-Presidential advertisements may lie elsewhere. The data indicates that Joe Biden's selection of Kamala Harris as his running mate played a major role. Harris is only the third woman to ever be selected as the Vice-Presidential candidate by one of the two major political parties[i]. In addition, she is the first woman of color to be selected as a Vice-Presidential candidate. These factors, combined with the growing role of social media and online advertising, become the exponent for the increase in attention on the Vice-Presidential candidate. In 2020 unlike most of the cycles ads, very few of the Vice-Presidential advertisements were attack ads, instead focusing mainly on promoting a party's candidate rather than criticizing that of the other party.

To establish context, I look first to the history of Vice-Presidential advertisements in previous election cycles. There has been very little research performed on Vice Presidential ads which most likely reflects an absence of VP advertisements in general. Some results surfaced for individual candidates, but they were mainly news articles mentioning new advertisements. When researching advertisements since the new millennium, articles regarding advertisements relating to Dick Cheney (Broder, 2020), Paul Ryan (Roca, 2012), and Tim Kaine (Klein & Scott, 2016) were readily found, these advertisements, however, are your run-of-the-mill attack ads, and limited to one or two instances. These contributed little to the respective campaigns, simply serving as one more individual attack ad. There also are few examples of advertisements providing a positive emphasis of a vice presidential candidates, most being a short bio. The one exception to the advertising practice of ignoring the vice president may have been Humphrey's classic *Laughter* ad poking fun at his opponent, Spiro Agnew (Laughter, 2016). Another memorable instance was John Kennedy's clip from an Eisenhower news conference where he ask to offer "one major idea that you have adopted in the role of decider and final..." Eisenhower responded, "if you give me a week I might think of one, I don't remember." (Dwight Eisenhower knocks VP Richard Nixon, 2014).

This chapter demonstrates that the 2020 Presidential election cycle, and particularly the Biden/Harris campaign, broke the mold of the past and injected VP into the process with a significant number of ads. It remains to be seen, and is doubtful, if this infusion of Vice-Presidential spots will endure in subsequent advertisement cycles.

Study Strategy and Results

This research was designed to account for possible themes or schemes found within the VP ads. A codebook was developed to account for the major characteristics from the examined sample. Categories were developed largely organically through examining the ads text and structures. Each advertisement was assessed as either meeting or not meeting each criterion. With the Kamala Harris spots, I recorded if the advertisement was pro or anti Harris, if the advertisement was outwardly anti-Trump, if the advertisement was released by a PAC or coalition as opposed to through social media or directly through the Biden/Harris campaign, if the advertisement focused on Joe Biden just as much as it did Harris if advertisement specifically mentioned Harris's race, gender, or political experience, if the advertisement directly mentioned COVID-19, and if it focused on getting out to vote. These categories allowed a focus on the characteristics and anomalies.

For advertisements focusing on Mike Pence I recorded if the advertisement was pro or anti pence, if the advertisement was released by a PAC or coalition as opposed to through social media or directly through the Trump/Pence campaign, if the advertisement mentioned Trump (in either a positive or negative light.), if the advertisement mentioned Pence's political experience, if the advertisement mentioned COVID-19, if it focused on getting out to vote, and if it was specifically against Joe Biden. This provided inclusive categories assessing campaign advertisements relating to Mike Pence. Finally, it should be noted that the sample size greatly differs between candidates. For Mike Pence, the sample consisted of 9 advertisements. For Kamala Harris, the sample size consisted of 72 advertisements. This differential number of ads may be due in part to the unique nature of Kamala Harris as a vice presidential candidate. Given these circumstances, I believe it is necessary to take this fact into account when assessing the study's results regarding Mike Pence advertisements, as there is a much smaller body of work.

(continues on following page)

Table 1: Distributions by Variable

Variable	Freq.	%
Pro-Harris	43	60.6%
Anti-Harris	28	39.4%
Anti-Trump	11	15.5%
Anti-Biden	1	11.1%
Large Organization and/or Super PAC	15	21.1%
Small Organization and/or Social Media/News clip	24	33.8%
Campaign/Party	31	43.7%
Gender	16	22.5%
Race	23	32.4%
Political Experience	31	43.7%
COVID-19	5	7%
Voting	11	15.5%
Joe Biden	23	32.4%
Anti-Pence	4	44.4%
Pro-Trump	2	22.2%
Anti-Trump	2	22.2%
Political Experience	1	11.1%
Distributed via Large Organization and/or Super PAC	3	33.3%
Distributed via Small Organization and/or Social Media/News clip	3	33.3%
Distributed via Campaign/Party	3	33.3%
COVID-19	6	66.6%
Voting	0	0%

We can begin to draw some general conclusions regarding the content found within these Vice-Presidential advertisements (See Table 1). Starting with advertisements concerning Mike Pence, we note first a few irregularities. Once again, the sample size of advertisements is smaller than Harris, but larger than most campaigns. With only 9 advertisements we can only draw limited conclusions. Additionally, five were not standard advertisements, three of which were produced by White House.gov; these highlighting speeches Pence has given around the globe.

The other two pro-Pence "advertisements" are news clips that the Trump campaign issued as social media entries, portraying him in a positive light. Thus, while we categorize these as "pro-Pence" for the sake of the above table, they are not television advertisements *per se*. Mike Pence drew less attention, negative or positive. It appears Pence was mainly seen as a calmed extension of Donald Trump. Furthermore, given the Trump campaign's history of his own centrality, this observation makes complete sense. Finally, the remaining Mike Pence advertisements in this sample are attack ads. These attack ads, however, are mostly designed to show the hypocrisy present in Donald Trump and Mike Pence's partnership. Particularly, The Lincoln Project published an advertisement, *Adultery*, comparing Donald Trump's sexual misdeeds alongside with clips of Mike Pence ironically condemning those who stray (Adultery, 2020). Overall, however, the number of ads produced for and against Pence may be indicative of Pence falling into the mold of previous Vice-Presidential candidates.

The sample of Kamala Harris advertisements provides the basis for many more observations. The Harris set is objectively large, with 71 advertisements. Broken down, 44% of these were directly from the Biden-Harris campaign, 34% were small news clips or social media-based advertisements, and the remaining 22% were from third party political organizations. This includes advertisements both in favor of and against Harris. Furthermore, roughly 60% of the advertisements in this sample were in favor of Harris, with the remaining 40% opposing Harris. Unlike the Pence sample, these advertisements are, in fact, conventional political advertisements, and thus we can consider these in the traditional form.

The sample of Kamala Harris advertisements stand out from previous Vice-Presidential candidates for a few key reasons. Mainly, Harris is a biracial woman. Thus, she easily provides representation to minority groups that have gone unheard in previous election cycles. This is exemplified in the sample of Harris related advertisements, almost a quarter of which bring focus to Harris's gender, while almost a third of the advertisements highlight her multiethnic background. These are noteworthy as this highlighting of Harris's diverse background allowed Biden/Harris campaign to signal minority groups. While these groups typically tend to vote for Democrats regardless, this may have helped recruit minority voters who voted for Trump in 2016 hoping for the "swamp" that is Washington D.C. to be drained. By emphasizing Harris's multiethnic upbringing, the campaign could better appeal to voters of similar origins which may have resulted in increased turnout.

There are a few more statistics worth noting regarding the Kamala Harris advertisements. First, almost 44% of advertisements focused on Harris's political experience. While this is lower than the aforementioned focus on race and gender it remained a significant theme. Pro-Harris commercials stressing credentials may have been attempts to define the candidate and/or inoculate against anticipated criticism.

Furthermore, due to the ongoing global pandemic, one would think that COVID-19 may be worth mentioning in an advertisement, whether it be disgracing the current administration's response, or promoting a new vision for the future. Surprisingly enough, COVID-19 was only a focus in 7% of Harris related advertisements.

Finally, the last major variable of interest when analyzing the Kamala Harris sample is the role of Joe Biden within the advertisements. In Table 1, the variable Joe Biden is meant to represent the frequency with which Joe Biden is a major focus of a Kamala Harris advertisement. From this sample, we observe that almost a third of Kamala Harris advertisements featured Joe Biden in just as prominent a role. This is informative, although the data regarding the use of Harris's race and gender suggests that the campaign wanted to emphasize her as an individual, we ultimately see that Harris is still meant to work in tandem with Biden, and the two of them creating a united front. In addition, some of these "joint" advertisements were attack ads, and thus they were meant to disparage the campaign.

Several of the pro-Harris ads, particularly those focused on background and career, were not issued by the Biden Harris campaign, but rather by Harris herself. An example would be Harris's ad *Unburdened* (2020) which celebrated her mother's cancer research and her tagalong learning her values. These efforts perhaps emanated from remnants of her primary campaign organization. They allowed an independence vis-à-vis Biden and potentially minor distancing for the main candidate. More likely it took advantage of available resources for targeted audiences.

This analysis suggests what Vice-Presidential advertisements mean in the grand scheme of Presidential advertising campaign. First, the advertisements, or lack thereof, focusing on Mike Pence are indicative of the past. Pence is simply an extension of the Trump administration, with the simple job of helping Donald Trump further appeal to Middle America. Thus, Pence is rarely a focus in advertisements as he plays a small role in the campaign compared to the "big fish" Donald Trump. On the other hand, Kamala Harris and the Biden campaign have balanced breaking the mold for Vice Presidential advertisements, while also maintaining a sense of normalcy on the whole. The campaign highlights the reasons why Harris stands out – by emphasizing her multiethnic origins and her gender, Harris helps appeal to those that may feel underrepresented in our government. While this may work when focusing on appealing to similar people, we must still factor in Harris's previous political experience, which in turn, helps humanize her as a candidate. While many of the anti-Harris advertisements focus on her being "the most liberal senator in Washington," pro-Harris advertisements focusing on her experience evoke a different tune. These advertisements focus on Harris's titles as proof of experience, without necessarily mentioning her policies enacted while in office. Furthermore, when Harris and Biden share the screen time within an advertisement, Harris's political experience and goals quickly become intertwined with her running mate's. Harris mentions how Biden was a father figure when she worked as an Attorney General alongside Biden's late son Beau. Furthermore, Harris falls in line with Biden as a more moderate candidate in these advertisements as well, as joint advertisements tended to emphasize Biden's "Build Back Better" message while also making little to no mention of Harris's more liberal tendencies. While this is arguably divergent from Harris's political background, it is ultimately necessary to create this united front for the sake of the greater campaign.

On the other hand, certain attack ads such as *Meet Phony Kamala Harris* criticize Harris for seemingly swapping her extreme liberal views in exchange for Joe Biden's more moderate stance, unseemly political gain (2020). Advertisements such as these are crucial to this analysis, as it shows the opposite viewpoint of Harris and Biden's newfound alliance. The abundance of positive advertising may have served to inoculate against the "too liberal" Harris.

Furthermore, it was noted that many of the Pro-Harris ads are coming directly from Harris's base herself, rather than from the joint campaign. This once again speaks to the individuality that Harris brings to the campaign. All in all, we see that while Harris's diverse background and experience are highlighted in a good portion of the advertisements within our sample, we ultimately see that these factors can only play a big factor to a certain extent, as Harris is frequently portrayed as simply an extension of Joe Biden and his more moderate agenda.

This 2020 election cycle provided some major developments in Vice Presidential advertisements. While advertisements relating to Mike Pence followed the traditional pattern, as most of these were cookie-cutter attack ads, the Biden/Harris campaign broke this mold while simultaneously embracing tradition. By focusing on Harris's diverse background, we finally see a Vice Presidential candidate playing a major role within a Presidential ad campaign. By balancing this with more traditional advertisements, featuring both Harris and Biden, the campaign was able to maintain a united front that could fit the previous molds. Thus, it is clear that by embracing Harris as a full-fledged member of the campaign, and not just viewing her as an extension of Joe Biden, the Biden/Harris campaign revolutionized the concept of the Vice-Presidential advertisement, which may have, in turn, contributed to their victory in the 2020.

References

Adultery (2020, August 26). The Lincoln project, YouTube. https://www.youtube.com/watch?v=F42TbMp9P08

Broder, J. M. (2020, July 31*). The 2000 campaign: the ad campaign; Cheney's votes are attacked.* The New York Times. https://www.nytimes.com/2000/07/31/us/the-2000-campaign-the-ad-campaign-cheney-s-votes-are-attacked.html

Dwight Eisenhower knocks V.P. Richard Nixon (2014, December 2). CBGP Television, YouTube. https://www.youtube.com/watch?v=F42TbMp9P08

Gersen, J. S. (2020, October 26). *We may need the twenty-fifth amendment if Trump loses.* The New Yorker. https://www.newyorker.com/news/our-columnists/trump-biden-election-twenty-fifth-amendment-mental-fitness

Klein, B., & Scott, E. (2016, October 4). *New RNC ad attacking Kane sparks controversy.* CNN politics. https://www.cnn.com/2016/10/03/politics/tim-kaine-rnc-death-penalty-ad/index.html

Laughter (2016, June 10). Museum of the Moving Image, YouTube. https://www.youtube.com/watch?v=0zHyH6PHFzc

Meet Phony Kamala Harris (2020, October 7). Donald Trump, YouTube

Roca, P. (2012, October 10). *Ryan ads may be misleading.* The Badger Herald. https://badgerherald.com/news/2012/10/10/ryan-ads-may-be-misl/

Unburdened (2020, October 17). Kamala YouTube. https://www.youtube.com/watch?v=x3fCeabLoO4&t=5s

---

[i] Kamala Harris with Joe Biden, Sarah Palin with John McCain and Geraldine Ferraro with Walter Mondale. *List of female United States presidential and vice-presidential candidates*, Wikipedia. https://en.wikipedia.org/wiki/List_of_female_United_States_presidential_and_vice-presidential_candidates

Chapter 21: Corruption Narratives in the 2020 Election Cycle

Maya Dalton and Mark Sucoloski

Maya is a Junior in Politics and International Affairs from Fairmont, WV and Mark is a Junior in Communication from Baltimore, MD

Introduction

Political corruption remains a staple within the American political culture. Always part of the daily vocabulary of elections, accusations of corruption permeated the 2020 election. In 2017 76% of Americans believed corruption to be widespread throughout the government while only 59% reported the same feelings in 2006 (Clifton, 2017). The Transparency International Corruption Perception Index offers an annual report of the degree of corruption in the world's countries and territories, scored from highly corrupt (0) to very clean (100). The United States has plateaued between 69 and 80 from 2011 to 2019 and was ranked 23rd out of 180 countries in 2019 (CPI, 2019). Between the developing disdain towards the presence of corruption and the indices of national ranks of corruption, the United States does not hold its once envious status on the global stage, and the minds of Americans are plagued with the corruption narrative even more so in the last two decades. In the chapter that follows, we discuss previous literature regarding corruption in political advertisements and assumptions of voter suppression in previous election cycles and present results of thematic content analysis of political ads ranging in topics from vote-by-mail debate to accusations of Hunter Biden's corruption.

There are a multitude of working definitions of corruption utilized in political science and in previous research based on standards of public interest, public opinion, and the law. A widely used definition of corruption is the "misuse of entrusted power for private gains" which takes legality and public interest into account (Fisman & Golden, 2017). When an action is illegal and abuses the power of an office, it is corrupt. Mark Warren introduces a more modern definition, stating that "corruption is always a form of duplicitous and harmful exclusion for those who have a claim to inclusion", hence, corruption must be defined by those conditions: exclusivity and duplicity (Warren, 2004). Therefore, corruption will be defined throughout this chapter as the abuse of public office for private gain, violating conditions of exclusivity and duplicity.

The paper is divided into two sections that examine discrete aspects of the corruption themes portrayed in the 2020. Section 1 examines voter suppression related schemes, while section 2 investigates scandals surrounding the candidate's persona and their families.

Section 1: Voter Suppression, the USPS, and Voting by Mail

Literature Review

Defining Corruption in Political Advertisements.

Political advertising has become the main way for candidates to communicate with voters over the last several decades, even more so in the unique nature of the 2020 election cycle which has been impacted particularly by COVID-19. This election cycle has brought forth plentiful accusations of corruption, from the United States Postal service scandal, to Vote by Mail fraud, to accusations against President-elect Joe Biden's son. Both political parties have spun a vicious narrative against one another to influence voters.

Previous literature supports the claim that corruption is not new within political advertisements. Scholars found that across newspaper ads in the 1964 presidential election, similar issues were displayed regarding the opposing candidate, such as education, health, elderly, and corruption (Mullen, 1986). In other countries, such as Taiwan, studies have found that political corruption issues are more visible in corruption propaganda during election times than in other years (Fell, 2006). The high-frequency of corruption advertisements combined with an "electoral cycle bias", certain media outlets, third party groups, and candidate campaigns try to affect voters when it matters most – prior to presidential elections (Moglie & Turati, 2019). Hence, the media can have an indirect effect on decreasing corruption, however, corruption narratives appear heavily in election years where groups want to frame their story to persuade voters.

The literature does not account for every confounding relationship of exposing corrupt candidates by the free media. Arguably the relationship may deter voters from holding politicians accountable and hence, decreases corruption. Also, media outlets often have their own ideological stance, which can imply bias in the supply of political news affecting the selection of both the topic to be covered and how it is presented and discussed. Such biased outlets try to create a corruption scandal of their own to "expose" through their own advertisements or use preexisting scandals to spin their own narrative in advertisements. Finally, because prior research does not directly explore the narrative of corruption advertisements, we conduct a thematic content analysis on the 2020 political advertisements.

Voter Suppression Narrative: Vote by Mail and the USPS Scandal.

Discourse surrounding voter suppression has been ongoing since before the height of the Civil Rights' Movement and the Voting Rights Act of 1965, which outlawed discriminatory voting practices, especially in southern states (Voting Rights Act, 1965). While voter suppression does not originate with the Civil Rights Movement, the passing of the Voting Rights Act was the first step to eradicating formal barriers to voting, even though informal obstacles remained in order to suppress minority communities from utilizing their right to vote. Other issues regarding voter suppression have surfaced since 1965, including the lack of election resources in states, allocation of poll workers, and restricted access to voter registration (Wang, 2012). Historically, voter suppression has risen when political organizations restrain the participation of certain demographics but cannot, politically or constitutionally, disenfranchise them outright (Keyssar, 2012). The voter suppression narrative has returned in the 2020 election advertisement cycle as millions of Americans were caught at a crossroad of risking infection of COVID-19 by going to the polls or turn to vote-by-mail sometimes associated with mistrust and fraud.

In the recent election cycle, vote-by-mail advertisements have been scarce or simply directed towards audiences that choose to vote by absentee ballot (i.e., military, university students, etc.). Voting by mail is not a new concept to US elections, for the last two federal elections, roughly one of every four Americans cast a mail ballot (Weise & Ekeh, 2020). A recent battleground poll conducted by CBS, it was found that 37% of citizens preferred voting by mail (Salvanto, et al., 2020). With this election cycle's unique circumstances, such as COVID-19, the influence on voter turnout and vote-by-mail requests increased greatly, making it is even more timely to explore the nature in which political candidates have influenced their supporters to turn to their mailboxes rather than election day voting.

Surrounding the surge of vote by mail campaigns has been claims of election fraud and discreditation, specifically by President Donald Trump, stating that mail ballots would create "the most CORRUPT ELECTION in our Nation's History!" (Dickinson, 2020). The President spun a very vicious narrative of election fraud through mail ballots, going as far as pushing to defund the

United States Postal Service (USPS) to avoid such fraud. In response to harsh criticisms and the threat of losing funding, the US Postal Service launched advertisements of their own to "educate the public on the Postal Service's role within the mail-in voting process." (Katz, 2020). The USPS went to great lengths to handle the 8-10% declines in mail delivery times due to COVID-19 and assure the American public that their ballots would be received in time to be counted (Katz, 2020).

Even so, Trump's reelection campaign continued to release advertisements to request that some mail-in ballots in many key battleground states such as Pennsylvania, Florida, Georgia, North Carolina, Iowa, Arizona, Maine and Wisconsin (Dickinson, 2020) not be counted. Many advertisements use different language than Trump himself, with no syntax of fraud or corruption through voting by mail, at least for absentee balloting (Dickinson, 2020). The twisted narrative between Trump himself, his campaign, and opponents in pushing Americans to vote, no matter the method is something truly distinctive from other election cycle narratives. Furthermore, the *Washington Post* reported ads presenting false information dissuading voters from using the USPS to vote by mail. Eventually advertisements were removed from Google and Facebook from groups such as Protect My Vote and FreedomWorks that allied with Donald Trump's reelection campaign (Stanley-Becker, 2020). The conflicting narratives regarding whether vote by mail ballots are fraudulent or a safe way to vote has brought a unique perspective to the 2020 election cycle which is analyzed in thematic content analysis.

Theories and Methodology

This research sought to observe political advertisements corruption narratives by conducting a thematic content analysis on the corruption advertisements in the 2020 election cycle. The sample of 25 advertisements was organized by date, duration, source, candidate/party mention, and common verbiage and/or themes. We look to discover recurring storylines of corruption in the USPS through vote by mail, as well as narratives regarding voter suppression. From such analysis we asked the research question: Do advertisements present recurring themes of suppressing a citizen's right to vote by mail?

Results

The results of the thematic content provide interesting results of the "corrupt" narratives with regards to voter suppression and the USPS scandal. As shown in Figure 1, the distribution of advertisements length has a positive skew. The mean average was 54.5 seconds being affected by numerous longer advertisements, with an outlier of 125 seconds. This would seem to suggest the sample largely abides by standard 30 second ad television but more extended messages of likely intended for social media outlets were produced.

Figure 1: Distribution of Ad Duration

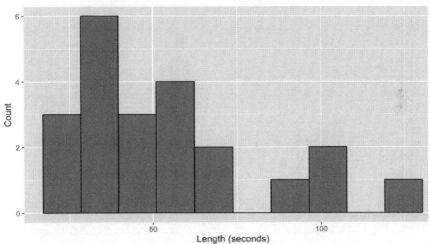

The visual of advertisement source is shown below in Table 1, with just under half, 40.91% being from third party ideological groups such as American Crossroads, Future 45, Make American #1, and Reclaim American, primarily conservative sponsors.

Table 1 – Frequency of Advertisement Source

SOURCE	NUMBER	%
(1) Primary Candidate Campaign	2	9.09%
(2) Sponsored by Political Party Group	1	4.55%
(3) Third Party Candidate Associated Groups	3	13.64%
(4) Third Party Ideological Groups	10	40.91%
(5) Third Party Interest Groups/Institutions	3	13.64%
(6) News Channel	4	18.18%
Total	22	100%

Interestingly, most of the advertisements mentioned President Donald Trump and the Republican party as shown in Table 2, 50% of the advertisements mention them in some capacity, whether it be a positive or negative fashion. While not a political advertisement, Donald Trump's response to criticism on cutting funding to the USPS on Fox News in September is an important piece in understanding the narrative.

Table 2 – Frequency of Candidate or Party Mention

CANDIDATE/PARTY	NUMBER	PERCENTAGE
(1) Joe Biden/Democratic Party	6	27.27%
(2) Donald Trump/Republican Party	10	50.00%
(3) Other	1	4.55%
(4) Both	2	9.09%
(5) N/A	2	9.09%
Total: 22	22	100%

In Table 3, the content analysis for common verbiage and themes is presented. Keywords and phrases found in the advertisements were sorted into five categories: Voting, USPS, Corruption, Voter Suppression, and Other. Of these categories, corruption and voting are the most frequent, with themes of voter suppression and the USPS scandal.

Table 3 – Common Verbiage and Themes in Advertisements

CATEGORIES	KEYWORKS & PHRASES	COUNT
(1) Voting	Vote by mail, voter registration, right to vote, counting votes, absentee ballots, mail-in ballots, universal voting, unsolicited ballots	25
(2) United States Postal Services	War on Mail, defunding USPS, destruction of mailboxes	7
(3) Corruption	Manipulation, cheating, fraud, false polls/votes, conspiracy theories, unsolicited, "fake"	23
(4) Voter Suppression	Voting safeguards, voter intimidation, suppression/depression	9
(5) Other	Pandemic/COVID-19	9
Total:		72

Discussion

President Trump claimed that ballots were being lost and discarded by the postal service, and the Democratic party is to blame for the "catastrophe" because they did not approve funding for the USPS. Trump's main argument within this set is that universal mail-in voting is sensitive to fraud and corruption. He reasons that absentee ballots are allowed, but mail-in ballots are not, which is illogical in the sense that the process for both is the same[i]. In his response to claims of destroying the postal service, Trump's argument of universal mail-in ballots as fraudulent and corrupt violates the definition of corruption we set forth for this study. If anything, universal mail-in ballots are the opposite of this definition: they are not abusing public office for private gain in any way, it is not exclusive, the process includes people who have the right to vote but may not be able to do so given the circumstances due to the year's circumstances, as some would argue not duplicitous. In an advertisement from AARP Florida from July, statistics of their state's population show that 93% of Americans trust the voting system, and 65% feel secure in voting by mail. These percentages, while not representative of the entire US population, give an idea of attitudes towards the USPS scandal being false in a key battleground state, at least before the rhetorical and advertising delegitimization campaign.

Further analysis found an interesting theme and concept to which this narrative can be described accurately as the "War on Mail". In an August advertisement from VoteVets, the organization expressed the importance of the postal service to military forces outside of the US. The troops rely on the USPS for medicine, communication with home, and their absentee ballots. The ad criticizes Trump for defunding the USPS and taking away the troops' access to home and their right to vote. Other advertisements, such as one from Defunding Democracy, call for an expansion to absentee voting to protect older citizens from COVID-19 and other health risks. Senator Gary Peters (D-MI) also stood up for postal service rights to be protected, criticizing Postmaster General Louis DeJoy's failure to give the US citizens answers.

Advertisements from conservative groups and news outlets pushed the responsibility of voter suppression to the democratic party with unfound claims of cheating, fraud, and corruption in mail-in votes. In an advertisement from the GOP (Republican Party) in May, they claimed that Democrats are working to radically change the voting process by removing voter safeguards and increase opportunities for fraud. Vernon Jones (D-GA) spoke at a Trump rally in early November claiming that liberals and the media are "suppressing and depressing" voters through false ballots and false polls. In a series of advertisements tailored to battleground states such as Arizona and Florida, The Lincoln Project put forth a warning to Republicans that they will be caught for intimidating voters and manipulating the election. This sample set of advertisements, regardless of political affiliation, provide support for the claims of corruption will violate the definition set forth and include themes of suppressing citizen's right to vote by mail through fear tactics such as COVID-19, the War on Mail, and unsolicited ballots.

Section 2: Sideshow Corruption Advertising: Character, Prominence, and Impact

Literature Review

What is an election without corruption? Whether it is a Clinton scandal, Trump's tax returns (or lack thereof), or Hunter Biden, elections of modern day have provided the average voter with a plethora of corruption content. Media has grown in a key role in discovering and amplifying this corruption as well, seeking to be first with breaking "news."

Corruption has taken on many meanings historically. Michael Johnston, author of *Political Corruption: Readings in Comparative Analysis*, claims, "In the 1900s, in the United States, corruption was one of the most frequently employed terms in the political vocabulary" (2017). This "aura" surrounding the word is what we focus on in this chapter.

Political corruption can rattle a candidate to their core, prematurely ending many a political career, the residue oftentimes unshakable. *Or…so we thought.* Now former United States President Donald J. Trump was the center of countless scandals involving women, money, and some of the most powerful people in the world. According to Timothy Kuhner, author of *Tyranny of Greed: Trump, Corruption, and the Revolution to Come* claims, "During his campaign and first presidential term, Donald J. Trump became a transparent catalyst for political corruption, crony capitalism, prejudice, and climate change" (2020). A Teflon presidency left many Americans scratching their heads at this one: How can a man involved in so many scandals win an election?

As we discover regarding this consignment of political corruption ads, everything may not be what it seems. Corruption likely matters to the American people, but voters seem willing to brush scandals aside and more heavily weigh other political factors (at least among Trump supporters). Regardless of how much money spent defacing the other on their "questionable" pasts, does it truly matter? The American people will see what they want to see, and they vote accordingly. Nam H. Nguyen, co-author of *Political Corruption and Mergers and Acquisitions* cites none other than President-Elect Joseph Biden claiming that "Corruption is a cancer: a cancer that eats away at a citizen's faith in democracy, diminishes the instinct for innovation and creativity; already-tight national budgets, crowding out important national investments. It wastes the talent of entire generations." (Nguyen et. al., 2019).

Through this paper, I argue that corruption in fact plays a role in the outcome of political elections. However, at times Americans are willing to overlook the transgressions of their own party figure.

Research Question and Methodology

Research Question: How did the candidate's advertising frame match up against their opponents? Data was collected via an independent set of 50 political advertisements focused on the corruption forms addressed in this section. The political ads were catalogued for three variables: Creator of Advertisement, Who the Advertisement Supports, and Length of Advertisement. Additionally, 3rd party advertisements were broken into Pro-Biden and Pro-Trump regarding their content. The content of each ad was further divided into ads about 1 – Biden's Long Career in Office, 2 – Hunter Biden, 3 – Biden as a "Pawn of Radical Left, 4 – Biden Scandal and 5 – Trumps General Actions and Scandal, 6 – Trump's Taxes and Money.

(continues on following page with Figure 2)

Figure 2: Ad Source

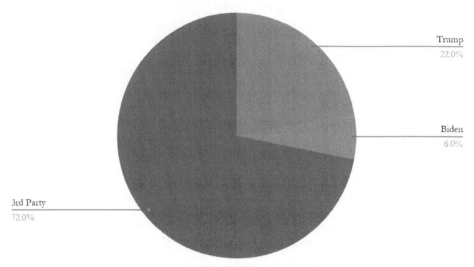

Results

Figure 2 shows the demographic of ad sponsor. The largest portion of persona-based corruption ads were produced by 3rd party PAC or organization. In volume the ads were more in favor of former President Trump (32, 58% pro-Trump, 18, 42% Pro Biden). The average length of these ads was over 57 seconds with the highest number of ad 30 seconds, the standard television ad space length, but many of the ads in support of Donald Trump ran long, the longest running over three minutes, indicating they were created for social media rather than television. Much of Trump's material came from speeches, meaning these videos were a little longer than his democrat counterpart. The sheer volume of ads supporting Trump was largely in the former President's favor.

Pro Trump spots (32) was a much larger set of ads than Biden (18). Trump friendly PACs and Trump himself paid more apparent attention to the (persona) corruption ads producing nearly double what supporters of Biden issued going after Trump's corruption. with this nearly 2:1 ratio of corruption ads in favor of Trump, Biden's time in the "corruption spotlight" was grim. This data does not account for the proportion of ads that actually ran on TV or were deployed on social media. The widely believed refrain of a "Corrupt

Trump" may account for needing less ads to make the case. It also could be that the eminent number of Trump ads was needed to tag Biden for the same reason, to counterbalance widely held public beliefs.

Third party ads were a major subset of these advertisements. It seems that nearly 70% of the ads in this set were created by third parties, significantly reducing the amount of resources the campaigns had to put into these corruption ads.

The ads were also categorized for their content (see Figure 3) that: 1-Biden's Long Career in Office, 2- Hunter Biden, 3- Biden as a "Pawn of Radical Left", 4 – Biden Scandal and 5- Trumps General Actions and Scandal, 6 – Trump's Taxes and Money. Trump's people typically went after the same two points. About a quarter of the anti-Biden ads went after his lying for 47 years in United States Government, and the other three quarters revolved around his son, Hunter Biden, and his "doings" in Ukraine and China. Biden claimed he knew nothing about what Hunter was doing overseas, but Trump's team believes otherwise.

Most of the ads against Trump were speaking to his aggressive tendencies with women, lack of productivity in office, and various "mini-scandals" in a compilation. Anti-Trump ads regarding his general scandal and behavior led all categories among themes. Both sides hit the same points over and over, ads within a category were largely repetitive.

The Hunter Biden scandal officially took hold in mid-October, only a few weeks before America chose their next leader. Biden's ads went after Trump's personality and the choices made in office. Biden's ads (of which he put out very little from his personal campaign) were rather vague and limited in number. Did it seem to matter? Trump and his PACs/donors spend millions of dollars on slander ads on the Biden corruption scandals, did it pay off in the long run?

Discussion

The original research question asked "How did the candidate's advertising frame match up against their opponents? The results from the data shows that while historically slander ads have a great impact on election results, former President Donald Trump wrote his own demise, without the help of Joe Biden, with his long list of previous corruption scandals. Americans can overlook past situations reconciling with that in their heads. In this partisan world, if their party sanctions something said, it is written in stone (forgiven) for many voters.

The major takeaway from this collection of corruption political ads is that people may not always be influenced, at least in this election cycle by the allegations made by politicians and PACs supporting the candidates. The main reason for this is the competing storyline structure of how this election transpired. Each day, it seemed like the United States was graced with another major political outrage. This caused many Americans to eventually become numb to scandals. With each side going after the other the perception is created of the "same degree" of blame for both campaigns.

From a point of view Donald Trump and company may have spent money bashing Biden all for nothing. The election was one of the most polarized in recent American history, most American voters were very much either for or against Donald Trump and his campaign. Of course, the ineffectiveness of ads was unlikely the case. They likely reinforced the converted, but more importantly they may have served to neutralize the shock or moral response to charges of corruption; if everyone is corrupt it then is no longer a defining issue. Despite the advertising push to further alienate or neutralize voters, over 80 million people, in part, rejected Trump's corruption counterpunch and voted for Joe.

The phenomena I examined, the political advertisements in the 2020 election cycle, centered on character indictments linked to the candidate. If a candidate has nothing to hide or distract from, there is no need to heavily play offense. What voter can conjecture from these ads is that Trump ads aimed to manage the narrative. If Biden had wanted to play offense, he would have had more ammunition. *The Atlantic* gives a few of the following examples of Trump's scandals, countless sexual assault scandals, beauty pageant scandals, racial housing discrimination, mafia ties, Trump University, bankruptcies, refusing to pay workers, etc. (Graham, 2020). Biden (relatively) chose to let the American people make their decision about who was more corrupt, leaving third parties to amplify those charges. Overall, the ads mirror how divisive America has become.

Conclusion

As anticipated advertisements presented recurring themes of suppressing citizen's right to vote by mail, defunding the USPS, and the never-ending debate on unsolicited mail-in ballots. Furthermore, the corruption narratives relating to vote by mail violated the definition set forth as the abuse of public office for private gain, violating conditions of exclusivity and duplicity. However, such advertisements relating to the Hunter Biden scandal leave room for claims of duplicitous abuse of public office for private gain. Additionally, we see that Donald Trump and his supporters attacked Joe Biden's campaign regarding corruption issues, by more than double what Biden's supporters attacked in Trump's campaign. While corruption is not tied to ideology in this cycle it may have been tied to a specific candidate. The 2020 election provided a plethora of corruption issues, whether it was Hunter Biden's laptop that Rudy Giuliani mysteriously "found" in a pawn shop, to Donald Trump paying lower taxes than nearly all Americans, we see both campaigns (and their respective third parties) attacking each other over the candidates alleged corruption scandals. Mainstream and alternative media often depict a partisan flavor regarding political corruption, yet both parties found reason to advertise to further their agendas. Corruption has impacted many narrative points in the 2020 election cycle allowing a unique opportunity for critique.

References

Camaj, L. (2013). The media's role in fighting corruption: media effects on governmental accountability. *The International Journal of Press/Politics 18*(2). 21–42.

Desilver, D. (October 2020). *Mail-in voting became much more common in 2020 primaries as COVID-19 Spread*. Pew Research Center. https://www.pewresearch.org/fact-tank/2020/10/13/mail-in-voting-became-much-more-common-in-2020-primaries-as-covid-19-spread/

Dickinson, T. (October 20, 2020). *As Trump demonizes Vote-by-mail, his campaign is urging people to vote by mail*. Rolling Stone. https://www.rollingstone.com/politics/politics-news/as-trump-demonizes-vote-by-mail-his-campaign-is-urging-people-to-vote-by-mail-1077953/

Fell, D. (2006). *Party politics in Taiwan: Party change and the democratic evolution of Taiwan, 1991-2004*. Routledge.

Fisman, R., & Golden, M. (2017). *Corruption: What everyone needs to know*. Oxford University Press.

Graham, D. A. (June 27, 2017). *The many scandals of Donald* (n.d.) The Atlantic. https://www.theatlantic.com/politics/archive/2017/01/donald-trump-scandals/474726/

Clifton, J. (June 27, 2017) *Land of the Free?* Gallup.com. https://news.gallup.com/opinion/gallup/212627/land-free.aspx

Johnston, M. (1978). *Political Corruption: Readings in comparative analysis*. Transaction Books, n.p.

Katz, E. (September 9, 2020). *USPS launches tv and direct mail campaign to assuage concerns about mail-in voting*. Government Executive. https://www.govexec.com/management/2020/09/amid-firestorm-usps-launches-tv-and-direct-mail-campaign-assuage-concerns-about-mail-voting/168335/

Kuhner, T. K. (2020). *Tyranny of greed Trump, corruption, and the revolution to come*. Stanford Briefs an Imprint of Stanford University Press.

Le Moglie, M., & Turati, G. (2019). Electoral cycle bias in the media coverage of corruption news. *Journal of Economic Political Corruption and Mergers and Acquisitions. Behavior & Organization, 163*, 140–57.

Mullen, J. J. (1968). Newspaper advertising in the Johnson-Goldwater campaign. *Journalism Quarterly, 45(2)*, 219–25.

Nguyen, N., Hieu V. Phan, H., & Simpson, T. (2018). *Political corruption and mergers and acquisitions*. SSRN Electronic Journal, 2018.

Our Documents – Voting Rights Act 1965 (2019). Ourdocuments.gov. Results – 2019 – CPI. https://www.ourdocuments.gov/doc.php?flash=false&doc=100. Accessed November 22, 2020.

Salvanto, A., De Pinto, J., Backus, F., Khanna, K., & Cox, E. (September 6, 2020). *Battleground Tracker: National, Wisconsin contests steady amid protests; more think Biden trying to calm situation*. CBS News. https://www.cbsnews.com/news/biden-trump-wisconsin-opinion-poll-protests/

Keyssar, A. (2012). Voter suppression returns, Voting rights and partisan practices. Harvard Magazine (July-August), 28-31.

https://www.harvardmagazine.com/sites/default/files/pdf/2012/07-pdfs/0712-28.pdf

Stanley-Becker, I. (2020, August) *Google allows misleading ads on mail-in voting to remain* – The Washington Post. https://www.washingtonpost.com/technology/2020/08/28/google-ads-mail-voting/

Starke, C., Naab, T. K., & Helmut Scherer, H. (2016). Free to expose corruption: The impact of media freedom, Internet access and governmental online service delivery on corruption. *International Journal of Communication, 10,* 4702–4722.

UNDP (2015). A users guide to measuring corruption. United Nation https://www.undp.org/content/undp/en/home/librarypage/democratic-governance/anti-corruption/a-users-guide-to-measuring-corruption.html

Wang, T. A. (2012). *The Politics of voter suppression: Defending and expanding Americans' right to vote.* Cornell University Press.

Warren, M. (2004). What does corruption mean in a democracy? *American Journal of Political Science, 48*(2), 328-343.

Weiser, W., & Ekeh, H. (2020, April). *The False Narrative of vote-by-mail fraud.* Brennan Center for Justice. https://www.brennancenter.org/our-work/analysis-opinion/false-narrative-vote-mail-fraud

---

[i] The media and much of Trump's advertising failed to draw a clear distinction between requested absentee ballots and more widely distributed (sometimes unrequested) mail in ballots.

SECTION 5: SURPRISING SIDEBARS IN THE 2020 ADVERTISING THEMES

Allan Louden, Editor

Every presidential campaign has unique twists and turns, but 2020 introduced more than most. This section examines sizeable ad sets that echoed previous campaigns but in intensity and messaging choice were exclusive to this cycle.

The section paradoxically opens with an analysis of political ads materials that were technically not political ads. Rafael Lima examines 82 videos issued by the White House Communication Office. This branch of the White House communication is charged to "promote the president's agenda throughout all media outlets." Typically, they document video events, presidential speeches and meetings, and, in its most political aspect, promotes numerous policy issues. The chapter makes a convincing case that under the auspices of the Trump administration the Whitehouse.gov produced video appeared, operated, and perhaps intentionally, were functionally political advertising in its classic form. The increased blurring of governing versus electoral pressures is changing the normative understanding of government's 'official' role in political intrigue.

(continues on following page with Figure 1)

Figure 1: Performance of Third-Party Candidates – 1892-2020

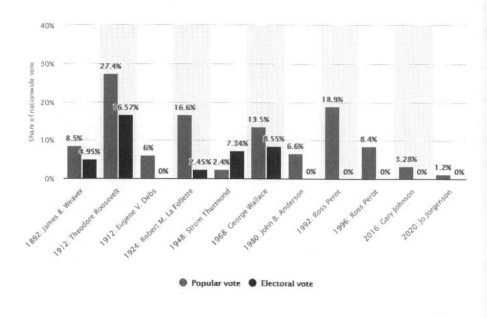

The 2020 campaign might be characterized as having more vocal elements for "crossover voting" than any prior election. The disaffected and the "Never Trumpers" (Never Trump Movement, n.d.). Historically third-party efforts such as Roosevelt's Bull Moose, Ross Perot's populist businessmen, and George Wallace's 1968 insurgency and perhaps John Anderson in 1980 "outsider" have influenced elections (See Figure 1; Statista, n.d.). Ostensibly those campaigns work to entice voters from both parties to their new effort.

At times candidates have ran ads asking voters to switch parties as with the *Confession of a Republican* prominent in the 1964 Lyndon Johnson/Goldwater campaign (Confessions, 1964). Landslide elections, as with this spot, seem to legitimize jumping ship messaging. Additional efforts such as "Democrats for Nixon" (Nixon & McGovern Campaign Ads, 1972) were orchestrated by the parties and asking for their presumptive opponents to change sides.

Dockery and Coelho research the idiosyncratic forms of "migration" messaging (changing party voters). Their analysis represents a fresh angle, laying bare the essential workings and assumptions of what heretofore had been minor entries in the presidential add sweepstakes. Their convenience sample informed that analysis.

Unlike any other election the 2020 cycle produced literally thousands of ads, more accurately video statements for social media, narratives asking members of their own party to defect and join in defeating the home team candidate. Republican Voters Against Trump posted voter created video (over 1500) sometimes sophisticated and often not. The RVAT group would feature non-sophisticated testimony for its enhanced relatability. The Republicans in these videos were asking fellow Republicans to vote for Biden or against Trump.

The WalkAway campaign testimonials were more often former liberals, sometimes Democrats, who had "seen the light" and asked those still indoctrinated to join them in voting for Trump. They posted just under two hundred testimonials. Other Republican groups also weighed in heavily often with migration messages, these included 43 Alumni for Biden (Ex-Trump administration officials) and Republicans for the Rule of Law, whose 30 ads dominated in the preconvention messaging.

Other groups also produced compelling narratives typically of moving from Trump to Biden. PACs like Priorities USA, American Bridge 21st Century, Really American PAC, and Pacronym. One ad, *Jennifer's story* (2020), from Pacronym illustrates the longer and highly produced testimonial spot – in this instance targeted state, Wisc., and occupation, farmer – often produced to air in that state and share on social media for the rest of the country.

The Trump campaign produced several of their own of lifelong Democrats now voting for Trump. He often issued video, as in *I Used to Be a Lifelong Democrat for Years…* (2020) of plainspoken Americans stating why they moved from Democrat to Trump, in this case a black retired Marine, offering a visual contrast to media portrayal of Trump supporters.

Jordan Hessinger examines 50 Supreme Court ads that followed the passing of Justice Ruth Bader Ginsburg. It has become routine for interest groups to weigh in with television ads during the Supreme Court confirmation process, and sometimes in conjunction with the election as with the Kavanaugh nomination. More traditionally the advertising, while political, has remained outside the election process and largely negative, in opposition to a nominee. The Amy Coney Barrett advertising however was front and center in late 2020. The Trump advertising predictably lauded her nomination and confirmation, but the bulk of the ads were positive character framing spots on behalf of Barrett, seemingly designed to inoculate the candidate against expected criticisms. Few ads attacked her directly, rather reinforcing the healthcare themes of the confirming Democrat Judiciary Committee members. The Amy Coney Barrett ads shared, along with their positive tone, character and experience referents with ads produced on behalf of Kamala Harris. An inevitability of outcome and perhaps a carefulness via gendered roles invited the positive tone.

The Lincoln project who issued over 150 presidential ads[i], was not the only influential independent player in the 2020 cycle. Although not addressed directly in this volume these included most notably Meidas Touch who produced nearly 100 spots. Especially the Lincoln Project had enough money to buy substantial airtime, and Meidas Touch was able to purchase ads later. Winslow films produced nearly 50 hard-hitting videos, often longer in length, shared across social media.

Caroline McClain provides a thorough accounting of the conception and purposes of the most influential group – The Lincoln project. Caroline culled the sample for representative examples of Lincoln project's entries. As she rightly notes the effectiveness of their advertising remains unknown, yet they spent upwards of 82 million during the 2019-2020 cycle (The Lincoln Project PAC Profile, 2020). Political science professor Lincoln Mitchell wrote that the group's "brutal" ads "seem to have been successful at getting inside Trump's head" and that their work is "attracting attention across and beyond the political spectrum" (2020). The Lincoln Projects spoke to an audience of one at 1600 Pennsylvania Avenue *and* to those seeking justification for Trump abandonment.

Maggie Moran examines the pre-and post-debate advertising from the 2016 (46 spots) and 2020 (33 spots) elections. Her findings apply William Benoit's Functional Discourse Theory finding that the negativity (attacks) of the political ads that follow a televised debate in both cycles were significantly less positive than the actual debates. One possible exception were "acclaim" ads on behalf of vice-presidential candidate Harris, perhaps part of a larger campaign establishing her aptitude.

Elizabeth Maline's explores at an aspect of social media in the Democrat primary. Her work reminds us that a more complete study of political advertising would include various social media outlets, but such a charge was beyond the time and resources available for this book. She looks at 28 Bloomberg's Instagram memes aiming to generate buzz for his nascent primary campaign. That the memes were specifically designed for social media is obviously the case. The intentionality of designing a political ad for a given platform is not so obvious for many groupings addressed in this book. Many ads, although designed for television, do not have sufficient money to buy television and hope to either narrowcast for their constituents, and if lucky to go viral. The line between televised political advertising and social media advertising is blurred or, as I would argue, without meaningful distinctions. Not only is Maline's work thorough in examining unique deployment of ads in this election cycle, but it also serves as a reminder that a comprehensive understanding of 2019 20 advertising will need to encompass social media as well.

Haleigh Cadd's focus is on language and political ads. She specifically looks at the word choice in Trump's pre-pandemic ads during the primary phase. Examining 44 ads she tracks the reasoning and choice of three emergent words that characterized the early ads – facts," "change," and "winning." Often political research is concerned with deployment and packaging of messaging. Messages are considered as containers of issue and image content, the local verbal structure often ignored. Words matter. Haleigh's effort engages in partially filling that gap.

References

Confessions of a Republican (1964). Democratic National Committee. http://www.livingroomcandidate.org/commercials/1964/confessions-of-a-republican

Jennifer's Story (2020, April 13). Pacronym, YouTube. https://www.youtube.com/watch?v=F-27VLS72Ec

Mitchell, L. (July 23, 2020). *How the Lincoln Project's brutal anti-Trump ads could remake US politics.* CNN. https://web.archive.org/web/20200724095713/https://www.cnn.com/2020/07/23/opinions/lincoln-project-anti-trump-ads-remake-politics-mitchell/index.html

Never Trump Movement, n.d. Wikipedia. https://en.wikipedia.org/wiki/Never_Trump_movement

Nixon & McGovern Campaign Ads (1972, November 7). C-SPAN. https://www.c-span.org/video/?25560-1/1972-nixon-mcgovern-campaign-ads

Performance of select third-party or independent candidates in U.S. presidential elections from 1892 to 2020 (2020, n.d.). Stratista. https://www.statista.com/statistics/1134513/third-party-performance-us-elections/

The Lincoln Project PAC Profile (2020). OpenSecrets. https://www.opensecrets.org/political-action-committees-pacs/the-lincoln-project/C00725820/summary/2020

---

[i] Numbers represent the ads collected for this volume

Chapter 22: WhiteHouse.gov Video as Political Advertising

Rafael Lima

Rafael is a Senior in Communication from Natal, Brazil

Introduction

Political advertisements are as old as political campaigns themselves in the U.S. Its roots can be traced all the way back to the 1800 presidential race between John Adams and Thomas Jefferson. Then, the two former presidential running mates turned political rivals resorted to all sorts of negative campaigning to best their opponent, including Adams likening Jefferson to a coward and weakling, and Jefferson referencing to Adams as a criminal and a fool (Kamarck, 2016, for an interesting take see Parton, 1873). In 2020, the tradition continued as positive and negative ads about President Donald Trump and former Vice President Joe Biden flooded TV channels and social media to the tune of over $14 billion in advertisement spending (Schwartz, 2020).

However, amid the seemingly unlimited cascade of political ads from both Democrats and Republicans, the White House official communication channel on YouTube stood out as an unusual source of political campaigning communication. Among the hour-long video transmissions of White House events, some of the videos posted on the channel displayed characteristics remarkably like political campaigning ads seen during presidential races. Some of the characteristics included appeals to voter's emotions, framing of salient issues, and prominently showcasing President Trump's traits that would present him a fitting candidate for office. These videos mirrored familiar political advertisement formatting including the use of constant frame succession, b-roll imagery[i], patriotic symbols, and robust background music.

According to Morey (2017), political ads – either positive, negative, or comparing candidates – have common features such as (a) the presence of one of the candidates in the ad, (b) an intended message objective (promote, praise one candidate or criticize, derogate the other), and (c) a clear appeal to emotional responses. Other researchers identify political ads, especially in electoral campaigns, as more likely to tackle issues of salience to the public, topics that are at the "top of the [public's] mind," as part of their messaging (Franz et al., 2020). Brader describes emotion appeals as essential to the work of political ads, focusing on fear and enthusiasm appeals as the main appeals that political ads convey to the public (2005).

This chapter analyzes how media produced by the WhiteHouse.gov functionally served the same purpose as political ads by breaking down similarities between the content released by the White House and common traits found in political campaigns. The research observed a definition of political ads on three main traits: (a) the prominence of a presidential candidate's persona; (b) the presence of salient political issues to the election; (c) use of emotional appeal (either fear or enthusiasm appeals). Furthermore, the analysis included formatting similarities between the official White House videos and traditional political campaign ads.

Literature Review

The literature around political advertisements has a broad focus wherein most researchers focus on usage of political ads or specific political outcomes seldom addressing those features which make an ad a political one. However, it is commonly agreed among political scholars that the main function of a political ad is to elicit political action by the audience through emotional appeals, as Brader prefaces in his analysis of emotion appeals in political advertising (2005). Building off this assumption of the centrality of emotional appeals, he focuses on "enthusiasm" appeals or "fear/anxiety" appeals as the two most persuasive ways of appealing to a voter's emotion through political ads. *Enthusiasm appeals* are aimed at provoking positive reactions from individuals by reinforcing the link between the candidate's platform and progress towards achieving the individual's personal goals (Brader, 2005). This is usually achieved by featuring the candidate's platform alongside content and imagery that are associated with success and good times (Brader, 2005). The American flag has increasingly become a staple of positive campaign ads – especially during the 2020 presidential race – as it appeals to voters' positive emotions of patriotism and national pride. Conversely, *fear appeals* link the opposition with content and imagery associated with threats, such as the use of the scream of a siren or violent images to capture the attention of crime-wary voters (Brader, 2005). As discussed further in the chapter, the use of *enthusiasm appeal* imagery and content was prevalent among the White House videos.

Political ads seek to link their candidate with positive emotional responses and the opposition or opposing view with negative responses. Thus, it is important for positive ads to present or allude to the candidate's persona, while negative ads should focus on the oppositional party or candidate (Morey, 2017). Regardless of the appeal of the ad, researchers argue that political ads tend to clearly favor salient issues – issues that are among the priorities of the electorate – as candidates tend to "ride the wave" of public opinion in their favor (Franz et al. 2020). Alternatively, political campaigns also often tend to highlight issues that have been historically associated positively with the party and candidate's image, described as ownership issues (Franz et al., 2020). This explains why Republicans tend to make arguments about the economy and taxes, while Democrats are more inclined to highlight environmental and social security issues.

As for delivery and format, most of the current scholarship on political ads is still concentrated on traditional media channels, with TV as its primary delivery platform. Yet, as social media increasingly becomes a more prominent aspect of people's lives (eMarketer, 2020) political ads have also migrated to social media platforms (Margetts, 2019). Social media advertising generally tends to have more condensed and direct-to-the-point messaging with most video ads ranging between five seconds and three minutes, a trend that political ads on social media have usually followed. Furthermore, while political ads can vary greatly in message and content, some of its formatting stays consistent across video platform. Political campaign video ads usually employ quick b-roll imagery transition, emotion-evoking background music and an eloquent narrator, as demonstrated by Dissolve's satire of campaign ads using only stock images (Dissolve, 2016).

Methods

The sample employed in research consisted of 81 videos from the White House.gov located in their YouTube channel between Sept. 3, 2019, with the first video observed to have political campaign messaging value (The Summer of Winning, 2019), and Oct. 27, 2020, with the appointment confirmation of Justice Amy Coney Barret just six days before Election Day (United States Supreme Court, 2020). This timespan encompasses most of the presidential election campaign season while also covering the channel's most active period in posting "ad-like" videos. The sample did not include all video content posted by the White House during the period – left out were some event transmissions (e.g., diplomatic events) and press conference recordings. It did however employ a comprehensive set of "political" video, providing an inclusive baseline for analysis and comparison. Two cycles of coding were engaged to determine whether the sampling resembles political campaign ads.

During the first round of coding, the aim was to engage the sample to find similarity patterns on content, issue focus, and formatting between videos. The definition of salient issues used for this analysis drew from topics discussed in other chapters of this book that have been identified as salient issues in political advertising during the 2020 presidential race. Those issues were the economy, coronavirus, climate/environment, the Supreme Court, law and order, social justice, among others. The second round of coding was aimed at theorizing about the patterns found across the White House videos and their similarities with traditional political campaign ads. The video coding was based on whether videos presented the three main observed traits discussed in Morey, Brader, and Franz et al.(2017) and/or whether they displayed the formatting features present in political campaign ads usually found on social media.

Findings & Discussion

Out of the 81 short-video samples extracted from the White House's official YouTube channel, 50 (63%) showed all three main observed content features (the prominence of a presidential candidate's persona, presence of salient political issues to the election, use of emotional appeal) commonly associated with political campaign ads. Sixty-six (81.6%) showed all the video formatting traits commonly found on social media political advertisement including the use of constant frame succession, b-roll imagery, and patriotic symbols, and strong usage of background music (Dissolve, 2016). Forty-five of the videos in the sample (55.5%) presented all the content commonly seen in political campaign videos while also displaying all the formatting traits expected from a social media political advertisement, making this set of videos in property and function very similar to other political campaign ads found on social media. This is especially surprising as it indicates over half of the videos in the White House sample to be of the close resemblance to political advertisement commonly used in social media. Table 1 provides a breakdown of the video sample by content and format.

Table 1: Video by Content and Formatting

Presence of political ads features	Present	At least one absent	Percentage	Total
All three content features	50	31	63%	81
All three formatting features	66	15	81.5%	81
Both formatting and content features	45	36	55.5%	81

Most of the White House videos also regularly engaged issues salient to the 2020 presidential election, with 59 of them covering at least one of the salient issues discussed in this book. This shows a link between the content found in these political ad-like White House videos and the "intention" to appeal to the electorate by discussing topics that framed the election. Among the many issues discussed by President Trump in the White House ads, the economy/jobs/energy/taxes block is by far the most frequent, being cited 27 times by the president or another White House official. This was anticipated, as the economy and the creation of jobs have been some of the main talking points of President Trump since he ran for office in 2016. The emphasis strong favoring economic issues reinforces the perception that this set of videos in the White House channel operates similarly to campaign ads, as political campaigns tend to favor proven issues ownership that is likely to strengthen the candidate's election bid (Franz et al., 2020). These ratios paralleled the emphasis in his partisan campaign (See Chapter 1). Other commonly discussed issues were the military/troops and social justice/race/law & order, with 17 mentions each. This is in line with the main messages of the Trump presidential campaign, as the president sought to claim the military and social justice reform as as accomplishments. The White House.gov was a perfect vehicle for issuing positive messages for these.

In addition to the country's economic recovery plan the White House also referenced his strong emphasis on law & order, amid civil unrest and the, nationwide protests against racial injustice. The economy, law & order (See Chapter 18), and the military (See Chapter 32) are also considered *ownership issues* of not only the president's platform but the Republican party in general, corroborating the notion that the choice of topics for these short videos resembles closely the issue selection found in an ordinary political campaign (Franz et al., 2020). Despite trailing in national polls for virtually the entirety of the presidential race, Trump still polled favorably among the electorate in his handling of the economy. Until mid-October, a little over 50% of voters approved the president's management of the economy (President Trump Job Approval, 2020), making it the last salient political issue where the Republican held the upper hand over his Democratic challenger (Silver, 2020). The military is also regarded in most elections as a group favorable to Republican candidates, even though the 2020 election showed a split between active personnel and veterans (Pickrell, 2020). Nevertheless, the President's heavy emotional appeal based on patriotic and nationalistic rhetoric tends to naturally resonate with the electorate. The choice of videos showcasing events such as the West Point graduation, the Mount Rushmore law & order speech, and the College Football National Championship Game also appeal more favorably to the conservative, rural and religious voters that compose Trump's main electoral based. A White House video issue in February brought together all the factors of patriotism, identification, constituencies in a highly dramatic video *President Trump Attends the Daytona 500* (2020). With video showing military flyovers and American flags Trump's voiceover intones, "NASCAR fans never forget that no matter who wins the race what matters most is God. In comparison, COVID-19 was only discussed 13 times, despite the U.S. going through a grim moment in the pandemic during the spring and early summer; five of those mentions were in the context of broader economic relief packages and not necessarily addressing the epidemiological side of the pandemic, which proved to be the biggest point of criticism of his administration in 2020 (Oliphant, 2020). Trump's ads on the political side were correspondingly thin (See Chapter 2). Climate/environment – considered an issue ownership of Democrats – was also only present in two videos in the whole sample.

Table 2: Distribution of Issues by Partisan Issue Ownership

Salient Issue	Times Featured	Party Issue Ownership
Economy/Jobs/Energy/Taxes	27	Republican
Military/Troops	17	Republican
Social Justice/Race/Law & Order	17	Republican[ii]
COVID-19	13	Democrat
Climate/Environment	2	Democrat

The issue choices presented in the sample (see Table 2*)* suggest that the White House, much like Trump's presidential campaign strategy, tended to focus on issues the president polled well at and avoided issues that could have been more easily spun in favor of the opposition. This could very well be a standard public relations strategy but does show that the video production behind these short posts was at least in tune with the voter dynamics in the 2020 election.

Additionally, the locations of choice for some of the presidential visit videos further strengthen this perception that the 2020 presidential race played a factor in the production of the White House's ad-like videos. Out of the 45 videos that matched both the content and formatting of political ads 12 were situated in key battleground states for the 2020 election. The YouTube channel featured visits to North Carolina, Texas, Georgia, Pennsylvania, Florida, Wisconsin, and Michigan, all, except for Texas, tightly contested states in the 2020 presidential race. While this could be just a side effect of the president's campaign trail itinerary, a look at the video activity of the White House channel under President Barack Obama in 2012 – during his reelection campaign against Republican Mitt Romney – showed little to no video activity linked to President Obama's campaigning efforts. Most of Obama era video were weekly addresses to the public by the president, lacking the regular formatting and delivery of political ads (Weekly address, 2012).

Another point of comparison between the White House videos and traditional political campaigns is the structural similarities between the two. There was a recognizable pattern among the 45 White House videos that resemble political campaign ads in both content and formatting. Most of such videos start with background music and one of President Trump's speeches in the background as a quick succession of b-roll images from the event or initiative being publicized. The majority of the images used present clear enthusiasm appeals such as the display of the American flag, a pleased crowd applauding the president, or an iconic U.S. landmark. The music continues to crescendo as President Trump continues to convey in his speech familiar talking points of his reelection platform such as the "call for justice and freedom" and the "creation of millions of high-paying jobs." The video then reaches its climax with the music instantly dropping while the president closes his appeal with one of his campaign catchphrases such as "the best is yet to come," "make America great again," or "America first." This White House video from December 2019 illustrates well this structure (Our Best Days, 2019). Likewise, this is the same video structure found in *America is Stronger, Safer, and More Prosperous Than Ever Before!,* an ad the Donald J. Trump for President campaign launched right before the 2020 election on Oct. 29 (America is Stronger, 2020). Aside from the b-roll imagery selected for both videos, all other aspects such as the content, the presence of enthusiasm appeal symbols and the use of music and the president's speech in the background are strikingly analogous between this campaign ad aired by the Trump campaign on national TV and the official White House video.

The ad-like videos found in the White House channel, however, differed from other campaign videos from the Trump campaign in the type of appeal they focus on. The White House spots focused more on positive, *enthusiasm appeals* with 57 videos in the sample presenting clear components of enthusiasm appeal (the American flag, enthusiastic crowd, national landmarks, people smiling, etc.). Negative, fear appeals (as in a representation or mention of a threat to people's lives or lifestyle), on the other hand, only show up in 14 videos and only five times as the video's main appeal; oftentimes the fear appeal is featured through the allusion of "the radical left" or an old political establishment coming for American jobs or threatening to erase their way of life, as seen in the video from the president's visit to the National Archives for Constitution Day (President Trump visits, 2020). The fear appeals found among the White House videos are, thus, less frequent and less directed towards the character of Joe Biden and more against left-wing politics in general. Given that the White House.gov channel is still an official government communication channel, an overt negative ad attacking Biden's character, as seen frequently among

Trump campaign ads, might too clearly cross the boundaries in the use of the office of the presidency. Yet, it is abundantly clear that some of the videos posted by the White House during the 2020 presidential election do serve the same campaigning purpose and function as traditional political ads.

Likewise, there is a clear contrast between the ad-like videos featuring President Trump and other posts by the White House that are not as politically charged, such as the series of 15 messages by First Lady Melania Trump (A Message from First Lady, 2020). These First Lady videos are less likened to political ads from the president's campaign efforts.

The use of the White House YouTube channel as an extended communication platform of the Trump campaign is definitely unorthodox and most likely a first in the government political communication sphere. There seems to be no equivalent under President Obama during his reelection campaign in 2012 and YouTube was yet to be publicly registered in 2004 when George W. Bush ran for reelection. With almost 1.8 million subscribers on YouTube, most of its videos scoring over 33,000 views and the most popular ones surpassing 100,000, the White House's official channel can reach a considerable number of voters without the heavy costs associated with traditional political campaign ads. Whether it is looked upon as an abuse of the presidential office and its official communication channels for private gain or simply a reinvention of the White House's political messaging outreach, it is undeniable that it broke with previous norms of what the White House communication efforts sought to be.

Conclusion

The sample of 81 videos produced by the White House YouTube channel shows a striking similarity to political campaign videos traditionally run on TV and social media. The formatting of videos no longer than three minutes with a quick succession of b-roll imagery, emotion-appealing background music, and an eloquent narrator follows the same formula employed in most political ads. When it comes to traits more specific to the purpose of the political advertisement genre, the White House videos consistently featured: the prominence of a presidential candidate's persona in the figure of Donald Trump (a); the presence of salient political issues to the election such as the economy and law & order rhetoric (b); and clear emotional appeal (c). Closer analysis also demonstrated that the overwhelming majority of the emotional appeal utilized *enthusiasm appeal* (Brader, 2005), as most of the videos reflected positively on the image of the president. This might be a conscious decision to mostly focus on Trump's platform. It could also be a case of having an unspoken limit to what kind of "ad-like" videos could be run on the official White House account, given that *fear appeals* targeting the opposition would more likely be frowned upon as crossing the line. This second explanation is further strengthened once one considers the numerous *fear appeal* political ads that Trump ran against Biden during the 2020 presidential race and against Hillary Clinton during the 2016 race.

Furthermore, the White House.gov sample frequently showcased issues salient to the 2020 presidential race with many of them discussing matters considered to be of Republican ownership such as the economy, the military, and law & order. Issues that are commonly associated with Democrat issue ownership such as the environment and, more recently, the response to the COVID-19 pandemic were visibly less present. The appropriation of direct campaign language makes the message found in both vehicles virtually indistinguishable. Alongside the resemblance of political ads features and the mirroring of their formatting, the characteristics of the White House videos make them hardly distinguishable from the myriad of political ads that ran on TV and social media. Perhaps the two main distinctions between the two were the strict preference for *enthusiasm appeals* in the White House videos and their lack of a legally required sign-off graphic of Trump approving the ad's message. Perhaps official White House issue automatically carries the presidential stamp of approval.

The advent of these "ad-like" videos indicates an unforeseen new use for official White House communication channels as a platform for an incumbent president's political campaign. It is possible that the White House Communication Office's invention will regress to a more normal fare, but that is not guaranteed. A discussion in the near future should include whether this political appropriation of official channels is beneficial, immoral, or even legal.

References

A Message from First Lady Melania Trump for America's Seniors (2020, April 15). The White House, YouTube. https://www.youtube.com/watch?v=mHUmZGbLpXM&ab_channel=The WhiteHouse

America is Stronger, Safer, and More Prosperous Than Ever Before! (2020, October 29). Donald J Trump, YouTube.

https://www.youtube.com/watch?v=MJds60ik694&ab_channel=DonaldJTrump

Brader, T. (2005). Striking a responsive chord: How political ads motivate and persuade voters by appealing to emotions. *American Journal of Political Science, 49*(2), 388–405.

Dissolve (2016, March 31). *This Is a Generic Presidential Campaign Ad, by Dissolve.* https://www.youtube.com/watch?v=rouDIzhgVcY&ab_channel=Dissolve

eMarketer. (2020, May 19). *Social networks see boosts in engagement among users, but not equally.* Insider Intelligence. https://www.emarketer.com/content/social-networks-see-boosts-in-engagement-among-users-but-not-equally

Franz, M. M., Franklin Fowler, E., Ridout, T., & Wang, M. Y. (2020). The Issue focus of online and television advertising in the 2016 presidential campaign. *American Politics Research, 48*(1), 175–196.

Kamarck, E. (2016, October). *Has a presidential election ever been as negative as this one?* The Atlantic. https://www.brookings.edu/blog/fixgov/2016/10/18/the-most-negative-campaign/

Margetts, H. (2019). 9. Rethinking democracy with social media. *Political Quarterly, 90*, 107–123.

Morey, A. C. (2017). Memory for positive and negative political tv ads: the role of partisanship and gamma power. *Political Communication, 34*(3), 404–423.

Oliphant, J. (2020, December 10). *U.S. election year shaped by pandemic and Trump's defiance.* Reuters. https://www.reuters.com/article/global-poy-usa-election-idUSKBN28K1FU

Our Best Days Are Yet to Come (2019, December 21). The White House, YouTube. https://www.youtube.com/watch?v=enJwnRjkE9g&ab_channel=TheWhiteHouse

Parton, J. (1873, July). *The presidential election of 1800.* The Atlantic. https://www.theatlantic.com/magazine/archive/1873/07/the-presidential-election-of-1800/307019/

Pickrell, R. (2020, October). *US troops favor Biden for president, but Trump has a big lead among veterans, polls show.* Business Insider. https://www.businessinsider.com/us-troops-prefer-biden-but-veterans-favor-trump-polls-show-2020-10

President Trump attends the Daytona 500 (2020, February 18). Trump White House Archived, YouTube. https://www.youtube.com/watch?v=3vU0RIY0crs

President Trump Job Approval—Economy (2020, n.d.). RealClearPolitics. https://www.realclearpolitics.com/epolls/other/president_trump_job_approval_economy-6182.html

President Trump visits the National Archives for Constitution Day (2020, September 17). The White House, YouTube. https://www.youtube.com/watch?v=kBQMUL14aQQ&ab_channel=TheWhiteHouse

Schwartz, B. (2020, October 28). *Total 2020 election spending to hit nearly $14 billion, more than double 2016's sum.* CNBC. https://www.cnbc.com/2020/10/28/2020-election-spending-to-hit-nearly-14-billion-a-record.html

Silver, N. (2020, October 6). *The economy was Trump's one remaining advantage. Now he might have blown it.* FiveThirtyEight. https://fivethirtyeight.com/features/the-economy-was-trumps-one-remaining-advantage-now-he-might-have-blown-it/

The Summer of winning (2019, September 3). The White House, YouTube. https://www.youtube.com/watch?v=MlmI43TPDEM&ab_channel=TheWhiteHouse

United States Supreme Court Associate Justice Amy Coney Barrett (2020, October 27). The White House, YouTube. https://www.youtube.com/watch?v=czzWyc_5-Rk&ab_channel=TheWhiteHouse

Weekly address: Preserving and strengthening Medicare (2012) The Obama White House, YouTube. https://www.youtube.com/watch?v=rnXk-uPmrz8&ab_channel=TheObamaWhiteHouse

[i] b-roll imagery is when a video uses supplemental imagery that is not in the main shot

[ii] Trump held mostly ownership of the law & order rhetoric, but not of social justice and racial relation issues. The way he framed the latter two issues as part of his law & order discourse is what is being discussed in this article as issues that traditionally owned by Republicans.

Chapter 23: Shifting Lines: Party Migration Voting & Political Ads in the 2020 Presidential Race

Madeline Coelho and David Dockery

David is an MA student in Communication from Cookeville, TN and Madeline is a Senior in Communication & Education from Hilmar, CA

The authors of this paper have interesting memories of the 2016 race. Both had frequent conversations with friends and family about the candidates. A recurring theme throughout them was that Trump was "the lesser of two evils." Four years later, it still feels as if this was the same mind set people had voting in the election. Biden and Trump were not the top choices the American population wanted, but somehow, they were the last two standing. Of course, voters often feel they must pick between two bad options. There is nothing new about bemoaning two-party electoral politics. What is noteworthy is the sheer amount of shifting between party lines reflected in the advertisements. The aim of this study is to examine the trends wrought by political advertisements aimed at getting voters to migrate from one candidate or party to another, a phenomenon more prevalent than one might expect.

An increasing trend in the election was party migration. Many voters who identify as Republicans or lean to the GOP voted for Biden rather than their party's own candidate, Trump. According to Pew Research, "4% of registered voters say they plan to vote for Biden and the Republican candidate for House in their district or Donald Trump and the Democratic House candidate" (Pew Research Center, 2020). Younger generations, including Gen Z and Millennials, are less likely to cast a straight-ticket ballot. Looking at a straight-ticket Republican ballot, "22% of Gen Z voters are voting this way, compared with nearly half (47%) of Silent Generation voters" (Pew Research Center, 2020). The lack of straight-ticket ballots has to do in part by the fact that these younger generations support third-parties: "13% of Gen Z voters favor non-major party candidates for either House or president, as do 9% of Millennial voters" (Pew Research Center, 2020). When not looking at third-party candidates, "3% of Gen Z voters and 4% of Millennials favor Biden and a Republican House candidate or Trump and a Democrat" (Pew Research Center, 2020).

There are many possible reasons for this sort of split-ticket mentality. One of them is that the identities of the two major parties are changing. One shift in the voting base was the trend of "Never Trump" voters choosing Biden over Trump. The movement that started in 2016 has produced groups like Republican Voters Against Trump (McManus, 2020). A reoccurring theme heard from groups like these is that "a vote for Biden is a vote against Trump." Those who are crossing party lines do not necessarily agree with much of Biden's policies, but they "can no longer support Trump." Everyday citizens are not the only ones who are against Trump. A number of Republican officials abandon Trump election. Some notable ones include Cindy McCain (John McCain's widow), John Kasich (past Ohio governor), Colin Powell (past secretary of state), and Mitt Romney (senator of Utah) (Paz & Martin, 2020). Of these people, some said they would be voting for Biden and others said they would simply not be voting for Trump (Paz & Martin, 2020). They are subscribers to the old Republican creed: Strength abroad, low deficits at home.

A second shift is the steady movement of minorities toward the Republican party. Bush outperformed Trump with minorities in 2004, but Trump has exceeded the performance of both McCain and Romney (Roy, 2020). Grassroots movements like Brandon Straka's #WalkAway movement created political ads aimed at traditional Democratic constituents, such as people of color and the LGBTQ+ community (*#WalkAway Campaign | Politics*, n.d.). There is evidence that Republican appeals to minorities had an effect. Based on the Edison and AP Votecast polls, "Trump gained 4 percentage points with African Americans, 3 percentage points with Hispanics and Latinos, and 5 percentage points with Asian Americans" (Gharbi, 2020). Trump also improved among white women, winning by 11% (Gharbi, 2020). Conversely, he lost support among college-educated white males (Gharbi, 2020). These numbers are hardly a sign that the GOP has become a bastion of intersectionality. They are, however, evidence of movement. Al Gharbi (2020) notes that this shift began in 2010 and has continued in every election since.

Joe Biden won the election of 2020. He did not, however, win in a landslide (Wolf, et al., 2020). His victory also cannot be credited to a surge in minority support- he underperformed Hillary in all categories (Wolf, et al., 2020). He won partly because a larger number of white men voted for him than the traditional political trends would suggest (Gharbi, 2020). These counterintuitive trends show that voter migration has occurred. Therefore, it is worth examining what political advertising strategies both sides employed to win over voters. This chapter conducts a thematic analysis of migration voter video ads. It creates a taxonomy of themes that underpinned the communication strategy of voter migration ads.

Literature Review

Voter migration ads are nothing new. As far back as 1964, Lyndon Johnson filmed the famous "Confessions of a Republican" ad, where a Republican actor got on camera and confessed his doubts about Barry Goldwater's candidacy (Confessions of a Republican (LBJ) (2019); Democratic National Committee, 1964). The same actor, William Bogert, was brought back by the Hillary Clinton to reprise his role in a 2016 ad against Donald Trump (Confessions of a Republican (Clinton, 2016; Rhodan, 2016). The ad is archetypical of the migration voter ad's genre conventions. Voter migration ads feature the testimony of someone who supported one party and then decided to vote for the other party this time around. The testimony usually explains what drove them away from their party's candidate, or their party more generally. Voter migration ads tend to be low production value. They trade polish for the perception that the ad is authentic. These advertisements offer an aura of "grassroots"-ness to the candidate that runs them. They assure the viewer that even the people on the other side agree their candidate is the wrong choice.

Of course, the world has changed since 1964. The political landscape was cratered by the twin impacts of Facebook and Twitter in the mid-2000s. Given that U.S. Presidential elections only occur every four years, we are only just beginning to see the long-term impact of social media on political advertisements. The existing literature on social media's influence offers some clues. In Sweden, an analysis of the political blogs showed that social media gives politicians the chance to connect more directly to their constituents than through the older media channels (Karlsson & Åström, 2018). The result is a more personalized politics since politicians no longer have to worry about mediating their messages through the usual channels (Karlsson & Åström, 2018). In Germany, Stier, Bleier, Lietz, and Strohmaier (2018) found that the public used social media for "political debates," discuss political philosophy, and commentate on "coalition formation" (p. 63). Politicians, on the other hand, used different platforms for different purposes (Stier et al., 2018). Twitter was their medium of choice for "political debate," but they preferred Facebook for "campaigning" (Stier et al., 2018). Assuming Karlsson & Åström, and Stier's results are generalizable to the United States, we might expect social media to result in a more personalized politics that cares less about policy and more about people. We may also expect social media to serve as a platform where the public can debate the merits of these politicians.

Voter migration ads are what we should expect of a vibrant political debate culture. As the public becomes more adept at creating videos and develops a desire to influence political opinion, it is not surprising some of them create voter migration ads of their own. Voter migration ads are also an excellent opportunity for political elites to filter their message into the public in an unobtrusive way. By expressing their message through the mouth of an "average citizen," they bypass the suspicions the public might have toward their message. Indeed, both Hillary Clinton's (2016) and Johnson's (Democratic National Committee, 1964) original "Confessions of a Republican" are examples of political elites astutely disguising their message in the form of personal testimony. Voter migration ads can arise from the grassroots or filter down from the top.

The 2020 Presidential race took place in the environment broadly described above. Biden ran against Trump in an era when it was easier than ever to produce voter migration ads. Consequently, both sides ran a substantial number of voter migration ads during the campaign. They deserve a close examination to determine what themes and values are reflected by these ads. Understanding them informs us not only of what the common man believed about the Presidential race, but about what message political elites wanted the masses to express. Therefore, we cannot overlook voter migration ads.

The present study relies on thematic analysis to engage the voter migration data. Thematic analysis is a widely used qualitative methodology in the social sciences (Gower et al., 2020; Levy and Sarmento, 2020; Talibian, 2020(Terry et al., 2017), but has not seen the same level of use and American political advertising studies.

Thematic analysis comes in a variety of forms depending on researcher philosophy and assumptions. Terry et al. (2020, p. 19) divide qualitative analysis into two broad traditions, the "critical" and "experiential" traditions. The former does qualitative research pursuing and understanding how communication is "creating" reality, whereas the latter sees communication as "reflecting" reality (Terry et al., 2017, p. 19). This study employs an inductive version of thematic analysis, engaging the data first to see what themes arise to avoid bias by using constructs foreign to the data set. We paid attention to what themes are most salient in the data.

Methods

Artifacts

The authors collected a convenience sample of 22 political advertisements from 9 political advertisers aired in the period between July 2019-November 11th, 2020. Political advertisement here refers to a video message created to influence the political choice of the public. The political advertisements in the sample all satisfied the definition of a migration voter ad, an advertisement that communicates primarily from a first-person perspective to convince voters to change sides.

Data Familiarization

In keeping with Terry et al.'s (2017) thematic analysis, we first familiarized ourselves with the data by repeatedly watching the ads. We took notes during the viewings and noticed emerging patterns. From these patterns, codes emerged to classify the data for a systematic analysis.

Coding

The advertisements were coded according to five distinct categories. The first, source affiliation, featured four designations: Trump affiliate, Pro-Trump non-affiliate, Pro-Biden non-affiliate, and Biden affiliate. These codes apply depending on the advertiser's relationship to the Trump and Biden campaigns. The Trump campaign, for instance, is coded as a Trump affiliate, whereas a grassroots campaign like #WalkAway would count as Pro-Trump non-affiliate. The second code category is affect, the feelings expressed by the advertisement. This dimension has two codes: Positive and negative. The individual emotions expressed by the advertisement are too vague to clearly demarcate into anger, happiness, sadness, etc. However, it was clear enough what was positive and what was negative. The third code category was identity, which covers the nominal variables of race and gender. The data only featured African Americans, whites, Latinos and Latinas, males, and females. These served as our codes for the nominal variables.

The fourth and fifth categories concerned the rhetoric of the advertisements. Arguments were coded as a distinct category, consisting of four codes: Issues, competence/incompetence, virtue/vice, and respect/disrespect. Issues refer to policies concerning topics like immigration, the deficit, healthcare, etc. Competence refers to the perceived ability of the candidates/party discussed in the ad. Virtue refers to the moral quality of the candidate. Respect refers to the attitude the candidate expresses toward certain constituents. These three codes share some similarity to Aristotle's (350 B.C.) elements of ethos, *arete, phronesis,* and *eunoia.* Moreover, each of these codes features a left (L)-right (R) alignment. Left-oriented codes apply that code exclusively to the Democrats and Biden, whereas right codes apply to Trump and the Republicans. For example, an ad that proclaims he is voting Trump because he cares about America would receive the (R) Respect code. If the same claim were made about Biden, it would receive the (L) Respect code.

The fifth category, narrative type, concerns the structure of the advertisements. Five distinct narrative structures emerged from the data. The first code, Decline and Fall, is the story of an individual who watches his country fall apart at the hands of a corrupt/incompetent leader. The individual then resolves to do something about the decline. It is prototyped by the myth of Nero strumming his lyre while Rome burns. The second code, Augustinian Conversion, is a biographical narrative where the subject experiences a moral awakening over a long period of time. It is prototyped by St. Augustine's story in *Confessions*. The third code, Pauline Conversion, is a pre-existing category developed by Bormann (1985).[i] It refers to an individual who has a sudden awakening and changes sides (Bormann, 1985). The fourth code, Angelic Helper, positions the subject as a character who has always been on the side of right. She now helps others join the right side. It is prototyped by the tales of angels helping the righteous in the Bible. Fifth and finally, the Crucible narrative positions the subject as someone holding firm to his principles in the face of a corrupt society. It is prototyped on Arthur Miller's play *The Crucible*.

Results

Code Frequencies

Of the ad sample, the majority (n=11) were Trump non-affiliates. The second highest category was Biden non-affiliates (n=9), followed by Biden affiliates (n=4) and Trump affiliates (n=2). Most ads featured a negative affect (n=18) compared to a positive affect (n=10). The most represented racial demographic was white (n=18), rather than African Americans (n=4) or Latinos (n=3). There were also more women (n=15) than men (n=9) represented.

In terms of argument, the most prominent argument was (R) Vice (n=9). The second most frequent was (L) Disrespect (n=8), followed by (R) Incompetence (n=7) and (L) Vice (n=7). These were followed by (R) Disrespect (n=6). (R) Issues (n=5) was followed by (R) Respect (n=4). (R) Virtue (n=5) is followed by (R) Competence (n=3) and (L) Virtue (n=2). (L) Issues, (L) Competence, and (L) Incompetence were all equally represented (n=1). The least common argument was (L) Respect (n=0).

The narratives appeared as follows: Decline and Fall (n=6), Augustinian Conversion (n=3), Pauline Conversion (n=8), Angelic Helper (n=2), and Crucible Narrative (n=3).

Theme Identification

The first major theme is *Attack Over Defense.* Notably, most ads featured negative emotions (n=18) over positive emotions (n=10). The most prominent arguments were also negative. Instead of arguing for a candidate or party's character, they focus on disparaging the opponent. The negative nature of these ads is evident from codes like (R) Vice (n=9), (L) Disrespect (n=8), and (R) Incompetence (n=7). Moreover, the second-most frequent narrative structure was Decline and Fall (n=6). In other words, most ads were interested in portraying the opponent as someone who will destroy the country. They were not primarily interested in propping up their allies' characters.

The second major theme is *Character Over Policy*. Most arguments focus on the character of the candidates or the party. The issues themselves were almost irrelevant, especially on the left. Left-wing issues only appeared once in the sample. Issues were more common on the right, but only because the ads advocated so strongly for free speech. Many arguments dealt with the character of the parties. The ads are concerned with portraying a leader worth following, not a policy worth passing.

The third and final theme is *Grassroots Participation, Not Candidate's Influence*. Most of the advertisers were not affiliated with either the Biden or the Trump campaigns. Unlike Clinton's (2016) "Confessions of a Republican" ad, most of these ads were not the candidates speaking through the mouths of the people. They were released by independent media groups or, in the case of most Trump supporters, individuals with cellphones. In the case of the #WalkAway group especially, the demographics of the group were notably non-elite. Their ads prominently featured members of the LGBT community, African Americans, Latinos, rural men, and women. These were people who did not have experience walking the halls of power, whether in Washington D.C., Madison Avenue, or Hollywood. In contrast, pro-Biden groups like *'43 Alumni* were notably composed of elites with political experience in Washington.

Discussion

The three major themes identified in this paper- *Attack Over Defense, Character Over Policy,* and *Grassroots Participation, Not Candidate's Influence*– suggest that the popular media portrayal of the race as a referendum on Trump are mostly correct. Amidst a media ecology that privileged personalized politics and political argument (Karlsson & Åström,

2018; Stier, et al., 2018), the public found an avenue to influence voters to switch sides. In the eyes of political advertisers, the key to winning was to convince the undecided voter that the other side was worse than theirs. The solution was to attack the opponent's character rather than focus on all the good deeds their candidate had done. In some ways, this is unsurprising. A presidential race is about choosing a president. However, the lack of contextualizing the parties to policies is unusual. There were no calls to Build the Wall, pass universal healthcare, or lower the deficit. The main point of stasis concerned the parties' characters and, more commonly, Trump's character. Watching the anti-Trump ads, one gets the impression that the testifiers fear Trump is rubbing off on the country. They do not want America to adopt Trump's character. In contrast, the anti-Democrat ads want the opposite. They feel that Trump is the epitome of American prosperity. To attack him is to attack the country.

The demographics in these ads are somewhat startling, as well. The demographic most commonly represented in the anti-Trump ads are white women, a demographic that Trump did well with (al-Gharbi, 2020). However, those women were also representative of the standard Never Trump ideology ads, a demographic with notable Biden voters. All of the African-Americans represented in the sample were featured in anti-Democrat ads, another demographic Trump gained with (al-Gharbi, 2020). More importantly, we see a divide between elites and non-elites in voter migration ads. Pro-Biden ads typically used the testimony of middle class to upper class individuals, some of them with notable political experience. Pro-Trump ads usually relied on the testimony of non-elites, individuals with limited access to powerful institutions like Congress, the White House, Hollywood, or Fortune 500 companies. These individuals were more likely to have been soldiers or worked blue collar jobs. The elite/non-elite divide in ad representation suggests that class, not race or gender, was the main tension between Trump and Biden voters. Both elites and non-elites feared that the values of the other would ultimately take over the country. Trump, then, truly was a populist hero in the eyes of pro-Trump migration voters. A singular hero able to check elite power over the public. In contrast, Trump was a source of corruption for the elite migration voters. There is, therefore, a surprisingly conservative cast to pro-Biden migration voter ads. For the elite migration voters, Biden represented the last, best hope to stop the republic from falling away from its democratic values. These elite migration voters, however, are often former Bush aides – precisely the sort of person who fits the definition of the "Deep State." The voter migration ads are a microcosm of class conflict.[ii]

The most important takeaway from these ads is the political instability they imply. The decision to target demographics outside of the parties' usual constituencies suggests that advertisers believed loyalties were wavering. Beyond targeted audiences, the testimonies in the ads themselves reflect a growing divide over the perceived moral character of the country. For the Left, Trump is a metonym for all the "isms" outside of their value systems. Not so for the Right, who see in Trump a torchbearer for the restoration of the country's prosperity to the people it rightfully belongs. The person of Trump is less important than the persona of Trump, glorified or castigated. Impressionistic data suggests that many testimonies were driven by resentment on both sides. Trump produces and is a product of that resentment, a fact the ads took advantage of.

Unfortunately, what we can conclude from voter migration ad data is limited. Studies of advertisements are just that – studies of advertisements. They tell us more about what advertisers hope to achieve than the actual psychology of their audience. It would be a mistake to draw too many general conclusions on audience from the artifacts. Moreover, the data sample in this paper was a convenience sample. One cannot draw general conclusions about the totality of political advertisements in 2020 from this limited data set. Rather, one should see this data reflecting themes underpinning some communication strategies used to reach wavering voters. There are likely many more waiting for discovery. Future research can expand on the data covered here.

Conclusion

In conclusion, this paper conducted a thematic analysis on 22 migration voter ads. It found that three major themes underpinned the communication strategy of these ads: *Attack Over Defense, Character Over Policy,* and *Grassroots Participation, Not Candidate's Influence.* These themes broadly reflect the popular narrative of the 2020 Presidential race as a referendum on Trump's character. Moreover, they broadly align with the exit polls conducted by AP Votecast and Edison.

References

al-Gharbi, M. (2020, November 14). *White men swung to Biden. Trump made gains with Black and Latino voters. Why? | Musa al-Gharbi*. The Guardian. http://www.theguardian.com/commentisfree/2020/nov/14/joe-biden-trump-black-latino-republicans

Aristotle. (350 C.E.). *Rhetoric* (W. R. Roberts, Trans.). The Internet Classics Archive. http://classics.mit.edu/Aristotle/rhetoric.2.ii.html

Bormann, E. (1985). *The force of fantasy: Restoring the American Dream*. University of Southern Illinois Press.

Confessions of a Republican (2016, July 18) Hillary Clinton, YouTube. https://www.youtube.com/watch?v=oeYKFRV34kY

Confessions of a Republican (2019, Feb 26). The LBJ Library, YouTube. https://www.youtube.com/watch?v=5tqTZW7pHzI

Democratic National Committee. (1964). *Confessions of a Republican*. http://www.livingroomcandidate.org/commercials/1964/confessions-of-a-republican

Gower, K., Cornelius, L., Rawls, R., & Walker, B. B. (2020). Reflective structured dialogue: A qualitative thematic analysis. *Conflict Resolution Quarterly, 37*(3), 207–221.

Hillary Clinton. (2016, July 18). *Confessions of a Republican | Hillary Clinton*. https://www.youtube.com/watch?v=oeYKFRV34kY

Karlsson, M., & Åström, J. (2018). Social media and political communication: Innovation and normalisation in parallel. *Journal of Language & Politics, 17*(2), 305–323.

Levy, H., & Sarmento, C. (2020). Understanding viral communism: A thematic analysis of Twitter during Brazil's 2018 elections. *Westminster Papers in Communication and Culture, 15*(1), 19–36.

McManus, D. (2020, November 1). *Column: Biden's secret weapon: Anti-Trump Republicans*. Los Angeles Times. https://www.latimes.com/politics/story/2020-11-01/bidens-secret-weapon-anti-trump-republicans

Paz, I. G., & Martin, J. (2020, September 22). *All the Republicans who won't support Trump.* The New York Times. https://www.nytimes.com/article/republicans-voting-for-biden-not-trump.html

Pew Research Center. (2020, October 21). *Large shares of voters plan to vote a straight party ticket for president, senate, and house.* Pew Research Center – U.S. Politics & Policy. https://www.pewresearch.org/politics/2020/10/21/large-shares-of-voters-plan-to-vote-a-straight-party-ticket-for-president-senate-and-house/

Rhodan, M. (2016, July 18). *Hillary Clinton Re-ups "Confessions of a Republican" Ad.* Time. https://time.com/4410286/hillary-clinton-re-ups-confessions-of-a-republican-ad/

Roy, A. (2020, November 9). *No, Trump didn't win 'the largest share of non-white voters of any republican in 60 years'.* Forbes. https://www.forbes.com/sites/theapothecary/2020/11/09/no-trump-didnt-win-the-largest-share-of-non-white-voters-of-any-republican-in-60-years/

Stier, S., Bleier, A., Lietz, H., & Strohmaier, M. (2018). Election campaigning on social media: politicians, audiences, and the mediation of political communication on Facebook and Twitter. *Political Communication, 35*(1), 50–74.

Talebian, S. (2020). Understanding the characteristics of broadcast media policy in Iran: A thematic policy analysis. *Global Media and Communication, 16*(2), 148–166.

Terry, G., Hayfield, N., Clarke, V., & Braun, V. (2017). Thematic analysis. In C. Willig & W. Stainton Rogers (Eds.), *The SAGE Handbook of Qualitative Research in Psychology* (2nd ed.). SAGE Publications. https://ebookcentral.proquest.com/lib/wfu/reader.action?docID=4882015&ppg=5

#WalkAway Campaign | Politics. (n.d.). #WalkAway Campaign. Retrieved December 13, 2020, from https://www.walkawaycampaign.com

Wolf, Z. B., Merrill, C., & Wolfe, D. (2020, November 7). *How exit polls shifted in 2016 and 2020.* CNN. https://www.cnn.com/interactive/2020/11/politics/election-analysis-exit-polls-2016-2020/

[i] Although we previously said we were not importing foreign constructs into the data, the Pauline Conversion was evident in the earlier phases of data analysis. Therefore, we felt justified in using Bormann's category.

[ii] We must be careful to not generalize too much from this sample. We cannot conclude from these ads alone that the class struggle I described is occurring in broader American culture. However, considering the January 6th Insurrection, researchers should consider elite resentment a live hypothesis.

Chapter 24: Supreme Court Political Advertisements in 2020

Jordan Hessinger

Jordan is a Senior in Communication from St. Petersburg, FL

Political advertisements regarding the Supreme Court applied during the 2020 election cycle were of greater number and fervor than in past elections due to unprecedented circumstances. On September 18th, less than two months before the conclusion of the widely contested presidential election, Justice Ruth Bader Ginsburg passed away. This kicked off a race for President Donald Trump to confirm a new Supreme Court nominee before the election in November. Many argue that it defies precedent, argued in 2016, that the Senate should wait until after a forthcoming election to confirm a new justice into the Supreme Court. Only 13 days passed between the time Amy Coney Barrett's nomination was sent to the Supreme Court to her first committee hearing. Amy Coney Barrett's Supreme Court nomination is the fastest confirmation time seen in 45 years. With the confirmation happening so close to a divided election, the fight over Amy Coney Barrett's nomination contributed to the content of several political ads (Miller, 2020).

In September, the ad wars of the 2020 election shifted to cover a new topic, the vacancy on the Supreme Court and President Trump's choice of Amy Coney Barrett to replace Justice Ginsburg following her death. Within 10 days of the passing of Justice Ginsburg, about $1.8 million has been spent on television advertisements specifically about the Supreme Court. These political advertisements directly referencing the Supreme Court nomination by President Trump, some in support and some in opposition, were produced by not only by both the Biden and Trump campaigns but other political groups as well (Biesecker, 2020). Of the 50 advertisements in this ad set, 38 were produced by conservatives and supported Trump's nomination of Amy Coney Barrett, and 12 were produced by Liberal groups. While only a small handful (3) of the advertisements run by Democratic groups were directly in opposition of Barrett and her beliefs, the other nine ads run by Democratic groups were either tributes to Ruther Bader Ginsberg and her legacy, or opposition to Trump appointing a Supreme Court Justice in general during an election year. The Trump Campaign, the Biden Campaign, Club for Growth, the Judicial Crisis Network, and the Democratic Coalition are the groups who created the most advertisements addressing the Supreme Court nomination.

In the set of 50 advertisements five distinct categories of advertisements emerged. These categories are health care, hypocrisy, the legacy of Ruth Bader Ginsberg, Pro-Barrett, and court-packing (see Table 1). Of these categories, advertisements praising the nomination and achievements of Amy Coney Barrett accounted for 24 of the 50 advertisements – almost 50%. Advertisements run about the hypocrisy of Republican politicians supporting the nomination of Amy Coney Barrett were tied for the second-highest number of ads in this set, with nine total advertisements. Hypocrisy advertisements were equal in number to advertisements expressing concern for Biden "court-packing" if he won the election and whom would be nominated if left to his administration. Next, five advertisements praise the legacy of Ruth Bader Ginsburg and her accomplishments in her career as a Supreme Court Justice. The final three advertisements were related to concerns about Amy Coney Barrett opposing the Affordable Care Act and how her nomination could potentially impede health care. These five categories of advertisements and the groups that funded them reflect the primary concerns and considerations of a nomination so close to a polarizing election.

Table 1: Judicial Advertising Distribution

Category	Count
Health Care	3
Hypocrisy	9
Ruth Bader Ginsburg	5
Pro-Barrett	24
Court-Packing	9
Political Affiliation	**Count**
Conservative	38
Liberal	12

Almost half of the ad set of Supreme Court advertisements during the 2020 election cycle were used to demonstrate Amy Coney Barrett's career successes, highlight her qualifications for the role, and to praise her nomination to the Supreme Court by President Trump. Many of these advertisements that fall into the pro-Barrett category were funded by the Judicial Crisis Network, the Trump Campaign, Americans for Prosperity, and Club for Growth. The Judicial Crisis Network, an American conservative advocacy group dedicated to strengthening liberty and justice in America, spent over $6.3 million in five weeks on national television spots supporting Donald Trump's nominee in the weeks leading up to the election (Biesecker, 2020). The Judicial Crisis Network also spent an additional $2.9 million on digital ads, direct mail, and text messages in support of Barrett. Many of the advertisements featured her background as a law professor turned judge who is also a devoted mother of seven with dedicated conservative family values. These advertisements also worked to frame any questions and attacks that may arise about Barrett's Catholic faith (Miller, 2020). While the Judicial Crisis Network spent a total of about $10 million on advertisements supporting the Supreme Court nomination of Amy Coney Barrett, it has not been disclosed where this money came from and who donated the money to the conservative organization. One of the most prominent ads funded by the group supporting Barrett includes a clip of President John F. Kennedy and defends Barrett's religious views, which came under attack by the Democrats.

Another prominent category of advertisements about the Supreme Court nomination during the 2020 election cycle includes ads relating to the hypocrisy of nominating a justice during an election year. With a total of nine ads in this set relating to hypocrisy, they were funded by groups such as the Lincoln Project, Medias Touch, the Democratic Coalition, and others. In a blistering ad, titled "Lindsey Must Go", the Lincoln Project created an advertisement using Senator Lindsey Graham's own words against him from a 2018 Atlantic interview. In the interview, Graham says, "if there's a Supreme Court opening in the last year of President Trump's term, and the primary process has started, we'll wait until the next election to confirm a new justice." The Lincoln Project advertisement used these words to point out the hypocrisy of Senator Graham in his push to quickly confirm a new Supreme Court Justice after the death of Justice Ginsburg (Papenfuss, 2020). Many of the other Supreme Court advertisements that fell into the hypocrisy category centered around Lindsey Graham, Mitch McConnell, and other GOP senators who blocked the confirmation of Barack Obama's nomination for the Supreme Court in February of 2016, nine months before the 2016 election.[i] This nomination was blocked as Republicans said it was too soon to the vote to replace such a critical position on the nation's highest court (Papenfuss, 2020).

Also, nine advertisements from the examined ad set is the category of assertions that speak on the issue of court-packing. The term court-packing is often used to describe changes in size to the Supreme Court, but it is better understood as an effort to manipulate the Supreme Court's membership for partisan ends. A party that attempts court packing will often violate the norms that govern who is appointed and how that process works (Moore, 2020). After the Death of Ruth Bader Ginsburg on the eve of an election, Trump's push to quickly nominate Amy Coney Barrett for the Supreme

Court came with much backlash from the Democratic Party. President Trump cited the fear of Biden "court-packing" if he was elected president and allowed the Supreme Court nomination for this rapid nomination and confirmation. Most of the advertisements with this message came directly from the Trump Campaign. The advertisements featured clips of reporters and debate moderators asking Joe Biden and Kamala Harris about their intention of packing the Supreme Court, and then the questions not being answered. The Judicial Crisis Network also released a powerful advertisement addressing the court packing issue. The ad gave a brief history of the Supreme Court numbers, stating that after the Civil War, nine justices became law. The ad then gave previous examples of court-packing attempts by presidents, specifically FDR, and then ended with a clip of Ruth Bader Ginsburg stating expressing that nine justices seem to be the perfect amount. The advertisements in the court packing category, funded by the Trump Campaign and Conservative political groups, used the fear of the future appeal demonstrate the unreliability of the Biden administration and to encourage the election of Republican Senators to prevent Court-Packing (Lovelace, 2020).

Another prominent category of political advertisements about the Supreme Court nomination was five advertisements praising the career of Ruth Bader Ginsburg and encouraging Americans to respect her legacy. These advertisements came from the Democratic Coalition, the Biden Campaign, Pacronym (a liberal political action committee), and the Lincoln Project. In an advertisement created by the Democratic Coalition, a narrator urges young people to get out and vote for Biden and uses images and soundbites of Ruth Bader Ginsburg in the ad. The message of this ad says that voting for Biden will honor Ruth Bader Ginsburg, who in recent years has become a popular figure among young voters. The Pacronym ad urges voters to be "ruthless" and vote for Biden. Using a pun that plays on Ruth Bader Ginsburg's name, the ad appealed to female voters encouraging them to vote for Biden to guarantee the protection of their reproductive rights. The ad released by the Lincoln Project in this category did not call anyone to action, rather it was simply a compilation of videos and soundbites of interviews from Ruth Bader Ginsburg speaking about the power of women and encouraging them to work hard and follow their dreams, arguing enthymatically. Interestingly, the advertisements in this set do not directly condemn Amy Coney Barrett, rather they are memorializing the life of Ruth Bader Ginsburg and encouraging Americans to vote for Biden to honor her legacy.

Finally, the smallest, but arguably one of the most powerful categories of advertisements in the Supreme Court ad set is the health care category, with a total of three ads. These ads addressing health care in relation to the Supreme Court nomination were made by the NARAL, Protect our Care, and the Independence USA political action committee. During Barrett's confirmation hearing, Democrats raised concern about how Barrett would rule on California V. Texas, which challenges the Affordable Care Act's mandate that people shall buy insurance (Chotiner, 2020). Amy Coney Barrett's conservative values and Catholic beliefs have also led Democrats to question whether she would attempt to overturn Roe V. Wade. Interestingly, Barrett's nomination hearing paralleled the Senate hearings going on about protection of the ACA. This parallel made the advertisements appealing to voters' concerns about Barrett and her stance on health care even more influential. The ad placed by Independence USA features clips of Democratic senators speaking about Amy Coney Barrett's Supreme Court nomination and what this could mean for the Affordable Care Act. In the ad, Senator Chris Murphy says, "Republicans… claim Amy Coney Barrett's nomination is about something other than the repeal of the Affordable Care Act." In Senator Richard Blumenthal's clip, he says, "Amy Coney Barrett is a clear and present danger and she will author a humanitarian nightmare if she joins others on the Supreme Court who have already indicated they want to strike down the ACA." Another ad on this category, produced by NARAL, a pro-choice group, says that reproductive freedom is under assault and features videos and soundbites of President Trump speaking about Roe V. Wade and then makes the assertion that a vote for Amy Coney Barrett is a vote against Roe V. Wade. All three advertisements in this set claim that by nominating Barrett, Trump is trying to undermine health care and the ads also make emotional appeals to female voters by addressing the issue of reproductive rights.

The death of Ruth Bader Ginsburg and the Supreme Court vacancy less than two months before the 2020 Presidential election, quickly created a new category of partisan debate for the already divisive election. The Trump campaign, Biden campaign, and political action committees wasted no time in creating print and television advertisements expressing concern, praise, and attacks surrounding President Trump's rapid nomination of Judge Amy Coney Barrett. Easily divided into five distinct categories, the advertisements targeted issues such as health care, Republican hypocrisy, and court-packing, and many praised Amy Coney Barrett's qualifications and achievements, and some honored the late Justice Ginsburg. What sets the advertisements covering President Trump's Supreme Court nomination apart from other political ads in the 2020 election are the intention of the advertisements. On the surface, the ads seem to be about whether Barrett should be nominated to the Supreme Court, however; the ads reveal to truly be about furthering party politics under the guise of discussing Barrett's nomination. Through these ads, the Democratic party and Liberal groups furthered their agenda of protecting the Affordable Care Act and revealing cases of hypocrisy in the Republican party. Similarly, the Republican party and Conservative groups used ads on the topic of Barrett's nomination to inform Americans about the Democrat's potential court-packing agenda and to counter the ads targeting

Republican hypocrisy. The Republican party and Conservative groups also used the ads to strengthen their stance on a strong family life and religious beliefs in politics. Finally, the Pro-Barrett ads were designed to overwhelm the public debate of her nomination and offered as inoculation against potential attacks on her beliefs (Compton & Ivanov, 2016). The advertisements presented in this set did not have the goal of persuading or dissuading politicians and the public of whether or not Barrett should be nominated to the Supreme Court or the legitimacy of this nomination, the ads were created to further the agenda of the respective political organizations on the eve of a contested election.

References

Biesecker, M. (2020, October 26). *Barrett ads tied to interest groups funded by unnamed donors.* AP NEWS. https://apnews.com/article/donald-trump-amy-coney-barrett-elections-us-supreme-court-courts-800810431929326355c9ef0a78bfee40

Chotiner, I. (2020, October 14). *How Amy Coney Barrett could affect the future of the Affordable Care Act.* The New Yorker. https://www.newyorker.com/news/q-and-a/how-amy-coney-barrett-could-affect-the-future-of-the-affordable-care-act

Compton, J., & Ivanov, B. (2016). Vaccinating voters: Surveying political campaign inoculation scholarship. *Annals of the International Communication Association, 37*(1), 251-283.

Lovelace, R. (2020, September 21). *Judicial Crisis Network spending $2.2 mil on ad blitz boosting forthcoming Supreme Court nominee.* The Washington Times. https://www.washingtontimes.com/news/2020/sep/21/judicial-crisis-network-spending-22-mil-ad-blitz-b/

Miller, E. (2020, October 2). *Political ads bombard airwaves in battle over Supreme Court.* OpenSecrets News. https://www.opensecrets.org/news/2020/10/supreme-court-vacancy-acb/

Moore, E. (n.d.). *What Is Court Packing?* https://www.rutgers.edu/news/what-court-packing

Papenfuss, M. (2020, September 20*). Supreme Court Hypocrite Lindsey Graham blistered by own words in Lincoln Project ad. HuffPost.* https://www.huffpost.com/entry/hypocrite-lindsey-graham-ad-lincoln

---

[i] Other ads ran attacking various senators for changing their procedural positions from the Cavanaugh nomination but were not included in the sample.

Chapter 25: The Lincoln Project – Success Story or Hype

Caroline McLean

Caroline is a Senior in Politics and International Affairs

The Lincoln Project, a political action committee formed in 2019 by current and former Republicans, generated significant media buzz in the 2020 United States Presidential Election. Though founders of the Lincoln Project identified as conservatives, they were determined to spark a nationwide movement with a singular mission: To "defeat Donald Trump and Trumpism at the ballot box." (The Lincoln Project, 2020). The Lincoln Project ads gained considerable viewership, despite the over-saturated media market of the 2020 election cycle. Indeed, their videos amassed millions of views. This chapter examines the history of the Lincoln Project, its purported mission, its tactics, and accomplishments, but it also investigates the core themes of Lincoln Project ads and analyze a subset that generated significant media attention in the 2020 election cycle.

History

The Lincoln Project was announced on December 17, 2019, in a New York Times op-ed by George Conway, Steve Schmidt, John Weaver, and Rick Wilson. Other co-founders include Jennifer Horn, Ron Steslow, Reed Galen, and Mike Madrid. The group states that they are "dedicated American protecting democracy" (Conway, et al., 2019). On their website homepage, the organization declares: "The Lincoln Project is holding accountable those who would violate their oaths to the Constitution and would put others before Americans" (The Lincoln Project, 2020). While the group acknowledges it has policy differences with Democrats, it also states that Democrats value constitutional values. "[T]he priority for all patriotic Americans must be a shared fidelity to the Constitution and a commitment to defeat those candidates who have abandoned their constitutional oaths, regardless of party," the mission statement reads. "Electing Democrats who support the Constitution over Republicans who do not is a worthy effort" (The Lincoln Project, 2020). The committee is named after Abraham Lincoln, who fought to keep the country unified. On February 27, 1860, Lincoln delivered his Cooper Union speech in Manhattan during his presidential campaign to be the first Republican president. Members of the Lincoln Project committee—

Schmidt, Wilson, Horn, Galen, Madrid, and Steslow—spoke in the same venue on the 160th anniversary of that talk, from the lectern that Lincoln had used (Williams, 2020).

While initially aimed to prevent the re-election of Donald Trump, the committee shifted to a pro-Joe Biden stance and announced its endorsement of Democratic presidential nominee Joe Biden in April 2020. Ron Steslow, one of the founders, even stated he would "vote blue no matter who" (Influence Watch, 2020). While the majority of the Lincoln Project's ads focused on the presidential election, the Lincoln Project also created ads backing Democrats in other races. The ads attacked Republican Senators Steve Daines, Cory Gardner, Martha McSally, Thom Tillis, Susan Collins, Joni Ernst, and Senate Majority Leader Mitch McConnell, all of whom were up for re-election in 2020. The Lincoln Project labeled this set of senators as enablers of Trump.

The Center for Responsive Politics found that the Lincoln Project raised $87,404,908 and spent $81,956,298 during the 2019-2020 election cycle. OpenSecrets.org reports that $51,406,346 came from individuals who had donated $200 or more, but the remaining amount came from small donors, an unusual proportion.

Tactics

What is the secret of the Lincoln Project's success? The founders argue that they simply used Republican strategies against potential Republican voters. Founder Rick Wilson said that they used "vernacular and language that is explicitly usually reserved for Republicans." (Dumenco, 2020). Joanna Weiss of Northeastern University's Experience magazine wrote that most of the ads: "pack an emotional punch, using imagery designed to provoke anxiety, anger and fear—aimed at the very voters who were driven to (Trump) by those same feelings in 2016", citing scientific research indicating that fear-mongering ads might be effective with Republican voters (Teacherken , 2020).

These tactics have been characterized as cutthroat and brutal. Wilson was not afraid to be vicious, saying, "Democrats play to win an argument; I play to win an election" (Williams, 2020). He went so far as to claim the Lincoln Project ads were "psychological warfare effort against the president and his administration and his lackeys and his campaign" (Dumenco , 2020). In Wilson's recent book, Wilson argued that Democrats must be willing to put "electoral realities ahead of progressive fantasies" (Williams, 2020). Many members of the staff of the Lincoln Project felt that Democrats were not willing to be vicious enough and saw themselves as filling that void. At one point, one of the founders, Edwards, tweeted: "We go low so you don't have to," but some of the Project leaders felt that it clashed with the idea of their goal to form a "coalition of the decent," and the tweet was deleted (Williams, 2020).

Presidential Ads

The ads generally revolved around four themes: COVID-19, the shattered economy, Trump's weakness on national security, and the President's "total disgracefulness." Economic inequality, climate change, and universal health care were not addressed, issues that the strategists did not think potential swing voters would care about. They chose to focus on a two-part strategy: blocking Republicans who had left the Republican Party from coming back and wedging or pushing voters away from Trump. Ads that the Project called wedges focused on the COVID-19 pandemic (Ferguson, 2020). Research showed it was powerful force of shifting voters away from Donald Trump.

The first Lincoln Project ad, *MAGA Church*, debuted on January 9th (The MAGA church, 2020). In this ad, the producers tried to reveal the hypocrisy of Trump's appeals to evangelical Christians. In the ad, Trump states that, "Evangelicals, Christians of every denomination, and believers of every faith have never had a greater champion—not even close—in the White House, than you have right now." As Trump comments, Matthew 7:15, a verse from the Bible, floats across the screen: "Beware of false prophets, which come to you in sheep's clothing, but inwardly they are ravening wolves." The video juxtaposes clips of Trump talking about faith and other crude comments made before and during his presidency. The clip also weaves lines of Evangelical Christian leaders praising Trump and praying over while Trump utters harsh, inflammatory lines such as "grab her by the pussy" and "If you don't support me, you're gonna be so goddamn poor." The ad was the only one of its kind that specifically targeted evangelical Christians but set the tone and style for the hundreds of other ads the Project would release. Rather than spending much of the ad highlighting what Democratic candidate Joe Biden stood for, the ads focused on attacking and destroying Trump and other Republican candidates' credibility. Usually, the ads used Trump or other Republican's words against them.

On March 17, 2020, the committee released a video, titled *Unfit*, which criticized Trump for his incompetent response to the COVID-19 pandemic (Unfit, 2020). This ad was one of the core themes the Lincoln Project chose to focus on throughout the 2020 presidential election. *Unfit* plays various speeches in which Trump proclaims the virus is a hoax and that he will quickly shut it down juxtaposed against the worsening pandemic and mounting death toll. It concludes with Trump stating: "No, I don't take responsibility at all" (2020). Once again, the ad flits back and forth between Trump's statements compared to reality. Other similar ads that focused on COVID-19 such as *Hospital, Covita,* and *Regeneron,* mocking Trump's responses to the pandemic.

The Project also sometimes re-worked former historic popular political ads, such as Ronald Reagan's "Morning in America." In 1984, Ronald Reagan framed his re-election campaign with the ad, showing that the economy had recovered from a severe recession and that he was responsible for the soaring employment rates and low housing costs. The video shows the quintessential prosperous American middle-class family. In early May, the Lincoln Project released a dystopian homage: *Mourning in America* (2020). The video recalled the narrator of the Reagan video, but with falling down houses, coronavirus patients, and unemployment lines. An American flag flew upside down. Republicans are reminded that Donald Trump has not delivered on the results of Ronald Reagan. While Reagan lifted Americans out of poverty following the recession, the Lincoln Project highlighted how Trump had failed, leaving only a ruined economy in his wake.

On June 5, 2020, the Lincoln Project released an ad, *Mattis,* that repeated criticism of Trump by former Secretary of Defense Jim Mattis, a retired Marine Corps general, following the Lafayette Square and Saint John's Church attacks against protesters. (Mattis, 2020). It shows the differences between "a coward and a commander," comparing "the coward Trump who dodged the draft" and "the commander Mattis lead American troops for forty years." The ad displays quotations of Mattis's op-ed piece in the Atlantic, where Mattis wrote: "Donald Trump is the first president in my lifetime who does not try to unite the American people—does not even try. Instead he tries to divide us." The ad asks its viewers: "Who do you trust: the coward or the commander?"

On June 17, 2020, the Lincoln Project released an ad entitled *#TrumpIsNotWell,* showing a video of Trump walking slowly and haltingly down a ramp at West Point and a video of Trump appearing to struggle to lift a glass of water, with narration suggesting that Trump was physically unfit (#TrumpIsNotWell, 2020). The voice-over said: "Something's wrong with Donald Trump. He's shaky, weak, trouble speaking, trouble walking. So why aren't we talking about this? …The most powerful office in the world needs more than a weak, unfit, shaky president. Trump doesn't have the strength to lead, nor the character to admit it." The ad is another example of using Trump's tactics against him. When Trump ran against Hillary Clinton in the 2012 Presidential election, he mocked Clinton's fainting episode as a 9/11 memorial event during a bout of pneumonia. Rumors spread amongst Trump's supporters that she had Parkinson's disease, advanced dementia, or bizarrely that she had died and been replaced with a body double.

Senate Ads

One of the most disturbing Lincoln Project ads that garnered considerable attention was the graphic ad titled, *Parasite* (2020). The ad has been called "shameful" by some, as the ad contains gross images of decaying animals and disgusting creepy-crawly bugs. "Some animals are parasitic," a sinister voice says. "They drink the lifeblood of their host, infect whatever they touch and spread like a virus. They're often right under our noses camouflaged, convincing their hosts they're not harmful at all." The disturbing ad refers to how Graham formerly was a follower of John McCain, calling Trump a "race-baiting, xenophobic, religious bigot." After McCain's death, Graham's rhetoric changed, becoming an outspoken supporter of Trump.

The Lincoln Project also released an ad targeting Maine GOP Sen. Susan Collins, who was up for re-election in November (Susan Collins, Do Your Job, 2020). The ad said: "Great, independent leaders rise from Maine's hard soil. Always have and always will," the ad begins over images of the state's past leaders. The ad then criticizes her as a "Trump stooge," saying: "Collins isn't an independent. She's a fraud. Mitch McConnell and Donald Trump control her voice. She makes excuses for corruption, for criminality, for cruelty, all while pretending she's worried." The ad warns voters, "Susan Collins doesn't work for Maine, she works for them. And Maine deserves a leader, not a Trump Stooge."

Reception

The reception for Lincoln Project ads has been decidedly mixed. Democratic strategist James Carville praised the group as being more tenacious than Democratic PACs, saying, "Let me tell you, the Lincoln group and The Bulwark, these Never Trump Republicans, the Democrats could learn a lot from them. They're mean. They fight hard. And we don't fight like that" (Sohn, 2020). The group has also been hailed as patriotic. Jennifer Rubin wrote that: "They made their careers helping to elect Republicans, but in the era of Trump, they have put partisanship aside in the cause of patriotism and defense of American democracy. Their ads have been the most effective and memorable of the presidential campaign, singling Trump in a way Democrats have not quite mastered."

Others, however, have been far more critical. Andrew Ferguson wrote in *The Atlantic* that the ads are "personally abusive, overwrought, pointlessly salacious, and trip-wired with non sequiturs." *The New York Times* wrote in October 2020 that "The Lincoln Project ads have been dismissed by some as "anti-Trump porn," more concerned with going viral than moving voters."

Indeed, Project members were routinely accosted by Trump supporters in angry calls and emails. A Las Vegas caller: "Get the fuck out of my country, bitches." A caller from Pennsylvania said: "Fuck every last one of you motherfuckers! And when a civil war happens…duck." Other leaders, while supportive of the Project's work, were less sure of the actual effectiveness of the ads. Dan Pfeiffer, a former Obama aide who is now co-host of Pod Save America, said: "I think [the ads] are helpful. I think they are not as helpful as a lot of people think" (Kafka, 2020). He felt that a lot of the ads that generated the most buzz were also the ones that would not sway an undecided voter. Pfeiffer said, "Negative ads can still work on Trump. But they have to introduce new information to people, and they have to reach people where they are" (Kafka, 2020). His hypothesis is supported through data. A survey experiment by political scientists David Broockman and Joshua Kalla suggests that prior to the election people had heard plenty about Donald Trump. What they were lacking was information about Joe Biden, hearing far less about him. Broockman and Kalla found that "both positive and negative messages about Biden have significantly larger effects on stated vote choice than either positive or negative messages about Trump" (Yglesias, 2020).

The researchers observed that: "Democratic ads are made by committed Democrats, the money to air them is raised by committed Democrats from committed Democrats, and the decisions about which ads to invest in are also made by committed Democrats. Committed Democrats probably find anti-Trump ads to be inherently more entertaining, and the mining of Trump's record of saying and doing terrible things to be more rewarding than talking up Biden's fairly banal Democratic Party ideas."

The effectiveness of Project Lincoln Senate ads is also highly questionable. Founder Rick Wilson insists: "We have very specific metrics in Arizona, Georgia, Pennsylvania, Michigan and Wisconsin, that we played a decisive role" (Dumenco, 2020). What do those polls show? Wilson claims that Lincoln Project ads, "[M]oved former Republicans, independents and current Republicans over what we call the Bannon Line. Steve Bannon, who is no fan of us, said, early in the process, if these guys can move 2% or 3% of the Republican vote, Trump is gonna lose. Well, from the metric we're showing, in the swing states, where we spent I would say 80% to 85% of our resources, we moved the Bannon Line, and crossover Republican voters, between 9% and 13%" (Dumenco, 2020).

The data appears to call Wilson's claims into question. Despite the Lincoln Project spending $12 million in seven Democratic candidates in key races to flip the chamber back to the Democrats, however, Republicans won in all seven races. Senator Lindsey Graham won by almost ten points and Senator Susan Collins won by nine points. Mitch McConnell, the Republican Senate leader from Kentucky, was also a prominent Lincoln Project target. He won by twenty points (Concha, 2020). Indeed, one wonders if the Lincoln Project would have been even more successful if they were less antagonistic against Trump and instead highlighted the strengths of candidate Joe Biden. While the ads discussed in this chapter were ones that went "viral" on social media, they were not necessarily the ones that won swing voters to their side. Indeed, the Democratic Super PAC Priorities USA found that "the better the ad did on Twitter, the *less* it persuaded battleground swing voters" (Wulfsohn, 2020). This is largely because the viral ads were meant to shock, dismay, and horrify viewers, but failed to concretely say why Joe Biden or other Democratic candidates would be better. Instead of providing an optimistic alternative, they left viewers feeling uneasy and sad. This was the fatal flaw of the Lincoln Project: Too often, the ads were geared towards voters that were already leaning towards voting for Biden, rather than targeting voters who cared more about the issues at stake than the character of the president.

While it will remain unclear how effective the ads were, the Lincoln Project is determined to continue its work after the 2020 election. Many of the founders, however, are no longer registered Republicans. *The New Yorker* observed: "The Project's scorched-earth approach distinguishes it from similar organizations: the founders, some of whom have entirely shed their Republican identities, have left themselves no clear path of return" (Williams, 2020). Wilson and Schmidt are now registered Independents (Williams, 2020). The Lincoln Project states that they are committed to concrete expansions of voting rights after Trump is gone. This includes advocating for automatic voter registration and a restored Voting Rights Act. They will also continue fighting against efforts that "make it difficult for black or poor people to vote."

The 2020 Presidential election ad cycle would be incomplete without mention of the Lincoln Project. This review found, however, that despite the significant media attention focused on the Lincoln Project, it is unclear how much of a difference the PAC made.

References

Concha, J. (2020, November 15). *Lack of influence means it's time to dismiss the Lincoln Project.* The Hill. https://thehill.com/opinion/campaign/525985-targeted-harassment-lack-of-influence-say-its-time-to-dismiss-the-lincoln

Conway, G. T., Schmidt, S., Weaver, J., & Wilson, R. (2019, December 17). *We are Republicans, and we want Trump defeated.* New York Times. https://www.nytimes.com/2019/12/17/opinion/lincoln-project.html

Susan Collins, do your job (2020, January 22). The Lincoln Project, YouTube. https://www.youtube.com/watch?v=PgmXzmwaDhU

Dumenco, S. (2020, December 9). *The Lincoln Project's Rick Wilson on the ads that actually worked.* AdAge. https://adage.com/article/campaign-trail/lincoln-projects-rick-wilson-ads-actually-worked/2300051

Ferguson, A. (2020, June 30). *Leave Lincoln Out of It.* The Atlantic. https://www.theatlantic.com/ideas/archive/2020/06/tactics-lincoln-project/613636/

Influence Watch (Accessed 12/15/20). The Lincoln Project. https://www.influencewatch.org/political-party/lincoln-project/

Kafka, P. (2020, August 20). *What's really going on with the Lincoln Project, the anti-Trump, Republican-led PAC that's pissing off lots of people.* Vox. https://www.vox.com/recode/2020/8/20/21376571/lincoln-project-trump-twitter-tv-ads-strategy

Mattis (2020, June 5). The Lincoln Project, YouTube. https://www.youtube.com/watch?v=oYa8mEr3sJA

Mourning in America (2020, May 4). The Lincoln project, YouTube. https://www.youtube.com/watch?v=t_yG_-K2MDo

Parasite (2020, 2020, September 9). The Lincoln Project, YouTube. https://www.youtube.com/watch?v=qrJsW3dZov0&t=5s

Sohn, P. (2020. August 1). *The sweet revenge (and brilliance) of the Never Trumpers.* Chattanooga Times Free Press. https://www.timesfreepress.com/news/opinion/times/story/2020/aug/01/sohn-sweet-revenge-and-brilliance-never-trump/528723/

Teacherken (2020, August 11). *New Lincoln Project: "Moving Day"*. Daily Kos. https://www.dailykos.com/stories/1968340

#TrumpIsNotWell (2020, June 16). The Lincoln Project, YouTube. https://www.youtube.com/watch?v=NVy_LWM091g

The MAGA church (2020, January 9). The Lincoln Project, YouTube. https://www.youtube.com/watch?v=yoglNFN5-Js

Unfit (2020, March 17). The Lincoln Project, YouTube. https://www.youtube.com/watch?v=7gJgmkWJ6es

Williams, P. (2020, October 5). *Inside The Lincoln Project's war against Trump*. The New Yorker. https://www.newyorker.com/magazine/2020/10/12/inside-the-lincoln-projects-war-against-trump

Wulfsohn, J. A. (2020, December 9). *Study finds that viral ads from The Lincoln Project failed to sway swing voters during election: report*. Fox News. https://www.foxnews.com/media/the-lincoln-project-study-2020-election

Yglesias, M. (2020, June 9). *Study suggests Democrats should be running more ads about Biden, fewer about Trump.* Vox. https://www.vox.com/2020/6/9/21284758/broockman-kalla-biden-ads-trump-ads

Chapter 26: From Delusional to Dominant: Debate Dialogue in Political Advertising

Maggie Moran

Maggie is a Senior in Communication from Spring Lake, NJ

Introduction

Presidential debates have been an integral part of Presidential politics since the first Kennedy-Nixon debate in 1960. Although debates have inevitably evolved both in form and content, the core of the institution remains the same: "two (or more) people on a stage discussing topics raised by interlocutors, televised into the homes of the public" (Schroeder, 2020). Vice presidential debates also play an important role in the election process, as they serve to "highlight the presidential candidate's decision making and provide insight into the abilities of the vice presidential candidate" (Benoit & Airne, 2005). More recently, the influence of the media has greatly shifted public perception and discourse surrounding political debates. As Schroeder (2019) notes, debates have a new home on social media, where viewers can become active participants tweeting real-time reactions, Instagram-ing satirical memes, or ranting in Facebook posts. It is no surprise then that the two most recent election cycles in 2016 and 2020 have resulted in historic public interest, attracting record debate viewership. McKinney (2018) asserts that they were "a most unconventional, unpredictable, unprecedented, and on many occasions rather "unpresidential" presidential contest."

Debates have received ample attention in traditional media cycles. From newspapers to the evening news, traditional journalism, too, has a great influence on political cycles, elections, and debate commentary. Post-debate advertisements have also become an important part of consumer media, with dozens of commercials airing within hours of a debate's conclusion. Although post-debate advertisements have become standard fare, there is little to no academic/journalistic research on the topic. This study performs a content analysis of post-debate advertisements from the 2016 and 2020 elections to determine how debate footage is used in contemporary political advertising.

Literature Review

Carlin & Bicak (1993) contend that presidential debates are a prime focus in the electoral process for "informing and persuading voters." Debates engage voters and provide a process for evaluating candidates (Jennings, Bramlett, McKinney, & Hardy, 2020). Benoit and Airne (2005, p. 226) introduce the three main uses of functional discourse. The first is acclaims, which identifies a candidate's strengths. The second is attacks, or criticisms of an opponent, showcasing their weaknesses and decreasing that candidate's desirability. The third is defenses, or responses to the attacks, to refute weaknesses (Benoit & Airne, 2005). Research on previous debates found that within the debate acclaims are more common than attacks, and attacks more common than defenses. Would post-debate advertising follow the same pattern? I therefore investigated if positive (acclaim) advertisements are similarly more frequent than negative (attack or defense post-debate advertisements.

Benoit's functional discourse theory also asserts that presidential debate research and discourse is focused on perceptions of two topics: character, or candidate image, and policy issues (Benoit & Airne, 2005; Jennings, Bramlett, McKinney, & Hardy, 2020) Research also found that the topics of presidential debates favor policy over character 3 to 1, and public opinion indicates that policy matters more to voters than does character (Benoit & Airne, 2005). A recent Gallup poll found that a majority of the American public view Donald Trump as having lower ethical standards than all presidents since Nixon, yet according to a poll from the Survey Center on American Life, 60% of Americans say their opinion of Trump is based more on what he has done as president, while only 39% say it is based on his character (Cox, Streeter, Abrams, Clemence, 2020; Trump rated worse, 2018). For this reason, I posit that policy-focused post-debate advertisements will be more frequent than character-focused post-debate advertisements.

Although they may be considered much less significant than presidential debates, research shows that vice presidential debates can influence voters' opinions, voters' perceptions of the candidates, and their voting intentions (Holbrook, 1994; Benoit & Airne, 2005). Carlin & Bicak (1993) argue that VP debates serve an important educational function, and "help voters confirm their leanings." Although the 2016 Pence-Kaine debate drew a relatively-small audience of 37.2 million, the 2020 vice presidential Harris-Pence debate drew approximately 57.9 million viewers, making it the second most viewed vice presidential debate after the Biden-Palin debate in 2008, which drew approximately 70 million viewers (Media advisory, 2020). Many contend that the 2020 VP race is among the most unusual and consequential, with two presidential candidates over the age of 70 amidst a deadly pandemic (Busette, 2020). For this reason, I theorize that there will be a higher frequency of Vice presidential post-debate advertisements in 2020 than from 2016.

Research Question and Methodology

I posit two research questions concerning post-debate advertisements:

> RQ1: How are presidential debates used as political advertising?
>
> RQ2: Did post-debate advertisements differ between the 2016 and 2020 election cycles?

Procedure

79 post-debate advertisements (46 from the 2016 election, 33 from the 2020 election) were content analyzed for subject (democratic candidate, republican candidate), messaging (positive messaging (acclaims), negative messaging (attacks), topic (policy issue, character), source (democratic, republican, third party), and form (straight debate footage, mixed footage). The findings were analyzed for frequency.

Variables

Year, Subject, Candidate Role

The following variables-*year*, *subject*, and *candidate role*-were either present or absent. The variable *year* obviously distinguishes 2016 from the 2020 election. The variable *subject* indicated whether the advertisement focuses on the democratic candidate or republican candidate. The variable *candidate role* distinguished advertisements between presidential candidate and vice presidential candidates.

Positive/Negative Messaging

Also measured was whether the tone of the post-debate advertisement is positive or negative (i.e., in favor of or opposing the subject). For this analysis, an advertisement may be labeled 'positive' if a single candidate discusses their achievements, character, or policies in a constructive and pragmatic way. An advertisement may be identified as 'negative' if a candidate or third-party attacks, insults, or belittles another candidate's achievements, character, or policies.

Source

The first source identified is the democratic party. For the 2016 election, this includes groups such as The Hillary Clinton Campaign, Hillary Clinton Victory Fund, Hillary Clinton for America. For the 2020 election it primarily included the Biden Harris Campaign. The second source identified is the republican party. For this analysis, this group mostly includes the Trump/Pence campaign. The third source is third party groups, including The Lincoln Project, Moveon.org, Correct the Record, among others.

Topic

The variable topic was split into two subgroups. The first topic is policy issue, meaning the advertisement focused on one or more specific policies. The second topic is character (bolstering/attacking). This group includes "acclaim" ads in which candidate's discuss their own character or accomplishments, or "attack" ads in which one candidate diminishes or attacks another candidate's character or failures.

Message Form

For this analysis, message form was also split into two subgroups, straight debate footage or mixed footage. Straight debate footage consisting solely of clips for the debate itself. Mixed message form will also include non-debate footage, including news clips or "outside" interviews.

Results

My first anticipation was that positive post-debate advertisements will be more frequent than negative post-debate advertisements. This supposition was backed with research from Benoit and Airne (2005) that claimed acclaims (positive discourse) are the most common use of campaign discourse. The Benoit and Airne findings were internal to the debate, extracted political advertising might (or not) follow that pattern. The results from Table 1 show that only 29.9% of post-debate advertisements from 2016 and 2020 had positive messaging or were centered on a candidate's acclaims. 70.89% of all advertisements analyzed contained negative messaging, including attacks or defenses from one candidate to the other regarding topics such as policy, character, or experience. Some of this disparity may be due to the goals of in-debate civility and more aggressive advertising, yet in the last two cycles the explanatory differences may have shifted making the two message forms more alike.

Table 1: Content Analysis Results

	Debate Usage in Ads (Total 79)		
Year	2016	44	55.70%
	2020	35	44.30%
Subject	Democrat	34	43.04%
	Republican	42	53.16%
	Both	3	3.80%
Candidate	Presidential	66	83.54%
	Vice Pres.	13	16.46%
Messaging	Positive	23	29.11%
	Negative	56	70.89%
Source	Democratic	17	21.52%
	Republican	17	21.52%
	Third Party	45	56.96%
Topic	Policy Issue	30	37.97%
	Character	49	62.03%
Message Form	Straight Debate	44	55.70%
	Mixed	35	44.30%

Although more negative than positive advertising does not support previous findings, it is consistent with media coverage and reports of the former president's aggression communication style, including insults, hand gestures, and facial expressions (Montez & Brubaker, 2019). Montez and Brubaker (2019) noted patterns of heightened aggression among trailing candidates against front-runners. They also concluded that Trump's nonverbal aggression may have "resonated with audiences out of familiarity with his persona," but nod to past research for future candidates that shows both verbal and nonverbal aggression does not resonate well with voters (Montez & Brubaker, 2019).

My second premise was the idea that public opinion indicates that policy matters more to voters than character (Benoit, 2007; Benoit & Airne, 2005). Question two predicted that policy-focused post-debate advertisements will be more frequent than character-focused post-debate advertisements. The results shown in Table 1 indicate that 37.97% of post-debate advertisements focused on policy issues, while 62.03% focused on character. These findings are again inconsistent with previous debate discourse research.

My third supposition theorized that there will be a higher frequency of post-vice presidential debate advertisements from 2020 than 2016. Although they see much less viewership than presidential debates, vice presidential debates can play an integral role. The results from Table 2 show that only 2.27% of post-debate advertisements focused on the vice presidential candidate in 2016, while Table 3 shows that 34.29% of post-debate advertisements focused on the vice presidential candidates. This data suggests that the 2020 vice presidential candidate was more consequential, at least as inferred from frequency. This may be due to heightened interest given the presidential candidate's age, as well as external factors including race, gender, and the COVID-19 pandemic. It may also intersect with the nature of advertising goals to uniquely drive these other issues.

Table 2 Results from 2016

Debate Usage in Ads- 2016 (Total 44)			
Subject	Democrat	18	40.91%
	Republican	26	59.09%
Candidate	Presidential	43	97.73%
	Vice Pres.	1	2.27%
Messaging	Positive	9	20.45%
	Negative	35	79.55%
Source	Democratic	10	22.73%
	Republican	11	25.00%
	Third Party	23	52.27%
Topic	Policy Issue	19	43.18%
	Character	25	56.82%
Message Form	Straight Debate	26	59.09%
	Mixed	18	40.91%

Table 3 Results from 2020

Debate Usage in Ads-2020 (Total 35)			
Subject	Democrat	18	50%
	Republican	17	50%
Candidate	Presidential	23	65.71%
	Vice Pres.	12	34.29%
Messaging	Positive	14	40.00%
	Negative	21	60.00%
Source	Democratic	7	20.00%
	Republican	6	17.14%
	Third Party	22	62.86%
Topic	Policy Issue	11	31.43%
	Character	24	68.57%
Message Form	Straight Debate	18	51.43%
	Mixed	17	48.57%

Discussion

Benoit's functional discourse theory claimed that candidates tend to use acclaims, or positive messaging more than attacks, and attacks more than defenses in debate rhetoric. However, the findings of this study, shown in Tables 1- 3, show that post-debate advertisements were overwhelmingly negative. This could be for several reasons, the first being President Trump's unconventional and unpresidential personality. Psychologists Steven J. Rubenzer and Thomas R. Faschingbauer found that Trump exhibits traits very unlike previous presidents: incredibly high extroversion and very low on agreeableness (McAdams, 2016). Research on the topic suggests that extroverts "tend to take high-stakes risks" and that less-agreeable people "rarely question their deepest convictions" (McAdams, 2016). These qualities could explain the president's inconsistent debating style. Furthermore, Montez and Brubaker (2019) believe Trump's aggressive discourse (verbal and non-verbal) heightened aggression among other candidates, providing a possible explanation for the significant percentage of negative messaging from 2016 and 2020 post-debate advertisements. In other words, the 2020 in-debate exchange may have been more like the aggressive political ads than in former cycles.

Functional discourse theory also posited that presidential debate discourse is focused primarily on character and policy issues. Benoit and Airne found that debate topics, as well as public opinion, favor policy over character. This claim is backed up by a public poll that found 60% of Americans judge Trump more on what he has done as president, and only 39% of Americans judge him based on character. It is worth considering, however, that respondents characteristically say they prefer issue-talk when in fact their major decision criteria are character-based (Brooks & Geer, 2007).

This research was again conflicting with the findings of this study. Tables 1-3 show that approximately 62% of post-debate advertisements from 2016 and 2020 focused on character, and only 38% focused on policy issues. The 2016 and 2020 debates were filled with character attacks focused on personal drama – Clinton's emails, Trump's sexual exploits, Hunter Biden's tax returns. A study conducted at the University of Amherst Massachusetts analyzed the language of past election debates, researchers found that the tone of Presidential debates has grown significantly more critical over the last three campaign cycles (SBS Students Find Increase, 2020). The study also found that Trump's strategy in all debates showed a strong reliance (around 65-75%) on personal attacks. This unprecedented shift in tone provides a basic explanation for the increase in character-related debate content, as the material used to create the advertisements is dependent on this content.

As noted previously, vice presidential debates can play an integral role in educating, influencing and shaping voters perceptions and intentions. While historically lower viewership among vice presidential debates suggests low public interest in the matter, record viewership, as well as an 32% increase in post-vice-presidential debate advertisement shows support for Q3. This data suggests that the 2020 VP race is more important to the public than in the past, perhaps due to the highly consequential nature of the presidential race.

Ultimately, this study answered RQ1 (How are presidential debates used in political advertising?) in unprecedented and unexpected ways. The data shows that post-debate advertisements shared predominantly negative messaging and focused more on candidates' character than policy issues. In response to RQ2 (Did post-debate advertisements differ between the 2016 and 2020 election cycles?), the data represented a large jump in vice presidential advertisements, showed a slight increase in positive messaging and a 12% increase in character related content.

While my three predictions were consistent with previous research, they were not reflected in the empirical data. One overarching explanation for this discontinuity may be the extreme circumstances of the 2016 and 2020 elections: the first female presidential candidate and the first black female vice presidential candidate, a president most widely known as a reality TV personality, national reckonings regarding race and gender, and a worldwide pandemic. These variables all undoubtedly impacted the nature of these two election cycles, making them unlike anything the nation has seen before. Thus, this analysis may ultimately be a process of comparing apples and oranges.

Conclusion

This study aimed to answer how presidential debates are used in political advertising throughout election cycles. While there is little to no literature on the topic, previous research surrounding presidential and vice presidential debates informed the hypotheses posited. This study provides evidence of evolving practice. The data from this study suggests that the 2016 and 2020 debates broke several norms, and seemingly strayed far from previous research including Benoit's functional discourse theory of campaigns, as well as years of polling data on public opinion. However, further analysis suggests that the collection of post-debate advertisements from the 2016 and 2020 election cycles exhibited a new era of debate dialogue, characterized by unusually dominant personas and the intersectionality of gender and race, as well as a nation under the distress of a pandemic. Together, these variables suggest that rather than this analysis contradicting previous research, it supplements it with new and incomparable data. In conclusion, the results of this study proved that external factors and events, such as global and national events, can make a significant difference in an election cycle. The COVID-19 pandemic, the modern civil rights movement 'Black Lives Matter,' and an emphasis on gender equality are just some of the factors that shaped the 2016 and 2020 presidential races. The last two election cycles have been among the most unpredictable, unpresidential, and unconventional in American history, and have thus generated a new category of data for study.

References

Benoit, W. & Airne, D. (2005). A functional analysis of American Vice Presidential Debates. *Argumentation and Advocacy, 41,* 2005, pp. 225–236.

Benoit, W. (2007). *Communication in political campaigns.* Peter Lang.

Brook & Geer (2007). Beyond negativity: the effects of incivility on the electorate. *American Journal of Political Science, 51*(1), 1-16.

Busette, C. (2020). *Did the Vice Presidential Debate matter? It did, and it wasn't good for Trump.* Brookings, 2020, https://www.brookings.edu/blog/how-we-rise/2020/10/08/did-the-vice-presidential-debate-matter-it-did-and-it-wasnt-good-for-trump/

Carlin, D., & Bicak, P. (1993). Toward a theory of vice presidential debate purposes: An analysis of the 1992 Vice Presidential Debate. *Argumentation and Advocacy, 30(2).* American Forensic Association, 119-130.

Cox, D.A, Streeter, R., Abrams, S.J., Clemence, J. (2020). *Socially distant: How our divided social networks explain our politics.* The Survey Center on American Life. https://www.americansurveycenter.org/research/socially-distant-how-our-divided-social-networks-explain-our-politics/

Holbrook, T. (1999). Political learning from Presidential Debates. *Political Behavior, 21*(1), Springer, 1999, pp. 67–89.

Jennings, F.J., Bramlett, J.C, McKinney, M.S., & Hardy, M. M. (2020) Tweeting along partisan lines: Identity-motivated elaboration and Presidential Debates." *Social Media + Society, 6*(4), 2020, 2056305120965518. doi:10.1177/2056305120965518.

McAdams, D. (2016). *The mind of Donald Trump.* The Atlantic. https://www.theatlantic.com/magazine/archive/2016/06/the-mind-of-donald-trump/480771/

McKinney, M.S. (2018). Political campaign debates in the 2016 elections: Advancing campaign debate scholarship. *Argumentation and Advocacy, 54*(1-2). 72–75.

Montez, D.J., & Brubaker P.J. (2019). Making debating great again: U.S. Presidential candidates' use of aggressive communication for winning Presidential Debates. *Argumentation and Advocacy, 55*(4), 282–302.

Media advisory: 2020 Vice Presidential Debate draws 57.9M viewers (2020, October 8). Neilson. https://www.nielsen.com/us/en/press-releases/2020/media-advisory-vice-presidential-debate-of-2020

SBS students find increase in use of personal attacks during Presidential Debates (2020. October 9). Univ of Massachusetts DACSS program. https://www.umass.edu/sbs/data-analytics-and-computational-social-science-program/news/research/sbs-students-find-increase-use-personal-attacks-during-presidential-debates

Schroeder, A. (2020). *From JFK to Trump: The evolution of U.S. Presidential Debates*. Routledge.

Trump rated worse than other modern-day Presidents on ethics (2018). Gallup. https://news.gallup.com/poll/242129/trump-rated-worse-modern-day-presidents-ethics.aspx

Chapter 27: Modern Political Campaigning: Assessing Michael Bloomberg's Use of Memes

Elizabeth Maline

Elizabeth is a Senior in Communication from Tenafly, NJ

The use of various forms of digital communication has grown rapidly to the point where social media has become one of the most popular internet services in the world. Social media platforms provide people with unlimited access to new information and supply users with an avenue for social and political participation, where they may not have previously found an avenue. One form of digital communication that has become of interest in recent years, especially in the realm of political communication, is internet memes. Combining aspects of language, society, popular culture and digital technology, internet memes have been described as "artifacts of participatory digital culture" (Ross & Rivers, 2017b). Memes can be powerful pieces of visual rhetoric packaged in a simple form. When considering the relationships between citizens' media use and their political decision-making, it is easy for memes to get overlooked because they may not appear to be as substantive as traditional media or even blogging. However, a successful interpretation of memes requires knowledge of current issues, recognition of the intended audience, and a universal sense of humor to strike the right chord with viewers. As Dan Pfeiffer, former White House Communications Director said, "Every policy, speech, interview, tweet, meme, video and photograph needs to be thought of as a piece of content that can be used to persuade voters" (CNN Business). While much of this content has previously been created by social media users, political campaigns, such as Michael Bloomberg's presidential campaign, sought to develop social media strategies and formulate content, like memes, themselves. Given their prominence in the digital sphere, it is useful to examine the role of memes in political messaging and how they portray candidates.

Review of Literature

A meme, in modern context, can be defined as a virtually transmitted photograph that is embellished with text and pokes fun at a cultural symbol, social idea, or person (Gleick, 2011). They take the form of captioned photos with block text or hastily constructed cartoons that are intended to by funny, often to publicly ridicule human behavior. Memes are often described as snarky, witty, angry, sarcastic, or poignant in tone and are more likely to mock a person or idea than to offer support (Huntington, 2017). The intention of many memes is to express a particular viewpoint, idea or to persuade, often through different forms of humor including irony, parody and sarcasm, which are often easier for people to relate to rather than overtly political or academic content (Ross & Rivers, 2017b). They are particularly popular among young people, as they reference pop culture and circulate quickly on social media. Though they are typically created by ordinary social media users, political campaigns have recently employed large-scale social media campaigns, which include the internal production of memes, in order to boost their candidate's popularity.

Memes can both be reflective of and contribute to larger public discussion about current issues. Social media users often employ creativity to create memes that introduce new ideas about culturally relevant people, while also creating memes as a reactionary tool to amplify certain events or actions by individuals. Additionally, meme consumers may be unknowingly engaging with political information in a format that feels more light-hearted or playful to them, which is significant given many citizens' citing of a lack of interest in politics. In general, people most often come into contact with memes on social media platforms like Facebook, Instagram and Twitter, though they can also be found on Google or Reddit and are often shared among groups of people via direct messaging.

Though internet memes are a contemporary phenomenon, the history of the study of memes dates back surprisingly far, to 1976. Richard Dawkins, a leader in the study of memetics, introduced the concept of 'memes' in his book "The Selfish Gene" (Fazal, 2018). The term meme originally comes from the Greek word "mimeme", which means "to imitate" (Fazal, 2018). As early as World War I, memes were used in the form of satirical texts, images, and artistic expressions. Poets and artists were hired to create cartoons and messages, which could be publicized through posters and newspapers (Leong, 2015). The use of humor and satire as political commentary is also well documented throughout history and has always been an important part of political discourse in society. Research says that political satire or entertainment matters when it comes to how people participate in and perceive politics (Huntington, 2017). Since the emergence of media, humor has been used as an instrument to comment and criticize politicians and political movements (Kulkarni, 2017). In fact, the history of humor being used as a tool formerly dates to stories and pictures in anti-Nazi comics (Kulkarni, 2017), although it likely adorned societies since the exchange of messages.

Studies show that political memes are a distinct internet meme genre not dissimilar to other forms of humorous political media (Huntington, 2017). A decade ago, the idea of using memes for political ends was a niche pursuit, largely employed by extremist internet groups (Haddow, 2016). They were viewed as vehicles through which activists could call out and embarrass the political elite (Haddow, 2016). Now they are popularized such that most any social media user can creating and sharing their own political memes. This is made easier than ever given social media's low barriers to entry. Through the creation of memes, citizens can express their political opinions and be a part of debates and discussions which cannot be had through traditional mediums (Shifman 2013). In fact, many political groups that gather on social media use memes to introduce new ideas to others with the hope of affecting real political change (Haddow, 2016). Various researchers mention that exposure to political humor increases political attention and helps people, especially digital natives, learn about and promote political issues important to them. This also leads to an increase in political efficacy and interest in politics, pointing to the reason why scholars have recently placed importance on studying political memes (Kulkarni, 2017). As memes are so rapidly created, manipulated, and shared, they provide an ideal tool for responding to current events through humor.

In the U.S., internet memes began circulating on a widespread scale in 2008 and 2012, but arguably reached a new level of creation and distribution in 2016 (Ross, Rivers, 2017). A study that analyzed the use of humor within Internet memes during the 2012 U.S. presidential election demonstrated how memetic campaigns can potentially impact how the public views certain candidates and even votes (Ross, Rivers, 2017). For instance, memes addressing Mitt Romney's "binders full of women", which highlighted and amplified his unpopularity with women voters (and how "unwoke," a term not yet invented, he was). Conversely, the series of memes known as "texts with Hillary," although not overtly political in nature, had a positive impact on the public image of Hillary Clinton (Ross, Rivers, 2017b). Another recent political meme includes the Ted Cruz Zombie Killer meme. Its influence is demonstrated in the fact that many voters really thought there was a connection between Cruz and the Zombie Killer (Tron, 2018). Whether this significantly affected voting patterns is something discussed later in this section. Regardless, researchers acknowledge that the sheer volume of memes to emerge as part of the 2016 election played a major role in influencing both popular and flailing campaigns.

A study, however, that examined the popular "Pepe the Frog" meme discussed how the 2016 election proves that internet memes are not always successful relational attempts (Riemensperger 2018). In 2016, many political communication campaign teams viewed memes as an equivalent to events such as a candidate's barbecue event to appeal to rural farmers, or an elementary school book reading to appeal to parents (Riemensperger 2018). These performative acts can help candidates form symbolic relationships with identities they do not necessarily hold, like memes, but can also backfire (Riemensperger 2018). For example, the Clinton campaign's attempts to identify with black and young voters were met with derision when she attempted to get voters to "Pokémon GO to the polls," and admitted that she actually carries hot sauce in her bag, tapping into a popular Beyoncé lyric (Riemensperger 2018). Riemensperger notes that the most successful memetic content during the 2016 election, measured by engagement, were memes originally created and distributed by ordinary people within political communities (Riemensperger 2018). This is how meme "lineages" (continuous reincarnations of a meme, like Pepe the Frog), which tend to spark significant engagement, can develop. The analysis finds that political campaigns benefit most by focusing on collaborating with these communities rather than broadcasting original content. Whether or not the candidate's own words are true or genuine, the third-party content creation is often perceived as more authentic.

Given the popularity of memes and their representation of significant aspects of pop culture, scholars point out that although politicians may not appreciate being the target of a meme, it does at least indicate that they are in some way culturally relevant. The 2016 U.S. presidential election was a demonstration in the continuously increasing use of media as a form of political engagement and active citizenship (Ross & Rivers, 2017b). In the 2016 election, internet memes provided researchers with insight into how they were employed during the Democratic presidential primary and the general election campaign to, on the surface, make a joke or a comment, but on a more critical level to engage with the political process and reveal a political position (Ross & Rivers, 2017a).

The growth in popularity of internet political memes must be viewed in the context of the growing popularity of social media as a political tool. A Pew Research study found that there have been increases in the number of adults using the internet and social media sites, as well as an increase in the number who engage with various forms of political activity on social media sites, using social media websites specifically for political activities (Anderson & Perrin, 2019). In 2016, more Americans named Facebook as the site they used most often for political information in the month leading up to election day than any other site, including those of high-profile news organizations such as Fox News, CNN, and major national newspapers (Garrett, 2019). Studies suggest that the number of adults who deliberately engage with political material is increasing, with percentages relatively balanced between those users who identified as Democrats and those who identified as Republicans (McClure, 2016). The shift in the public's media allegiances toward digital sources has rendered social media a far more viable and effective political tool (Owen, 2019). Political campaigning on social media platforms, whether on behalf of voters or political campaigns themselves, has become a core feature of contemporary political systems around the world (Dimitrova and Matthes, 2018). Arguably most relevant is that researchers have found, across a variety of different models, that well-executed social media campaigning seems to help win votes (Bright, Hale, Ganesh, Bulovsky, Margetts, & Howard, 2017).

Not only do an increasing number of people use social media to consume and share political information, but there is also a growing trend of people who use social media to create original political content. Media companies are no longer the sole creators of news and entertainment. Instead, digital media technologies and social networks allow regular people to contribute to the collection of publicly available media content through their online actions (Huntington, 2017). Further, traditional media platforms are covering what happens on social media platforms, through a process sometimes described as inter-media agenda setting (Bright, Hale, Ganesh, Bulovsky, Margetts, & Howard, 2017). Therefore, social media attention can often lead to attention from other media, which helps expose the candidate to additional audiences.

One of the many benefits political campaigns see in campaigning on social media is that they can amplify their messages to even larger audiences. Political campaigners use memes as a medium for communicating with digital native eligible voters. Attracting the support of young voters can be a key ingredient for success, as voters ages 18 to 24 make up about 12% of the U.S. electorate according to U.S. Census Bureau data. As young people continue to use social media to communicate and share ideas with others, candidates can best convey their messages to younger voters by meeting them on the platforms they use. As Elia Rathore notes in the *New York Times*, "The language of social media is different than other medias…the younger generations, like millennials and Gen Z, are more likely to use pop culture in their language…so pop culture now affects political language," (Rathore, 2019).

Though political memes are intended to influence how people feel about important political issues, there is consensus among researchers that people who encounter political memes are not moved ideologically by the memes. A recent study from Texas A&M University finds that memes favor extreme perspectives, given that they poke fun at a politician or party, therefore isolating a large portion of the electorate (Haddow, 2016). Participants whose political ideology matched that of the political memes they saw, as well as those who stated they agreed with the ideas presented by the memes, rated the memes as being more effective messages than did participants whose ideology differed from that of the memes, or than those who disagreed with the memes (Huntington, 2017). Results suggest that while memes hold potential for enhancing political engagement among a citizenry that is often seen as depoliticized, youths' perceptions of the memes do not allow for deterministic conclusions about their efficacy in this regard. There are also the possibilities participants will interpret memes differently or misinterpret them all together, as each viewer brings their individual experiences with them when they view the meme (Huntington, 2017). This complicates measuring their effectiveness. However, while politicians will likely not see voters' opinions or minds changed on specific issues, memes are instead beneficial and even made for the purpose of creating viral moments and generating earned media. Creating viral moments during a campaign is crucial, as media attention is expensive and name recognition is a vital ingredient for electoral success (Yasseri & Bright, 2016). Regardless of the message presented, a viral meme will launch the candidate into the popular culture and political conversation thereby putting the candidate on the voter's (specifically younger voters') radar.

Finally, researchers examined aggregate measures of online influence in the form of "clout scores" in the context of the United States 2012 elections. They found that politicians with more clout, meaning influence or power, were more successful. They also argued that candidates' social media use significantly increased their odds of winning in the 2010 US House of Representatives elections (Bright, Hale, Ganesh, Bulovsky, Margetts, & Howard, 2017). Obama's use of social media helped him achieve celebrity status among millennials, which contributed to his success (Chin, 2019). Young voters place value on and respect candidates they perceive as having clout, which can often be achieved by connecting with voters using the platforms and content they engage with, such as memes. As political scientist Bruce Bimber points out, "The exercise of power and the configuration of advantage and dominance in democracy are linked to technological change" (Owen, 2019). Who controls, consumes, and distributes information is largely determined by who is best able to navigate digital technology (Owen, 2019). Social media have emerged as essential intermediaries that political actors use to assert influence and attract younger voters.

Social media has increasingly become an integral aspect of campaign strategy and is a significant factor in determining the success of a campaign. While politicians have previously benefited from the content social media users have created about them, before recently they had not attempted to create this content themselves. However, Michael Bloomberg's 2020 presidential campaign garnered attention for producing memes as part of a larger social media campaign. While previous research on this topic has focused exclusively on how individual social media users interact with and share political memes, there is much to be explored regarding how political campaigns can leverage this trend and have begun to launch their own meme campaigns. Given that political campaigns are beginning to recognize not only social media, but also memes as a significant form of political communication, it is critical that this subject receives attention, and will be the subject of this study.

Research Question and Methodology

As social media use in campaigns has become a more mainstream practice, candidates are constantly struggling to find new ways to exert themselves in the crowded world of digital media, whether it's using new features of the various platforms or publishing groundbreaking content. Additionally, as social media trends are ever changing, campaigns must constantly keep up with what platforms and content are most popular to effectively campaign on social media, specifically with younger voters. Michael Bloomberg, a candidate for president of the United States in 2020, ran one of the most sophisticated, wide-spread, unique social media campaigns of any candidate. Part of this large campaign was a more specific and targeted campaign made up of memes. The Bloomberg campaign collaborated with Jerry Media, which manages a large portfolio of internet "influencers", or extremely popular content creators, whose followers amount to 60 million. Bloomberg paid the meme creators to post memes that took the form of direct message conversations with Bloomberg on Instagram.

The meme campaign was an ambitious and risky endeavor. While it is unclear whether or not the meme campaign was successful or unsuccessful given lack of information regarding voters' feelings about the campaign, it is clear with the benefit of hindsight that Bloomberg did not receive a high number of votes on Super Tuesday and ended his campaign for president the following day. As a candidate, he did not resonate with voters as he hoped he would despite his efforts and after exhibiting a promising start to his campaign.

This leads to a fundamental question: How did the use of the meme campaign portray Michael Bloomberg to the public? To answer this question, I conducted a close textual reading of 28 Bloomberg memes, assessing how they presented the candidate to the audience, in an effort to understand the social media commentary after a post. This was a comprehensive review of the campaign, as the memes I reviewed encompass the vast majority, if not the totality of all memes created. Specifically, I analyzed the text of the memes, any images present and how Bloomberg questioned and responded to the influencer. I obtained as many memes as possible from their original source on social media but relied on news articles and images on search engines for those I could not find in their original form. Since many of the memes have since been deleted, I relied on mainstream media outlets' reporting of the meme campaign and the specific memes to gather data. While many of the memes were created by the Bloomberg campaign team but posted by influencers who they paid, the campaign prompted a spin-off movement, in which influencers who were not included as part of the campaign created memes as well. These memes were viewed and analyzed but not emphasized as heavily as those created by the actual campaign.

Results

The analysis of the memes led to several conclusions about how Michael Bloomberg was portrayed. First, a Bloomberg campaign aide noted that the campaign wanted the memes to be self-referential and that the goal was to create a self-aware, ironic personality around Bloomberg (NPR, 2020). Though the campaign was meant to poke fun at Bloomberg's extreme wealth and emphasize his awareness of his fortune, the memes ultimately portrayed him as elitist. Bloomberg's excessive campaign spending and large fortune had already been discussed as part of the campaign, though Bloomberg tried to frame his spending as an act for the greater good in defeating Donald Trump. However, as can be seen in the content of the memes and in social media users' responses, the jokes about Bloomberg's wealth portrayed him, rather than diffusing the wealth issue, some saw the memes as trying to buy the election.

(continues on following page with Figure 1)

Figure 1

The first meme discussed (Figure 1) is Bloomberg's hyperbolic pitch which includes the promise "I'll give you a billion dollars", an outlandish amount of money to post a meme (Tiffany, 2020). In a meme that is not pictured because it was deleted from Instagram, an influencer says, "Of that [the meme] will cost like a billion dollars," before Bloomberg shoots back, "What's your Venmo?" The comments on these memes ranged from, "Billionaire trying to buy his way in *vomit emoji*", "Dude thinks he can just buy the presidency", "Bloomberg flexing a billion bucks like an Arab prince" "This is a clear example of what wealth can get you votes…Bloomberg's a billionaire and is able to pull in endorsements like this" and even "Oligarch inbound to buy our election". According to Vox, many of the negative comments specifically called out Bloomberg for his wealth, labeling him an "oligarch" (Ghaffary, 2020). This characterization reveals the extent to which Bloomberg is, perhaps unintentionally, portrayed as a wealthy elitist. Additionally, according to the Pew Research Center, most Americans want to limit campaign spending and say that big donors have greater political influence (Jones, 2018). Bloomberg is a billionaire who funded his own campaign, which may explain the negative feedback from social media users. However, this is not to say that the feedback was all negative. Other users recognized Bloomberg's self-deprecating humor regarding his wealth and responded, "F****** baller" and "Kind of a flex tho". Therefore, in attempting to make a light-hearted joke about his wealth, Bloomberg drew further attention to his privilege and elitism, which he was already trying to defend on the campaign trail. This meme exemplifies the way in which Bloomberg discusses money and contributes to the elitist stereotype of himself.

Figure 2

Figure 3

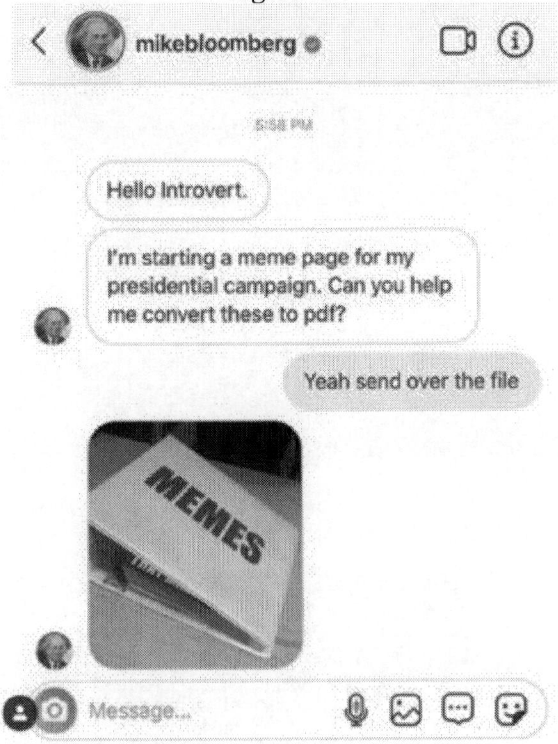

mikebloomberg
5:58 PM
Hello Introvert.
I'm starting a meme page for my presidential campaign. Can you help me convert these to pdf?
Yeah send over the file
MEMES
Message...

(continues on following pages)

Figure 4

Aside from being elitist, Bloomberg is also portrayed in the memes as old and not very in tune with social media. To acknowledge Bloomberg's age (78), it was likely the intention of the campaign to portray him this way in an effort to make him seem self-aware. This portrayal can be identified throughout a few of the memes. One of the influencers produces a meme (Figure 2) of Bloomberg reading a newspaper alongside the text "When you're researching meme influencers to target young voters." Figures 3 and 4 show Bloomberg keeping his memes in paper form in a binder, using a typewriter to write his memes, openly telling the influencers he does not understand the meme and telling one of the influencers to fax the meme to him before the markets close.

He also asks one of the influencers to post a viral video of him playing "Solitaire for iPhone" a reference to how his granddaughter showed him the meme accounts (Figure 5).

Figure 5

Finally, in many of the memes, Bloomberg addresses the influencers by Mr. or Mrs., which to any social media user is recognized as clearly too formal. The comments on the memes also reflect the idea that Bloomberg is portrayed as old and out of touch. They range from, "How do you do, fellow kids", "Mike Boomer" and "Wow, I had no idea Bloomberg was so hip and in touch with us youngsters!" It is possible that these memes resonated with voters, because although Bloomberg is attempting to connect with younger voters using memes as a method, it is unrealistic to believe he knows as much about them as a millennial or Generation Z voter would, given his age.

Figure 6

The third significant result I drew from my analysis was that Bloomberg is portrayed in many of the memes as desperate for online attention. In the beginning of most of the staged conversations with the meme influencers, Bloomberg asks them if they can make him "seem cool" for the upcoming Democratic primary (see Figure 6). This request implies that either he is not already cool, or at least recognizes that voters do not view him as cool. This could have been potentially problematic with voters, as young voters prefer a candidate they believe as having clout, as discussed in the Review of

Literature. In some of the other memes (see Figures 7, 8 and 9) Bloomberg asks if the meme influencers will promise to follow him back, reassure him that the meme is viral, or reassure him that the meme will make him look cool. This text relays a sense of insecurity and lack of knowledge of how to achieve his goals.

Figure 7

Figure 8

Figure 9

Social media users responded to these memes by commenting "Embarrassing", "Weak strategy. Sorry Mike this demographic has already chosen its old white man #bernie2020", "This guy is desperate AF", "Bernie is above this" and "This guy is trying so hard".

Though there is no data at present indicating whether or not the memes were "successful" in helping Bloomberg attract more votes, the level of exaggeration and inappropriateness (in terms of social media etiquette) signal that they were not received favorably among social media users. Given that the memes were texting conversations between Bloomberg and social media influencers, they did not follow many of the typical characteristics of a meme, which can be identified as images with block text over them. However, they do work to get the attention of social media users by attempting to critique and recontextualize beliefs social media users hold that Bloomberg is too old and not social media savvy. If the campaign's goal was to raise awareness of Bloomberg's candidacy to the youngest voting bloc, it would seem as though that goal was achieved given that the memes generated significant buzz on Instagram, as well as in various news outlets that reported on the social media activity. Regardless, the memes served as a vehicle the campaign used to reach voters who may not ordinarily be engaged in politics or support a candidate like Bloomberg based solely on his political history and apparent characteristics.

The campaign also intended to portray the candidate as aware of recent social media trends, though he is not an active social media user. The memes place emphasis on the image the candidate can create by engaging with prominent social media influencers, though this approach can be viewed as disingenuous given the focus on appearance rather than genuine characteristics. The strategy is indeed unconventional, given that political candidates of the past have sought to connect with voters on a personal, genuine level to attract their votes. Bloomberg appears to be taking a different rout of using sarcasm and humor directed at himself to connect with voters. Though there is a level of respect social media users attribute to those who can poke fun at themselves, based on comments on the meme posts, these acts were seen as over the top and even manipulative, as the end goal was to procure more votes that would only benefit Bloomberg.

Conclusions

It is evident that Bloomberg uses the meme campaign to engage with and attract youth and millennial voters by meeting them on the platforms they use and producing content they resonate with. This type of social media campaigning is unprecedented and experimental, as many of Bloomberg's fellow candidates utilized more traditional forms of media such as television interviews and advertisements or relied on user-generated rather than campaign-generated memes. Bloomberg's public asking of meme influencers to make memes for him places him in sharp contrast with his competitors, namely Bernie Sanders and Andrew Yang, who received this attention organically from their bases and without paying. Since Bloomberg had not previous benefited from user-generated content, he was forced to manufacture it by paying for it. Unlike some of his opponents, Bloomberg had never has never held federal office and may not be as well known to the average voter. Regardless of whether the memes helped to attract voters, judging by the number of media outlets reporting on the memes, they did generate buzz around the campaign.

In the memes, Bloomberg embraces the irreverent tone of social media. Though the campaign likely intended to portray Bloomberg as humorous, it is clear from the analysis that he was ultimately portrayed as elitist, old and out of touch and desperate for online attention. These attributes together to promote a negative candidate image of Bloomberg that many social media users were critical of. Ultimately, the memes made Bloomberg the target, in many of the users' comments, of the internet culture he was seeking to tap into and be viewed favorably by. Though sarcasm, irony and self-incrimination are essential elements of effective internet memes, they are only received positively among the public when the subject is within his or her bailiwick, or legitimate area of influence. Rather than working within the persona that voters already attributed to Bloomberg, he sought to insert himself into an alternative arena of which he is not normally a part, which backfired. It is possible that the negative image portrayed in the meme campaign contributed to Bloomberg's failed presidential campaign and lack of voter support, though that conclusion cannot be explicitly drawn. While the campaign certainly garnered attention on social media and helped portray Bloomberg as a prominent candidate, that attention did not translate into support from voters, which is clear given Bloomberg's dismal Super Tuesday performance. In fact, it may have contributed to a lack of support. Regardless of how successful the campaign may or may not have been in attracting voter support, the critical textual reading reveals that the campaign portrayed Bloomberg in a negative light and thus prompted negative reactions from social media users.

As social media and its features continue to evolve and develop, campaigns are constantly trying to stay ahead of trends and appear tech-savvy by utilizing these features. Additionally, with the abundance of political news in the world, candidates struggle to rise above the noise. While an intelligent social media campaign can certainly help a candidate, a poorly executed one can just as easily hurt a candidate. It is vital that campaigns consider the most effective ways to use social media for it to enhance the campaign. This study reveals future room for research in campaign-created meme and social media content. As other candidates seek to distinguish themselves from their competitors by making use of social media features, it may be useful for them to reference Bloomberg's approach as a model for this type of campaigning.

References

Bright, J., Hale, S., Ganesh, B., Bulovsky, A., Margetts, H., & Howard, P. (2019). Does campaigning on social media make a difference? Evidence from candidate use of Twitter during the 2015 and 2017 U.K. Elections. *Communication Research, 47*(7), 1–28.

Chin, C. (n.d.). *Social media and political campaigns.* http://www.gpprspring.com/social-media-political-campaigns#test-copy-of-retweets-hashtags-and-political-campaigns

Fazal, M. (2018, May 8). *Richard Dawkins told us what he thinks about memes.* Vice Australia. https://www.vice.com/en_us/article/d35ana/richard-dawkins-told-us-what-he-thinks-about-memes

Garrett, R. K. (2019). Social media's contribution to political misperceptions in U.S. Presidential elections. *Plos One, 14*(3), 1–16.

Ghaffary, S. (2020, February 14). *Bloomberg's Instagram meme ad campaign is backfiring.* Vox. https://www.vox.com/2020/2/14/21137102/mike-bloomberg-instagram-meme-ad-campaign-backfiring

Gleick, J. (2011, May). *What defines a meme?* Smithsonian Magazine, https://www.smithsonianmag.com/arts-culture/what-defines-a-meme-1904778/

Haddow, D. (2016, November 4). *Meme warfare: How the power of mass replication has poisoned the US election.* The Guardian. https://www.theguardian.com/us-news/2016/nov/04/political-memes-2016-election-hillary-clinton-donald-trump

Huntington, H. E. (2017). *The affect and effect of internet memes: Assessing perceptions and influence of online user-generated political discourse as media.* Dissertation, Colorado State University.

Jones, B. (2018, May 8). *Most Americans want to limit campaign spending.* Pew Research Center. https://www.pewresearch.org/fact-tank/2018/05/08/most-americans-want-to-limit-campaign-spending-say-big-donors-have-greater-political-influence/

Kulkarni, A. (2017). Internet meme and political discourse: *A study on the impact of internet meme as a tool in communicating political satire.* SSRN Electronic Journal, 6, 13–17.

Leong, P. P. Y. (2015). Political Communication in Malaysia: A study on the use of new media in politics. *JeDEM – EJournal of EDemocracy and Open Government, 7*(1), 46–71.

McClure, B. (2016). *Discovering the discourse of internet political memes.* New Prairie Press. In Proceedings. Adult Education Research Conference (pp. 291–293).

Memes are infiltrating the 2020 presidential election. CNN. (2020, February 27). https://www.cnn.com/videos/politics/2020/02/27/2020-presidential-election-memes-trump-bloomberg-cillizza-the-point.cnn

Owen, D. (2019). *The past decade and future of political media: The ascendance of social media.* Openmind. https://www.bbvaopenmind.com/en/articles/the-past-decade-and-future-of-political-media-the-ascendance-of-social-media/

Rathore, E. (2019, April 23). *Living in the age of political memes.* New York Times. https://www.nytimes.com/2019/04/23/style/india-pakistan-political-memes.html

Riemensperger, K. A. (2018). *Pepe's power: Internet memes, constitutive rhetoric, and political communities.* Master's thesis, Wake Forest University.

Ross, A. S., & Rivers, D. J. (2017a). Digital cultures of political participation: Internet memes and the discursive delegitimization of the 2016 U.S Presidential candidates. *Discourse, Context & Media, 16*, 1–11.

Ross, A. S., & Rivers, D. J. (2017b). Internet memes as polyvocal political participation. In *The Presidency and Social Media* (pp. 285–308), Shill, D., & J. A. Hendricks (Eds.), Routledge.

Sarwari, K. (2020, February 28). *The Bloomberg memes say he's got enough money to take risks. But what do they say about democracy?* News@Northeastern. https://news.northeastern.edu/2020/02/28/the-bloomberg-memes-say-hes-got-enough-money-to-take-risks-but-what-do-they-say-about-democracy/

Tiffany, K. (2020, February 28). *You can't buy memes.* The Atlantic. https://www.theatlantic.com/technology/archive/2020/02/bloomberg-memes-instagram-ads/607219/

Tron, G. (2018, October 5). *Where did the Ted Cruz-Zodiac killer meme come from?* Oxygen: True Crime Buzz. https://www.oxygen.com/martinis-murder/where-ted-cruz-zodiac-killer-meme-come-from

Perrin, A., & Anderson, M. (2019, April 10). *Share of U.S. adults using social media, including Facebook, is mostly unchanged since 2018.* Pew Research Center. https://www.pewresearch.org/fact-tank/2019/04/10/share-of-u-s-adults-using-social-media-including-facebook-is-mostly-unchanged-since-2018/

Shifman, L. (2013). Memes in a digital world: Reconciling with a conceptual troublemaker. *Journal of Computer-Mediated Communication, 18*(3), 362–377.

Chapter 28: Word Choice in Trump's 2020 Primary Advertisements

Haleigh Cadd

Haleigh is a Senior in Communication from Greensboro, NC

Professor Stefan Sonderling of the University of South Africa offered in 2017 that, "communication is war" (Chibuwe, 2017, p. 30). Regarding the 2019 presidential candidate campaigns, that is exactly how journalist Julie Wong for *The Guardian* described the primary Democratic candidates, whom were "battling each other." While Democratic candidates were at war, Wong says that Brad Parscale, the then campaign manager for Trump's campaign, was working to build strategies to target conservative voters (One Year inside Trump's Monumental Facebook Campaign, n.d.).

In general, political advertising is thought to "play a key role in electoral politics and in the engineering of consent in any polity…It enables politicians to gain votes or 'engineer consent,' while enabling the citizenry to make informed political decisions" (Chibuwe, 2017). Chibuwe argues political advertising's purpose is twofold, to influence voting and help "citizenry" be aware of facts demonstrated by the politician. It is up to the audience, to perceive the political advertisement as reputable. In the last election cycle, however, many in America labeled Trump ads "disinformation" (Romm, Stanley-Becker, Timberg, 2020); Chibuwe's essential claim nonetheless stands: political advertisements "enable politicians to gain votes."

As can be assumed, there is not enough manpower or access to assess the direct effectiveness of Trump's 2020 digital campaign (Corasaniti, 2020). All that is known with certainty is that Trump energetically was deemed according to some to have "ran the single best digital ad campaign has ever seen from any advertiser" (Bogost, Madrigal, 2020). This is despite the advertisements being labeled as "simplistic" not exactly "quality" (Ecarma, 2020).

This study's been rationale for focusing on the word choices in Trump-endorsed political advertisements is because language choice "attracts attention, motivates desire, evokes interest, creates conviction and gets action" in an advertisement (Zhihong Bai, 2018, p. 842). In other words, Bai argues that an advertisement cannot be rendered effective if the language choices are ineffective.

In a study conducted by Switzer, examining the effect of generic words on genders, it was concluded that "language choices have a profound effect on clarity and on any given message" (Switzer, 1990, p. 69). Switzer's conclusions support the idea that the effectiveness of ads can hinge on word choices. I have therefore examined word choices used in Trump's 2019-20 primary period advertisements. This study can inform additional understanding of online campaign reasoning–which due to coronavirus, in part, were forced to move online (Corasaniti, 2020).

Online political advertisements were prominent part of the 2020 presidential candidates' campaigning tools. There was, theoretically, a better chance of encountering more cultivated and strategized political ads. This study aims to present some insight on the 2020 "war like" communication.

Rationale

There is little research on word choices in political advertising. One study focusing on language, Professor Albert Chibuwe of the University at Johannesburg, studied political advertisements utilized by the Zimbabwe African National Union-Patriotic Front (ZANU-PF). In this context, these political advertisements were produced by the ZANU-PF to demonstrate and reclaim power in the government for the July 2013 elections. Chibuwe's findings illustrate that the ZANU-PF legitimized its rule by negatively framing the opposing party in its advertisements with words (Chibuwe, 2017).

In specific regards to word choices affecting the interpretation and reception of messages, a study done by Jo Young Switzer at Indiana University studied the differences in reception of generic words across both males and females, concluded that variations in language choice "clearly affect the degree to how stories were told…" (Switzer, 1990). In other words, Switzer's findings alluded that word choices influence the audience's reception of an idea or concept.

As mentioned earlier in this chapter, there is not an easy or conclusive way to measure the success and impact of Trump's political ads. For example, in an article discussing Trump's digital advertising strategy in his 2016 campaign, journalist Nick Corasaniti agrees that "…the overall impact of the ad campaigns that result from these findings would be nearly impossible to assess at scale" (Corasaniti, 2020).

On the other hand, in a journal article discussing the scope of the effect of word choice on economic behavior, Farrow, Grolleau, and Mzoughi reference the idea that the wording of, specifically, the Brexit referendum gave the Leave campaign the wherewithal to tap into "voters' cognitive biases much more effectively than did the Remain campaign" (Farrow, 2018). Brexit languages encouraging them to vote 'Leave.' Farrow, Grolleau, and Mzoughi (2018) go on to say "Although the impacts associated with words can sometimes be subsumed under framing effects, we believe there is sufficient evidence to suggest that words can generate behavioral impacts that are distinct from framing effects."

Intuitively and based on supportive research there is reason to believe that word choices impact the results of an audience's behavior–specifically in how they vote. Furthermore, this evidence suggests that word choices in Trump advertisements had an influence in how audience members of the Trump ads voted in the 2020 election.

Terms

For this study "word choice" relates to the lexicon of the Trump advertisements. "Word choice frequency" relates to the most frequent words that were utilized in the advertisements–excluding pronouns, conjunctions, and prepositions. "Advertising," on the other hand, refers to a form of communication for marketing and is used to encourage or convince audience members to take some new actions (Bai, 2018). In this context, political advertising refers to the advertising of a political candidate for a public office via videos released on social media sites. Political advertising uses tools, such as word choices, to rhetorically affect their audience.

Method

Procedures

Forty-four Trump-endorsed advertisements released in preconvention primary period in 2019 and 2020 for his re-election campaign were analyzed for this study. The ads were obtained online from YouTube. Some were originally were aired on Facebook and as TV ads (Fowler et al., 2020).

Three steps were taken to assess across Trump ads released during the selected period. First, the forty-four ads were watched to obtain an idea of what words stood out or reappeared to the researcher. Next, the researcher made a list of words that frequently appeared across the Trump ads. The researcher, then, watched the same forty-four ads and put a tally mark next to the word for each time it was said in the ad. The researcher was focused on how many ads a specific word appeared in, not how many times a word was used in the ad. If a specific word was used in an ad–regardless if it was used once or multiple times in an ad–it was be assumed that the ad intended a particular rhetorical effect.

Results

Summary of findings

After coding word choice, the top three words that were utilized in Trump political advertisements were: "facts," "change," and "winning." As presented in the bar graph below, the word "facts" was also measured to include numerical words–such as percentages or numerical amounts.

Figure 1

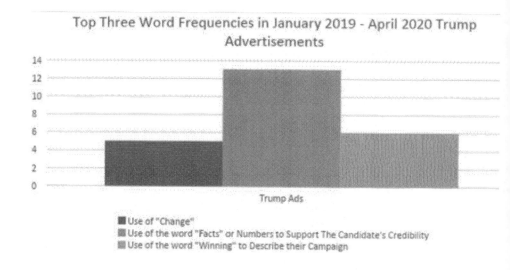

Discussion

Practical Implications

The purpose of this study was to discover word frequencies in the word choices Trump's campaign is to appeal to voters. For instance, in a study done on the veteran vote influencing the 2004 election, Jeremy Teigen states that "Candidates need votes to win elections, and one way to attract support is to draw straightforward links between the candidates and potential voters" (Teigen, 2007). This statement points out that presidential candidates utilize motifs to make themselves more relatable and appealing to voters. For instance, in a campaign ad released in 2019, one of Trump's ads is voiced by a narrator with this transcript:

Fact: Joe Biden pressured Ukraine to fire its prosecutor. Fact: The persecutor said he was forced out for leading a corruption probe into Hunter Biden's company. Fact: Democrats want to impeach President Trump for discussing this investigation with Ukraine's president. Fact: Donald Trump won but Democrats want to overturn the election. Do not let them (Sherman 2019).

This transcript of a Trump ad displays how prevalent the use of facts is in his ads, as the word "facts" also appear in 13 out of 44 of the ads. Thus, it seems Trump might have been attempting to appeal to his specific audience by "drawing straightforward links" from Trump-endorsed facts to his audience.

The word "change" can be seen in a myriad of former President Barack Obama's political advertisements. In fact, Obama's campaign has been said by NBC News to have been "buoyed by the 'hope and change' optimism of his first presidential campaign" (Bacon, 2016). There is yet to be significant research on the rhetorical effect of the word "change" used in political advertisements; however, there is expectation that a frequency of this word is across many if not most political ad campaigns. This is especially the case if a presidential candidate is running to replace an opposing party member in the same office. In Trump's deployment, "change" would probably be welcome by the presidential candidate's party. For instance, Trump's ads that use the word "change" are mostly alluding to the fact of how Trump will bring about change for families in America. For instance, one of his ads depicts a mother helping her daughter get ready for school. In the ad, the mother passes a sign in her suburban neighborhood that says, "vote Republican." The voiceover–portrayed as this mother's voice–says: "Things are starting to change. There is more opportunity to invest in the ones that matter." In this quote, the word 'change' is referring to a change from a pre-Trump era to a Trump era, where, according to the ad, "[there will be] more opportunity to invest in the others that matter."

The most surprising aspect of this study was the frequency of the word "winning." For example, one of his ads titled "American Heroes Online" brings in a clip from a speech Trump gives, when he says "We're winning. We're winning all over." If we reference once again Chibuwe's work, we can understand that political candidates and parties running for office, or competing for "dominance," usually justify their "dominance" on "the basis of their achievements" (Chibuwe, 2017, p. 30). The word "winning," therefore, would allude to Trump's dominance as a presidential candidate.

Conclusion

In conclusion, the three words "facts," "change," and "winning" were utilized by the Trump campaign in ads released from January 2019 to April 2020 to appeal to the audience in different ways, based on their individual rhetorical effects. For example, "facts" is used to draw links between Trump-endorsed facts and the audience. "Change" is utilized as a word to encourage the idea that Trump can positively impact and change the state of the country once he is voted into office. Additionally, "winning" is a word that blatantly portrays the idea in the ads that Trump is superior to the other presidential candidates.

References

Bacon, P. (2016, December 26). *Hope and Change? Obama's legacy at a crossroads.* NBC News. https://www.nbcnews.com/storyline/president-obama-the-legacy/hope-change-obama-s-legacy-crossroads-n697691

Bai, Z. (2018, July). *The characteristics of language in cosmetic advertisements.* ResearchGate. https://www.researchgate.net/publication/326269494_The_Characteristics_of_Language_in_Cosmetic_Advertisements

Bogost, I., & Madrigal, A. (2020, April 18). *How Facebook works for Trump.* The Atlantic. https://www.theatlantic.com/technology/archive/2020/04/how-facebooks-ad-technology-helps-trump-win/606403/

Casselman, B., & Tankersley, J. (2019, October 29). *Why the economy might not sway 2020 voters*. New York Times. https://www.nytimes.com/2019/10/29/business/economy/survey-politics-economy.html

Chibuwe, A. (2017). Language and the (re)production of dominance: Zimbabwe African National Union-Patriotic Front (ZANU-PF) advertisements for the July 2013 elections. *Critical Arts: A South-North Journal of Cultural & Media Studies, 31*(1), 18–33.

Corasaniti, N. (2020, April 28). *How a digital ad strategy that helped trump is being used against him*. New York Times. https://www.nytimes.com/2020/04/28/us/politics/Facebook-Acronym-advertising.html

Ecarma, C. (2020, April 28). *Trump's 2016 Digital-ad mastermind is now working to defeat him*. Vanity Fair. https://www.vanityfair.com/news/2020/04/trump-facebook-mastermind-james-barnes-working-against-him

Farrow, K., Grolleau, G., & Mzoughi, N. (2018). What in the word! The scope for the effect of word choice on economic behavior. *Kyklos, 71*(4), 557–580.

Fowler, E., Franz, M., Ridout, T., Bogucki, C., Oleinikov, P., Neumann, M., Page-Tan, C., Baum, L. (2020*). Trump spends big on tv ads while Biden holds back*. The Wesleyan Media Project. https://mediaproject.wesleyan.edu/releases-070220/

Wong, J. (2020, January 29). *One year inside Trump's monumental Facebook campaign*. The Guardian. https://www.theguardian.com/us-news/2020/jan/28/donald-trump-facebook-ad-campaign-2020-election

Sherman, A. (2019, October 11). *Donald Trump ad misleads about Joe Biden, Ukraine and the prosecutor*. PolitiFact. https://www.politifact.com/factchecks/2019/oct/11/donald-trump/trump-ad-misleads-about-biden-ukraine-and-prosecut/

Romm, T., Stanley-Becker, I., & Timberg, C. (2020, February 20). *Facebook won't limit political ad targeting or stop false claims under new ad rules*. Washington Post. https://www.washingtonpost.com/technology/2020/01/09/facebook-wont-limit-political-ad-targeting-or-stop-pols-lying/

Switzer, J. Y. (1990). The impact of generic word choices: An empirical investigation of age- and sex-related differences. *Sex Roles; New York, N.Y.*, *22*(1), 69–82.

Teigen, J. M. (2007). Veterans' party identification, candidate affect, and vote choice in the 2004 U.S. Presidential Election. *Armed Forces & Society*, *33*(3), 414–437.

2016 Presidential election results. (2018, November). New York Times. https://www.nytimes.com/elections/2016/results/president

SECTION 6: FOREIGN POLICY ADVERTISING SIDETRACKED

Allan Louden, Editor

There is a sense in which across presidential campaigns that foreign policy advertising often is less about foreign than the domestic political implications. Foreign policy ads typically, absent a pending war or bragging rights, is more hinted than highlighted. Aspects of national security and procurement costs make their way into ads, but more as a signature of strength or weakness. One of the more famous Roger Ailes' 1988 spot is of leather-helmeted Michael Dukakis galloping about in a tank. Ostensibly, the ad was to inform who supported special weapon systems, who was strong on Russia, but soon became about persona, a joke indicting "goofy" Dukakis' readiness (Cillizza, 2014).

A major theme that arose during the campaign was the China threat, an issue that some said represented little more than political diversion. *The Washington Post* reported that "President Trump's campaign is preparing to launch a broad effort aimed at linking Joe Biden to China, after concluding that it would be more politically effective than defending or promoting Trump's response to the coronavirus pandemic" and with little real-world fallout (Bandow, 2020).

The researchers who approach the 39 China ads are Chinese nationals studying at Wake Forest University. Yuxuan (Sandra) Wang on campus and Liyan Zhu back home in Shenzhen due to Corona constraints. They independently conducted content analysis, examining different aspects. First, Wang looks at the way US domestic conditions created an appetite for the Chinese ads while Zhu explores the way "trade war" becomes an organizing idea for the China ads. Although subtle, the Chinese authors characterize the ads as influenced by US domestic politics, seemingly insulated from actual or potential Sino-US relations.

Itamar Lewin-Arundale offers an original take on the foreign policy advertising. Namely the use of foreign entanglements of the candidate's adult children as surrogates, thereby incriminating the father's. He reports on 13 of the political ads selected among the 42 foreign policy ads. As with other issues foreign policy the ads in this set often degenerated into character indictments or corruption charges. He explores the ways in which the ads work as well as their propriety.

The Trump campaign also made positive/political use of his children and son-in-law in his advertising. Jared Kushner, late in the campaign, was often featured in Trump videos showing excerpts from press appearances. He became the primary spokesman for standard pro-Israel ads and claims of success in the Middle East state-to-state diplomacy (President Trump Has, 2020). He also became a spokesman on the coronavirus rollouts. Of course, the opposition, not so much Biden, but groups like the Lincoln project went after Kushner on both fronts. Perhaps the most dramatic being an ad entitled *Evil* reporting on a Corona meeting, "Evil was in that room." And the *evil* was Jared. (2020). In another instance the Lincoln project reviewed the *Secretary of Failure* labeling Jared as incompetent the "pampered Princeling." (Secretary of Failure, 2020).

An echo of the Cold War, and a staple of presidential campaigns, has been Russia. Resolve and strength were needed to contain the "Russian Bear." Russia became an important subset of ads which openly discussed the reliability of the commander-in-chief and his fidelity with the military. Following the *New York Times* story "Russia Secretly Offered Afghan Militants Bounties to Kill U.S. Troops…" (Savage et al. 2020) the quote military" ads began to flow, often from independent groups like VoteVets.

All hell broke loose in September when *The Atlantic* published the article "Trump: Americans Who Died in War Are 'Losers' and 'Suckers'" (Goldberg, 2020). Scores of advertisements played out over a month and a half, dramatically showing open scorn for Trump's disrespect for the troops. This large number of ads which aired and occupied social media were about the military but not foreign policy, they were about narcissism's risks in the sensitive arena of foreign relations. Yanlin Zhang brings a fresh perspective and a thorough accounting to the 74 "military" ad set.

Trump's response, substantially lower in volume, was to invoke patriotism and the trappings of the Commander-in-Chief, a combination which made for powerful video. "Support the Troops" a nearly universal and popular political posture, not so subtly transformed into a version of "Support the Troops, support Trump."

Virginia Witherington has the honor of closing this volume with another "domesticated" foreign policy spots collection. The issue she explores was one of the more standard/predictable sets from the campaign (37 ads). Immigration ads were some of the least surprising as they tracked an expected course with Trump warning of societal overrun and Biden lamenting the callousness of US immigration policy. She illustrates that while standard immigration ploys from Trump – the Wall, jobs, security – were aired, immigration was more muted than in the 2016 or 2018 elections. She finds, however, the tone of the anti-Trump immigration ads strident, inhabited with "children in cages" and attendant misery-imagery dominating. Additionally, several of the ads were produced by independent groups, less to influence voters, more to influence future policy.

References

Bandow, D. (2020, May 5). *China to Become a Political Piñata in 2020 Presidential Campaign. China-US Focus.* https://www.chinausfocus.com/foreign-policy/china-to-become-a-political-piata-in-2020-presidential-campaign

Cillizza, C. (2014, August 5). *Who really made the Michael Dukakis 'tank' ad? It's* really complicated. The Fix, Washington Post. https://www.washingtonpost.com/news/the-fix/wp/2014/08/05/who-really-made-the-michael-dukakis-tank-ad-its-complicated/

Evil (2020, August 24). The Lincoln project, YouTube. https://www.youtube.com/watch?v=SgXg36ztMCg&t=2s

Goldberg, J. (2020, September 3). *Trump: Americans Who Died in War Are 'Losers' and 'Suckers'.* The Atlantic. https://www.theatlantic.com/politics/archive/2020/09/trump-americans-who-died-at-war-are-losers-and-suckers/615997/

President Trump has set the stage in the Middle East to accomplish this historic breakthrough (2020, August 13). Donald J Trump, YouTube. https://www.youtube.com/watch?v=8Wq1idptWYE

Savage, C., Schmitt, E. & Schwirtz, M. (2020, June 26). *Russia secretly offered Afghan militants bounties to kill U.S. troops, intelligence says*. New York Times. https://www.nytimes.com/2020/06/26/us/politics/russia-afghanistan-bounties.html

Secretary of Failure (2020, August 5). The Lincoln project, YouTube. https://www.youtube.com/watch?v=xcxt7gUCgKY

Chapter 29: Correlations between China Campaign Ads and US Social Issues

Yuxuan (Sandra) Wang

Yuxuan is a Senior in Communication from Shenzhen, China

Background

The waning relations between China and America created heated debates in the 2020 presidential advertising. The advertising itself may have encouraged the relational erosion. For months, the candidates and their supporters continually railed about US relations with China, attacking the opponents for their attitudes and relevant foreign policies. In these political advertisements, China was chiefly portrayed as the antagonist. Any candidate who offered positive comments on China was castigated. The content of the advertisements covered a broad spectrum of policy woes including job loss, trade deals, Coronavirus, as well as candidates and their immediate families' relationships with China. Granted, the presidential election plays out to an audience of US citizens; citizens who seemingly have little or no connection with a country thousands of miles away.

Many of the issues mentioned in the campaign advertisements are closely related to the American voter's circumstances, and the advertisements draw attention to the candidates by targeting audiences from different social classes, cultures, and domestic geographies. Much of the current research primarily has been focused on the trade war/general relations between China and the US. Only a few commentaries addressed the influences advertising had on the presidential campaign in the US. In this analysis, the China advertisements are assessed from the perspective of relating US social problems with China. The assumption of the targeted audience is considered and compared according to the content and sponsors of the advertisements.

Method

The study was conducted through direct observation, classifying advertisements into categories for analysis. The advertisements were first divided on positively or negatively orientation toward the candidate. The mechanics for determining which candidate is being supported is based on the content, whether the information provided is in favor/disfavor of the two major candidates. For instance, an advertisement regarding Ivanka Trump's personal relationship with China is considered a pro-Biden advertisement since it conveys information that is in favor of Joe Biden.

Additionally, ads were assessed based on issue content. The resulting three categories included economy/jobs (Econ), coronavirus (Covid-19), candidates' personal relationships/attitudes (PR/Attitudes) toward China. Frequencies for the categories as they appeared in campaign advertisements were collected.

Another category assessed sponsorship, including the affiliated groups: candidates' political parties, candidates themselves, and allied and independent supporting groups. The sponsors and content of each advertisement were recorded for analysis.

Results

Relations with China and Xenophobia in the American Society

The first area analyzed focused on the content of each advertisement: economy/jobs, Covid-19, and personal relations and attitude toward China. According to the data, candidates' personal relationships and attitudes about China are mentioned most often in both Biden and Trump advertisements (See Figure 1). Specifically, the advertisements present, as a criticism, the close connection between candidates and China's government. The idea conveyed was whichever candidate discussed could potentially be a threat to the US, as they would not be tough enough in confronting China.

Figure 1: China Ads Content

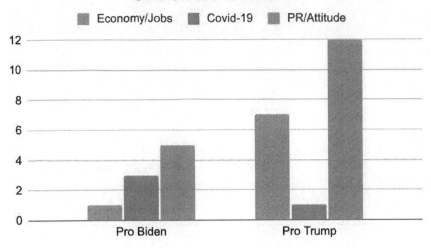

In the Pro-Trump advertisements regarding Biden's PR/Attitudes toward China, Biden's past comments about China, especially during his term as the vice president, have been quoted most frequently. Specifically, a speech that was given by Joe Biden while visiting China as the Vice President of the US served as evidence of Biden being *too* friendly and close to China (If Biden Wins, 2020). In the speech, Biden, as the Vice President suggested a prosperous and closer tie between the US and China by saying "what a beautiful history we wrote together". The speech was given during the Vice President's Asia trip on August 11, 2011. During the time, the Obama administration and China's government maintained a relatively friendly relationship with more collaboration and connection in many fields; however, the two countries have developed more tension upon Trump administration's multiple restrictions and sanctions on China. The hostile attitude toward China has grown during the Trump administration. Hence, Biden's friendly speech that was given nine years ago under a completely different political climate offered as a potential weakness for Biden. Other than Joe Biden himself, his son Hunter Biden's business relationship with China has been mentioned several times that helps prove the Biden family's scandalous connection with China (See Chapter 31).

On the other hand, in Pro-Biden's advertisements, Donald Trump was also criticized for having a "too-close" connection with China. Among the Pro-Biden advertisements, half of them mentioned Trump receiving help from China's government in many areas including the presidential election, the economy, his daughter Ivanka Trump's fashion business, and bank loans (Chyna, 2020). In addition, in these advertisements, Donald Trump was described as China's puppet multiple times (How Trump Got Played, 2020).

Both candidates were targeted by their opponents' supporters regarding their close connection with China to attract potential voters. One right group, America First Action Super PAC, even produced an anti-Biden spot in Chinese with English subtitles (Toast of China, 2020)

In multiple Pro-Trump advertisements, Biden's objection to the Travel Ban against China was quoted serving as further evidence of Biden-China connection. The quote is from one of Biden's campaign rallies in which he claimed the travel ban and other restrictions on China due to Covid-19 was "Trump's hysteria xenophobia" (Responsible, Joe Biden, 2020). The quote comes from Biden's campaign rally in Fort Madison, Iowa on January 31 while the Covid-19 has just started to become a serious epidemic in China and a few parts of the world. Biden's criticism of the Trump government's travel ban against China has been considered a form of protection on behalf of China and conveys the idea that Joe Biden does not put American interests first.

The large proportion of the advertisements illustrating candidates' relationship with China reflected that xenophobia, especially toward China which became more and more popular. Most of the China advertisements condemned candidates and their families for being "too friendly", any friendly comments on China were framed as threatening and dangerous.

The candidate's families' relations with China, such as Ivanka Trump's fashion line as well as Hunter Biden's personal business, appear to be a disadvantage even though the candidates themselves may not be involved, and it further suggests the China fear is deeply planted inside American society. For instance, Ivanka Trump-owned company does business with China in the fashion field, associating that judgment to Trump. The relationship could also be an indirect critique of Trump's transactional decision-making.

Figure 2 – Attitudes Toward China – Pew Research Center

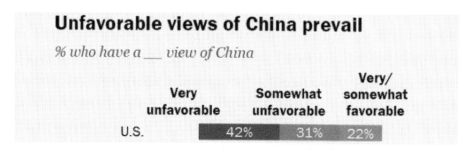

Furthermore, the candidates' past China comments were condemned even though they were expressed in a different political environment. These positive comments on China were popular and generally accepted by the public in the former context. To influence or create public opinion, the campaign advertisements celebrate xenophobia that appears to permeate American society. The Pew Research Center observed "[I]n the U.S., negative views of China have increased nearly 20 percentage points since President Donald Trump took office, rising 13 points since just last year" (Silver, et al., 2020). The widespread appearance of China campaign advertisements, unique to the 2020 cycle, may echo a growing fear toward China (See figure 2).

Job Loss and China's Threat to US Economy

The economy was a prominent theme in candidates' advertising. Most of the Pro-Trump videos blamed Biden for job loss, especially in the manufacturing industry outsourced to China. Trump ads emphasized the "weak, job-killing trade deals with China" through the five decades of Biden's political career, the ads having a distinct "Rust-Belt" Midwest swing-state flavor. For example, the number of job losses in Michigan was deployed multiple times in Trump ads aiming to blame Biden for helping China steal American jobs (Poor Michigan, 2020). Also, other advertisements mentioned Biden's trade deal costing Wisconsin nearly 88,900 jobs. In addition, the number of job losses in Pennsylvania, 137,300, Ohio 15,600 pictured with closed factories, demonstrations of Biden and China's shady collaboration on trade. Other Biden's policies that appeared in the Pro-Trump advertisements including NAFTA and TPP, also presented as evidence of Biden's efforts regarding China impairing the American economy (Joe Won't Stand Up, 2020).

Similarly, the advertisements against Trump targeted the "failed" trade war. Trump was criticized for harming farms and triggering small businesses' bankruptcies, conditions predicated on favorable China policies.

Although the American economy had largely recovered from the 2008 subprime crisis, the overall job market still faced challenges, particularly with Covid unemployment. The states mentioned in the advertisements, replete with aging factories (Michigan, Wisconsin, Pennsylvania, Ohio), are part of the rust belt in the US, a region sustained by manufacturing. As businesses moved their factories into developing countries to advantage cheaper labor, the states faced economic challenges and political stirrings. As the US economy experienced waves in recent years, the job market and employment rate of the US has been a crucial issue and a *scapegoat* was needed. In fact, just 10 years ago, China's "existential" threat was not part of the popular political conversation. China had purchased a large number of American Treasury Bonds in order to help boost the economy. While China was a financial crisis helper it was now seen as the chief culprit. This may explain why many of the advertisements conveyed the idea that China stole American jobs and blamed candidate's policies.

Ads Sponsors and Target Audience

Figure 3: Pro Trump Sponsors ad

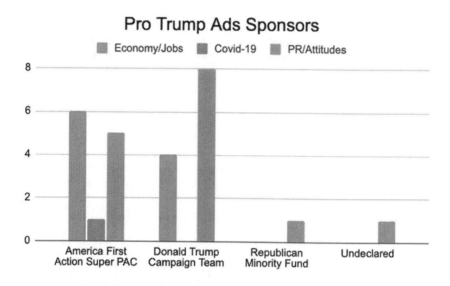

The data revealed multiple sponsors for the advertisements and each of them tended to favor categories of content in their videos. In the Pro-Trump advertisements, there are four groups sponsored advertisements regarding issues with China including American First Action Super PAC (America First Action), Donald Trump Presidential Campaign Team, Republican Majority Fund, and Undeclared sources (see Figure 3).

Among the advertisements sponsored by America First Action and the Donald Trump Campaign Team, Economy/Jobs and PR/Attitudes were mentioned more than Covid-19. The group America First Action was created by Donald Trump and was the only Trump-related group allowed to receive unlimited donations. The majority targeted were Trump's loyal supporters, according to Trump's digital and data director in 2016, "Some of the same like-minded individuals who put their energy into getting Mr. Trump elected" (Brad Parscale). Since many of Trump voters come from the middle class – factory workers, farmers, and other small business owners – America First Action focused on presenting Biden's weak trade deals that caused job loss among American blue-collar workers.

On the other hand, sponsors for Pro-Biden China advertisements were more diverse consisting of eight groups. According to the data, PR/Attitudes is discussed the most following by Covid-19 related content. In the PR/Attitudes advertisements, Trump's connection with China is being depicted as a superior-subordinate relationship. Unlike the Pro-Trump advertisements in which past quotations of Biden were cited, Pro-Biden advertisements focused on presenting China's manipulation of Trump's weakness. Additionally, Covid-19 ads continued to gain attention. Among the eight sponsors of those advertisements, The Lincoln Project presented the most advertisements against Trump. The Lincoln Project is founded by several anti-Trump

Figure 4: Pro Biden Sponsors

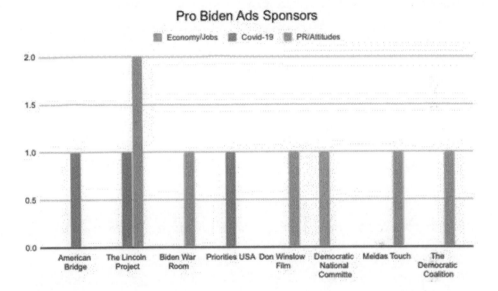

republicans in 2019, aimed at "Electing Democrats who support the Constitution over Republicans who do not is a worthy effort." Through China-related advertisements regarding PR and Covid-19, The Lincoln Project illustrated the image of weak and failed Trump and targeted swing Republican supporters.

Discussion

As China develops, the competitive relationship between America and China has increased in intensity. Nevertheless, being fearful and hostile to another country has often unintended harm for American society. The ads are evidence of how the policy positions can be corrupted to serve partisan politics. Both parties recognize subliminal prejudice based on social conditions, in turn, advantaging prejudicial feelings among voters. Social conditions render voters open to what some might argue to be biased policy-lite solutions, often unfair interpretations wherein serious foreign policy considerations are abandoned for the expedient.

Notably, the China foreign policy advertising's subtext emphasized economic and military threats, yet these ads were in the end about candidate image. The presence of the larger-than-life Trump persona, the "invention" of China as a central campaign issue, and convenient Don Quixote enemy, almost remove them from a traditional understanding. Foreign policy political advertising in 2020 was seldom about foreign policy yet was endlessly political.

References

Chyna (2020, June 17). The Lincoln project, YouTube. https://www.youtube.com/watch?v=wuAHz4i3_x8

How Trump got played by China (2020, September 5). Joe Biden, YouTube. https://www.youtube.com/watch?v=6MqCRcLQzGQ&t=65s

If Biden wins, China wins and America loses (2020, August 19). Donald J Trump, YouTube. https://www.youtube.com/watch?v=flf4OhQ2Zhc

Joe Biden, The China candidate (2020, September 24). Coalition for American Veterans. https://youtu.be/_1-cb-7CBUY

Joe Won't Stand Up for Us (2020, August 19) Donald J Trump, YouTube.

Poor Michigan (2020, May 15). American First Action Super PAC, YouTube. https://www.youtube.com/watch?v=Fwx-72A7wLo

Responsible, (2020, May 11). Joe Biden, YouTube.

Silver, L., Devlin, K., & Huang, C. (2020, October 6). Unfavorable views of china reach historic highs in many countries. Pew Research Center.

https://www.pewresearch.org/global/2020/10/06/unfavorable-views-of-china-reach-historic-highs-in-many-countries/

Toast of China (2020, May 15). America First Action Super PAC, YouTube. https://www.youtube.com/watch?v=VIpScYKKg8Q

Chapter 30: "Trade Wars" Define 2020 Campaign China Advertising

Liyan Zhu

Liyan is a Junior in Communication from Shenzhen, China

Introduction

The 2018 to 2020 Trade war between China and the United States became an economic conflict with long-term implications for both America and China's economic, technology, and resources fields. This trade war continues to impact people around the world and roil economic markets. The politicization of China within the presidential election gained electoral traction and was emphasized in both Donald Trump's and Joe Biden's political advertisements. Each candidate talked frequently about the trade war. This paper analyzes how the trade topic played a role in the 2020 China advertisements.

This project decoded the sentences and terms that relate to the trade war as deployed by the respective campaigns. There are five themes that emerged from the analysis of 50 advertisements. These include fear of the growing China economy, negative side of the trade war, blaming between presidential candidates, each candidate's relationship with China, and the preference of the Chinese government. All five aspects are attack points for both candidates of assigning blame.

Method

The method utilized in the research is thematic analysis. In the initial state of coding, all advertisement content was considered. After the first review, the discussion of trade stood out and was chosen as a focus for this project. The distinct themes that arose were recorded as lists including the fear of the trade war and negative effects, assigning blame, past and future relationships between China and America, the weakness of the president, enacted policies, etc.

I then watched the advertisements one by one and wrote down the words and sentences that connected to overarching themes on the lists. It was found that 25/39 of overall advertisements talk about jobs, technologies, manufactures. Also, sixteen of Donald Trump's advertisements include speeches disparaging Biden for his praise of China. Ten of Donald Trump's advertisements also point out the business deal between Biden's son and Chinese government. Another eleven of Donald Trump advertisements expressed concern of the "ownership of America" by China. In addition, I recorded the title of each advertisement, and the length of time those words and sentences appear in the advertisements. Next, I identified the words and phrases that relate to the themes, words such as "own, prefer, job, supplies". Using the list, I went back to each advertisement and identified an overview idea about each highlighted theme present. Then I noted if it encompassed positive sentiments or negative sentiments; was it praising or censuring in disclosing certain meaning. For example, the word "jobs" were always connected with negative words which shows the jobs persecution. I then grouped themes to help identify trends. I then sorted for the themes fear and blame. Finally, using the identified themes I wrote down global arguments about the role of trade terms in the China advertising.

Analysis

The first theme that was identified is the fear of the impacts of increasing economic power in China. The "If Sleepy Joe wins", trumps hyperbole overtly states that "China would own the United States" (If Sleepy Joe wins, 2020). The China dominance phenomenon was especially pertinent in Donald Trump's advertisements, warning of the fatal repercussions of a Biden administration. Since the word "own" implies a process of occupancy/occupation, Trump was trying to instill fear that China is a strong enemy and may colonize America if the president, such as Joe Biden, is weak. The sentiment within these advertisements seems to exaggerate the effect of the trade war by likening it to complete ownership of a country. In a speech extraction turned into social media video, Trump said, "If Joe Biden became president, China would own the United States. They own every one of these people. They own this building because Biden will give them anything." This shows that he is using the misinformation to arouse the audience's anger toward Biden and China. Even though it is obvious that owning the United States is impractical, the sentiment is an effective fear tactic. In addition, in another advertisement, Trump said, that "China would own this state, you're gonna have to learn to speak Chinese." He is suggesting what would occur if China were to own the State and accentuate one facet of life that would change drastically. It is the case currently that the world learns to speak English, it is dispirited if they start to learn Chinese, especially for children and those not receiving higher education. Speaking Chinese is far away from the trade war it is still terrifying for the listeners. Therefore, Trump is using extreme rhetoric to evoke people's fearfulness and anger. Since Trump blamed Biden for the lifestyle changes that would occur, it is easier for some to support him instead of Biden.

Second, the advertisements spotlight the fear of losing the trade war and the negative effects for the United States. The most obvious loss was jobs, manufacturing, and technology. The word "jobs" were mentioned 23 times across the ad set, a staggering 46% of all the advertisements analyzed. Upon further analysis, By decoding those sentences I discovered that words before and after jobs are always negative sentiments, such as "loss", "kill", "empty", "plunder", "take", "regard", "destroy them", "cost, "steal", "ship", "weak", "risk". The words invoke a fearful feeling that China is causing a large damage to America's employment rate. In addition, I also found that there are 8/24 times when numbers and cities together with the jobs. In several of the advertisements, it mentions that "Joe [Biden] trade deals with China costs Wisconsin 88,900 jobs," "Lost 112,400 jobs were sent to Chinese business and Chinese factories," "137,300 jobs left in Pennsylvania," "China has been stealing on manufactory, lost Wisconsin 19000 jobs", "Biden shoot 10,000 of our jobs overseas", "Workers to compete against people making pennies had resulted the loss of 160000 jobs", "Biden emptied Ohio factories 156,000 jobs lost", and "By 2016, 5,000,000 manufacturing jobs vanished." All the numbers that are mentioned in the advertisements are staggeringly large. Therefore, it evokes the audience's fear of losing more jobs and causes them to blame China for the job loss. Even though there is no definitive evidence saying that all the numbers are correct or due to China trade – citations not provided – nonetheless specific enough that the audience believe it. The specificity of job loss and links to cities conveys a certain authority.

Second, the word "manufacture" has also been mentioned nine times in the advertisements. As with the word "job", the word before and after "manufacture" also brings negative senses, such as "recession", "hurt", "steal", "close", "vanish", "decrease", "regard." These words can imply that the trade war is causing negative effects on American manufacturing, effective messaging to evoke audience anger toward China and the trade war. There are also some terms that mentioned in the advertisements the audience a closer feeling such as "manufacturing in a recession", "hurt by inferior trade with China", "stole American manufacturing", and "stealing on manufactory". Again, and parentally China is the one to blame. Additionally, from, many who see those advertisements may be working in manufacturing. Therefore, when they are "informed" and reinforced by the idea that the trade war may cause them to lose security, they are more likely to choose the l benefits their profits.

Similarly, there are several other statements that relate to the negative side of the trade war. For example, "China is killing our jobs, stealing technology", "Economic rival to the United States is exported, and is manufactured. It takes 'American jobs, China is having negative effects on the US economy". These statements insinuate that the trade war is causing sizable losses for America.

Biden's advertisements were enabling an audience to know that Trump is the one who started this war and he is to blame for the loss. Pro-Biden advertisements often expressed, "Trump's business war left farms and small businesses bankrupt." There is a specific Biden's advertisement that purports to convey China's view of Trump, "Trump is pretending again; he said he is the one to take actions on China. They know Trump is weak, corrupt, and ridiculed. China beats him every time. Trade Negotiation. China won. They laugh at Their Trump taxes. Trump's business war left farms and small businesses bankrupt." From this entry, we see that Biden was illustrating that Trump inability to compete against China.

On the other hand, Donald Trump also characterized Joe Biden as "too weak" to contest against China, and say *he* is the one who helped America to win in the competition between China and America. As he mentioned in the advertisement that "In 2019, the economy of China was going to be bigger than the US, except it did not happen because I got elected, and I turned it the opposite way" and "Donald Trump has been clear to bring back manufacture to the US in decreasing our country's reliance on Chinese supply chains." He is showing his audience that Biden does not have the boldness to help America restore growth. Even though both presidential candidates find a way to use the trade war to support their own standpoints, each in their own way invites the American people to be terrified by trade war losses.

The third theme that arose from the data was (policy) blaming. Both Donald Trump and Joe Biden talked about their policies and solutions toward this trade war and attacked each other's policies. Donald Trump references that he "put 20% tariff on China", "I did tax", "bring back manufacturing", "decreasing reliance on Chinese supply chains", "toughest ever actions". When mentioning his actions toward China, it provides his supporters a feeling that he strength/resolve to help America gain back confidence and profit from the trade war. He also inspires confidence in the audience and communicates that he can lead them in the stand against China. However, Joe Biden advertisements, when countering Trump's rhetoric, labels him as "weak, corrupt and ridiculed". Biden is saying that China always "won" in the trade war during Trump's presidency. This casts his policies as ineffective.

Audiences become afraid that China is winning the trade war leading them to vote for the one they trust will win. The trade war is never a win or a loss proposition, since it brings net loss for both countries, yet it turns out to be a win/lose position in the ads. Keeping in mind the language used against one another, it is easy to see how both candidates use opposing policies to assign blame. Even as specific policies mentioned were different the ads functionally adopted parallel strategies in the arena of China ads.

The fourth point that evidenced from the trade war advertisements is the importance of the *relationship* between the presidential candidate and China. In these advertisements, many examples about praising China are used to show the candidate's' support to China and friendships with China. Whoever expresses positive sentiments towards China invites the notion that the candidate has a close relationship with China. Therefore, suggested support for China instead of America is commonplace in the advertisements. For the Joe Biden set, his speech exhorting Chinese friendship was played 3 times in the overall 29 Trump's advertisements. In the speech, Joe Biden says that "They are not bad folks", and "no competition for us." The image of Joe Biden and Xi Jinping, the Chairman of China, cozying up to one another is emphasized in the speech. This speech utilized as a point of vulnerability for Trump's exploitation, a narrative that Joe Biden does "not make sense." Even as China inflicts damage Biden praises and collaborates.

The word "Xenophobia" was shown eight times by Trump regarding Biden's initial response to his China's travel ban. The definition of "Xenophobia" is a strong feeling of dislike or fear of people from other countries which is indeed what is occurring. In the advertisements Biden expresses his dislike regarding the travel ban, but he is trying to support China's travel to the United States as a welcome foreigner policy. The hypocrisy is apparent as the travel band also is an important point of vulnerability for the Trump campaign, since the band fed within Xenophobia

As if the campaigns were keeping pace with each other, and similar accusations somehow neutralized the issue, there were one of Joe Biden's ad that showed how "cozy" Donald Trump was with China. In these advertisements, Trump says that he has a great relationship with President Xi, and China "did a great job" to control the Coronavirus. It simultaneously recruiting the negative sentiments about Coronavirus, declaring that Trump did not prevent or improve the pandemic.

Both Joe Biden and Donald Trump not only use praise when showing the close relationship with China, but also the policies they support and enact. The advertisements from the Trump campaign said Biden had a record in advantaging China, for example, "supporting trade with China", "voted for weak job Killing trade deals", "give a pass on trade", "voted for permanent trade", "committing with Chinese government", "selling out America to China", "protected China's feeling", "called China travel ban Xenophobia", "pass the green new deal", "supporting bad trade deals", "entry into the world trade organization", and "trade deal favoring Shanghai." All those terms are the "positive" policies that Biden has pushed toward China illustrating Biden's amicable stance. There are three things that have been mentioned twice in each Trump's advertisements, "support china entry into the world trade organization", "voted for permanent trade with China", and "criticizes China travel ban". The unstated premise is that these actions are largely beneficial for Chinese trade and the Chinese economy. Even though the trade market has positive effects toward both countries, it still evokes American people's anger toward Joe Biden. Voter ought to believe that Biden's policies should not reflect anything positive for China. On the other hand, there is an advertisement that disclosed "a bank account" that Donald Trump has in China. In the advertisements, they say that Trump took nearly "25 million-dollar cash from sources linked to China." This revelation that Trump also has some undisclosed business relationships with China, hints at impropriety. In addition, Joe Biden's advertisement said, "Trump would benefit Beijing."

An important policy that has been mentioned in both Trump and Biden's advertisements are "the supplies sent to China, such as masks" in the Coronavirus period. The Trump advertisement mentioned, "Since the outbreak, the communist party has been mobilizing overseas organizations to buy local supplies and send them to China." This sentence was spoken twice. On the other hand, Biden advertisements are were that Donald Trump "sent 17.8 tons of masks and supplies to China." From those claims, it seems that no matter the political party, "sending masks and aid" signified a complicit relationship, aid sent to China leverage to condemn.

Both Donald Trump and Joe Biden's off-spring were also "exposed" in the advertisements. Even though what the Trump and Biden families had done may be within normal trade relationships, the audience is asked to interpret "secret" business deals as nefarious. For Joe Biden's son, Hunter Biden, he was accused of having "a billion-dollar deal with an energy bank of China." This was mentioned seven times in these advertisements and an interview of Biden, and his son were shown (See Chapter 31). This aroused a misleading message surrounding Biden's son's business with China, since the nature of the "deal" was unclear. The audience could easily perceive that Biden's son collaborates closely with China and assure and therefore so does former Vice President Biden. They think that Vice President Biden supports China instead of America because of his familiar business relations.

Similarly, Donald Trump's daughter Ivanka Trump has also been criticized regarding secretive trade with China that aired in Biden's advertisements, such as "New trade mark for her fashion brand", "Chinese government gave her free new trade mark on April 6th". This has the same effect as Biden's son's advertisements. Since it is covered with detail and includes picture, it is easy for the audience to conclude that Ivanka has been given handouts from Chinese government. Thus, people will think that Ivanka Trump stands with China and assume Trump also stands with China. Both those advertisements disclosed the trade between the candidate's daughter and son to "document" candidates closeness with China.

Finally, the preference of the Chinese government was a theme in these advertisements. Since the preference of Chinese government seems to relate to the support and benefits that they can get from the president this is intentionally a persuasive point. Therefore, the candidate that the Chinese government prefers should not be chosen because the candidates and Chinese leadership are perceived as having ulterior motives. In these advertisements, mentions include "China prefers Joe Biden" five times, two times after pointing out Biden's son's trade deal with China[i]. Another two times the term "unpredictable" was used to describes Donald Trump's relationship with China. Therefore, it seems like if China "prefers" Joe Biden to win, Joe Biden brings profits to China which helps China grow and therefore is bad for the American people. In addition, the phrase "If Biden Wins, China Wins" has been occurred for three times. The winning of Biden and China tied together to show a closer connection. The phrase is also short and strong not asking voters to think deeply about it. Since the investigation shows that China wants Joe Biden to win, it becomes an attack point for Donald Trump through which he can emphasize the closeness between China and Biden. Earlier advertising was discussed that showed China's Trump preference reflected their sense of his weakness and disposition toward strongman leaders.

Conclusion

Analyzing the presidential candidate China ad set reveals that "the Trade War" played an important role. The fearfulness of an increasing Chinese economy's threat to the international status of America permeates these spots. The fear of losing the trade war, argued to be determinant in job loss, technological inferiority, and shrinking manufacturing dominated these ads. Blame was established by showing that supported policies were associated with risk. The relationship between China and the presidential candidates and family was assessed by business deals articulated toward China. Finally, the preference of Chinese government for this debate seemed to be evidence of closeness.

The orientation of the China advertisements leads the audience to misunderstanding. Rather than explore the nuances of China/US trade, the implication is there would be adverse impact on the American economy. No mention is made of the idea that more effective relationship between two countries is collaboration rather than competition, potential win-win outcome. China and America can support each other, cooperation restraints. A large percent of those advertisements coalesce around that blaming China shows the candidate's strength. Intentionally, China is the enemy, advertising is political, and the "lesser of two evils" celebrated.

References

If Sleepy Joe wins, China will own the United States. (2020, October 15). Donald Trump, YouTube. https://www.youtube.com/watch?v=s2qq5Aa7Rfg

If Biden wins, China wins and America loses (2020 August 19). Donald Trump, YouTube. https://www.youtube.com/watch?v=flf4OhQ2Zhc

---

[i] Editor's Note: There were many more than two ads of Hunter Biden's dealings in China, but most were assigned to another research set. This article correctly identifies the theme in the direct China advertising.

Chapter 31: Why the Children? Foreign Policy Advertising in 2020

Itamar Lewin-Arundale

Itamar is an MA student in Communication from Weston, MA

An uncommon variation of the 2020 campaign enterprise was the severity and "importance" with which campaigns targeted candidates through their children's lives. Naturally the lives of the president's family have always drawn public's interest, yet the aberration that occurred in 2020 elevated to a pivotal position familial scandals as evidence of candidate's unsuitability for office. This chapter focuses on the divergence from previous elections and how the messages about children were constructed as to influence public perception of the candidate themselves.

The papers in this section were designed to investigate advertising trends having to do with foreign policy, including China. China was of heightened, sometimes manufactured, concern this cycle, the subject of scores of ads, therefore China was assigned in its own sub-category. This portion focuses solely on the foreign policy ad-set which excluded the China spots and makes a narrower claim about why the ad-set, and plausibly the 2020 presidential campaign, focused on defaming children of presidential candidates.

The data was analyzed using a linguistic rhetorical approach. Each advertisement was noted, and its themes identified. In total, the foreign policy ad-set contained 42 entries among which were a scattering of themes. It was found that five of the original 42 advertisements (11.9%) were about the candidate's adult children. After identifying the theme, advertisements outside the original research set were taken up to bolster data points from the emergent theme regarding presidential children. With the addition of these advertisements nine total advertisements were used[i]. Both these groups of advertisements were then analyzed further due to the unique nature of the children's targeting and being used to indict an opponent's suitability in office.

During the 2020 election, Hunter Biden, Jared Kushner, Ivanka Trump, and Eric Trump experienced unprecedented levels of press coverage and public scrutiny. From unverified stories of drugs and sexual exploits to full-on family scale corruption, the rhetoric during the 2020 electoral campaign centered on transitioning blame from child to candidate.

White House Children

An appreciation of the 2020 emphasis begins with an awareness of how presidential children White House lives were covered in prior campaigns. There are many Chronicles of presidential children causing a ruckus around the White House, tales of curiosity nearly as long as the presidency itself. Tad Lincoln sprayed dignitaries visiting the White House with a fire hose (Thomas "Tad" Lincoln, n.d.). Theodore Roosevelt's daughter Alice became a matinee public figure as soon as the Roosevelts moved into the White House. She was known for smoking on the roof of the White House, drinking, partying, using voodoo dolls, walking around with a snake in her purse, and was coined "Princess Alice" (Alice Roosevelt Longworth, 2020). The trend continued, during Barrack Obama's tenure in office, a scandal involving his daughter when smoking marijuana at a party broke out (Halper, 2016). The difference from the examples is that in the past, children's mishaps were divorced from discussions about a president's fitness for office. During the 2020 election, a marked shift occurred as the presidential children's narratives were deployed to influence the president's image. This deviation has substantive implications.

Presidential "Kids" in 2020

The candidate's children during the 2020 election were older than the above-mentioned examples. They were not living in the White House, presumptively considered "independent" from their political parents. Resident children's transgression's, like "spraying dignitaries with a fire hose," were juvenile hijinks, amusing asides, not signifiers of serious consequence. Perhaps the 'of-age children' permitted different political judgment, but the past is replete with older children who did not draw nearly the political fire. Ronald Reagan's adult children, Patti, Ron, and Michael attracted attention and gossip, the W. Bush twins, Truman's daughter Margaret (surely one of John Taylor's 16 children must have caused a ruckus) did not elevate as the centerpiece of campaign advertising. Simply being of age does not reconcile the fact that in 2020 there was an advertising-based upswing of child attacks.

An argument can be made that the children of the 2020 electoral candidates were intimately involved in politics and therefore were fair game. Naturally, political connection, serving the candidate invites their inclusion in the electoral conversation. This has not always been the case, however, as presidents throughout history gave their family trusted political positions. John Adams appointed John Quincy Adams as minister to Prussia and the Netherlands (Hogan, 2017). Rutherford Hayes son was appointed at the age of 20 as the president's private secretary (Webb Cook Hayes, n.d.). Alice Roosevelt also helped broker the Sino-Japanese treaty during her tenure working for her father in Japan. While sometimes scandalous that a president would engage in overt nepotism, there is no documentary evidence to suggest they were ever talking points during elections on this scale (Presidential libraries, 2021).

This study assesses the shift in political advertisements by identifying the language used to transition negative sentiment from the child to the candidate.

The Trump Children

The language used in referencing Trump represented the Trump family as an immoral collective. That sentiment then bleeds over conditioning voters to conceptualize Trump as the family figurehead and susceptible to the criticisms superficially made solely against his children. For example, Meidas Touch, an organization dedicated to preventing Trump's re-election, ran an advertisement attempting to conflate the Trump family as a corrupt global crime syndicate (Trump Crime Family, 2020). The advertisement begins, "The family is a criminal enterprise. Russian mobsters and corrupt oligarchs use Trump's properties not only to launder vast sums of money, but even as a base of operations for their criminal activity… according to the *Times* tonight, president Trump has a previously undisclosed bank account in China." The advertisement then proceeds to talk about how Jared and Ivanka Trump made over 82 million dollars as unpaid advisers, and that Ivanka received patents in China the same day as she had dinner with Xi Jinping. Throughout the advertisement the claims were focused on Trump's children and their dealings in nefarious situations. The advertisement used language such as criminal enterprise, money laundering, criminal activity, prostitution rings and illegal trafficking, undisclosed assets, charity fund allocation, and finally *crime family*, which was reinforced multiple times. The emphasis was not on demonstrating specific wrongdoings by President Trump, but rather the association with criminal signifiers, under the salient umbrella *crime family*.

Similarly, Meidas Touch ran another advertisement called *#byeEric,* focusing on similar crime syndicate imagery (Bye Eric, 2020). The advertisement shows Eric shouting, "they want to get rid of your first amendment" followed by Donald Trump saying, "I call the fake news the enemy of the people." The crime-syndicate imagery is communicated by showing a video of the police injuring a news employee filming the riots as the Trump voiceover continues to run. The enthymeme argues that Donald Trump is truly the one who is threatening free speech. In this advertisement, the police are Donald Trump's soldiers and his children are his consigliere (Trump Crime Family, 2020).

The crime family persona is further emphasized by associating Donald Trump with QAnon, a radical far right group that believes the world is being controlled by a secret group of Satanist pedophiles who engage in a global sex trafficking cannibal scheme (Roose, 2021). When asked what he thought about QAnon's traction and their looking to him for leadership, Donald Trump's voice asked, "Is that a bad thing?" (Bye Eric, 2020). The purpose of framing Donald Trump's statement with Eric was to paint the entire family as untrustworthy and then point out that Donald Trump sanctions the crimes that makes the family untrustworthy. Showing Donald Trump expressing indecisive sentiment towards alt-right organizations such as QAnon communicates tacit support. This expression is then contextualized by Eric's statements regarding the imminent dangers to our first amendment rights. In attempting to show Donald Trump's stance on QAnon, Meidas Touch debunks, disseminating a substitute narrative that the Trump family are felonious and not to be trusted, through the lens of Eric's statements.

Jared Kushner also experienced criminally focused attacks on his persona in advertisements crafted against Donald Trump. One advertisement begins by suggesting that lacking administrative experience his appointment was the solely the result of overt nepotism. The advertisement starts with an awkward interaction where Jared says that his team on the Middle East is highly qualified, to which the individual he is talking to laughs and exclaims, "How is that?!" Jared responds, "I was joking" (He Went to Jared, 2020). The advertisement then shifts to depicting Jared as a white-collar criminal. Advertisements said things like, "The [Saudi] crown prince is boasting that Kushner was quote is in his pocket" and focused on the fact that he and Ivanka made millions as unpaid advisors. Emphasizing that Jared made millions of dollars in an unpaid position amplifies the criminal undertones in Jared's criticisms. By painting Jared as greedy and felonious, negative associations occur on the familial level and then specifically on Trump for hiring him.

Hunter Biden.

Advertisements covering Hunter Biden likewise defaulted to a criminal narrative, although tonality varied. Questions surrounding his connection with the Ukraine energy company Burisma and why he was chosen to have a silent board position spread. One of the ads explained, "Hunter Biden had no energy experience, no knowledge of Ukraine, no policy experience, he didn't even speak the language. The reason Hunter got the job? Five letters, his last name B-I-D-E-N (Biden/Ukraine, 2020)." Hunter becomes minimally the grifter if not an outright white-collar crook, a theme similar to those adhering to the Trump children. Hunter was accused of immorality, but the highlight of the accusation was his last name, those associated with his immorality. The purpose of defacing Hunter was to identify the moral indecency in the Biden *family*, and then transition the blame to Joe Biden. By underscoring the Biden family's impropriety, the Trump campaign estranged voters from the "criminal enterprise."

Efforts to represent Joe Biden as deceitful is also observed in other Trump advertisements. For example, one clip-video depicted Trump personally attacking Joe Biden's ethos through Hunter Biden. During the advertisement Trump claims, "[Joe] lied about his involvement in his son's corrupt business dealing [Burisma]" (Trump calls the report, 2020). The statement was not that he was a part of the corrupt business deal, but rather that he lied about it. Biden, it is suggested, engaged in a cover-up. Wrongdoing was implied, but the message directly confronted Joe Biden's persona, painting him as a candidate who would lie. By representing Joe Biden, and his son, as lawbreakers, Trump striped Joe Biden of being the palpable decorum alternative

Joe Biden's campaign strengths were fundamentally centered on characteristics distinct from the Trump campaign, helping to explain strategy variation between the campaign will. Biden's position as the alternative to the Trump likely invited the Trump counterattacks on family. Having already played their hand once, Americans knew that the full Trump family played central roles in the administration. Any attacks having to do with his children inherently adhered to Trump. The allegory 'Crime family' perfectly weaponizes Trump's familial associates as dangerous staples of what a future Trump administration would look like. On the other hand

On the other hand, Joe Biden's decorum-filled alternative to the "Don" meant any personal association or attempt at covering up his son's business dealings would patently contradict the platform from which his campaign was built. Biden's persona functioned as both his avenue to election and his opponent's optimal target of offense. The Trump attacks aimed to neutralize or inoculate the drumbeat of attacks on his family.

Nonetheless, not all child-oriented advertisements attempted to push a criminal narrative. In other circumstances Trump's children were weaponized to obviate his shortcomings as president. In an advertisement titled Bye Ivanka, Ivanka is pictured explaining, "your journey to this day did not come without challenges, sacrifices, determination, grit, sweat and likely a few tears" (Bye Ivanka the Sequel, 2020). The images then flash to police shooting tear gas at protesters. The advertisement then continues with Ivanka discussing measures taken across the country to protect American citizens, all the while juxtaposing images of police brutality. The advertisement communicated that what Ivanka sees is not what is happening in America. The words coming out of Ivanka's mouth are in stark contrast with the videos of events occurring on the streets. The advertisement emphasizes over-extensions of authority and force, specifically highlighting that Donald Trump is the reason for the police brutality and that Ivanka is "unaware." The "Lie" a deep seeded corruption within the Trump family. Undoubtedly, the fear that Trump shares the same disjointed reality as his daughter or perhaps worse, that he taught her to think the way she does. The desired outcome of framing Ivanka as having lost touch is to provoke the consumer to inquire why she lost touch in the first place.

Conclusion

The 2020 presidential campaign produced numerous advertisements focusing on the candidate's children, birthing the researcher's investigative curiosity. Salient trends in the language became clear; police corruption, criminality, incompetence, conflict of interests, and international syndicate narratives were added to the strategies weaponized during the 2020 presidential campaign. The themes became evident focusing on defaming the opposition rather than communicating policy. In fact, all but three of the advertisements had no mention of policy, including elucidation on their own administration's prospective viewpoints. The question begs itself, if not foreign policy, what are the advertisements communicating to their audience? What are the specific goals of foreign policy advertisements during a presidential campaign? The answer is that foreign policy becomes a container for battles fought on different grounds. Individuals were deployed using corruption, deception, illicit and immoral activity as an added avenue to impugning the opponent's character. Foreign policy advertisements have transitioned from policy to persona, a locus of slander and the 2020 presidential campaign irreparably reinforced that trend. The prominence of the children demonstrates the trend of attempting to slander individuals through superficial "foreign policy" advertising.

References

Alice Roosevelt Longworth: Topics in chronicling America: introduction. (2020, October 21). Library of Congress. https://guides.loc.gov/chronicling-america-alice-roosevelt-longworth

Biden/Ukraine (2020). Donald J. Trump, YouTube. https://www.youtube.com/watch?v=2AApjerH2TE

Bye Eric: A total phony (2020, August 22). Meidas Touch. https://youtu.be/sX7Q8fKQoQ4

Bye Ivanka the sequel: Trump family nepotism exposed. Meidas Touch, YouTube. https://www.youtube.com/watch?v=c-8-SHFzp1I&feature=emb_logo&ab_channel=MeidasTouch

Dedicated Americans protecting democracy. The Lincoln Project. https://lincolnproject.us/

Trump interrupts Biden's tribute to late son to raise unfounded accusations (2020, September 30). Guardian News, YouTube. https://www.youtube.com/watch?v=vaioeewn5CY&ab_channel=GuardianNews

Hogan, M. A. (2017). *John Quincy Adams: Life before the presidency.* Miller Center. https://millercenter.org/president/jqadams/life-before-the-presidency

Leonard, T. (2020, October 15). *Shocking pictures of Biden's son and damning emails emerge.* Daily Mail. https://www.dailymail.co.uk/news/article-8842709/Joe-Bidens-son-crack-pipe-new-low-dirtiest-election-writes-TOM-LEONARD.html

Halper, D. (2016, August 19). *Obama 'furious' at Malia for appearing to smoke pot.* New York Post. https://nypost.com/2016/08/19/obama-furious-at-malia-for-appearing-to-smoke-pot/

He Went to Jared: Jared Kushner's failure (2020, July1). Meidas Touch, YouTube. https://www.youtube.com/watch?v=nkeyFUe6WdU&ab_channel=MeidasTouch

Felsenthl, C. (2014, December 3). *A presidential daughter you could pick on.* POLITICO Magazine.

https://www.politico.com/magazine/story/2014/12/first-daughters-alice-roosevelt-113302

Trump Crime Family (2020, October 23). Meidas Touch, YouTube. https://youtu.be/A_ticL9p_NE

Presidential libraries and museums of the National Archives. (2021, January 20). National Archives. https://www.archives.gov/presidential-libraries

Roose, K. (2121, February 4). *What Is QAnon, the Viral Pro-Trump Conspiracy Theory?* New York Times. https://www.nytimes.com/article/what-is-qanon.html

Rubinstein, D. (2020, October 15). Times Square billboards with Ivanka Trump and Jared Kushner stir skirmish. *The New York Times* (2020, October 25). https://www.nytimes.com/2020/10/25/nyregion/billboard-ivanka-trump-jared-kushner.html

Thomas "Tad" Lincoln – Abraham Lincoln Bicentennial Foundation. (n.d.). Abraham Lincoln Bicentennial Foundation. https://www.lincolnbicentennial.org/resources/abraham-lincolns-life/lincolns-family/thomas-tad-lincoln.

Trump calls report on hunter Biden a 'smoking gun' (2020, October 14). *Bloomberg Politics, YouTube*. https://www.youtube.com/watch?v=ETTmhCsz2Fw&ab_channel=BloombergPolitics

USA Today. (2020, September 29). *President Trump slams Hunter Biden at first presidential debate. USA Today*. YouTube. https://www.youtube.com/watch?v=2kycW_uv7OM&ab_channel=USATODAY

Webb Cook Hayes. (n.d.). Rutherford B. Hayes Presidential Library & Museums. https://www.rbhayes.org/hayes/webb-cook-hayes/

---

[i] A substantial number of ads attacking Hunter Biden are analyzed in the China chapters 30 and 31. They were not included in this study.

Chapter 32: "Losers" & "Suckers": 2020 Presidential Campaign Military Advertising

Yanlin Zhang

Yanlin is a Senior in Mathematical Economics from Shanghai, China

Introduction and Literature Review

2020 was one of the most dramatic years entering into the 21st century, filled with natural disasters, global health crisis, perplexed international affairs, unexpected deaths of celebrities, and what we focus on here, the new round of selecting a president. This chapter examines the military ads offered during the 2020 presidential election period.

Political advertising in the United States has been among the most common topics of political communication research. Johnson and Kaid in their 2002 comprehensive study of techniques, strategies, narratives, and symbols used in televised political spots in US presidential campaigns find that issues ads are more common than image ads, that attacks are more common in issues ads, and that image ads focus primarily on candidates' credibility. However, this is updated by Mahone (2009) based on empirical estimation of US election ads in 2004 and 2008. He concludes that North American political advertising might be shifting from a policy focus to a character focus.

This chapter focuses on the cross-comparison of the strategies, techniques, narratives, and various elements of the political ads surrounding military themes and issues. Very few literatures have touched on this topic, with most studies focusing on political ads generically or in another issue arena. A likely reason for the dearth of attention is the simple fact that advertising regarding military were far and few between in previous cycles.

The United States has an especially liberal environment regarding political advertising regulation. There is little regulation of content, allowing campaign to advertise and invent messaging at will. The Bipartisan Campaign Reform Act of 2002 pointedly did not enforce the verifiability of content of political advertising (Bipartisan Campaign Reform Act, n.d.). Therefore, it is not entirely surprising to see melodramatic ads, some of them even uncomfortable to watch.

Appealing to emotion is an important aspect in political ads. Research on the role of emotions in political persuasion (Brader, 2005) shows that presidential candidates use campaign ads to elicit emotions and thereby influence the political behavior of viewers in predictable ways. From a historical perspective, the campaign ads and political ads tend to address the negativity of the opponent more often than the positivity of the sponsoring candidate (Krupnikov, 2014).

Methodology

To analyze advertisement's themes, I created codebook that consists of seven variables: *Sponsorship, Timeline, Standpoint, Slant Form/Style, Type of Organization*, and *Theme*. Frequency distribution and cross-tabulation among variables were the primary analysis outcomes. 74 ads were scrutinized.

Sponsorship refers to which groups of presidential candidate, political organizations or activist groups officially endorsed the video message. Many of the ads are from the direct endorsement of either presidential candidate, and therefore I denote them as "Biden" or "Trump." There are also a solid number of endorsements from political action committees (PAC) like Lincoln Project and VoteVets. Lastly there are video clips from media sources like Fox News, presented as political ads, typically by the Trump campaign.

Timeline is where I classify all the advertisements according to specific months in 2020. Some of the months were when key events or "turning points" happened, for example, was variable when the conventions for both parties took place.

The Standpoint variable consists of five values: "pro-Biden", "Biden-affiliated", "pro-Trump", "Trump-affiliated", and "independent." One of the purposes is to categorize each ad according to their general standpoint. If the ad is a direct endorsement from either presidential candidate, then it would be marked as "pro-Biden" or "pro-Trump." If the ad producer itself is an activist group or political organization, mostly PACs, whether it publicly endorses either presidential candidate will determine if it is affiliated or independent. For example, The Lincoln Project is categorized as "Biden-affiliated" because the organization officially announced to endorse Joe Biden for president on Twitter, Apr. 8, 2020. VoteVets, on top of endorsing Joe Biden, urged Biden to name Senator Tammy Duckworth as his Vice-Presidential candidate. Trump-affiliated organizations include Turning Point Action, an affiliate of Turning Point USA and the PAC that campaigns against Democrats during the 2020 election season [i]. To determine whether a group is independent or not is a little more nuanced task. Organizations like Patriots for change, though posted ads that went directly against Trump administration, did not officially claim their endorsement to the other extreme and they are therefore considered independent. A cross-table between *Standpoint* and *Sponsorship* will be presented and explained later.

Slant, different from *Standpoint*, is to address more of the political tendency that the content of specific ads reveals. There are five possible entries: "neutral", "pro-Biden", "anti-Biden", "pro-Trump", and "anti-Trump." However, of all 74 ads in the Military-Troop-Arlington dataset, none of them employs an "anti-Biden" strategy in the content, and therefore only the remaining four entries are present. As aforementioned, ads from Patriots for change, although the organization itself is most likely to be independent, the content of its ads is consistently criticizing Trump's behaviors and policies. The same rule applies to Stand Up Republic and Really American PACs. Therefore, those ads, or observations in the dataset, will be denoted "independent" in Standpoint yet "anti-Trump" in Slant. Besides, there are also a decent number of ads that technically are also against Trump but convey the message mostly based on supporting Biden's policies and plans, such as one ad by Unite the Country. Those ads, in terms of Slant, will be denoted as "pro-Biden." There is a peculiar ad, a short video clip of Trump addressing police and military issues from Fox News, is classified as "neutral" since it is part of Trump's statement that should be objective. One may argue the clip is cropped and perhaps aimed to degrade or ascend Trump's image, but I do not go that far. Therefore, it is treated as an outlier and was removed it from the sample.

Form/Style is a general categorization of the form or style of those video advertisements. They are annotated as "Speech" if they are highly unedited video clips of Trump, Biden, or Congressmen. They are annotated as "Documentary/Narrative" if they use montage or other types of editing styles, oftentimes accompanied by background music, and may use actors/actresses to play out the plots instead of real clips. They are annotated as "Testimonial" if they are highly unedited video clips of veterans themselves talking about their political opinions. For example, almost every ad from Lincoln project is "documentary/narrative" since the production and content are highly artificial and original. A few ads from Republican Voters Against Trump (RVAT) and Veterans for Responsive Leadership (VFRL), on the other hand, are based on "Testimonial."

Type of Organization is a variable that classify the groups or organizations that produced the ads. An ad is "Political Party" if it is directly endorsed by either presidential candidate, "Political Organization" if it is produced by PACs or, literally, political organizations like Lincoln Project or Pacronym,

"Activist Group" if it is produced by non-political organizations like RVAT, or "Media"[ii] if it produced by cable channels like Fox News or news channels like Bloomberg News (See Table 1).

Table 1. Sponsorship: relative frequencies

Source	Number	Percent
American Bridge	1	1.35%
Biden	20	27.03%
Nat Sec for Biden	1	1.35%
Pacronym	1	1.35%
Patriots for Change	2	2.70%
Really American	1	1.35%
Stand Up Republic	1	1.35%
Unite the Country	1	1.35%
Trump	7	9.46%
Turning Point Action	1	1.35%
Lincoln Project	12	16.22%
RVAT	2	2.70%
Meidas Touch	3	4.05%
VFRL	2	2.70%
VoteVets	15	20.27%
Bloomberg	1	1.35%
Fox News	2	2.70%
Tulsi Gabbard	1	1.35%

Theme is the last variable that describe what is advertisement is generally addressing. There are instances like hostages, Russia, veterans' opinions, etc., but the most frequent is the "general" category, which is essentially addressing military/troops in general rather than focusing on one or two specific themes/issues.

Data Description and Result

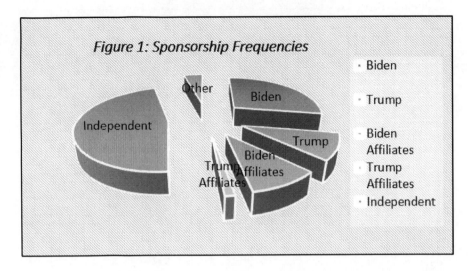

Figure 1 shows the frequency distribution for sponsorship. Notably, 27% of the ads are sponsored by Biden team, 20.27% are from VoteVets, and 16.2% are from Lincoln Project. It is not surprising to see that, for the general theme of military and troops, most of the ads are from organizations, like VoteVets, that either focus on the interests and rights of veterans, or those themselves less affiliated with the military but actively uses Trump's disparaging of the US military as an effective weapon to reproach Trump administration and thereby supporting Biden. There are also 9.46% of the 73 military-related ads that are sponsored by Trump team, focusing generally on Trump's behaviors that honor the courage, patriotism, and utter devotion of the US military.

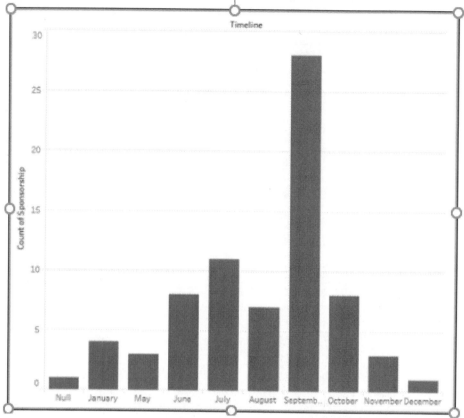

Figure 2. Timeline: relative frequencies

Figure 2 shows the frequency distribution for *Timeline* from January to December 2020. 38% of the ads were posted in September 2020, when Trump was accused of nixing a visit to France's Aisne-Marne American Cemetery and Memorial in 2018, the absentee ballots to voters were started to mailed out in North Carolina, various presidential and vice presidential candidates attended 911 memorial ceremonies, Supreme Court justice Ruther Bader Ginsburg died, the first presidential debate took place, etc. Ads published in June, July, August, taking up roughly 35% of the ads in total, when both parties' primaries and conventions took place, reactions to the George Floyd killing varyingly intensified, Trump's tax records got subpoenaed, Kanye West announced campaigns, etc. Not to take away from October, when 11% of the ads were posted, Trump and Melania tested positive for COVID-19, candidates attended multiple town halls, deadlines of absentee ballot got extended, second presidential debate took place.

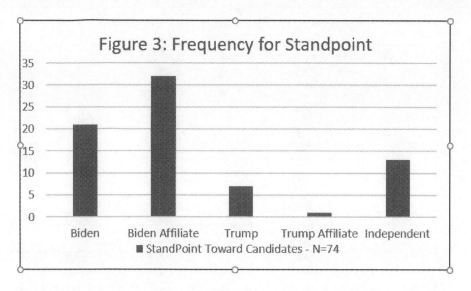

Figure 3 shows the frequency distribution for *Standpoint*. Ads that endorsed directly by Biden or created by Biden-affiliated organizations make up of more than 70% of all the military-themed ads, in contrast with only 10% ads from Trump or Trump-affiliated sources. Those percentages explain themselves, showing how military-relevant themes and contents leave Trump open to a variety of charges and accusations, and subsequently how pro-Biden ads utilize such vulnerability to touch up Biden's propositions and to strengthen his legitimacy. In the Slant frequency distribution right after, and the cross-table of Standpoint versus Slant in later sections, we further see how independent groups align themselves with Biden or at least demarcated themselves from Trump in terms of military scenarios.

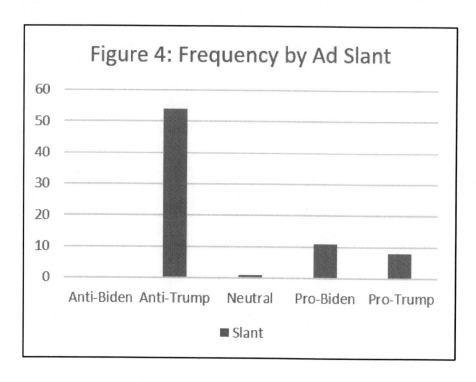

Figure 4 shows the frequency distribution for *Slant*. There are 73% of the ads, overwhelmingly, present anti-Trump content relevant to the military themes. Many of them focus on veterans' opinions, John McCain, families of military, or the general rhetoric that built up various materials that Trump reprimanded war heroes, veterans, sacrificed troops. On the contrary, significantly fewer military ads support Biden without including Trump's self-aggrandizing demeanor. I go into specific examples of advertisements later, yet Trump is vulnerable in public opinion battleground of military issues.

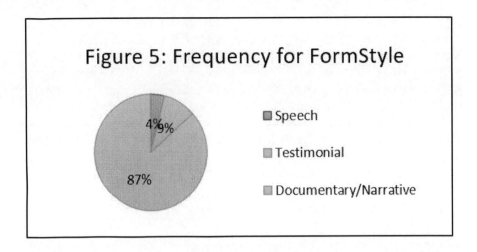

Figure 5 shows the frequency distribution for *Form/Style*. Not surprisingly, 86.5% of the ads fall into the category of documentary/narrative as it is a favored mode for establishing credibility with campaign advertising. These ads are exquisitely produced, rehearsed, and even micro-films, with melodramatic background music, classic or in some cases formalist style of editing, testimonial, speech, or documentary fragments, resulting in a synthetic rhetorical device. Though small in numbers, nearly 10% of the ads featured less-edited clips of the statements and opinions from veterans or families of US military. Therefore, regardless of which side specific ads were supporting, the overall advertising strategy consists of 90% of artificial documentary/narrative and 10% of more "realistic" materials. I will go into specific examples later. Figure 5, likewise, shows the highly skewed distribution of what video style the ads utilize.

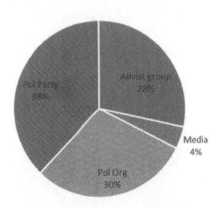

Figure 6
Freq by Type of Organization

Figure 6 shows the frequency distribution for Type of Organizations. 28% of the ads are created by activist groups including RVAT, Stand Up Republic, VoteVets, VFRL, and NatSecForBiden. Just to note that NatSecForBiden, fully known as National Security Officials for Biden, should be part of the activist group Defending Democracy Together 29.1% of the ads are created by political organizations, mostly PACs, including American Bridge, Lincoln Project, Meidas Touch, Pacronym, Patriots for Change, Really American, Turning Point Action, and Unite the Country. 37.8% of the ads are endorsed by presidential candidates directly. Last there are 3 ads, taking up 4% of the 74 military ads, are from the media sources.

Table 2 Frequency Distribution for Theme

Absentee Vote	1	1.35%	Deceased	2	2.70%
Hostages	2	2.70%	Military Families	5	6.76%
Jim Mattis	1	1.35%	General	18	24.32%
John McCain	3	4.05%	Gen.'s Opinion	3	4.05%
McConnell's Silence	1	1.35%	Healthcare	1	1.35%
Russia	8	10.81%	Mil. Base Name	1	1.35%
Russia Police	1	1.35%	Military Vote	1	1.35%
Spanish Troops	1	1.35%	News vs Trump	1	1.35%
Tammy Duckworth	1	1.35%	Pandemic	2	2.70%
Tom Tillis	1	1.35%	Police & Military	1	1.35%
Vietnam	1	1.35%	Protest	1	1.35%
Women	1	1.35%	Veterans Opinion	12	16.22%
Captured Heroes	1	1.35%	Veto Threat	1	1.35%

Lastly, Table 2 shows the themes addressed. A variety of themes and topics were touched on, while topics of Russia, veterans' opinion, families of military are addressed multiple times, representing 11%, 16%, and 6.7% respectively. There is also notably 24% of the ads that may not have a specific topic, discussing general or a combination of military-relevant issues. The nature of those small-numbered items in the table is that there was a variety of different ways to talk about the issue beyond Arlington, such as Vietnam War, women in the military, as well as a combination of two or three individual topics, like a June Stand Up Republic ad, with Russia, police, and military combined (Donald's Betrayal, 2020).

Effect of negativity in political advertising

Figure 7: Standpoint vs Slant 1

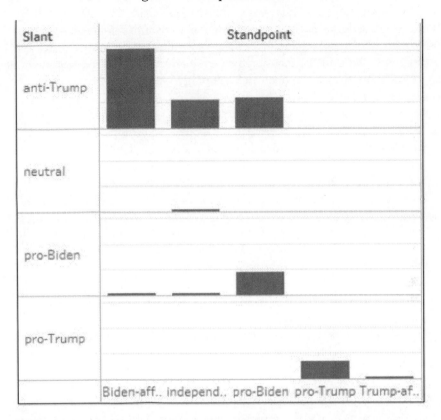

Figure 7 is a cross-tabulation of *Standpoint* versus *Slant*, the political stance versus actual content of the ads. This is trying to build upon the individual frequency distribution of Standpoint and Slant content, showing that regardless of the political stance of an organization (except for pro-Trump ads), the general rhetorical strategy is consistently anti-Trump, attacking his inappropriate statements toward US military or suspected misbehavior with Russia. Those military ads are rhetorically strong and distinctive, criticizing Trump in a multi-faceted manner.

Let us consider one short statement by Joe Biden in *A Betrayal* (2020). It is a short clip of Biden criticizing Trump regarding his alleged connection to Russia. The context is the FBI and several US congressional committees have been investigating links between Russia government officials and individuals associated with Donald Trump, in part resulting from the investigation of the Russian interference in the 2016 US elections (Borger, 2017). Following Trump confidant Roger Stone dropping his appeal of seven felony convictions which detailed ties between the Trump campaign and Russia, the final reported released by US Senate Select Committee on

Intelligence on Aug. 18, 2020, stated that there were significant ties between 2016 Trump presidential campaign and Russia (Gerstein, 2020). Specifics revealed transactions between several Russians as a back-handed way to relieve his personal debt and tax issues. Regardless of the actual case, his affiliation with Putin and Russian businessmen has been condemned both in speeches and writings for years and inevitably is an opportunity to exploit for Biden and his supporters.

In Biden's June 28 video, he framed his words concisely addressing this topic, "Not only did he fail to sanction or impose any kind of consequences on Russia for this egregious violation of international law, Donald Trump has continued his embarrassing campaign of deference and debasing himself before Vladimir Putin…he sought to invite Russia to rejoin the G7…It's betrayal of the most sacred duty we bear as a nation to protect and equip our troops when we send them in a harm's way." Biden commentary works in the way to scapegoat Trump, while consensus is signaled by supporting advertising from other anti-Trump ads groups.

It is not uncommon to see one candidate form his or her own message by attacking another candidate. Geer & Vavreck (2014) points out that in a polarized political environment, exaggeration by candidates in attacking an opponent creates more value for negativity. Geer (2006) and Ansolabehere and Iyengar (1995) demonstrate the statistical correlation between polarization and negativity. Such polarization in the US bipartisan atmosphere is exacerbated after Trump's 4-year effort in creating an iconoclastic style of politics with Biden portraying an imminent need for a national leader with expertise, establishment, and pluralism. Therefore, instead of yielding confusion and misinformation, anti-Trump negativity worked to capture the Trump backlash.

Table 3: Sponsorship & Standpoint vs Type of Organization

Sponsorship	Standpoint	Activist Group	Media	Political Organization	Political Party
American Bridge	Biden-affiliated			■	
Biden	pro-Biden				■
Bloomberg	independent		■		
Fox News	independent		■		
Lincoln Project	Biden-affiliated			■	
MeidasTouch	independent			■	
NatSecForBiden	pro-Biden	■			
Pacronym	Biden-affiliated			■	
Patriots For Change	independent			■	
Really American	independent			■	
RVAT	Biden-affiliated	■			
Stand Up Republic	independent	■			
Trump	pro-Trump				■
Tulsi Gabbard	Biden-affiliated				■
Turning Point Action	Trump-affiliated			■	
Unite the Country	independent			■	
VFRL	independent	■			
VoteVets	Biden-affiliated			■	

Table 3 is a cross-tabulation of *Sponsorship*, *Standpoint* versus *Type of Organization*. It shows the military-themed ads were dispensed by a varied collection of political organizations, including Lincoln Project, Meidas Touch, Pacronym, Patriots for Change, Really American, Turning Point Action, Unite the Country, and activist groups, including NatSecForBiden, RVAT, Stand Up Republic, VFRL, and VoteVets, and for both categories there are mostly independent and Biden-affiliated organizations.[iii]

Those different activist groups or political organizations are founded by both political and non-political people, varying in size and initiative, but most of them are anti-Trump republicans or right-leaning individuals. Patriots for change is a group of former reporters, video producers, political veteran, website developers, and others who are harnessing social media to reach American voters and sought to replace Donald Trump and nine GOP Senators in the election. Meidas Touch is a PAC formed by three brothers to stop the re-election of Trump. Really American is an anti-Trump PAC, as is Pacronym and Stand Up Republic, more progressive leaning PACs. Unite the Country is a PAC founded by several former aides to Joe Biden to support his presidential campaign (Meyer & Severns, 2019). Republicans Vote

Against Trump (RVAT), the name speaks for itself, focuses on hundreds of testimonials of republicans, conservatives, moderates, and right-leaning independent voters. Except for Unite the Country that is more directly Biden-affiliated, other independent or republican organizations use essentially similar rhetoric in their ads, calling Trump "betrayers" due to his actions relevant to Russia, criticizing his attitude towards John McCain, etc.

One of the few pro-Trump ads was issued by college Republicans, Turning Point Action's ad (Gold Star Families, 2020), a cropped Fox News video clip praising Trump for supporting Gold Star Families. The spot shows an interview with Brittany Jacobs, a Gold Star widow who expressed her gratefulness of what Trump had done for her family. She specifically mentioned the effort Trump made to help eliminate the SBP-DIC Offset (Survivor Benefit Plan/Dependency and Indemnity Compensation Offset (Phased Elimination, 2121).

The Trump campaign, however, did use the military extensively in its general advertising. Some ads were predominantly aimed at the military issue, for example his *Commander in Chief* spot where the central actor Trump dominates the scene surrounded by military venues. He lauds accomplishments, radiates leadership, and in "bigger than life visuals" his voiceover proclaims being Commander-in-chief "it's more than just a job, it's a sworn duty, to keep America safe" (2020).

As compared to the various anti-Trump ads showing multidimensional content, the pro-Trump ads were relatively standard in the sense they reinforce already well-known leadership virtues, not nearly as the "shocking" revelations from opposing quarters. Both in terms of strategy and numbers, pro-Trump ads in the realm of military issues seemingly were at a disadvantage.

Is September 2020 pivotal?

Table 4: Timeline vs Sponsorship & Theme

Theme	Sponsorship	Janu..	May	June	July	Augu..	Sept..	Octo..	Nove..	Dece..
911	Lincoln Project						■			
Absentee Vote	Lincoln Project								■	
captured heroes	Lincoln Project						■			
deceased	Trump		■				■			
families of military	Biden						■			
	Lincoln Project		■							
	Turning Point Action						■			
	VoteVets					■	■			
general	Biden	■		■	■		■		■	
	Bloomberg	■								
	Lincoln Project					■	■			
	Pacronym				■					
	Really American						■			
	RVAT						■			
	Trump					■	■			
	Tulsi Gabbard	■								
	Unite the Country	■								
	VoteVets					■				
generals opinion	Biden							■		
	Lincoln Project		■							
	VoteVets						■			
healthcare	Biden				■					
Hostages	Trump					■				
Jim Mattis	Lincoln Project			■						
John McCain	Lincoln Project							■		
	MeidasTouch						■			
	RVAT						■			
McConnell's silence	Patriots For Change						■			
military base names	VoteVets			■						
military vote	VoteVets						■			
newspapers vs Trump	Fox News						■			
pandemic	MeidasTouch							■	■	
police military	Fox News				■					
protest	VoteVets				■					
Russia	Biden			■						
	Lincoln Project			■						
	VFRL			■						
	VoteVets					■	■			
Russia Police	Stand Up Republic			■						
Spanish Troops	VoteVets						■			
Tammy Duckworth	VoteVets			■						
Tom Tillis	Patriots For Change						■			
veterans opinion	American Bridge						■			
	Biden						■	■		■
	NatSecForBiden							■		
	Trump						■			
veto threat	VoteVets				■					
Vietnam	Lincoln Project						■			
Vindman	Lincoln Project					■				
Women	VFRL							■		

Table 4 is a cross-tabulation of *Timeline* versus *Sponsorship* and *Theme*. Note that all ads from the refined sample were posted in 2020. Earlier Figure 2 revealed that September was most concentrated with military ads, we also see ads by organizations including Lincoln Project, VFRL, RVAT, VoteVets, and American Bridge 21st Century, centralizing their advertising within the August-October period. Ads by Biden were posted throughout the year, and there are also ads by Stand Up Republic, for example, scattered out a little more and not necessarily targeting 3-month period. Besides, we also discern a variety of different themes being addressed in the September period, including 9/11, families of military, bounties, deceased, military vote, Spanish language troops, Vietnam, and veterans' opinion.

September 2020 appeared to be crucial considering concurrent happenings. The trigger event appeared September 3 when *The Atlantic* published an article by Jeffery Goldberg claiming that Trump did not want to join other heads of state visiting France's Aisne-Marne American Cemetery and Memorial in 2018 to honor US troops buried there. He said, according to *The Atlantic* reporting, they were "losers" and "suckers" (Goldberg, 2020).

The occurrence of Trump calling sacrificed troops losers and suckers became a signature event that inflamed the US military families, veterans, opposing politicians, and organizations. The Lincoln Project ad *9/11* (2020) addressed the dedication and sacrifice of the US military, simultaneously reprimanding Trump's ignorance of the military. The *9/11* ad explicitly linked 9/11, COVID-19, and Trump's transactional core, creating strong comparisons the daily death of the pandemic and the total casualties of 9/11. The ad replays a Trump statement "that he now had the tallest building in New York" after World Trade Center collapsed. The ad tallies the virus deaths, "a 9/11 death toll every three days, because of the fool that sits behind the president's desk."

The *9/11* ad also implicitly points out Trump's arrogance in the aftermath civil unrest of the George Floyd incident. The death of George Floyd in police custody contributed to the public's examination of racial inequality across society, but also within the US military (George Floyd's Death, 2020). The fear was people might become more disbelieving of the authorities linked with maintaining social order, including the military.

In a VoteVets' Spanish language spot *Mi País*, former military veteran Pablo Pantoja reveals he received his military ID on 9/11, 2001, yet Donald Trump made him a "double loser", "treated us as if we were worthless." He intoned, "we cannot stop the hurricane, but we can stop Donald Trump." In the latter VoteVets Spanish ad, the combat of hurricane Laura was brought up, a way of implying Trump administration's history of politicizing disaster responses and the inability to deal with crises, where military is all about crisis.

Trump also threatened to deploy the army to quash the upheaval (Zurcher, 2020), undermining the military's reputation as it might be compelled to turn against American citizens. These spots illustrate how ads associated with military became fiercely demarcated via Trump repute. These ads also are discerning examples of how campaign's put together different, perhaps irrelevant, pieces together to target Trump.

At a White House press conference (President Donald Trump, 2020), Trump referred to *The Atlantic* article, as a "hoax." The former ad makes a defensible point regarding a hoax in the sense he is calling out hyped "out-of-context" piling on. From that reading of what he said the latter statement by Trump might not be as flat as it seemed to be. Nonetheless, a few "trivial" enactments, disavowals of accusations, could be easily outweighed by multiple kinds of anti-Trump permeations. As Trump himself described it in the press conference, the media puts so many "unrelated things" together when it got closer to the election, and at least in the realm of military-Arlington-troops, those accusations/criticisms/ads/evidences become rhetorically compelling.

Giving September some leeway, we see on Oct. 2, 2020, Trump was tested positive for COVID-19 coronavirus (Baker & Haberman, 2020), a pivotal incident undercutting his effort to shift the campaign focus away from the pandemic. It was made it even more sarcastic was Trump suggesting Gold Star families might be whom to blame for his infection and the spread of the coronavirus at the White House (Steinhauer, 2020).

Forms and Styles

Table 5: Theme & Sponsorship vs Form/Style

(continues on following page)

Theme	Sponsorship	documen..	Speech	Testimo..
911	Lincoln Project	■		
Absentee Vote	Lincoln Project	■		
captured heroes	Lincoln Project	■		
deceased	Trump	■		
families of military	Biden			■
	Lincoln Project	■		
	Turning Point Action			■
	VoteVets	■		■
general	Biden	■		■
	Bloomberg	■		
	Lincoln Project	■		
	Pacronym	■		
	Really American	■		
	RVAT	■		
	Trump	■		
	Tulsi Gabbard		■	
	Unite the Country	■		
	VoteVets	■		
generals opinion	Biden	■		
	Lincoln Project	■		
	VoteVets			■
healthcare	Biden	■		
Hostages	Trump	■		
Jim Mattis	Lincoln Project	■		
John McCain	Lincoln Project	■		
	MeidasTouch	■		
	RVAT			■
McConnell's silence	Patriots For Change	■		
military base names	VoteVets	■		
military vote	VoteVets	■		
newspapers vs Trump	Fox News	■		
pandemic	MeidasTouch	■		
police military	Fox News		■	
protest	VoteVets	■		
Russia	Biden		■	
	Lincoln Project	■		
	VFRL			■
	VoteVets	■		
Russia Police	Stand Up Republic	■		
Spanish Troops	VoteVets	■		
Tammy Duckworth	VoteVets	■		
Tom Tillis	Patriots For Change	■		
veterans opinion	American Bridge	■		
	Biden	■		
	NatSecForBiden	■		
	Trump	■		
veto threat	VoteVets	■		
Vietnam	Lincoln Project	■		
Vindman	Lincoln Project	■		
Women	VFRL	■		

Table 5 is a cross-tabulation of *Theme, Sponsorship* versus *Form/Style*. Most military ads exhibited an editing style of documentary/narrative, while a few testimonial focused ads also have their own power. For example, a Republican Voters Against Trump ad films a less edited clip of Scott, a Republican Veteran of North Carolina sharing his views of John McCain and Donald Trump (Army Vet, 2020). Along with showing respect to John McCain, he called Trump a "coward" running away from Vietnam. And the short clip of Trump saying "I like people that weren't captured" is included and repeatedly incorporated in other anti-Trump ads. Like other testimonial-based ads, this one is sliced together with other fragmented elements and intertwined with montages, designed to enhance the persuasiveness. These ads worked as "fact-based with emotional appeals."

On the other extreme, most documentary/narrative style military ads in our dataset are more "emotional-based with factual supplements." A good example would be a Meidas Touch ad addressing John McCain as well. Biden's honoring of and Trump's presumptuous statements of John McCain alternate in this one minute and a half video, intersected with edited documentary short clips, Fox News short clips, and stills which combined organically biting montage of Biden praising and Trump disapproving (Arizona Knows Honor, 2020).

One potential reason the combination of two different styles has strength is they target both the audiences' heuristic processing and systematic processing. Schwartz (2000) finds that in the realm of political advertising, positive moods lead to greater reliance on existing beliefs or heuristics, whereas negative moods lead to greater reliance on systemic processing [iv]. Similarly, Brader (2005) suggests that negative images and music elicit meticulous reasoning while positive messages encourage fidelity to prior beliefs. Moreover, Geer and Vavreck (2014) point out that the public learns more from attacks, and attacking an opponent is an implicit way of offering one's own position on the issue, and therefore a pure, entirely negative campaign would not be as effective. Therefore, since overt negativity leads the voters to the central route of information processing inevitably, it is important combine the emotional appeals with at least partial facts in the form of statistics, documentary clips, testimonial statements, etc. In terms Aristotelian modes of persuasion, documentary/narrative-type ads are primarily utilizing *Pathos*, the appeal to the audience's emotions, but the contents are also supplemented with *Ethos*, the appeal to the credibility of the argument and source.

Conclusion

This chapter discussed the content, form, context, and strategy employed by the political/campaign ads relevant to the US military. The empirical result found that anti-Trump ads are fewer and less rhetorically diversified, in part due to the prevailing media narratives which put Trump at a serious disadvantage. Considering "standpoint and slant," the overt and cutting negativity in anti-Trump ads fueled by 2020 turbulence, combined with Trump's iconoclastic persona likely had an impact.

Military ads were generally a late campaign phenomenon with most airing in September, a timeline associated with news stories ("losers" and "suckers" from *The Atlantic*). Other media shocks earlier drove advertising, for example, the Russian bounties on US troops in Afghanistan.

Most of the ads took the form of documentary/narrative, an emotion-appealing approach deployed with military ads. Those ads are more of less backed up with reason-based evidence, asking voters to think about the ads message, an approach aligned with the cognitive principles of persuasive messaging.

Previous literatures on US military advertising have been scarce.[v] This analysis, largely demographic in scope, represents a beginning effort to understanding the military ads in 2020.

References

A betrayal. (June 28, 2020). Joe Biden for President, YouTube. https://www.youtube.com/watch?v=io769-0T9dM

Arizona knows honor (2020, September 23). Meidas Touch, YouTube. https://www.youtube.com/watch?v=3YBK32GH1GA

Army vet and lifelong Republican Scott (2020, September 10). The Republican Accountability Project, YouTube. https://www.youtube.com/watch?v=aGpZsZbH6x0

Baker, P., & Haberman, M. (2020, December 31). *Trump tests positive for the Coronavirus.* The New York Times. https://www.nytimes.com/2020/10/02/us/politics/trump-covid.html

Bipartisan Campaign Reform Act (n.d.). BallotPedia. https://ballotpedia.org/Bipartisan_Campaign_Reform_Act

Borger, J., & Ackerman, S. (2018, February 9). Trump-Russia collusion is being investigated by FBI, Comey confirms. *The Guardian*. https://www.theguardian.com/us-news/2017/mar/20/fbi-director-comey-confirms-investigation-trump-russia

Brader, T. (2005). Striking a responsive chord: How political ads motivate and persuade voters by appealing to emotions. *American Journal of Political Science, 49*(2), 388–405.

Budryk, Z. (2020, July 1). *Liberal veterans group urges Biden to name Duckworth VP*. The Hill. https://thehill.com/homenews/campaign/505484-liberal-veterans-group-urges-biden-to-name-duckworth-vp?rl=1

Commander in Chief (2020, August 13). Donald J Trump, YouTube. https://www.youtube.com/watch?v=WtRaVJaamso

Donald's betrayal. (2020, June 29). Stand Up Republic, YouTube. https://www.youtube.com/watch?v=bFVrYwb3uhE

Franz, M. M., & Ridout, T. N. (2007). Does political advertising persuade? *Political Behavior, 29*(4), 465–491.

Frickel, S., & Rea, C. (2020). Drought, hurricane, or wildfire? Assessing the Trump Administration's anti-science disaster. *Engaging Science, Technology, and Society ,6*, 66-75.

Geer, J. G., & Vavreck, L. (2014). Negativity, information, and candidate position-taking. *Political Communication, 31*(2), 218–236.

Geer, J. G. (2006). *In defense of negativity: Attack ads in presidential campaigns.* Chicago, IL: University of Chicago Press.

George Floyd death makes military face "own demons" on race (2021, January 28). Los Angeles Times. https://www.latimes.com/world-nation/story/2020-06-05/george-floyd-death-pushes-military-face-own-demons-on-race

Gerstein, J. (2020, September 8). *Roger Stone drops appeals of felony convictions*. Politico. https://www.politico.com/news/2020/08/18/roger-stone-felony-appeal-397548

Gold Star Families. (2020, September 8). Turning Point Action, Youtube.

Goldberg, J. (2020, September 4). *Trump: Americans who died in war are 'losers' and 'suckers.'* The Atlantic. https://www.theatlantic.com/politics/archive/2020/09/trump-americans-who-died-at-war-are-losers-and-suckers/615997/

Goldstein, K., & Ridout, T. N. (2004). Measuring the effects of televised political advertising in The United States. *Annual Review of Political Science, 7*(1), 205–226.

Krupnikov, Y. (2014). How negativity can increase and decrease voter turnout: The effect of timing. *Political Communication. 31*, 446-466.

Lopatto, E. (2020, September 15). *Conservative group used a bunch of teens to evade Twitter and Facebook moderation.* The Verge. https://www.theverge.com/2020/9/15/21438897/troll-farm-turning-point-teenagers-moderation

Markus P. (2001). Weighted content analysis of political advertisements. *Political Communication, 18*(3). 335-345.

Meyer, T., & Severns, M. (2019, September 29). *Ex-Biden aide forms Unite the Country super PAC.* Politico. https://www.politico.com/news/2019/10/29/ex-biden-aide-super-pac-unite-the-country-061096

Mi País. (2020, September 23). *VoteVets, YouTube.* https://www.youtube.com/watch?v=yw4Cpd96uB8

Petty, R. E., & Cacioppo, J. T. (1977). *Communication and persuasion: Central and peripheral routes to attitude change.* Springer Series in Social Psychology.

Phased Elimination of the SBP-DIC Offset Begins in January of 2021 (n.d.). Defense Finance and Accounting Service. https://www.dfas.mil/RetiredMilitary/newsevents/news/Survivor-SBP-Newsletter/Phased-Elimination-SBP-DIC-Offset-January-2021/

President Donald Trump on The Atlantic Story. (2020, September 4). Trump, YouTube. https://www.youtube.com/watch?v=EJwtj2YXa5Q

Schwartz, B. (2019, May 20). *Pro-Trump college GOP activist Charlie Kirk will launch a new group to target Democrats in 2020.* CNBC.

https://www.cnbc.com/2019/05/20/pro-trump-activist-charlie-kirk-to-launch-new-group-to-target-democrats.html

Schwarz, N. (2000). Emotion, cognition, and decision making. *Cognition & Emotion, 14*(4), 433–440.

Serhan, Y. (2020, November 5). *What the U.S. Election proved about populism.* The Atlantic. https://www.theatlantic.com/international/archive/2020/11/what-us-election-proved-about-populism/617003/

Sharma, V. (2020, November 11). *Veterans showed up for Biden this year — and Trump wants to dump military ballots.* Now This. https://nowthisnews.com/news/veterans-showed-up-for-biden-this-year-and-trump-wants-to-dump-military-ballots

Stanley-Becker, I. (2020, September 15). *Pro-Trump youth group enlists teens in secretive campaign likened to a 'troll farm,' prompting rebuke by Facebook and Twitter.* The Washington Post. https://www.washingtonpost.com/politics/turning-point-teens-disinformation-rump/2020/09/15/c84091ae-f20a-11ea-b796-2dd09962649c_story.html

Steinhauer, J. (2020, October 8). *Trump suggests Gold Star Families may be to blame for his infection.* The New York Times. https://www.nytimes.com/2020/10/08/us/politics/trump-coronavirus-gold-star-families.html

Zurcher, A. (2020, September 28). *Hunter Biden: Republicans release report on Joe Biden's son.* BBC. https://www.bbc.com/news/election-us-2020-54268887

9/11. (2020, September 11). Lincoln Project, Youtube. https://www.youtube.com/watch?v=-KLyOuWAzns

---

[i] See Issac Stanley-Becker's article on *The Washington Post* on Sept. 15, 2020. He explained how Turning Point USA paid young people in Arizona to post anti-Democrat content without disclosing their affiliation with Turning Point USA.

[ii] Editor's Note: These are usually candidates sponsored ads, using excerpts from the media production.

[iii] Editor's Note: More independent actors took at least one shot at Trump's "military problem" than perhaps any other grouping considered in this volume, lending support for the notion that the military opportunity was apparent and at least somewhat productive. Versha Sharma writing for the military times "cited exit polling from Edison Research that showed 52 percent of military and veteran voters preferred President Donald Trump to Biden, who 45 percent preferred. That margin is much narrower than in 2016, when Trump enjoyed a 26-percent advantage, pulling in 60 percent to Democratic presidential nominee Hillary Clinton's 34 percent (Sharma, 2020).

[iv] According to the Elaboration Likelihood Model (ELM), people process incoming information by using either, or a combination of central route and peripheral route (Petty & Cacioppo,1977), where the former is when audience carefully processes the information with high level of elaboration, yet the latter is when audience makes a simple judgement about the merits of the advocated position.

[v] There are several possible directions for future investigation of military themes in campaign advertising. For example, it would be useful encode the categorical variables with Likert Scales or other methods to quantify the relationships between variables. One may investigate more details of the words and phrasing of the ads by methods like NLP (Natural Language Processing), given that the sample size is much larger. In terms of the form and style of ads, the relationship between ads and characteristics of contemporary culture could be explored.

Chapter 33: An Examination of Immigration Political Advertisements in the 2020 Election

Virginia Witherington

Virginia is a Junior in Communication from Fairhope, Alabama

Immigration has remained a divisive topic throughout U.S. history, even as immigrants make up a "majority" of the U.S. population. In recent years, immigrants comprised almost fourteen percent of the population. The "right", although not all conservatives, tends to view immigrants and refugees as a threat to the American way of life, while the liberal left sees immigrants and refugees as predominantly positive additions to our society. According to the Pew Research Center in 2015, "45% of adults say immigrants in the U.S. are making American society better in the long run, while 37% say they are making it worse" – generally coalescing with party affiliations (Brown, 2015). Cultural changes, perhaps some arising, in part, from increased immigration have contributed to an adverse and politicized reaction.

Many Americans imagine that immigrants "fill the jobs that American citizens do not want" ones citizens believe they are above or too good for (Krogstad, Lopez, Passel 2020). Others reason immigrants steal jobs from Americans. Republicans and Democrats have evolved too late markedly distinct perspectives which often promote isolated outlooks on the creation and enforcement of government policy.

President Trump exacerbated the divide with an approach to immigration incredibly divergent from other Republican presidents – starting with the New York Trump Tower elevator ride and the announcement of the border wall – contributing further to polarizations in political affiliation.

In 2020 incumbent President Donald Trump and Vice President Joe Biden publicly offered polar-opposite perspectives. As suggested above these contentious election positions fed off, in part, a lack of consensus within the country. Immigration political advertisements intentionally created and reinforced difference. They were largely unequivocal in endorsing or distrusting immigration, positions predictable from their authorship. According to CNN, "Candidates and committees have shelled out more than $150 million on campaign ads dealing with immigration so far this year, a major increase over recent election cycles," further exhibiting how disputed immigration remain (Shoichet, 2018). Each party worked to reinforce their public's sanctimonious sense of the right and moral, yet it seems as if neither tried very hard to alter beliefs.

After an initial push of immigration messaging in the primaries, the issue became less central until September and October, late in the campaign. Even then immigration ads took a relative backseat to other issues in the campaign, their bases were reinforced but not much political game was to be had. According to the *Wall Street Journal*, the issue of immigration barely made the list of the top ten topics most highlighted in this election's political advertising (Siddiqui et al., 2020). Yet, there was media discussion about immigration ads, but often they were independent actors and not the campaigns. For example, a series of ads dubbed *Words Matter* released by political action committee Immigrant's List Civic Action Corporation issued varying by subtitles in Korean, Chinese, and Vietnamese (Words Matter – Korean, 2020), focused on incumbent President Trump's "controversial rhetoric" about China and the transmission of coronavirus (Madan, 2020). The ads were prompted as they claimed by the "2,100 anti-Asian American hate incidents related to COVID-19 … reported across the country over a three-month time span between March and June…", and through self-indictment sought to demonstrate President Trump's distaste for the Chinese (Madan, 2020). These ads were examined by the *Miami Herald*, and discussed in the media as "aiming to sway the Pacific Islander voter population to vote against Trump" as well as targeted them, because that population is "often overlooked" (Madan, 2020). Similarly, an article hosted by *Vox* stated that Trump used "nativist language around immigrants in 54 percent of his ads… while Democrats, on the other hand, are talking about fundraising and other policy issues, but not immigration", showing an interesting disconnect between the two parties (Stewart, 2019).

Results

Both the Republican and the Democratic parties produced ads that built on the innate fears that members of their parties hold. For Republican party, these fears include viewing immigrants and refugees as a threat and seeing the border as a secure means of protecting Americans from dangerous criminals. In a Trump social media release, using an excerpt from one of his stump speeches (a mode often used by Trump to create quick ads emphasizing the moment) he capitalized on the fears of Republicans is an ad titled "Biden has promised a 700% increase in the importation of refugees" (Biden has promised, 2020). This augmented an ongoing narrative that if Biden won, he would open the borders, overrun the country, and destroy the culture with a stream of violent, dangerous criminals as well as immigrants that take jobs from "deserving" American citizens. This ad states that, if elected, Biden's nation (specifically Minnesota) will be "flooded with a rampant Somalian population", demonstrating the scare tactics and fear appeals the ad utilizes.

For many Democrats, their fears regarding immigration include threats from the Republican administration's blocking the entry path for many immigrants, the treatment of immigrants in the United States, ICE policies of arrests, deportations, and detainments. An ad that reflects the capitalization on the more liberal, Democratic fears is an ad titled "Cruel" sponsored by the Lincoln Project (Cruel, 2020). This ad, supporting Joe Biden's candidacy, aimed to add to the ever-growing outrage many Democrats held about the way the Trump administration has treated immigrant children and families. The ad utilizes startling – cages, prisons, lonely despondent children – imagery, with words such as "trauma", "sick", and "inhumane" to elicit moral outrage and into an obvious solution, elect Biden. The Democratic ad set appears to beg the presidency to stop the current insanity and treat immigrants as what they are – people. In

The Chicago Council on Global Affairs stated statistically parties divergence, "self-described Republicans are far more likely than Democrats to view immigration as a critical threat (78%, compared to 19%), to believe that restricting immigration makes the United States safer (78%, compared to 24%), and to support the use of US troops to prevent immigration at the US-Mexico border (81%, compared to 23%)" (Affairs, 2020). They also make it clear that "Republicans are also far more likely than Democrats to consider strict immigration policy measures effective, like carrying out more arrests and deportations (82%, compared to 29%) and separating immigrant children from parents when they are accused of entering the US illegally (40%, compared to 10%).", and "Likewise, Republicans are more likely than Democrats to view increasing border security (93%, compared to 55%) and imposing new fines on businesses that hire illegal immigrants (83%, compared to 54%) as effective policies." (Affairs, 2020).

With the immigration ads, I found recurring themes. On the Republican side, the main themes were an emphasis on border security, freedom, illegality, and the violence and corruption that immigrants allegedly bring to America. Another major theme of the Republican backed flank was the "freedom and opportunity" that paradoxically restrictions provide for legal Americans. Regardless of age, race, ethnicity, class, or socioeconomic status, Republican ads emphasized that opportunity and freedom was attainable through hard-working, law-abiding, legal status. By emphasizing the preference and respect for legal immigrants, the Republican ads isolated and ostracized illegal immigrants and their families. The more conservative ad set also portrayed America as a safe haven protected from violent, dangerous immigrants only by border laws and restrictions, and aimed to demonstrate how immigrants would "ruin" that America. These ads also focused on the crime, violence, drugs, and trafficking that immigrants would potentially bring to our country.

Among ads supporting Joe Biden, the major themes were the potential for change, possibilities an opportunity *for all*, and compassion. One of Biden's major platforms was "Change is possible", and this was evident throughout his ads as well as ads produced by other entities supporting him. According to the ads that supported Biden, he aims to change the immigration system, and reform it into a more equitable and humane system for all that has a high regard for human life, as was stated in many of the ads that supported his candidacy. These ads also focused on the possibility and potential of all people, including immigrants. The ads are more generically safe in their language and tone. While maintaining compassion for all, these ads demonstrated how Biden hoped to reform the immigration system and make it increasingly fair and reliable. Another major theme was the plethora of opportunities available to all Americans, including immigrants, in the United States. The ads supporting Joe Biden's candidacy demonstrate how immigrants matter to America, not a faction to be mistreated or forgotten.

In the immigration set, there were 39 ads that were relevant to my research. I chose to focus only on ads for the two actual presidential candidates rather than including primary ads.

In the immigration ad set, a major trend was the repetition of certain words in the ads to portray a specific ad's message and narrative. Ads supporting Trump, the most utilized word was "illegal", with 13 mentions in 15 political advertisements surrounding immigration. The word "alien", similar to "illegal", was also used very frequently, being mentioned 6 times in 15 pro-Trump advertisements. The word violence was used 5 times, and the words "border" and "security" were utilized 3 times each. This demonstrates that for Republicans, there was a major focus on illegality, laws, and border security. The words terrorist and terrorism also deserve mention. They were often used in the ads supporting Trump, as well as a means of inciting fear and wariness to the audience by preying on already present fears about foreigners and acts of terrorism.

The words utilized most to indict Biden in the Trump and affiliate ads supporting President, were extreme, radical, and weak. This echoed much of the "popular" Republican opinion that Biden was unfit to be in office. For ads supporting Biden, words utilized often were "change" and "violence", with 6 mentions each in 24 political advertisements surrounding immigration. The word used most frequently was "caged" to describe the separation of immigrant children from their families, with 7 uses in 24 pro-

Biden advertisements. The words "progress" "possibility", and "opportunity" were also utilized, with each being repeated 4 times within the 24-count ad set. From the Democratic standpoint, there are more issues to discuss than the Republican side. Therefore, they have more freedom and leeway to create more advertisements and focus on many different issues and problems. The words utilized most to describe Trump in the ads supporting Biden, sponsored by various sources, were un-American, criminal, hateful, and inhuman, showing the common perspective of President Trump's suspicious character.

A common word utilized throughout the overall ad set was "violence". For pro-Trump ads, this was directed towards immigrants and the "terror" and "criminality" they supposedly would bring to America. For pro-Biden ads, this was directed toward President Trump and his violent and discriminatory policies towards immigrants. The word violence was used about 11 times in the 39 political advertisements.

The most common ad formulization in the set was exaggerated opponent auditory and visual clips, by both campaigns, to capitalize on the already present fears and stereotypes. These ad forms employed strong imagery, metaphors, and comparisons to evoke emotion from their audiences and appeal to their beliefs. For example, Trump was often portrayed to be unkind and uncaring surrounding the issue of immigration, while Biden was conveyed as too weak or radical to stop the country from being destroyed by immigrants. Throughout the set, 31% of the ads focused on exaggerated opponent auditory and visual clips.

An ever-present theme, as indicated above, were attacks on the character and competency surrounding the candidate themselves, not their policies or positions. This aspect of the advertising seems consistent with other ad categories where issues serve more to reveal or seal the perception of candidate's persona than to signal issue positions. These character attacks have definite effects on the audience's perception of each candidate, but often not the desired effect – a vote against the attacked candidate. According to "Character Attacks and Their Effects on Perceptions of Male and Female Political Candidates" in the *Political Psychology* journal, it was found that "participants tended to rate the candidate who attacked his/her opponent as having less integrity than a candidate who did not attack his/her opponent…", demonstrating this unfortunate, but understandable, effect of attacking a candidate's personality and honor (Schultz & Pancer, 1997, p. 95). While a backlash may occur in a race so vicious and with so many venues it is unlikely this occurred with immigration ads.

Third party ads are often much more vicious and cutthroat because they have no actual affiliation with each candidate's party and campaign, going for the jugular. Such was the case for ads groups such as The Lincoln project, Don Winslow film savaging Trump, and on the other side groups such as America First Action Super PAC use testimonials of legal immigrants opposing illegal immigration (Cristina, 2020).

Most third-party ads however were not of the attacked variety, but rather were aiming to influence future policy in the immigration arena. For example, the Immigrants' List Civic Action PAC, mentioned earlier, issued ten often on behalf of national/state groups, for example Puerto Rican, Haitian, Vietnamese. Unions also produced immigration ads, primarily the Service Employees International Union (SEIU) were more partisan, speaking for immigrants from central and upper South America (Change is Possible Yarleny, 2020).

Narratives and testimonials are also a common form in the immigration ad set, especially in the third-party immigration ads. They utilize "genuine" people, living true stories, to convey the reality of their messages and appeal to different audiences. Narratives and testimonials are likely the most convincing because we tend to relate to real people. They were also deployed from the left more. The third parties working on the policy used narratives more, with a 34% increase. Within these narrative ads from third parties, a certain prominent figure was utilized in each – with a 52% rate of the use of immigrants telling their stories.

Conclusion

Through analysis of this ad set, I found many differences in the ads that supported Biden and the ads that supported Trump that focused on immigration. On the more conservative side of the spectrum, the ads portrayed America as a safe haven that immigrants, especially illegal immigrants, would overrun and destroy. These ads even used narratives from immigrants themselves to emphasize that point such as the ad titled "Peruvian immigrant on why she supports President Trump", which was produced by Donald J. Trump for President, Inc. (Peruvian immigrant on why, 2020). The ads supporting President Trump also used stronger, more forceful language such as "criminals" or "aliens" and were less optimistic about the future – focusing on the negative aspects of immigration. Meanwhile, with ads that supported Joe Biden's campaign, the ads differed in the way that they seemed to have more agency with their content as well as the forms the ads took. These ads also targeted Trump and his immigration policies and plans, focusing a lot on his character (or lack thereof). Yet, there were also certain similarities between the polar sides of the campaign. Similarities include the emphasis on violence on each polar side of the ad set, character attacks on each candidate, and the widespread use of exaggerated audio and visual clips of opponents disgracing themselves and their party, as well as convincing and relatable narratives and testimonials.

References

Affairs, C. C. O. G. (2020, February 3). *Republicans and Democrats in different worlds on immigration.* Chicago Council on Global Affairs. https://www.thechicagocouncil.org/publication/lcc/republicans-and-democrats-different-worlds-immigration

Biden has promised a 700% increase in the importation of refugees (2020, September 18). Donald J Trump. https://www.youtube.com/watch?v=Be7n9QD44FQ

Brown, A. (2015, September 28). *Key takeaways on U.S. immigration: Past, present and future.* Pew Research Center. https://www.pewresearch.org/fact-tank/2015/09/28/key-takeaways-on-u-s-immigration-past-present-and-future/

Change is Possible Yarleny (2020, October 16). SEIU, YouTube. https://www.youtube.com/watch?v=6tFQTNkwSnE

Cristina (2020 August 26). America First Action Super PAC, YouTube. https://www.youtube.com/watch?v=TTjqfpkzubM

Cruel (2020, October 28). The Lincoln Project, YouTube. https://www.youtube.com/watch?v=1bVqWcuGpk0

Krogstad, J. M., Lopez, M. H., & Passel, J. S. (2020, June 10). *A majority of Americans say immigrants mostly fill jobs U.S. citizens do not want.* Pew Research Center. https://www.pewresearch.org/fact-tank/2020/06/10/a-majority-of-americans-say-immigrants-mostly-fill-jobs-u-s-citizens-do-not-want/

Madan, M. (2020). *Miami immigration group ad highlights Trump's COVID rhetoric about Asian Americans.* Miami Herald. https://www.miamiherald.com/news/local/immigration/article245300920.html

Peruvian immigrant on why she supports President Trump (2020, August 20). Donald J Trump, YouTube. https://www.youtube.com/watch?v=D-NrzM9R0

Schultz, C., & Pancer, S. M. (1997). Character attacks and their effects on perceptions of male and female political candidates. *Political Psychology, 18*(1), 93–102.

Shoichet, C. C. E. (2018, October 15). *Immigration campaign ads surge in leadup to 2018 midterms,* CNNPolitics. https://edition.cnn.com/2018/10/14/politics/immigration-campaign-ads-midterms/index.html

Siddiqui, S., Hackman, M., & Day, C. (2020, October 27). *Trump campaign tones down immigration messages that dominated 2016 election.* Wall Street Journal. https://www.wsj.com/articles/trump-campaign-tones-down-immigration-messages-that-dominated-2016-election-11603796411

Stewart, E. (2019, April 16). *Trump 2020 campaign targets older people with immigration Facebook ads.* Vox. https://www.vox.com/policy-and-politics/2019/4/16/18410513/facebook-ads-trump-campaign-immigration-2020

Words matter – Korean (2020, October 20). Immigrants' Civic Action PAC, YouTube. https://youtu.be/85sNTp7Is1I